CW00571980

HEYSEL STADIUM BRUSSELS:

EUROPEAN FOOTBALL'S DARKEST HOUR

PAUL MCCALLAM

PAUL MCCALLAM BOOKS

Copyright © 2022 by Paul McCallam

All rights reserved.

No part of this book may be reproduced in any form or by any electronic or mechanical means, including information storage and retrieval systems, without written permission from the author, except for the use of brief quotations in a book review.

ISBN: 978-1-7397077-1-2

Published by Paul McCallam Books

For my mum and my wife. Apologies for the pre-occupation.

TABLE OF CONTENTS

INTRODUCTION

Santa Marinella is a tiny seaside resort about an hour north of Rome. In a good way, nothing much seems to happen there, and it is definitely not somewhere I would have expected to have an epiphany.

When I lived there, Wednesdays were the big evening on the Santa Marinella social scene, because it was karaoke night at Monkeys English Pub. Monkeys is one of those English pubs you find in foreign fields that are about as English as Zola Budd, but—to be fair to Monkeys—it became a lifeline for me. The staff were friendly and the food was fine. It was also the place where I was figuratively slapped about the face with "the tragedy that dares not speak its name". And that tragedy is, of course, Heysel.

On a Wednesday evening in Monkeys many years ago, I was on a first date with a local woman. To my complete surprise, she turned up with her brother, who was acting as a modern-day chaperone—although in their defence, I could have been a Scouse Ted Bundy for all they knew. Her brother had one drink with us; the fifteen minutes or so he stayed turned out to be some of the most awkward in my life. During the formalities of the introductions, when he asked me where I was from and I told him I was from Liverpool, he said something like:

"Oh, Liverpool. You're a hooligan."

Even to this day, I am still surprised by his apparent rudeness. First, I did not know him from Adam; second, I was on a date with his sister; and finally, I had picked the tab up for his drink. I wish now that I'd had the sense to say, "Come on, fella. That's a bit rude, isn't it?"

But of course, I did not. Instead, I started listing reasons as to why the Heysel Stadium disaster had happened, and the list certainly did not include hooliganism. I cannot remember my litany of excuses, except for one, and that was:

"The Pope had just visited Brussels, so on the day of the match all the full-time police officers were on holiday, and if they hadn't been, they would've controlled the crowd better."

Until that evening I had given no real thought to the events that had unfolded in Belgium. Dr Rogan Taylor, a lecturer in football studies at the University of Liverpool, told the BBC that because the disaster happened abroad, it was not something English supporters—or the authorities—could analyse and come to terms with, in the way they might have done had it happened in the UK. Dr Taylor remarked:

"It was a tragedy that happened in a foreign land."[1]

This quote now helps me understand why the UK has never given much thought to such an appalling event. Narrowing the geography down from the UK to Liverpool, my recollections are that the city forgot about the tragedy relatively immediately. In spite of the fact that my hometown is famous for having a big heart, Heysel was buried and people did not talk about it, despite the tragic loss of life. Sadly, the same is true nearly forty years after the tragedy. That 'big heart' has to reconcile itself with the horrors—otherwise, our 'big heart' theory needs to be buried as well.

After that evening in Monkeys and my line about the Pope, my conscience began nagging away at me. I could not believe how brainwashed I had been since that terrible night in Belgium. I still feel embarrassed to this day by what I said, and it is the main catalyst that has driven me to write this book.

The second trigger came in 2015, during the thirtieth anniversary of the disaster. Throughout this period, I read articles on the tragedy, and found some really informative pieces written by journalists such as Oliver Brown, Jamie Jackson and Ed Vulliamy. However, it is difficult to read too many articles on the subject because they do not exist. Predictably, when you do find them, they are often titled something along the lines of "The Forgotten Tragedy". As I continued to read, I became more and more uncomfortable with what I was setting my eyes upon. Pieces written by local people made me feel the most queasy and ashamed. The cold-heartedness shown by some LFC fans towards Juventus supporters and the people of Turin has been nothing short of scandalous. I was left with this growing sense of injustice because of what was being dished out— and is still being dished out—to the people of Turin by some cruel people from my hometown.

Football journalist Tony Evans said in 2016: "It had been bugging me for years, the lack of empathy or contrition among certain sections of the Liverpool support."[2] And he's a Red.

By March 2017, I had reached the same conclusion. I

had arrived at a juncture where I thought somebody born and bred in the city needed to redress the balance—because it is crystal clear from the point Tony is suggesting that from the beginning some LFC supporters have shown no respect to the victims, and by an unfortunate association with these people, it dishonours our city. On top of this, there is something more subtle at play regarding Heysel, in that the denial of some Reds means Brussels will forever be off the conversational menu.

Allow me to give you a couple of examples of this lack of empathy. In the immediate aftermath, one Red wrote:

"I must also point out, although some people will find it distasteful, that there were two basic National characters highlighted during this sad affair. Although both sides were – as far as fighting goes – fairly equal in number, when the Italians charged the Liverpool fans, the latter stood their ground. When the Liverpool fans counter-charged the Italians, the Italians turned and ran."[3]

To rub salt into the wound, he went on:

"Both sets of fans were equally to blame for the fighting, but only one set panicked. It was not the Liverpool fans who crushed the Juventus fans – but the Juventus fans themselves." [4]

In more recent times another fan, Chris Tyrrell, wrote:

"Well what happened was loads of Juventus fans kicked off then legged it causing a wall to collapse then tragically 39 people lost their lives [...]"[5]

Hand-in-hand with this lack of contrition is denial. For me, the refusal to face up to historical fact has the same consequence as the malice, in that it also brings immense shame to the city.

Daniel Fieldsend came out with this:

"We're experienced in Europe and see it as a mate-making exercise, rather than a 'lets kick seven shades out of the locals and sing England songs' alternative (like you, Leicester)."[6]

Leicester? Can you imagine how gob-smacked Daniel will be when he finds out about Heysel? Forgive my sarcasm, the "mate-making exercise" is bad enough, but it's the Leicester bit that annoys me the most. How can he in a million years criticise Leicester fans? Sometimes you just laugh at the ridiculousness of it. Daniel would certainly be laughed out of town in Leicester. Unfortunately, other times you are taken over by humiliation and you think to yourself, "What must they think in Turin?"

Another Red, Steven Walmsley, wrote:

"Liverpool and Europe were meant to be together. It suits us. We're at our most comfortable descending on mass to new cities, taking over the bars, the roads, the rails, creating friendships and memories with a little help from a bevvy or 12. We know what we're doing."[7]

Once more, I don't want to criticise Steven, but the "we know what we're doing" bit, well... By using this language, fans such as these seem to have obliterated all conscious knowledge of Heysel from their minds. How otherwise, do we explain it? The common denominator that binds these men together is an unconditional love for a football club, which is highly unfortunate for the rest of us in Liverpool. Gentlemen, how about some love towards the city itself, and not just a football club? And how about some respect for the people of Turin and Brussels?

With LFC having national support, fans that weren't born in the city sometimes feel like they have more to prove in their dedication to the club, but their views only humiliate our city further. One, Rob Gutmann, wrote, "To this day I am none the wiser as to where precisely the true weight of culpability lay for the Heysel disaster."[8] Rob, I therefore implore you to read my findings on the subject, because I feel they will probably fill in some of the blanks for you. I feel Rob needs the situation clarifying, because he continues his thoughts with: "But I know that my club ultimately took responsibility for it."[9] If blaming others, not facing up to the tragedy for twenty years and only acknowledging it because you were forced to means taking responsibility, then I agree with you. He finishes by stating: "we as supporters remain haunted by the spectre of those events to this day." [10]

That is true, Rob, though your first two sentences reveal to me that you are haunted by it for all the wrong reasons.

It is at this point that I would like to say to LFC fans to try and give this book a chance. The book contains hundreds of referenced sources. I have attempted to make it as accurate as I can, which means it is going to be a hard read for you. To be honest, some parts will be a hard read for everyone. I also need to stress to everyone, and forgive the pretentiousness, that I didn't go looking for Heysel. Heysel found me, on a date, in a bar, in a country whose citizens went to a football match and never returned.

After carrying out in-depth research into Heysel, I have drawn the following conclusions:

1. Throughout the preparations, Liverpool FC Chief Executive Peter Robinson had grave reservations about the ticketing policy and the lack of segregation between fans. His concerns

were ignored. There's no question that both these aspects played a major part in the tragedy.

2. The stadium was a deathtrap. It was a disaster waiting to happen. The tragedy would not have happened had the dilapidated stadium been kept in an appropriate state of repair. Despite high-profile games having been held in the stadium in the past, the final should never have been held there. It was an insult to both the clubs and their fans. As the *New Civil Engineer* magazine reported the week after the game, the arena broke all European footballing safety rules.[11] In addition, a visiting British engineer commented that the ground would not have received a safety certificate under British safety laws: "The crush barriers and fences were unsafe and the stadium would never have passed the Safety at Sports Ground Act. It would have been closed immediately."[12]

3. The year before, Liverpool supporters had been viciously attacked at the European Cup Final in Rome by Roma fans. Liverpool player Alan Kennedy, who scored the winning penalty in Rome and who because of injury became the squad's unofficial lookout in Brussels, said: "I am sure what happened was, in some way, related to events in Rome the previous year. Our supporters then were pelted with stones, bricks and bottles by Roma fans."[13] This meant some Reds in Brussels were more tense in comparison with previous European trips, whilst others were seeking revenge because Juventus, like Roma, is an Italian club. One

suspect, when asked by Merseyside Police in June 1985, "You said to [name blanked out] that trouble had been expected in Brussels after the trouble in Rome," answered: "That's right we were anxious about it."[14]

4. With Heysel being one of the great unspoken tragedies of British sport, it is relatively unknown that Juventus supporters at the other end of the ground caused severe problems for the Belgian Police before the tragedy even happened. If the deaths hadn't happened—and yes, I am fully aware that is a massive *if*—Juventus could have possibly been banned from the following season's tournament.

5. Fans from any English club who played in Europe at the time would have been capable of the violence on show at Heysel.

6. From a British perspective, Heysel was sadly inevitable, and the fact it took place in 1985 is no twist of fate. In the months leading up to the final in May, English football had hit (near) rock bottom after decades of strife. The violent scenes at Luton Town vs Millwall, Chelsea vs Sunderland, Liverpool vs Manchester United, and Birmingham City vs Leeds United were horrendous. These four games in particular emphasised how little control the football and state authorities had over the English Disease. The tragic fire at Bradford City, which had nothing to do with hooliganism, highlighted how little attention the authorities paid to protecting supporters from the potential dangers within stadiums. The neglect was

criminal, and the national game was fast becoming yesterday's sport.

7. The conduct of fans during the afternoon in Brussels city centre is a standalone event in itself. All English clubs could have been banned from European competitions due to this event alone. LFC probably would have been. The empire mentality on display was nauseating. Englishmen plastered on strong Belgian lager and xenophobia brought havoc to unsuspecting locals and Italians. As one bar owner said after seeing his place wrecked: "What is wrong with you British? Have you become an angry tribe?"[15] Unfortunately, this "angry tribe" took their behaviour on the metro from the city centre to the stadium with them.

8. The men who tore down a fence at the stadium and/or harmed innocent people fell into several categories. Some were simply football hooligans doing what they do. Others were seeking a misplaced nationalistic revenge for the attacks in Rome the previous year. Some took intergroup behaviour to deadly levels. Others were caught up in the madness of the crowd. Some were drunk. What bound them together, along with a love for a football club, is that the vast majority came from backgrounds where fighting publicly, whether in a pub, a pub car park, a nightclub or on the street, was the norm.

9. The deaths were caused by a stampede, following an assault. The press of large numbers squashed and suffocated innocent people. The collapsed wall, often used as self-exoneration by

Liverpool fans, actually saved lives. Let me repeat that: the wall actually saved lives; the deaths were caused by a stampede because fans were fleeing from an attack.

10. The events of and reasons for the disaster are not complicated to understand. When all is said and done, it was down to appalling behaviour, followed by the weight of history, a perfect storm of related events and gross mismanagement by the Belgian FA, UEFA and the Belgian Gendarmerie. The causes I have just presented, of course, need discussing and explaining, but they aren't complex.

11. In the days and weeks following the tragedy, the *Liverpool Echo*'s coverage was journalism at its best. As you can imagine, it was very raw and their eyewitness writers used words such as "murder" and "slaughter" to describe the reality of the events at Brussels. They also allowed fans to give two contrasting pictures of how the events had unfolded. There were Kopites in Belgium who supported the views of the *Echo*, i.e., that Liverpool fans caused the destruction. Through no fault of its own, it also afforded plenty of column inches to Reds who blamed infiltrators.

12. Liverpool FC made the situation much worse by blaming Chelsea fans for causing the riot. Additionally, they appealed their ban. Initially, they were banned for three years longer than other English clubs, who were all banned. LFC's punishment was reduced from three years to one on appeal. The appeal document

they sent to UEFA on 8 August 1985 is shocking beyond belief in its selfishness. I am now convinced the club's response was tied up in LFC's historical roots. For those who are unaware—and as we will see later—LFC's roots are bedded in sectarianism and Conservatism, which flourished in north Liverpool in the 1890s when the club was formed. Oh, and by the way, that's definitely a big "C". Here, the Tory origins of the club are not important; what is significant is the founding fathers would have made Ian Paisley Senior blush. Therefore, for me, the club's reaction in 1985 was the Orange rallying cry of "No Surrender". At the end of day, roots are roots, and LFC's will always be Blue and—more pertinent here—Orange.

13. If, God forbid, anything similar should happen in the future, the local media and civic leaders must show more moral leadership and not act sheepishly or feel in any way inferior to large city institutions, in this case Liverpool FC. To give the *Liverpool Echo*, the city council and church groups credit, they tried to lead the city along the correct path. Sadly, they were browbeaten within weeks by the club's foul attitude and the denial of many supporters. In addition, the city delegation who visited Italy in June 1985 seeking forgiveness only succeeded, it would seem, in setting the benchmark for 'how not to do reconciliation'.

14. As a city, we denied the Heysel families any genuine sense of justice. One misconception about Heysel is "fourteen fans went to prison,

so justice was done". Justice was not done, and as a city this was not our finest hour. In the wake of the tragedy, the Belgian Interior Minister, Charles Nothomb, said, "[...] people should know they can't cause death and violence and then run home."[16] Unfortunately, some Reds well and truly tried. Several years later, at the end of the trial of the LFC fans in Brussels, Otello Lorentini, who lost his son Roberto in the tragedy, said: "Eventually only a few were convicted. And one by one they slowly slipped away during the trial. At the end, the court was empty, and nobody protested or stopped them."[17]

15. Most importantly, schools and parents have a duty to educate future generations of Liverpool kids about the atrocities and criminal behaviour carried out by people from our city during that afternoon and evening. We are happy to tell people we have a great waterfront and are home to one of the best music scenes the world has ever seen. By the same token, we have to admit that people from our city destroyed families forever. On this point about education, Reds have to understand that you cannot keep kicking the can down the road for eternity. Awful things happened that day. In fact, worse than awful. Acts which were so beyond the pale it makes you lose faith in humanity. And as we will see, many of these were witnessed by Reds from the city and printed by the *Echo*.

16. We owe Turin big time. We have to seek genuine reconciliation. The city council and

Liverpool FC have an immense responsibility to reach out to Turin. One idea would be for Everton, Liverpool, Juventus and Torino to play in a pre-season tournament. The possibility of using the two Turin and two Liverpool teams to forge closer links between the cities was first suggested by Signor Catella, the regional head of the Olympic Committee, in June 1985. Our city is full of statues, so a statue could possibly be a second and easier option. If a statue is ever built, it would have to be in a prominent site, slap-bang in the middle of town. Before reaching out, however, we first need to show Turin that we have come to terms with Heysel ourselves, and that, regrettably, is a long way off at the moment.

17. Ex-Liverpool player Mark Lawrenson, who played in the game, once stated: "Heysel is never ever mentioned. Very, very, rarely is Heysel ever mentioned. It's kind of been glossed over a little bit, which of course it should never ever be. But it doesn't get a mention and as ex-players, and there's an awful lot of us who live very close together in Southport and when we see each other and go and have a beer, we don't talk about it, nobody talks about it, nobody talks about Heysel, absolutely nobody. I find it really, really strange, I really do."[18] Lawrenson went on: "It's just really odd that there's never been that discussion about Heysel, and you feel a little bit like it's a dirty secret in many ways."[19] He's 100% right; it is a dirty secret in Britain and especially in Liverpool. Ironically, the rest

of the world knows what happened and we don't.

18. The point above leads me to academic Rob Steen's quote: "A sociologist colleague recently told me, somewhat sheepishly, that it would be 'career suicide' for him to reassess Heysel, to reopen this Pandora's Box."[20] I understand where Rob's colleague is coming from, because there has been a blanket of intimidation thrown around Heysel in the UK. It is not referred to as the *Forgotten Tragedy* and the *Tragedy that dares not speak its name* for nothing. In part this was because of Liverpool FC and even Juventus FC; were both trying to forget the event themselves. However, today, I am sure Rob's colleague is not afraid of upsetting either club when he speaks about "career suicide". However, as soon as he reopens the Pandora's Box, he knows full-well what would happen. I have to confess that I am truly mortified when you have a situation where academics are cowering under their desks due to people from my hometown. There has to come a point when you have to stop shooting the messenger.

19. When I started this project, my plan had been to write a single book, but after completing the first draft, I realised that was an impossibility. This story is just too vast, and the main reason for this is nobody in Britain has ever written a book fully devoted to the events that occurred in Belgium, though an Italian author, Francesco Caremani, has written an acclaimed book on the subject. It has become clear to me that, with

a couple of notable exceptions, very few people in our country have the faintest idea about what transpired and, just as important, why it happened. So, considering the enormity of the topic, I will be writing a follow-up to this book. This book will deal with the tragedy itself, as well as the preceding events and immediate aftermath. The second will focus on the police investigation, the trial, LFC supporters' response, and our hopes for reconciliation with Turin.

PART ONE
WHY IT HAPPENED

ONE

A SHARED UPBRINGING

For the unaware, Liverpool faced Juventus in the European Cup Final at the Heysel Stadium in Brussels on Wednesday 29 May 1985. It had the potential to be one of the all-time great finals, a game that should have taken its rightful place in the annals. Liverpool were Europe's number one club, and Juventus had the opportunity to become the first club to win all three European Cup competitions. Juventus had lost their two previous finals, to Ajax in 1973 and Hamburg in 1983; in both games, they had conceded goals in the first ten minutes of each game. In contrast, the Reds had won all four of their previous finals, beating Borussia Monchengladbach, Bruges, Real Madrid and Roma. If Liverpool had won the game, they would have kept the cup. *Guardian* football journalist David Lacey, who was in the stadium, summed up perfectly what was at stake for both teams and countries:

"This really was a match to regain some kind of Italian presence in Europe or confirm the English domination of Europe. We were all looking forward to an outstanding football occasion."[1]

The man in the Liverpool dugout was Joe Fagan. Fagan was managing his last ever game, after deciding to leave halfway through the 1984–85 season. He had taken over Liverpool, aged sixty-two, in the summer of 1983, having the unenviable task of following on from the football mastermind that was Bob Paisley. As Merseyside football journalist John Keith astutely remarked:

"It was akin to walking on stage after Frank Sinatra. Just how do you follow a genius called Bob Paisley? Well, Joe came up with a way and landed the first treble in the history of English football."[2]

The coach of Juventus was the legendary Giovanni Trapattoni. Trapattoni had retired from playing in 1972 after a glittering career at AC Milan, winning two Serie A titles and two European Cups, before winning Serie A as manager of both Inter and Juventus. During his near forty-year career in management, he also managed Italy, the Republic of Ireland, Fiorentina, Bayern Munich, Benfica, Red Bull Salzburg and the Vatican City's football team.

Ian Rush, who played for Liverpool in the game and would later play for Juventus, told the press on the eve of the game it was a "logical final, it will be a clash between two of the best European clubs".[3]

The line-ups of both teams were packed with international players, superstars and characters. Juventus had Italian World Cup winners Marco Tardelli and Paolo Rossi, Polish great Zbigniew Boniek, and possibly the greatest midfielder of his generation, Frenchman Michel Platini. For Liverpool there was the elegant Scottish centre-half Alan Hansen, their greatest ever player, Kenny Dalglish, and in goal was the charismatic South African Bruce Grobbelaar.

On the morning of the game, Brussels woke up to

glorious sunshine. To the backdrop of gorgeous weather, the excitement of the occasion and a feeling that this was what life was all about, fans of both teams were mingling happily on the streets of a European capital. Juventus supporter Simone Stenti, a twenty-year-old student at the time, travelled to the match with his father. He recalled:

"I love so much those moments that come before such an important match when there is the excitement, the build-up. There were lots of English people; I still have a Liverpool scarf I exchanged with an English supporter."[4]

Like Simone, LFC fan Barry O'Hara witnessed supporters swapping scarves; he also saw fans buying each other drinks and kissing each other.[5] It all sounds perfect.

Regrettably, just a few hours later, BBC radio football commentator Peter Jones was informing the nation: "This is war correspondent stuff here."[6]

So, how did we go from fans kissing one another and exchanging scarves to "war correspondent stuff" within a few hours?

IN 2015, on the thirtieth anniversary of Heysel, a group of LFC supporters were discussing the tragedy on a podcast. One panellist, Mike Nevin, understandably said: "I'm a bit all over the place with Heysel."[7]

Mike's sense of psychological turmoil in never coming to terms with Brussels surfaces as he goes on to say:

"I can say with my hand on my heart there was a lot of people at that game—I don't want to put a number on this, certainly in the hundreds if not thousands—that came from different parts of the country."[8]

He continued, "The train was full of people that I

would never have associated with being Liverpool supporters."[9]

After drudging up the diversionary route of Chelsea and the NF, fellow guest, Peter Hooton, shows Mike a photo of LFC fans gathering next to the fence dividing both sets of supporters and informs him, "You look at the photograph and that's mostly Liverpool's known, active hooligans." [10]

Peter then informs his fellow guests he used to interview hooligans in his capacity as a writer for the 1980s magazine *The End* and so he knew some of the men in the picture.

It would therefore be logical to lay the blame for Heysel squarely on the shoulders of your common football hooligans. However, the tragedy is not that clear-cut. You see, many of the men who attacked Italians in Belgium were not just "Liverpool's known, active hooligans". Rather, the hooligans were supplemented by a large group of Englishmen, mainly from Liverpool, who had different rationales for attacking Juventus fans. The two common denominators that united both factions during the fifteen minutes of madness were, of course, the love of a football club, and—just as significant—the English working-class upbringing shared by the vast majority.

I believe that this shared heritage led to the scenes witnessed in Brussels city centre earlier in the day, the conduct in and around the stadium, and the tragedy that enfolded on the terraces. In short, violence and the suspension of conventional norms was a standard occurrence for the hooligans and ditto for the considerable majority of the second group. And I know because I came from a similar background to those who were arrested.

From a theoretical perspective, allow me to introduce

you to a key academic theory that supports what I am saying. The Leicester School, based at Leicester University, is an important academic movement in the study of football hooliganism. Paradoxically, that is not important to me. What is important, however, is the roots of their football hooligan theories are fundamentally associated with working-class structures. Structures that also apply to the second group who took part in the rampage.

Leicester argue that lower-working-class communities [myself, I wouldn't be splitting hairs too much here about lower-working-class and other working-class communities in Liverpool] bestow prestige on males who can fight. Correspondingly, there is a tendency for these males to acquire a love for fighting and to see it as a central source of meaning and gratification in their life. The central difference in this regard between lower-working-class communities and their counterparts in other classes in society appears to be that, in the latter groups, violence in the face-to-face sense tends to be condemned while in the former it tends to be normalised. A further difference is in the latter, violence takes place 'behind closed doors' while with lower-working-class communities, violence tends to occur to a greater extent in public. Further underpinning of this system comes from the regular feuds between families, neighbourhoods and, above all, street gangs.[11] Which, of course, is all very public.

Consistently, they highlight how important fighting is and the significance it can play in a male's self-confidence and status in such an environment. On this point, I'm sure in many schools, the old-fashioned "cock of the year" was looked up to—and fortunately the lad in our school was a decent lad. Besides this, our district had lads who loved to fight, and it is important to stress that many of these lads went nowhere near Goodison Park or Anfield, never mind Stanley Park in its heyday. So, when it came to fighting, the attitude was very much "it's what boys do".

Leicester's point regarding families, neighbourhoods and street gangs is also nail-on-the-head stuff. One fight I witnessed as a teenager was five lads against five others, although I would definitely not call the lads who took part in this fight 'street gangs', more like lads who knocked around together. Their fight had clearly been arranged, because there was an audience of scores of other teenagers from the estate.

The ten paired off into twos and lined up facing each other. We the crowd were standing around a small fence and the poor guys were inside, and then on some sort of cue they began fighting one another. The crowd certainly enjoyed it. There was no sign of the police despite the din and in spite of the fact the police station wasn't that far away. In saying that, it wasn't the kind of place where people would ever phone the police, because if you did it was highly likely you would have "Grass" sprayed on your house. I'm sure anyway the police attitude was simply, "Let them kick lumps out of each other. What do we care?"

Of course, not everybody will agree with my take on the police. However, a brilliant, in-depth study of working-class youth cultures in Britain was carried out by David Robins and Philip Cohen between 1972-1974. They gathered most of their material while they were working on the Black Horse disco project in inner-city north London. They believe that people in middle-class residential areas directly experience only the welfare aspects of police work, while people in working-class districts experience police behaviour in full contradiction of itself.[12] And from my early lived-experience, Robins and Cohen are on the money. Although, I have to put up my hand and say now that I've moved towards the first category. A consequence of this "behaviour in full contradiction of itself" means there is little or no respect shown towards police officers by many working-class people.

This disrespect was evident at Heysel, for when Belgian police attempted to control rioting LFC fans on the terraces, some fans simply took the batons from officers and chased them with their own weapons. This is hardly surprising for as McGregor, Assistant Chief Constable of Operations from the British Transport Police at the time, remarked, the Belgian police, with the exception of the Ostend Gendarmerie, appear to have treated the presence of football fans with great apprehension.[13] This resulted in them displaying a lack of determination to control the rowdy element from mid-afternoon onwards. This, in turn, allowed the situation to deteriorate to the scenes witnessed in the stadium from 6 p.m. onwards.

Coming back to the fight I witnessed, I knew some of the lads involved, and I would imagine the fight was over something relatively petty and that a middle-class person would not understand that something so trivial could lead to a gang fight—or in this case a 'group of lads who knocked around together'-type fight.

From an academic standpoint, a study from across the Atlantic that took place in the Near West Side of Chicago carried out by Gerald Suttles (Suttles influenced the Leicester School profoundly) supports the point I'm putting forward. Suttles took up residency there in the summer of 1963 and left a little less than three years later. He observed that an insult, confrontation or rivalry would be judged against a background of 'facts' that would be inadmissible in most courts of law or seem trivial to a non-resident.[14]

Suttles' findings very much mirror what happened growing up in working-class Liverpool, and no doubt throughout other UK working-class districts. The bottom line is, as Robins and Cohen note, that being able to settle disputes with your fists also ensures that your words need no further emphasis![15] In relation to Heysel, lots of the lads that charged Italians and neutrals in Block Z would certainly have lived by Robins and Cohen's viewpoint.

TWO
US AND THEM

No crowd is homogenous. The LFC fans in Block X and Y certainly were not. Narrowing it down, the people who attacked Juventus fans were not homogenous in their intentions, despite all having a love for their football club. As I stated in the introduction, the men involved fall into several categories. Some, LFC's hooligans and those seeking revenge for Rome, had clarity of mind and pre-planned motives. However, the testimony from several suspects would suggest that the "mob mentality" played a role in explaining the actions of others. Going by evidence from LFC fans involved and those who were witnesses, some Reds' behaviour at Heysel would support the psychological research into the behaviour of crowds and groups we are about to discuss.

On the theme of psychological studies, we will journey back to the 19th century, travel through the 20th and finish in this one. As with all concepts, there are pros and cons, detractors and exponents for each study. As we will see, none of them are completely watertight; however, when used together, they help us put the building blocks in place, which makes Heysel understandable.

From my perspective, I want to attempt two things. First, to clarify what happened by using psychological ideas to explain the behaviour of some fans. And second, to hopefully help LFC fans who still have the mentality of "I'll never understand what happened that night."

With crowd theories, there is only one place to begin and that is with Frenchman Gustave Le Bon. Le Bon wrote his seminal book, *The Crowd*, in 1896, based on an era of extreme social disorder in France. It is worth stressing that when looking at Heysel through the lens of Le Bon and some other social psychologists, we are not discussing the Reds who were hooligans or those seeking revenge for Rome. We are referring to the fans who ordinarily may not have acted violently, but on this occasion became caught up and participated in the hostility.

According to Le Bon there are special characteristics of a psychological crowd, and he asks the question: "What constitutes a crowd from a psychological point of view?" He suggests that there is a disappearance of an individual's personality, a lowering of their intelligence and the complete transformation of their sentiments. One of his most famous quotes highlights this:

"By the mere fact he forms part of an organised crowd, a man descends several rungs in the ladder of civilisation. Isolated, he may be a cultivated individual; in a crowd, he is a barbarian—that is, a creature acting by instinct."[1]

Le Bon's sentiment is echoed perfectly below by the statement of one LFC fan at Heysel. The supporter recalls:

"Suddenly, I snapped and lost my head, I joined in. I ran towards the Italian who had pulled out the knife in front of me and I started fighting with him. I started hitting him. He ran away and for some reason I chased him. I wanted him. I caught up with him again halfway up the terracing. He had nowhere to run. I started hitting him, I lost my head. I started hitting any Italian who was anywhere near. It didn't matter who as long as they were Italian. I must have been enjoying it or I wouldn't have done it."[2]

The last few sentences capture the 'barbarian' Le Bon speaks about. The Red continues:

"I stood there and looked around at the Italian fans. I started to cry, I wasn't the only one. One minute I was acting like a yob you see on TV, the next I was crying. One young Liverpool supporter who I had seen fighting, his eye cut, just stood there and said, 'Oh God, what have we done, this wasn't supposed to happen.' An Italian family stood with us. The mother and father were trying to get their two children out of the ground. I gave a young girl my scarf and tied it around her neck. My friend did it also to the other young Italian. Without saying anything we lifted the two children up to the Italians on the wall. All we could keep saying was sorry. Their mother and father thanked us. For what?"[3]

We can now see the civilised individual when he cries, when he realises the extent of the tragedy developing and, of course, when he helps the children to escape the carnage.

Le Bon goes on to claim that the most striking peculiarity presented by a psychological crowd is that it does not matter what individuals compose it. It is not important what their intelligence or background is, the fact they have been transformed into a crowd puts them in possession of a sort of collective mind which makes them feel, think and act in a manner quite different from that in which each individual would feel, think and act were he in a state of isolation. He stated different causes lead to the appearance of these characteristics peculiar to crowds that are not possessed by isolated individuals.

The first is that the individual forming part of the crowd acquires, solely from numerical considerations, a sentiment of invincible power, which allows him to yield to instincts that, had he been alone, he would have kept under restraint. The second cause is contagion. For Le Bon, contagion is a phenomenon easy to establish but not easy to explain.[4]

Allow me here to move away from Le Bon for a moment to put 'contagion' into a modern environment and help to clarify the "not easy to explain" part. Academic Gary Slutkin, who wrote about the 2011 London Riots, believes that violence is an epidemic—it behaves with the characteristics of an infectious disease. He suggests that violence as an epidemic is not a metaphor; it is a scientific fact.[5] Slutkin cements his thoughts by referring to the work carried out by cognitive psychologist Aaron Beck. Beck describes the synchrony of the group reaction as an "emotional contagion" that ripples throughout a crowd driving them toward (often violent) action.[6]

One Heysel suspect gave an example of this 'contagion'. When arrested by Merseyside Police, he said, "I didn't want to fight. I ended up running with everyone else because there was nowhere else to go."[7]

The last point the suspect makes is interesting. For me, it supports Beck's point that a crowd drives people toward action. The Red clearly feels he had nowhere to go, so was it "emotional contagion"? Probably for you and me, it seems he could have stayed where he was or moved in the opposite direction, away from the chaos. I would imagine the fan in question understood this not soon after the fifteen minutes of madness was over.

Coming back to Le Bon, a third cause he observes is that an individual immerged for some length of time in a crowd in action soon finds himself—either as a consequence of the magnetic influence given out by the crowd or from some other unknown cause—in a special state that resembles the state of fascination a hypnotised individual finds himself in. He moves on to say that the activity of the brain is paralysed in the case of a hypnotised subject, who becomes a slave to all the unconscious activities of his spinal cord, which the hypnotiser directs at will.[8]

Staying with this theme of "the hypnotiser directs at will," Le Bon points out that as soon as a certain number of living beings are gathered together, whether they're animals or men, they place themselves under the authority of a chief. With human crowds, the chief is often nothing more than a ringleader or agitator, but as such he plays a considerable part. Further, Le Bon says that the multitude is always ready to listen to the strong-willed man who knows how to impose himself upon it.

When I read the list of the named suspects that had been charged with causing the riot, I recognised one name immediately. In 1980s Liverpool, it was said that this man was the leader of LFC's hooligan crew, and so he would have been highlighted as a chief by Le Bon.

It is on the theme of leaders where Sigmund Freud joins the debate, and despite some criticisms of Le Bon, Freud described his work as a "[...] brilliantly executed picture of the group mind."[9] Freud argued that the crowd 'unlocks' the subconscious. He held the view that society's moral standards uphold civilised behaviour because they are fixed in the human psyche as the super-ego. In crowds, though, Freud thought the super-ego is superseded by the leader of the crowd, who now acts as the hypnotist controlling unconscious and uncivilised impulses. Crowd leaders have this result due to a deep and primitive instinct in all of us to revert, in crowds, to the 'primal horde'—the original brutal human group at the dawn of existence.[10]

In a podcast quoted at the beginning of Chapter One, Peter Hooton mentioned "Liverpool's main hooligans". It is possible that these hooligans acted as leaders, fitting Le Bon and Freud's theories, and that some other fans were led astray and became part of the 'primal horde'. This contention is affirmed by one fan:

"We had been misguided by pride, by the older ones."[11]

Likewise, one arrested fan told Merseyside Police: "Not long after this I saw an older man, who I'd watched, shouting at other Liverpool supporters to attack Italians and stick together."[12]

Staying with Freud's theme of the 'primal horde', British psychologist William McDougall is another significant early theorist who suggested the most common instinctive emotions are the simple primitive ones (e.g., fear and anger), and that these would therefore be the most common and widely shared emotions in any human collective. More complicated emotions would be rare and less commonly shared. Stimuli eliciting the primitive simple emotions would therefore cause a strong consensual reaction, while those causing more multifaceted emotions would not.[13] He goes on to state that primary emotions spread and strengthen quickly in a crowd, as each member's expression of the emotion acts as a further stimulus to others—a snowball effect called 'primitive sympathy'.

The police statement below from one LFC fan who was arrested would certainly support McDougall's theory. The Red disclosed: "I just wanted to get over there, to sort them out, anyone who wanted to know."[14]

McDougall believed that the effect of 'primitive sympathy' is not easy to control, as individuals feel depersonalised and have a lowered sense of personal duty.

Underneath is part of the statement from the above suspect, after being shown a video of himself by Merseyside Police. We can witness this lowered sense of personal duty in practice:

"Yes, that looks like me, but there are people cowering and I'm putting the boot in. I can't believe that's me. I honestly didn't know what I was doing." [15]

Asked what was going through his mind, he could only say, "It must have been madness, absolute madness." [16] Asked what he was thinking at the time, he said, "I don't know. I was there, but I wasn't." [17]

Another suspect had similar feelings. He admitted: "I got carried away. I lost control. We all panicked."[18]

Forgive the long quote, but we are going to need it to understand the next example from the stadium. McDougall summed up the crowd as:

"[...] excessively emotional, impulsive, violent, fickle, inconsistent, irresolute and extreme in action, displaying only the coarser emotions and the less refined sentiments; extremely suggestible, careless in deliberation, hasty in judgment, incapable of any but the simpler and imperfect forms of reasoning, easily swayed and led, lacking in self-consciousness, devoid of self-respect and of a sense of responsibility, and apt to be carried away by the consciousness of its own force, so that it tends to produce all the manifestations we have learnt to expect of any irresponsible and absolute power. Hence its behaviour is like that of an unruly child or an untutored passionate savage in a strange situation, rather than like that of its average member; and in the worst cases it is like that of a wild beast, rather than like that of human beings."[19]

We could select any of the language above, and unfortunately it would still not do justice in explaining this:

"I saw a young Italian girl, she couldn't have been more than 15, the same age as my son, stuck on the top of a safety fence dripping in blood. Do you know what the bastards did? They tried to 'help' her over the fence by chucking bricks at her."[20]

Liverpool supporter Jim Montgomery gave the above description. If I had to select any quote of McDougall's, it would be: "in the worst cases it is like that of a wild beast, rather than like that of human beings". Later we will come across more modern theories who disagree with the "madness of the crowd", but Jim's eyewitness account informs me that there has to be something in this concept.

Another theory inspired by Le Bon was put forward by Festinger et al. in the USA in 1951. Like Le Bon, they note that people indulge in forms of behaviour in which, when alone, they would not. They make the point that individuals act as if they were submerged in the group. Such a state of affairs may be described as one of *de-individuation*; that is, individuals are not seen or paid attention to as individuals. In other words, many of the behaviours which the individual wants to perform but which are otherwise impossible to do because of the existence, within themselves, of restraints, become possible under conditions of de-individuation in a group.[21]

In much more everyday English, Chris Allison, Temporary Assistant Commissioner of the Metropolitan Police, defined it like this:

"People use the cover of the crowd to do stuff that they would never have the bottle to do as an individual, but when they were in that crowd they felt they had the power to do it, they had the mentality, they were willing to take a step further."[22]

The work of Festinger et al. is enhanced by other psychologists such as Phillip Zimbardo. Zimbardo was chiefly concerned with the relationship between *anonymity* and *aggression*. Zimbardo advocates that the "diffusion of responsibility" that goes with deindividuation facilitates this relationship. He is saying that as well as feeling lost in a group, individuals also feel less responsible for any damage that is a consequence of their behaviour and so it is more likely that there will be more acts of individual violence.

When you watch news footage from the night of the Heysel disaster, both Festinger et al. and Zimbardo's models were certainly on display. You see Reds attacking Italians and then running back and hiding in the massed ranks of Reds.

AS WE HAVE JUST SEEN, in the 1920s William McDougall and Sigmund Freud put their weight behind Gustave Le Bon's ideas about the psychology of the crowd. However, in the same decade, alternatives to Le Bon arose too.

As Reicher et al. note, Allport in particular dismissed the notion of reversion to a primitive group mind.[23] His work started a tradition that explains crowd action in terms of the character of those individuals drawn to the crowd. According to this perspective, if crowds are violent it is not because peaceable individuals are transformed in the mass but because violent individuals are drawn to crowd events where they can express their true nature. If the classic view, in popular parlance, might be called the 'mad mob' approach, then this latter view is the 'hooligan' approach. So despite the differences between Le Bon and Allport, they both came to the same conclusion that crowds are fundamentally dangerous.

The evidence from Brussels would suggest some individuals lost their mind to the mob, and I propose this is true because they tell us they did. If they did not lose their senses, how do we explain Jim Montgomery's eyewitness account?

However, when it comes to Heysel, it was not just a matter of people falling into Le Bon or McDougall's primitive crowd mentality and suddenly becoming the personification of the English Disease. It was accurate for some, but not all. Many knew exactly what they were doing, even though they did not expect such dire consequences. One obvious group of people is the football hooligans themselves; they were doing what they do. On top of the hooligans, it would seem there were Reds who, although not part of a hooligan crew, were seeking revenge for Rome in 1984, where Liverpool fans were attacked by Roma ultras. Peter Hooton makes this distinction between the two:

"I don't think there was much of a revenge element there because in Rome actually it was the innocent, the women and the children who got picked off in Rome. Liverpool's known hooligans actually went into the city centre that night and there was trouble, but it was regarded as they weren't completely obliterated. And you've got to put it in context, they weren't after revenge because I don't think they [were], maybe your average fan may have been, thinking there were so many stabbed in Rome."[24]

We will now discuss another psychological phenomenon which was on view in Brussels. One which is easier to follow than the "madness of the crowd", which covers the two groups Peter Hooton has just mentioned and everyone else who was involved in the mayhem. It is a psychological phenomenon which, when mixed with an English working-class upbringing, can have deadly effects.

Although he's not speaking about Heysel directly, Jason Marriner, a Chelsea fan, hits the nail on the head when it comes to group minds and Belgium. Jason appeared in an episode of *The Real Football Factories*, hosted by Danny Dyer. As you might imagine, given the subject, it was full of exaggerated Cockney patter and hard-case walks; however, Danny and his production team did a brilliant job.

The documentary includes interviews with academic Peter Marsh and with Ian Stuttard, the director of Hooligan, the famous Thames TV football documentary about West Ham's ICF (Inter City Firm). It also includes an interview with Jason, a member of Chelsea's infamous Headhunters. When asked by Danny why he became a hooligan, Jason simply says:

"I believe it starts from an early age. I've always maintained that schools fight schools, different boroughs fight different boroughs, different housing estates fight different housing estates, and so on."[25]

The reason I believe Jason nails it is that his words are a pure textbook example of a psychological concept called intergroup behaviour. And for me, intergroup behaviour is fundamental to comprehending why some LFC fans ran riot. We can understand intergroup behaviour as the idea that:

"Whenever individuals belonging to one group interact, collectively or individually, with another group or its members in terms of their group identification, we have an instance of intergroup behaviour."[26]

Therefore, struggles between nations, political groups or, like Jason says, "different housing estates" and fans are all illustrations of intergroup behaviour. One of the classic concepts of intergroup behaviour is that of "ethnocentrism". In 1906, William Sumner was the first to use the term, together with those of "ingroup" and "outgroup".[27] For Sumner, ethnocentrism was a "syndrome" in the sense that it encompassed "a number of (mutually related) attributes of social life"; it played a function in group formation and intergroup competition, and it was universal. Sumner described ethnocentrism like this:

"A view of things in which one's own group is the centre of everything, and all others are scaled and rated with reference to it. Each group nourishes its own pride and vanity, boasts itself superior, exalts its own divinities, and looks with contempt on outsiders. Each group thinks its own folkways the only right one. Ethnocentrism leads a people to exaggerate and intensify everything in their own folkways which is peculiar and which differentiates them from others."[28]

Sumner's ideas explain a few things to me. First, ethnocentrism is part of the explanation for LFC supporters' behaviour at Heysel, i.e., they attacked Juventus fans because they were simply another group. Second—and forgive me because this is a debate for another day—it enlightens me on the attitude of some LFC fans today who still will not accept culpability. Sumner's quote, "[...] one's own group is the centre of everything, boasts itself superior, leads a people to exaggerate and intensify everything in their own folkways which is peculiar and which differentiates them from others", could have literally been written to describe the sort of Red Tony Evans was talking about when he said: "It had been bugging me for years, the lack of empathy or contrition among certain sections of the Liverpool support." Additionally, it fits hand in glove with your Daniel Fieldsend and Steven Walmsley types of this world as well.

One of the first landmark studies of intergroup behaviour was carried out by Muzafer Sherif. During his youth in what is now Turkey, Sherif witnessed interethnic violence between Turks, Greeks and Armenians that claimed tens of thousands of lives, and these experiences inspired him to seek answers to prevent further atrocities occurring in the future.[29]

He conducted three famous field experiments in 1949, 1953 and 1954 at summer camps for young boys in the United States.[30] When the boys arrived at camp, they were divided into two groups. The groups were separated from one another and then later brought together to participate in sporting and other activities. This produced passionate competition and intergroup antagonism and aggression, while at the same time manufacturing camaraderie within the groups themselves. During Sherif's trials, basically all intergroup activities deteriorated into intergroup conflicts. For example, when the groups dined together, the meals turned into an opportunity for the groups to fling food at each other. Intergroup rivalry became so vicious that a lot of the experiments were cancelled.

Now, whilst food fights might sound comical, there was plenty of similar intergroup conflict occurring, before the fateful charges, on the dividing line between Block Z and Y at Heysel. For example, one LFC fan believes it started with fellow Kopites firing rockets at Italians. He recalls:

"The first provocative incident, aimed at the mixed section of fans of Z Section [...] was the firing of rockets right into the fans' faces. The fireworks came from various parts of both X and Y section. The fans in Z Section offered little in the way of retaliation other than the verbal abuse."[31]

As we can see from Sherif's trials and the eyewitness example above, there seems to be an innate trait inside people that encourages an "us and them" mentality that leads to conflict. If we supplement this inherent character-istic with the environment we grow up in and the education we receive, it is easy to appreciate part of the reason that countries go to war, never mind groups of hooligans attacking other supporters.

THREE
KLEE VS KANDINSKY

The research we are now going to turn to (well, at least at the beginning of the chapter) demonstrates that conflict is not even necessary to stir up intergroup behaviour, which makes Heysel even easier to comprehend.

In 1971, Henri Tajfel and his colleagues (Billig, Bundy and Flament) devised a novel way to demonstrate what has become known as minimal group paradigm. The aim of the study was to assess the effects of social categorisation on intergroup behaviour when, in the intergroup situation, neither calculations of individual interest nor previously existing attitudes of hostility could have been said to have determined discriminative behaviour against an outgroup.[1] In short, Tajfel et al. were attempting to show that you do not need prior hostility between groups for prejudice and conflict to occur. Therefore, it was a move away from earlier conflict theories such as Sherif's.

Tajfel's et al.'s research used Bristol schoolboys who believed they were taking part in a study on decision making. They carried out a pilot study and two subsequent studies. During their second experiment, the criterion for intergroup categorisation was adopted by using the paintings of artists Paul Klee and Wassily Kandinsky.

Twelve coloured slides were chosen, six being reproductions of paintings by Klee and six by Kandinsky, all of which were fairly abstract. The participants were informed that they would be asked to express their preference between paintings of "two foreign modern painters, Klee and Kandinsky". The slides were shown one at a time, in 12 successive pairs and in various combinations, without the participants being informed which of them were reproductions of Klee and which of Kandinsky. After each pair, the participants were requested to tick their preference on prepared answer sheets and were then placed into groups based on their preferences.[2]

When you think about it, what is significant is that Klee and Kandinsky were modern artists, so it is not pushing the boundaries of the imagination to say the boys were more interested in the Gas and the Robins (today, unfortunately, it would be Liverpool or Manchester United—or am I so behind the times it could be Chelsea and Manchester City?) than painters from Switzerland and Russia, and so, therefore, the groups they joined were meaningless in their importance.

During the experiment, the boys only knew which group they belonged to and so had no idea as to the identity of outgroup and fellow ingroup members, who were masked by the use of code numbers. The boys went into private booths where they were presented with a matrix where they had to assign monetary value to either an ingroup or an outgroup member. They did not assign this monetary value to themselves; therefore, their own greed did not come into play.

The most powerful force found in the study was ingroup favouritism, i.e., participants wanted to make sure that their group got more than the other group. In fact, the most chosen monetary value was the maximum difference between the ingroup and the outgroup. There was also a tendency to choose fairness, but there wasn't a propensity to distribute money and give it to the outgroup.

As Tajfel et al. note themselves, the main finding confirmed in all three experiments is clear: in a situation devoid of the usual trappings of ingroup membership and of all the vagaries of interacting with an outgroup, the participants still act in terms of their ingroup membership and of intergroup categorisation. Their actions unambiguously favour the members of their ingroup against the members of the outgroup. This happens despite the fact that an alternative strategy—acting in terms of the greatest common good—is clearly open to them at a relatively small cost of advantages that would accrue to members of the ingroup.[3]

Two further aspects of the findings are even more important. First, the participants act in this way in a situation in which their own individual benefit is not affected one way or another. And second, as was shown in the second experiment and in the pilot experiment, when the participants have a choice between acting in terms of maximum utilitarian advantage to all (Maximum Joint Profit) combined with maximum utilitarian advantage to members of their own group (Maximum Ingroup Profit) as against having their group win on points at the sacrifice of both these advantages, it is the winning that seems more important to them.

Tajfel et al. conclude that the crucial results of the study can be simply restated as follows:

"[...] in a situation in which the participants' own interests were not involved in their decisions, in which alternative strategies were available that would maximise the total benefits to a group of boys who knew each other well, they acted in a way determined by an *ad hoc* intergroup categorisation."[4]

According to Tajfel, the finding that intergroup discrimination can be caused by a "minimal" social categorisation retains a considerable robustness. A count made for his review resulted in a conservative estimate of at least 30 studies which used minimal or near-minimal categorisations with diverse populations of participants, independent variables and dependent measures, and which all show ingroup-favouring bias.[5]

Likewise, Hogg and Vaughan suggest the robust findings from hundreds of minimal group experiments conducted with a wide range of participants are that the mere fact of being categorised as a group member seems sufficient to produce ethnocentrism and competitive intergroup behaviour.[6]

Now I understand if some of you are thinking: how are Bristol schoolkids connected to the horrors of Belgium? Well, Michael Billig, one of Tajfel's colleagues during the experiments, later went on record as stating that although Tajfel may have begun his research career by addressing technical questions of perceptual judgement, he was soon using this research as a basis for understanding the nature of prejudice. Billig added that for Tajfel academic research for its own sake was insufficient. Tajfel was of Polish-Jewish background and had lost many family members and friends during the years 1939-1945. With this in mind, as Billig highlights, Tajfel would tell his students that behind his work lay one question: "How is genocide possible?"[7] Therefore, if someone as academically renowned as Tajfel was looking for answers as to why six million humans were killed by another group, I would say it is more than fair to employ his studies and conclude that intergroup behaviour was a massive cause of the disaster in Brussels.

WE ARE GOING to continue with the journey from Tajfel's social categorisation research in Bristol and move to the wider social identity approach, which led to the social identity model of crowd behaviour.

Today, social identity research is now the pre-eminent approach in ingroup psychology and for its exponents it has thoroughly dismantled the particular belief of identity which underlies the classic crowd psychologies that we discussed in Chapter Two.

As Reicher et al. point out, as its name suggests, the social identity tradition rejects the idea that people only have a single personal identity.[8] Rather, it argues, identity should be seen as a system in which different parts govern our behaviour in different contexts. Certainly, there are times when we do think of ourselves in terms of our personal identities: what makes us unique as individuals and different from other individuals. But at other times, we think of ourselves in terms of our group memberships (I am British, I am a police officer, or whatever) and of what makes our group unique compared to other groups. That is, we think of ourselves in terms of our social identities. Psychologically, the shift from personal identity to social identity is what makes group behaviour possible.

In addition, as Reicher et al. point out, when people shift from seeing others as individuals to seeing others as group members, their relationships with them undergo a fundamental transformation. Common ingroup members are treated with warmth and respect; they are trusted, supported and they receive cooperation [in our case LFC fans]. This rarely extends to outgroup members [Juventus fans]. The reason for this fundamental transformation is that once people define themselves in terms of a group membership, the fate of the group as a whole (and hence of others in the group), its well-being, prestige and reputation becomes the individual's fate, their well-being, their prestige and their reputation.[9]

This social identity theory has its historical origins in the 1950s and, especially, the 1960s when, as Drury and Stott state, many of the ideas of 'crowd science' were challenged and it was again the prominence of the 'violent crowd' that prompted the need for alternatives.[10] The epicentre of these challenges to academic orthodoxy was in the USA. During this period, there was the development of the civil rights movement, anti-Vietnam protests, and especially the riots which occurred throughout urban American cities.

For many of the social scientists that studied the urban ghetto riots, 'the social problem' was not the crowd, but deep-seated inequality and racism in US society.[11] Additionally and importantly, as Reicher et al. note, the early theorists of the crowd were essentially on the outside looking in at alien behaviour. But the theorists of the 1960s were often involved in some events themselves—such as the Vietnam protests on college campuses—and at the very least, they were interested in participants' own accounts and reasons, and not just their behaviours.[12]

From a British outlook, Reicher's study of the 1981 St Pauls riot in Bristol paints an impressive picture of the social identity model of crowds. While the immediate cause of the riot was a police raid on a café, the relationship of ongoing antagonism from the police towards St Pauls, a predominantly black district of Bristol, was also key to the understanding of what took place. Reicher's interview and archive study showed that the identity of "members of the St Pauls community" was defined in terms of locality, "freedom" and the antagonistic relationship with police. These features made sense of the distinctive pattern of the riot, which was one of the first of a wave of urban riots affecting UK cities in the 1980s.

As Drury et al. suggest in relation to St Pauls, the crowd's behaviour was clearly in line with the definition of their identity: the targets of attack were the police and certain kinds of property. Banks, the benefits (social security) office, the rent office and the post office were singled out as agents of the community's continued powerlessness, whereas local shops and homes were actively protected from rogue elements. Second, there were clear limits to who got involved; only those who shared the identity were influenced by other crowd participants. Relatedly, the most influential people were those who were seen to best embody the crowd identity—in this context, older Rastafarians.

Reicher's SIM (Social Identity Model) proposed that commonality in crowd behaviour, rather than being because of contagion or social facilitation, is due to participants sharing a common social identity. The St Pauls study, along with Reicher's experimental research on anonymity in groups, was a powerful riposte to the 'irrationalist' tradition, from Le Bon to de-individuation.

IN TERMS OF FOOTBALL CROWDS, one study by Stott et al. investigated social identity and inter-group dynamics during social disorder at the 1998 World Cup Finals in France.[13] Of course, the back-story and the pattens are different to Heysel, however their study helps us to understand how powerful intergroup dynamics work at football matches. Stott et al. called their theory the Elaborated Social Identity Model of Crowd Behaviour (ESIM).

From a theoretical viewpoint, Stott et al. point out how crowd events are characteristically intergroup encounters. As such, identity processes within a crowd do not simply determine collective action in a one-way process; rather, identity processes involve the dynamics of intergroup relationships. These intergroup dynamics function to change the nature of the social relations facing crowd participants, which in turn redefine their initial social identity and its associated norms, thus changing the shape of collective action. Therefore, rather than context being seen as something merely external to identity, the context in which any one group acts is formed by the identity-based actions of other groups. In Brussels, Reds looking for revenge would certainly fit into this group.

Stott et al. would have been kept busy in France, because during their research at least 32 people were injured during three days of rioting and violence when England met Tunisia in Marseille in their opening game on 15 June. As the BBC reported, after some isolated trouble on the Saturday night, Sunday saw 400 England followers involved in pitched battles with Tunisian fans, local youths and police during seven hours of violence.[14] Police fired tear gas to break up groups of several hundred England and Tunisia supporters. There was a constant hail of bottles and missiles, and as fans retreated, they destroyed shops and premises.

Sir Brian Hayes, former deputy commissioner of the Metropolitan and the English FA's security advisor at the tournament, stated:

"The English fans didn't start it. Some of the African population started lobbing cans of beer at England fans, and even if England fans don't start a fight, they are up for one. I had seen occasions where England fans started trouble but in Marseille I can say they didn't—from what I saw. They were heavily provoked. It was not a good experience."[15]

Kevin Miles of the Football Supporters' Association said English fans were caught up in the tension between locals and French riot police:

"What happened was a war on the streets of Marseille between the local Arab population and the police for their own reasons about French politics, not English football. English fans have been caught in the middle of that with no protection from the police."[16]

On top of this, Hayes acknowledged during a television news interview that the majority of those English supporters involved in these incidents of disorder were not known to the British police's intelligence unit (NCIS) prior to the incidents themselves.[17]

How was it, then, that many individuals not previously known to have engaged in violent acts in football came to engage in acts of collective violence during their time in Marseilles?

Stott et al.'s analysis claims that the episodes of collective conflict witnessed in Marseilles were imbedded within a developing intergroup context that had important implications for the normative structure of collective action. As they arrived in Marseilles, increasing numbers of English supporters understood themselves as being confronted by persistent taunts, threats and at times unprovoked violence from large groups of local youths. They also experienced policing that appeared to go from one extreme to another; from police inactivity during situations of outgroup provocation and violence to 'heavy handed' indiscriminate intervention against ingroup members in situations of English retaliation/defence.[18]

Moreover, supporters not directly witnessing these events soon came into contact with those who had, and an understanding of illegitimate outgroup action became common currency between ingroup members.

This form of intergroup context and interaction led to variation in the nature of the social identity driving collective action among sections of the English support. Initially, English supporters who had not previously been engaged in conflict came to understand violence as proper social action and gathered with other ingroup members, particularly those that were prepared to confront, and therefore provide defence from, local youths. The intergroup context was such that it changed hooligans from a violent and confrontational out-group to prototypical category members able and capable of exerting a normative influence among increasingly larger numbers of English supporters. This is part of the key to understanding Brussels because non-hooligan fans followed the influence of full-time hooligans.

We spoke earlier about the power of leaders during crowd disturbances through the works of Le Bon and Freud. During their study in France, Stott et al. noted that the norms of the group were now such that certain individuals were empowered and became disproportionately influential in structuring collective action. Violent individuals previously seen as marginal were seen as prototypical and were able to provide by their violent action an instantiation consistent with the current collective identity. For me, Stott et al.'s findings on this point seem to me to support the older theories that espoused this view over a hundred years ago, therefore supporting my belief that some Reds became intoxicated by the crowd and the leaders within it.

A criticism of ESIM is that it does not consider the possibility of emotion in the crowd. As we have already mentioned, and as we will see later, evidence from the stadium would support this criticism. But for me, it is when we put all the theories together that they cover all bases in describing what occurred.

In the next few chapters, we will move away from psychology to history, which when combined with what we've just learned will help us construct a clear picture of the scenes of Brussels.

FOUR

"WE HAVE COME TO EXPECT IT FROM ENGLISH PEOPLE."

Britain has had problems with football hooliganism since day one. As early as 1885, during an Aston Villa vs Preston game, the *Saturday Night* reported:

"On the North End team leaving the field, they were mercilessly attacked by a gang of, if appearances go for anything, bona fide *Brummagem* roughs, who mobbed them and used sticks, stones and every available missile with which to wreak their vengeance on the visitors."[1]

Speaking of *Brummagem* roughs, in 1899, Small Heath (now Birmingham City) played West Brom in a derby match. The *Birmingham Daily Mail* reported:

"The lower elements of the Small Heath Football Club partisans are a particularly objectionable lot. Not content with resorting to disgusting expletives, they not infrequently molest strangers when the chances of the Coventry Road team are vanishing."[2]

These problems continued into the 20th century both before and after the Second World War; however, they were seen as isolated incidents.

From a historical perspective, as Marsh et al. describe,

the 1960s saw a colourful transformation in the style of fan support.[3] Football fans became more organised, with carefully arranged waving displays, songs, chants and slogans, and were more mobile. Regular support of away games helped to disperse the differing styles across the country. By 1964, the core troublemakers were perceived to assemble in groups with no allegiance to either team, and could no longer be seen as simply overly ardent supporters. These groups identified and named themselves separately from the teams and used match days as a place for clashes with rival groups.

By 1967, the sport of 'taking ends' appeared as the favourite pastime of young male fans. The aim was to charge at supporters of the opposing team, drive them away from their viewing area behind the goal, take as much of their team gear as possible (flags, scarves, etc.), and land a few good kicks and punches before police arrived. While on film these charges looked really aggressive, in reality serious injuries seldom happened. Moreover, with intimidating threats and waved fists, the blows exacted were largely symbolic.[4]

By the 1970s, these groups became increasingly sophisticated in their cohesiveness, organisation and 'scoring' systems, which, among other means, used press coverage to determine which group was on top in the hierarchy of hooligan 'firm' rivalries.[5] This cohesiveness and organisation led to a massive upturn in football hooliganism and a move away from the more innocent notion of only 'taking ends' and 'symbolic blows'.

As Rob Steen observes, in the 1970s 'firms' multiplied the length and breadth of England, Scotland and Wales.[6] No club suffered more blows to its reputation than Manchester United, whose fanbase was easily Britain's biggest, and whose Red Army was among the most feared and reviled. In September 1975, the players organised a bonding session with their younger fans. Winger Willie Morgan said:

"We, the players, are sick to death of listening to the complaints about a small section of our so-called supporters."[7]

He went on to say:

"We do not need these villains, they should go somewhere else."[8]

When the Red Army rumbled into London for a match against Millwall in 1975, all police leave in the New Cross area was cancelled, shops were boarded up and pubs shut. Come Christmas, at the behest of the FA and the Football League, Man United would become the first club to make away games all-ticket affairs.[9]

A truly horrendous incident happened on 24 August 1974, when Blackpool fan Kevin Olsson was stabbed to death when fighting broke out at a Blackpool vs Bolton match. The then Bolton manager, Jimmy Armfield, who was making his return to the club he had served as a player from 1954 to 1971, responded to the tragic event by saying:

"It was the worst Saturday night of my life—Alan Waldron, one of my players, had suffered a horrific broken leg. I went from visiting him in hospital to calling on the family of the dead boy."[10] He added, "As a Blackpool man, I had to visit them."

Dennis Howell, the then sports minister in the Labour government, visited the murder scene, saying he would consider identity cards for football fans. Blackpool introduced segregation for fans on their Kop and fenced them in; other clubs followed suit. A juvenile was acquitted of Kevin

Olsson's murder at Lancaster Crown Court. No one else was ever charged.[11]

In Scotland, during the first Old Firm match of the 1975–76 season, journalist Stuart Cosgrove remembers that the game "was fraught with tension".[12] Police reported:

"Two attempted murders, nine stabbings, two cleaver attacks, one axe attack and thirty-five common assaults, all of which were connected to football. One Rangers fan was badly injured when he was thrown off a bridge near Ibrox."[13]

———

I RECKON anyone who went to a game in the 1970s or 80s must have witnessed violence either inside or outside the ground at some point, which made the scenes in Brussels, unfortunately, not as surprising as they should have been. Off the top of my head, I can recall two incidents I witnessed inside of stadiums. One was between Everton against Chelsea, taking place in the Upper Bullens stand at Goodison. I think it was when Chelsea won 4–3, and we went onto win the title. Not sure if Jason from the Headhunters was there.

The other was when we played Stoke City away, and again there was fighting in the stand behind the goal, not a terrace. In fact, I can now think of another time where Everton fans were scrapping with Stoke fans, and that time it was in the corner of the stand that ran along the side of the pitch. Not so long ago, I was travelling to Leicester by train and we stopped at Stoke, and it looked to me like the station hadn't changed a great deal. Alas, this led to flashbacks of barking Alsatians and police escorts. Horrible.

There are three incidents I can remember outside

grounds in the mid-1980s, and they all involve Manchester United. The first was in 1983 when Everton played United in the FA Cup at Old Trafford, which Everton lost—and very unluckily, I may add, 1–0. After the game, directly outside the ground, there were a few punches thrown, but nothing major. We were then put on buses to take us to the station, and whilst we were waiting to leave, United fans were rightly reminding us of the score.

One group in particular were dressed in the casual clothes of the day, and you would recognise them as possible hooligans or—more than likely, considering what happened —wannabe hooligans. Next minute, to everyone's delight on our bus, the Red Devils took to their heels because a mob of Everton fans came up from behind them and began chasing them down the road (cue *Benny Hill* music). Everybody on our bus began banging the windows with a sense of, I suppose, pride. Give me a break, I was fifteen.

The second happened outside Goodison in the mid-'80s. It was the time of the police escorts, and a Man United fan was wandering around looking lost. For those who know Goodison, this happened opposite where the club shop is now, right next to Stanley Park. The poor United fan was straight out of the 1960s, with his big red scarf and the look of the Dick Emery character "Dad I think I got it wrong again". A Scouser tapped him on his shoulder, and when the Man U supporter turned around, the Everton fan put the old "Kirkby kiss" on him. The guy's legs buckled, and then a right hand put him to the ground. It was terrible to witness, but it was the way it was then.

The next was at Old Trafford in 1984 after a League Cup game. Both sets of fans left the ground, and it was pitch black. I was walking with a friend, and we happened to be walking with guys I'd noticed at Goodison who were hooligans. I'll always remember one of them saying, "There's going to be a stabbing here." It made me so nervous. Thankfully, I did not witness one, but a few days later in the *Daily Mirror* there were pictures of a United fan who had been cut to ribbons.

I attended the Feyenoord vs Everton game in Rotterdam in 1995 and saw the same guy again who'd predicted the stabbing. My friends and I did not have tickets for the game, so we had to buy them from a local tout outside the ground. Unfortunately, they were for the Feyenoord end. We were sitting right next to the Everton fans, who were separated from us by some type of netting or plastic. Now, of course, this did not prevent both sets of fans from giving it the big one with each other—and who did I see leading the charge from the Everton end towards a lower tier filled with Feyenoord fans? Exactly: the Everton fan from Old Trafford. I was sitting there thinking, "Nothing changes."

Incidentally, we stayed in Amsterdam for a few days with a friend who lived in the city centre at the time. One morning I received a parking ticket, and a couple of days later my car was broken into and my passport was stolen. I wouldn't mind, but we lost—Everton, hey!

IF ON A SATURDAY evening after an Everton or Liverpool game, someone on our estate told me, "I hear so-and-so sparked a West Ham fan out today at the match," I would have believed it, even if I knew the person in question who had thrown the punch wasn't a football hooligan, because as we saw previously, in many working-class districts violence is casual. Not to offend West Ham fans, I would have also believed "I hear so-and-so was sparked out by a West Ham fan today at the match."

With this in mind, I just want to pick up on the casual football hooligan and the more full-time football hooligan type because both were on display in the Belgian capital. In the street next to where I grew up, there was a football hooligan I knew personally; he was a few years older than me. The guy was always dressed immaculately, so clothes were clearly part of the attraction to him, like they were for many hooligans. Now, of course, he was one of Everton's "known, active hooligans"—therefore, the violence obviously played a part too. I always respected this guy and let me explain why.

In March 1982, I went to my first away game, where Everton drew 1–1 with Man City at Maine Road. I went with a group of other lads from school. I told my mum and dad I was going with one of their fathers, which of course was not true. Our tickets were for the Kippax, that peculiar standing terrace which ran along the side of the pitch.

Throughout the game, Man City fans were throwing objects at us. Now, I am sure Everton fans were throwing things back too, but I do not remember that, because during the match an object struck me, and it is this experience that has since dominated my attention. With one other lad, I was escorted to the first aid room, which happened to be in the City part of the Kippax. They put some kind of plaster on my head, and that was that. I always remember, during half-time, bumping into the well-dressed local football hooligan, who was standing with other Everton hooligans. He did not give it the big one and ignore me; he actually said hello, and we had a small conversation, and I always respected him for that.

On the train back to Lime Street, I witnessed more

hooliganism—this time Scouse, not Manc. The train was one of those old football specials with wooden tables. For some reason (actually, I shouldn't say that, after all those concepts I've been serving up), a few of the lads I was with started smashing up the tables, and they threw them out of the window. Of course, I knew this was wrong and I wished it was not happening (honestly!). However, I should not have been too surprised, because in doing research for this book, I have since found out that between 1955 and '56, Liverpool and Everton fans were involved in several train-wrecking exploits.[14] In addition, Scouse supporters held the record for the worst cases of train-wrecking to and from matches in the early '6os.[15]

One time at Lime Street Station, after Everton had played Manchester United in 1985, I saw another lad from the same street as the full-time hooligan.

It shocked me to see him, because I am sure he didn't even like football, and I do not know to this day whether he is a Red or a Blue. The gentleman in question had a reputation not only on our estate, but throughout the city, not for football hooliganism but a general type of violence. And then, of course, the brain kicked in, and it was clear why he and the lads he was with had been to Manchester that day... and it was not to see Derek Mountfield and Gordon Strachan score goals in a football match.

The reason I am mentioning these two guys I knew is to reinforce the point that lads from Liverpool, or any other big city in Britain, can commit such atrocities similar to the acts of brutality that occurred in Brussels, even though they were unintended in size and horror.

CONTEXTUALLY, it is absolutely impossible to fathom the events of 29 May 1985 without considering English fans' experiences abroad, and LFC supporters' experience in Europe too. In the decade before 1985, English clubs had dominated European football. Remarkably, between 1977 and 1984, an English club had won Europe's biggest foot-balling prize for seven out of those eight years. Along with Liverpool, who were Europe's pre-eminent team during this period, Nottingham Forest won it twice under the enigmatic Brian Clough, and in 1982 Aston Villa beat Bayern Munich to take the trophy back to Birmingham. In 1981, Ipswich won the UEFA Cup, as did Tottenham in 1984, and just two weeks prior to Brussels, Liverpool's Grand Old Team lifted the Cup Winners' Cup in Rotterdam. Although English clubs were topping the European trophy league, we were also, sadly, head and shoulders above any other nation for hooliganism. Scarily, followers of the national team had an even worse reputation than the club sides.

In Rotterdam in May 1974 during the UEFA Cup Final, Spurs and Feyenoord fans kicked off massively. Fifty fans were arrested and two hundred were hurt; the *Daily Mail*'s headline the next day screamed, "Rioting Fans Shame Britain".[16]

Commentator Gerald Sinstadt informed watching viewers at home:

"I'm sorry to say, but during this half-time, we've had some disgraceful crowd scenes here. With spectators ripping up seats on the top-tier and throwing debris over onto the crowd beneath them. The Tottenham chairman, who had appealed before the game over the public address system for good behaviour, came onto the loud-speakers again and addressed the Tottenham fans and said, 'you are disgracing yourselves as Tottenham supporters, you are disgracing the British people,' and he went on to add 'the Tottenham club would undoubtedly face the possibility of a heavy fine'."[17]

Reflecting at a later date, Tottenham's then manager Bill Nicholson recalled:

"It was very bad to think that Tottenham Hotspurs couldn't control their supporters. Mind you, I fail to see how any government can control supporters who want to act in the way that they acted. There are so many reasons for it, a lot of our people's fault; they weren't completely and entirely to blame. A lot of people thought the police out there were to blame; the poor old police always catch it, don't they?"[18]

Curiously and ominously, Dutch journalists and academics refer to this match as the spark for a major rise of football-related hooliganism in the Netherlands.[19] Spurs had to play their next two European games away from White Hart Lane.

In Paris at the 1975 European Cup Final, Leeds United supporters went on the rampage following their controversial 2–0 loss to Bayern Munich. Leeds were denied a blatant penalty after a challenge on Alan Smith, and they also had an obvious goal chalked off because of an atrocious off-side decision. In saying that, they should have been down to ten men after only two minutes when Bayern defender Bjorn Anderson was cruelly chopped down by Terry Yorath. In the eighty-first minute, Gerd Muller put Bayern two ahead; it was at this point that Leeds fans began causing trouble. The violence continued, with many looking to get out of the city and get home as soon as possible. Reports of further incidents cropped up over the following few days. Local papers led with the headline: "Les Animaux Anglais".[20]

The stadium director at the Parc des Princes announced:

"It was no surprise to us, we have come to expect it from English people. Over the last three days Leeds followers have attempted to break in and damage our premises. Their match behaviour was disgraceful. I have never seen anything like this and I hope I never do again."[21]

The *Yorkshire Evening Post* ran with the headline, "Shame of Paris".

Duncan McKenzie, who was in the Leeds squad that evening, used this classic line to describe the disappointment of losing and on hearing the news of the mayhem in Paris:

"We also had the terrible news to go to in that our fans had wrecked Paris and all that they'd left was the Eiffel Tower."[22]

For the record, UEFA banned Leeds from European football for four years, which was subsequently reduced to two years on appeal.

Former General Secretary of the FA, Ted Croker, believed the first major incident regarding England fans was in the Grand Duchy of Luxembourg in 1977. Croker proclaimed that a rabble of so-called supporters ran riot in the city causing damage to property and then later to the stadium itself. Croker thought the newspapers exaggerated some accounts, but the FA felt the obligation to pay £2000 in compensation to the Luxembourg people.[23]

Rene van den Bulcke, president of the Luxembourg Parliament and also president of the FA, said he never wanted England supporters back in his country.[24] Unfortunately for van den Bulcke, on Wednesday 16 November

1983, England played Luxembourg away in the European Championship again. Denmark's victory over Greece earlier in the day meant England finished second in their group and could not qualify for the 1984 European Championships in France. The stadium director at the Parc des Princes probably said, "Thank fuck for that."

On Tuesday, the day before the game in Luxembourg, about twenty English men beat up a railway employee in Belgium, and four police officers needed hospital treatment after fighting broke out among drunken fans who got off a ferry in Ostend.[25]

After the game, on Wednesday, some England fans went onto the streets. Six hundred police and soldiers, almost the entire resources of the country's security forces, were not enough to prevent them from causing havoc. It was the worst outbreak of hooliganism Luxembourg had ever seen. Cars were overturned, windows were smashed, shops looted and local residents terrorised. At night, sirens rang out in the usually quiet city as police tried to round up the troublemakers. Forty English fans were detained and the rest bundled onto trains bound for England, leaving behind a city in a state of shock.[26] At the height of the night's violence, riot police from neighbouring West Germany had to be drafted in to help the over-stretched Luxembourg forces. Weapons seized included axes and aerosol cans filled with tear gas.[27]

Emile Krieps, then Luxembourg's sports minister, declared:

"Our people, they can't stand it because there was a lot of damage done. I would say that if our football league would try to have another game here against a British team, our mayors of the various towns, they could refuse the use of their grounds and that would put certainly the end to any next game."[28]

By coincidence, the rest of Europe's sports ministers were meeting in Rotterdam that evening to discuss just such problems; they had watched similar scenes from the Feyenoord-Tottenham match just a fortnight earlier (we can safely say Spurs and Feyenoord have a historical problem with one another). Afterwards there was unanimous support for an initiative from Britain's sports minister, Neil MacFarlane, aimed at wiping out football violence. The ministers agreed on a coordinated campaign of action across Europe to stop the thugs.[29]

The best laid plans and all that.

BEFORE BRUSSELS, Liverpool had had a great reputation for good behaviour abroad in comparison with other English clubs such as Leeds United, Manchester United, Spurs and, of course, how could we forget the national team. Domestically, Reds were nowhere near the top of the hooligan league, which at the time in the mid-'80s was particularly dominated by London clubs. There is a huge *however* though, and it's twofold. First, who wouldn't have had a great reputation when compared with the aforementioned. Second, people hadn't been paying attention. However, the *Liverpool Echo* had. The evening after the night before, its editorial on the front page nailed the reality. It stated:

"Last night's scenes of sickening violence were witnessed by 400,000,000 television viewers throughout the world. What we saw was a sickening extension of something which has been building up insidiously over recent years. It has been masked by the exemplary behaviour of the majority of Merseyside soccer fans and by the acceptance of lower standards of behaviour by society in general. The obscenities, the stoning of coaches, the gangs in Stanley Park, the fights in Manchester this year, the drunken brawling in Paris in 1981. The cancer has been there, spreading slowly and now erupting."[30]

In part the *Echo* was of course talking about Everton fans here too, but like I said, people hadn't been paying full attention to the exploits of LFC hooligans. Let's begin with Paris on 27 May 1981, an episode which has totally been eliminated from the history books.

Liverpool faced Real Madrid in the European Cup Final, a game they won courtesy of an Alan Kennedy goal. What has been lost in the passage of time however is the behaviour of some Reds in the French capital during the build-up to the game. The day before the match, the *Liverpool Echo* ran with the headline: "Rioting Reds Fans Banned by Hotels".[31]

The *Echo* reported that Parisian hotels began refusing entry to LFC fans because around thirty supporters had trashed a hotel. Fire extinguishers were torn from walls, carpets slashed, and cans of paint were used to dub LFC slogans on the walls and escalators.[32] The deputy manager said:

"Some people on the third floor were throwing bottles onto the road and urinating on passers-by. They were acting like animals; the police came and arrested 30 or more. I don't know how much the damage there is going to be."[33]

He continued:

"The hotel, along with others on the Rue d'Amsterdam next to the St Lazare railway station, has told all Liverpool people to leave."[34]

Police raided the hotel after the manager was threatened, and dozens of fans escaped onto a nearby railway platform. One LFC supporter who was on the platform recalled: "Apparently only a few lads had paid for the rooms and the rest were dosing down on the floor."[35]

The *Echo* went on to report that the vandalism in the hotel happened several hours after French and Liverpool youths fought on the streets close to the hotel. During the clashes two French youths were slashed with Stanley knives, one of them across the throat.[36]

The Parisian police were also concerned with the number of ticketless fans and had launched a big operation to quell any trouble, as the *Echo* reported:

"Meanwhile at the Parc des Princes Stadium hordes of supporters have ignored constant warnings to stay away and many have pledged to get into the ground no matter how."[37]

One fan who arrived without a ticket said, "We are looking everywhere, we haven't come here for nothing. If the worst comes to the worst, we'll be over there," referring to the specially designed grey spiked railings which surrounded the stadium.[38]

Another fan added:

"I reckon there'll be about 30,000 Reds fans here – but only 12,000 have guaranteed tickets. I dread to think what will happen when kick-off time nears and thousands are still outside."[39]

For me, Paris shows what some Red hooligans could do, and I would imagine for most of you this is the first time you have read about this incident. And that's because if you say something enough times it becomes the truth, i.e., "Before Brussels we hadn't brought trouble with us".

Another huge hooligan incident occurred at Goodison Park, Liverpool, on 13 April 1985, when Liverpool met

Manchester United in the FA Cup semi-final. Let's not forget that this was a mere seven weeks before Brussels. For the record, the match finished 2–2, but that was not the major news from the day. As the *Independent* later reported:

"Two fans were stabbed during running battles in the streets outside, a flare was fired into a terrace packed with United fans and United winger Jesper Olsen was hit by a missile when he went to take a corner."[40]

This was also the year manager Ron Atkinson likened going to Anfield to being in the Vietnam War after United's coach was attacked with tear gas before a league game.[41]

Of course, Big Ron was exaggerating; however, the scenes in L4 on the day of the semi-final were brutal, as Tony Evans recalls:

"It is difficult to explain what happened at Goodison that day. Supporters from both sides fought, stabbed and hurled missiles at each other throughout the day. Inside the ground, there was brawling in every section, with magnesium flares fired into crowds from close range and golf balls studded with six-inch nails flung at the opposition pens. These were not gangs of elite, hard-core hooligans that had become a fixture in the popular imagination; these were ordinary men—and some women—caught up in the madness."[42]

As we can see, Tony's last sentence is an example of the psychological theories we mentioned previously. Like with Brussels, it would seem usually well-behaved LFC and Manchester United supporters succumbed to the insanity of the crowd.

During a podcast in October 2017, a LFC and a Manchester United fan were reminiscing about the game.

Their recollections, like Tony's, give us a taste of why Heysel was not so much of a surprise.

LFC FAN: I don't think I've ever seen anything like it. Walton, the streets of Walton around Goodison, it was like a war zone, wasn't it? This was of the time, like Steve said before about the societal influences, were much as part of the rivalry. Certainly, in the violence stakes, they were tough times, weren't they? Basically, teenagers got their kicks through this sort of thing, but erm [...] A mate of mine from school actually wore a [...] I don't know where he got this scarf from, he wasn't one of the cool cats, he'd wear a scarf, whatever, and it had like a tinge of black on. And in those days United favours were red if you like, white and black, and if anything ours were red, white and yellow and he got his head absolutely stoved in by Liverpool fans. He was screaming "I'm a Liverpool fan, I'm a Liverpool fan, look at my scarf?" It had Liverpool FC on it, but it had a tinge of black on and that was the reason enough for him to get a massive kicking. There were incidents like that going off all round the ground before and after the game. During the game I think we fired a flare, didn't we, into your end?

United fan: The big events there, the flare that got sent into our end.

LFC fan: It hit the scoreboard and then dropped down, didn't it?

United fan: It was a shit shot really. I think Jesper Olsen got hit by a missile on the pitch. There were people getting slashed and knifed outside.

LFC fan: Golf balls with nails?

United fan: The spikey golf ball was what you

brought to Maine Road [Man City's old ground]. I don't recall the spikey golf ball being at Goodison, which is largely because I didn't see anyone getting hit by one, but it doesn't mean they weren't there. Maine Road was that one. It's pretty evil when you think about it that people were going to that level and thinking, it's a step up from the days of, 'have you got your wallet, rattle, and your flat cap and scarf'. You know what, 'have you got your knife, yes, check, spikey golf ball, check'.[43]

Hardly the romance of the cup, is it? The LFC fan recalls LFC supporters beating one another up—we will come across this more than once again during the day in Brussels. The replay took place at Maine Road, Manchester, a few days later. Interestingly, Tony Evans said this:

"Liverpool lost and thoughts turned back to Brussels. On the trains, in the bars, it was said over and over: 'It won't be like Rome'."[44]

Will we cover Rome in Part Two.

On top of the fighting against Manchester United, from a personal perspective during the same season (1984–5), I was standing on the Kop for the derby game. On that day, there was a bit of fighting literally a few metres from where I was standing. It was hardly Hagler vs Hearns and probably looked worse than it really was. Nevertheless, and as I said earlier, this violence had been increasing in the years before Heysel, but people had not been paying attention.

FIVE

WASTED OPPORTUNITIES

It would be an understatement to say Heysel in tandem with repeated acts of the English Disease at home and abroad brought grave embarrassment to the UK's political rulers. In the wake of Heysel, the government unsurprisingly brought in a raft of legislation to hopefully prevent such a scenario from reoccurring. So, at face value, well done. However, prior to Brussels there were lost opportunities by governments and football authorities to implement recommendations from various reports that could have prevented the chaotic scenes witnessed throughout the 1970s and '80s, and—who knows—possibly even the ugly events that happened in Belgium.

History seems to show that after every major football hooliganism incident or crowd disaster, politicians and representatives from football's governing bodies appear in the media, scratching their heads, saying things like "we have to investigate the causes", "this cannot be allowed to happen again", "I have demanded a report", whilst old reports with recommendations are gathering dust in a filing cabinet in Westminster.

On 19 May, less than two weeks before the match and in the wake of the Bradford City fire on 11 May 1985, the *Sunday Times* wrote an editorial titled: "Putting the boot in". It opened by stating:

"Yesterday's Scottish and English cup-finals should have marked the triumphant finale of the 1984-5 football season. Instead, Britain's national game is wallowing in the lowest reputation it has ever held. Throughout the season, football hooligans brought thuggery and blood to the terraces."[1]

You couldn't really argue with that.

It then moved onto its infamous line of:

"British football is in crisis: a slum sport played in slum stadiums and increasingly watched by slum people, who deter decent folk from turning up."[2]

The editorial was full of disdain for the sport, and as we can see from the above, for the people who attended. However, it suggested the government should lay down strict requirements for the safety of all football grounds, from fire to safety to violence, and clubs should be given a minimum period to meet those requirements. For me, that is a fair comment. Unfortunately, given how important football teams are to a town's local pride and sense of community, it continued by saying those who fail should be closed down. The piece also highlighted that football stadiums should have similar safety regulations as theatres, cinemas, hotels and restaurants. Amen to that.

For me, the *Sunday Times* editorial, although in some ways forward-thinking because it was talking about a product that would eventually become the Premier League, seems to be written by a person who did not have a historical knowledge of how we got from the forming of the league in 1887 to the fire at Bradford. I will try to explain why.

From the inception of the league, football and its fans have been placed in a precarious position. The setting of stadiums was reliant on the availability of low-cost land near to urban conurbations. And as Johnes proposes, the result was that many chosen sites were unsuitable, with little room for expansion or improvement of facilities as crowds grew.[3] In particular, entrances were often along narrow side streets that were prone to overcrowding. Even when they weren't in side streets, there was still danger afoot.

Ton Pentre FC's ground in the Rhondda was perched precariously on a hillside. In 1911 iron fencing gave way in the general rush to leave the ground, and a number of men fell into the river below sustaining head injuries.[4] Johnes goes on to observe that clubs and the sports authorities were run by a mixture of small businessmen and gentlemen whose full-time professions lay elsewhere. They were far from knowledgeable about crowd management, and nor did they employ such expert advisors. Therefore, it would have been legitimate, even in the era of laissez-faire, for the state to impose safety regulations on football clubs in the way it did (to varying extents) on theatres, music halls, railways and shipping.

The first report connected with serious crowd chaos in the British game was called the *Shortt Report*, and it arose from the disorder that occurred at the FA Cup Final of 1923, the famous "White Horse Cup Final" between Bolton Wanderers and West Ham. After the disarray, the then secretary of state for the home department asked Edward Shortt to form a committee to inquire into, amongst other things, arrangements made to deal with the abnormally large attendances on special occasions, especially attendances at sports grounds.[5] The official attendance was 126,047, but some estimates put the crowd at 250,000. The overcrowding caused thousands to spill on to the pitch, delaying the match. Miraculously, no one was killed but there were about 1,000 injuries. Had there not been free access to the pitch from the bottom of the terraces, the casualties would have been colossal.[6] As we will discover later, egress was a major problem in Brussels.

The chief constable of Birmingham told the inquiry that grounds were not always constructed in the best possible manner and were subject to frequent overcrowding. He thus felt that they should be subjected to a licensing system similar to other places of entertainment. The attitude of the FA to such intervention, in what it regarded as an internal matter, was demonstrated by its refusal to give evidence to the inquiry.[7] The inquiry's main findings were that if more than 10,000 persons were at an event, "the control should then pass into the hands of the senior police officer present", and "we consider it desirable in the interests of safety that, for the purpose of handling a crowd, stewards should be employed in any case where the crowd is likely to approach the capacity of the ground".[8]

The second official report was called the *Moelwyn Hughes Report*. It was named after Liberal and Labour politician Ronw Moelwyn Hughes. It was commissioned following the disaster at Bolton Wanderers on 9 March 1946, when what began as an exciting afternoon ended up in tragedy. Hundreds of people were injured and 33 fans—one aged just 14—lost their lives in horrific circumstances. Authorities had expected around 55,000 people to attend the game at the 70,000-capacity stadium but it is estimated that 85,000 actually managed to find a way in.[9] Like many grounds, the facilities at Burnden Park were rudimentary, as one person commented:

"The bank was pretty crude, just dirt really, with any old bits of flagstones they could get for steps. When it rained, the gaps filled with water and the mud spilled out, but people didn't mind."[10]

The turnstiles were closed at 2.40 p.m. as it became clear that there were simply too many people in attendance. But more people managed to trickle into the ground, climbing in from the railway entrance, clambering over the closed turnstiles and rushing through when a locked gate was opened to let out a father and son who could not deal with the crowd.[11]

According to Molloy and McDonnell, as the size of the crowd increased, supporters began to be pushed inward towards the pitch and a number of barriers collapsed, causing a crush which left people trapped underneath.[12] The game was already under way but was stopped when the fans burst onto the pitch and then again at 12 minutes when the barriers collapsed. Referee George Dutton stopped play while authorities tried to determine what had happened. He then spoke to a Bolton police officer who informed him that there had been a fatality. Together with the two teams' captains, the decision was made to halt the game. Shockingly, it was restarted again just half an hour later, with the bodies of some of those who had died in the crush laid out at the side of the pitch and covered over with coats. Some accounts suggest the corpses were so close to the pitch that new touchlines had to be drawn in sawdust before the game could begin again.

Hughes highlighted that grounds had outgrown their original origins, and he recommended inspections of the enclosures, scientific calculation of the maximum number to be allowed entry, counting those entering the ground by mechanical means and central coordination of the system, all to ensure the admission of a safe number of spectators.[13] In relation to future regulations, he announced:

"No ground of any considerable size should be opened to the public until it has been licenced by, I suggest as an appropriate licencing authority, the local authority."[14]

He went on:

"The issue of the licence would depend upon satisfying the authority as to the construction and equipment of the ground, its compliance with regulations, and the proposed maximum figures of admission to the different parts."[15]

In addition, the report said:

"Compliance with the recommendations of this Report will cost money. They will involve grounds in a loss of gate money on popular days [...] The insurance for greater safety for the public demands a premium."[16]

As Oliver Popplewell states in his 1986 report on crowd safety and control, Hughes' suggestions "fell on deaf ears".[17] It was wretched that it did so, because similar tragedies to Bolton were to occur again.

The next report was commissioned in June 1966, and it was called the *Chester Report*. The secretary of state for education and science appointed Norman Chester from Oxford University. It's with this report that we first come across the spectre of football violence and not just the subject of crowd disasters.

Chester made this observation about crowd behaviour:

"In recent years there has been an increase in disorderly behaviour by spectators. During the period 1946-1960 there were 195 cases brought to the attention of the FA, an average of thirteen per season. In the following six seasons 148 cases were reported, an average of twenty-five per season. The matter was discussed some time ago at a meeting between representatives of a number of police forces (including the British Transport Police), the Football Association and the Football League. Both these governing bodies have been very concerned at this development."[18]

Regrettably, Chester went on:

"We have not been able to devote the time and resources to the study of this problem which its complexity deserves."[19]

The *Harrington Report* was the next to follow in 1968. Harrington described the behaviour of some fans:

"Some spectators carry knives, hammers, sticks and spikes, choppers, and other offensive weapons like powdered pepper, which are not necessarily used for violent purposes but may be used in threatening displays. There is also the problem of singing or chanting bawdy or obscene songs and phrases, some of which are also threatening and provocative."[20]

In relation to riots at games, the report declared:

"While such riots must be regarded as almost unknown accompaniments of football in this country, their potential seriousness and danger were exemplified recently by football riots in Turkey, where many people were reported killed [43 people died, I also read 40 fans too and 300 injured during a match between Kayserispor and Sivasspor]. While comparable riots seem unlikely here, it would be foolish to rule out the possibility of much more serious crowd disturbances at football matches than we have yet experienced."[21]

These words from Harrington were certainly prophetic, for after his report, "crowd disturbances" exploded over the next two decades. Harrington went on to criticise the inactivity of implementing previous reports. Moreover, he censured clubs and the football authorities, noting:

"We think that those responsible for club management and the governing bodies of football should accept far more responsibility for keeping their crowds in order. This applies not only within the stadium itself, but to club supporters travelling in groups to and from matches. One gets the impression that some clubs disclaim any responsibility for the behaviour of their supporters, and if the atmosphere of a Roman holiday is not deliberately fostered, it is looked on with considerable tolerance."[22]

In terms of a solution for hooliganism inside stadiums, he stated:

"The solution of the problem of hooliganism in the football stadium is ultimately the responsibility of individual clubs, who must each deal with it in the light of local circumstances. While a few clubs are exemplary in their attitude to the problem, others are *laissez-faire* and need persuasion to take a more active role in trying to control hooliganism in their own grounds. This *laissez-faire* attitude does not help the police in their attempts to deal with the matter."[23]

Just after the *Harrington Report*, the connected *Lang Report* was published. A Working Party under the chairmanship of John Lang, and including a number of distinguished members, was appointed by the minister with special responsibility for sport. It was to examine the problems involved in football crowd behaviour to which attention had been called a few months previously by the *Harrington Report*. Lang's report was presented on 21 November 1969. The introduction read:

"The Working Party has not found a single simple solution for a problem which is often due to a combination of factors."[24]

The members of the inquiry witnessed the demonstration of CCTV equipment, and reported:

"The view was formed that closed-circuit television could be of value in the general subject of crowd control and would be an important factor in preventing misbehaviour by spectators at grounds. It was a refinement which most of the top-class clubs could be expected eventually to have as a matter of course."[25]

On the subject of alcohol—he could have been writing about Belgium here—the report said:

"There can be no doubt that consumption of alcohol is an important factor in crowd misbehaviour, both because it stimulates quarrelsomeness and because empty bottles are dangerous missiles. There would be no advantage in refusing licence facilities to football club grounds—this would merely stimulate spectators to bring their supplies from outside."[26]

It is ironic and disheartening that Harrington denounced the lack of implementation of previous recommendations, and condemned the clubs, plus the footballing authorities, for not taking enough responsibility for the problem of hooliganism, for it seems clear that the reports from Harrington and Lang were similarly and negligently ignored.

Two years after the Lang's 1969 report came the *Wheatley Report*. In February 1971, Lord Wheatley was asked to investigate the disaster at Ibrox Stadium in Glasgow, where sixty-six spectators had died in January 1971.[27] In March 1972, Lord Wheatley completed his report; he ended it by saying:

"I trust that this Report may be of assistance to you in deciding what should be done to solve this important question of crowd safety in football grounds. One thing is certain. The public demand for something to be done has been growing over the years. I am sure I am reflecting public opinion when I say that something must be done now. The evidence certainly supports that view."[28]

Sadly, during a session of the Belgian Senate on 14 June 1985, just a couple of weeks after the Brussels tragedy, one senator used the Glasgow disaster for political capital, and unfortunately, he had little idea about the subject. The senator claimed:

"Crowd violence at football matches is something which has emerged over the last 20 years. It is a phenomenon particularly associated with matches involving British teams. At Glasgow in 1971, 66 deaths occurred; the death toll has increased since then until now crowd violence has spread even as far as China."[29]

Following the Wheatley report, the Safety of Sports Grounds Act 1975 was passed. A licensing system involving the issue of a safety certificate for designated grounds was introduced, and supporting guidance was published. It is noteworthy that we are back to the issue of "licensing"—a subject the *Hughes Report* had highlighted decades earlier, which "fell on deaf ears".

The final official report before Brussels was produced by the Department of the Environment Working Group in 1984. It was set up following serious incidents of violence involving English supporters at England's matches in Luxembourg in November 1983 and February 1984. Regarding domestic football, the report stated:

"The Football Association had issued a 'blueprint' detailing the precautions which league clubs should take against violence, which was circulated to clubs at the beginning of the 1983–84 season."[30]

The *Working Party Report* said that the blueprint "[...] has not been rigorously adopted by all clubs. Since it represents the collective wisdom of football clubs, many of whom have successfully countered serious threats of violence, its implementation should have prevented some of the violence in grounds last season."[31]

The report recommended that matches between high-risk clubs should be programmed so that the risk or threat of violence could be reduced. It said:

"It is more likely to take place at the beginning and end of the season and at holiday periods, particularly at seaside fixtures, when other groups of young people sometimes also clash with football supporters."[32]

The report went on to recommend the introduction of club membership, CCTV and closer links with the community.

In terms of closer links with the community, some clubs really did try, and none more so than Millwall. The reason I am mentioning Millwall is the club gets a lot of stick for their fans' behaviour, but it is clear how much they have tried over the years to remedy the problem. During a BBC *Panorama* documentary aired in 1977, you could really appreciate the connection between the club and local community; the bond seemed genuinely huge—for instance, the club ran a market on a Sunday for local residents.[33] Moreover, it was obvious how much effort the club was spending to prevent trouble, especially at away games; they hired their own trains and ran a membership scheme. You could see that the club treated their fans with absolute respect. Their manager, Gordon Jago, nailed it on the head when he said:

"The answer to me is one thing only. If you could have had a 25,000 or 20,000 all-seater stadium here and all sold as a season ticket sale to Millwall supporters, that would suit me fine."[34]

We have seen in recent years the vast difference all-seater stadiums can make to the behaviour of fans. Another feather in Millwall's cap is what presenter Charles Wheeler says at the end of the programme:

"We want to thank the Millwall club for their help; alone amongst the several clubs we approached, they were willing to co-operate with us. Millwall, in fact, is going some way to meeting the trouble of violence constructively— they're hoping to build a sports centre with the idea of diverting the youngsters' energies from fighting to active sport, and that may be closer to a real solution for the problem of football violence than putting up fences."[35]

The reports we have just discussed highlight the wasted opportunities we had to attempt to make conditions for fans in stadiums a more pleasurable experience. As we will see in the next part of the book, Heysel Stadium was in a worse condition than the vast majority of UK stadia. In fact, it was in a worst state than most Belgian stadiums, for during the Belgian parliamentary debate on 14 June 1985, which we mentioned just before, one deputy claimed:

"The Heysel Stadium, unlike the stadia of other many large Belgian clubs, did not comply with UEFA standards."[36]

SIX

A VIOLENT NATION

It seems to me that whenever you meet a foreigner (the age of the person appears to be irrelevant), you get the impression that they love Sting, Mr Bean, Queen, Midsomer Murders, and Dire Straits. Now of course, I am clearly exaggerating, but the point I am clumsily trying to make is that as a nation, we possess an unbelievable amount of soft-power throughout the world due to our creativity. All the cultural products we send around the globe, especially the language (yes, I am aware Mr Bean doesn't speak), allow us to be perceived as a cultured nation, particularly by ourselves. However, our history is crammed with events that are far closer to 'savage' than 'civilised'.

In the immediate aftermath of the Heysel disaster, journalist Charles Glass wrote a very pertinent and insightful article on the connections between our violent past and the killings on the terraces at a European Cup Final. The subheading to his article was "An English tradition of butchering foreigners".[1]

Glass noted that English bloodlust is legendary in the histories of most other countries and was once prized as a virtue by the English themselves. Glass's observations are very much supported when you consider, as Mallinson observes, that of the 192 member states of the United Nations, the British Army has fought in well over half of these states or their predecessor polities.[2] Now, I am sure we seldom—if ever—consider this, but Glass's ideas now resonate with me, not only because of my research into this topic, but also because of a conversation I was involved in personally. About seven years ago, I was discussing Brexit with a couple of Brits and a few foreign people. One of the British guys said, in such a British way, "It's better for Britain to stay in the EU because then we can keep an eye on the Germans."

One of the foreign chaps replied, "It's not the Germans we need to worry about—it's the British."

A silence filled the room. By now, us Brits were disorientated and attempting to understand exactly what had just been said. It was one of those moments where you are literally speechless and you are not sure where the conversation might lead, so you employ another British characteristic and change the discussion in another direction as quickly as possible—I forget now, but I think we moved on to Sting's latest release. Afterwards, the conversation made me realise that Glass's remarks from 1985 still resonate in the foreign consciousness today: i.e., they still think we are aggressive.

Glass's article begins with a tale about our behaviour during the Crusades. He writes:

"The Arabs still remember what happened when Richard the Lionheart conquered Acre on the Palestinian coast in 1191. Richard, in the words of Sir Stephen Runciman, 'ordered the massacre of the twenty-seven hundred survivors of the garrison at Acre'. His soldiers gave themselves eagerly to the task of butchery, thanking God, so

Richard's apologists gleefully tell us, for this opportunity to avenge their comrades who had fallen before the city. The prisoners' wives and children were killed at their side. When the slaughter was over the English left the spot with its mutilated and decaying corpses."[3]

Now unlike Glass and me, some people, particularly Reds, will now say, "You're stretching the point there, aren't you?"

You might be right, although I do not think you are, because I am now totally convinced that what took place in Brussels, especially in Grand Place, is completely tied up with our empire-building mentality, plus our very primitive inclination for fighting. Soon, we will discuss more instances from our military history that show our propensity for fighting, but first allow me to give you two examples from football to demonstrate the point I am making—one involving the national team, the other from LFC fans regarding Heysel, and both in relation to Italians.

At the 1990 World Cup, England played Holland in Sardinia. A few hours before the game, a couple of thousand England fans were heading to the stadium. Up ahead, more than 7,000 armed Carabinieri, Italy's feared antiriot police, had thrown a roadblock to re-route the march. What happened next is described by football academic Rogan Taylor:

"As we approached the armoured cars and riot shields, various comments emerged from those at the front. 'Do you fancy a go, lads?' 'They're only Italians.' 'We'll go through them like a bayonet through butter.'"[4]

Just contemplate the language for a moment. *"Do you fancy a go, lads?"* is a pure example of our disposition towards scrapping. *"They're only Italians"* is full of the stereotype of Italians being cowards. *"We'll go through them like a bayonet through butter"* could not be any more imperial.

Taylor goes on to say:

"I remember thinking afterward, 'If I were in the British Army, halfway up the Khyber Pass in 1863 when the Rules of Association Football were first written with a horde of Pathan warriors ahead, these are the boys I would want with me'. They're strong and fit; they will act together with focused violence; and they're not afraid of anybody, especially not foreigners. These are, at least, some of the characteristics that built the British Empire."[5]

There cannot be many nations on the planet that fit these historical, sporting, linguistic, and character qualities as we do. Although Taylor's next line was talking about the fans in Sardinia, he could have been describing Kopites in Brussels:

"It may have crumbled long ago, but the empire still strikes back, albeit in such a perverse and anachronistic way."[6]

In the immediate aftermath of the tragedy, one LFC fan said something similar to Taylor's *"They're only Italians"*. In a letter to Liverpool's CEO, Peter Robinson, in relation to the attacks, the fan wrote:

"[...] and to my complete amazement the Juventus supporters just began to retreat and retreat instead of standing their ground."[7]

The letter above was written in the immediate aftermath, and if we are being generous we could say the person who wrote it could not see the wood for the trees because he was in some sort of shock. However, another LFC supporter wrote something similar on a forum decades later:

"as far as I'm concerned, juve fans are as much to blame as us. They pelt us with halfies [bricks] and spit at us then are surprised when they get charged. fuckin sums up the shithouse eyeties in my opinion. if it would've been, say, a dutch or german team we were playin that night it wouldn't have happened cos if we would've charged any of them, they would've stood their ground and fought back instead of shitting themselves and running away."[8]

Now, of course, the letter above is revolting. But it allows us great insight into the way a lot of LFC fans feel about Heysel. Some Reds still believe in the idea that Italians are cowards and they somehow brought the disaster on themselves—it really is the world turned upside down.

As Charles Glass, Rogan Taylor and I have mentioned, the British Empire mentality is key to understanding English football fans when they are abroad. In 2000, after more trouble involving English football fans, Jack Straw, then foreign secretary, also concurred with this view. He suggested football hooliganism and racism are largely caused by English people with a distorted and racist view of their nationality. Moreover, Straw had stated in the past that the English have a propensity for violence, and he attributed racism and xenophobia in part to the baggage of empire, saying the relative smallness of Wales, Scotland and Northern Ireland had allowed them to develop a fuller culture.[9] This English colonial mentality Straw speaks of was at its rampant worst in Brussels.

FROM ACRE IN 1191, we will now venture, relatively briefly, seven hundred years later to southern Africa in the 19th and early 20th centuries to the Boer War. This will help us to comprehend why Glass's opinions linking the wickedness displayed in Brussels and our history are so perceptive and no coincidence. Without going into details, we didn't go to Africa for the weather, more for the jewellery. In the end the war cost Britain over £200 million.[10]

The human cost of the war was even higher. The Boers lost at least 7,000 of approximately 88,000 who served in the field (which included 2,100 foreign volunteers and 13,000 rebels from the Cape and Natal).[11] It is impossible to calculate the extent of the damage exactly, but approximately 30,000 homesteads were burned, and several million cattle, horses and sheep were either destroyed or carried off. As many as 63,000 Boer families made claims for compensation.[12] Eventually 28,000 Boer women and children and at least 20,000 black people died in the [concentration] camps.[13]

From a British perspective, there were approximately 100,000 thousand British and Imperial casualties, including 22,000 dead. About 6,000 were killed in action, while the remaining 16,000 perished as a result of wounds or disease. In a war that many expected to be "over by Christmas" but which actually lasted nearly three years, Britain and her empire eventually sent 450,000 men to fight.[14]

Interestingly, back home and with the status of football rising, the sport acknowledged its appreciation to the fallen. Without the Boer War and without the battle of Spion Kop, which took place between 23–24 January 1900, the Kops at Anfield, Hillsborough and other grounds would never have existed.

As the *Berkshire Chronicle* reported, the conduct of our infantry during the battle was magnificent. Nothing could have exceeded their obstinate bravery during the truly desperate fighting, which lasted the whole day without a minute's cessation.[15] Officers and men suffered alike. As the *London Evening Standard* reported, there was no escape from that deadly plateau. Men hardly dared to raise their heads to return the enemy's fire, or if they did, fell back the next moment, to lie quiet forever. Shells were exploding amongst them, maiming those who escaped death.

The *Standard* goes on to report that there was a scarcity, too, of water. None for the men so pluckily facing death, none for the wounded whom the ambulance bearers could not reach and had to be left where they fell. The pangs of thirst added to the pain of their wounds.[16] One Boer, H. J. van Wyk, wrote:

"[...] the whole air smelled of human blood and the continuous moaning and groaning of dying English soldiers was indescribable."[17]

After the battle, seventy men of the Lancashire Fusiliers were found dead in a trench with bullet holes in the right side of their heads. One admiring burgher remarked:

"The British troops attacked us, but time and time again they were mowed down."[18]

As we will discover in Part Four, the Spion Kop at Anfield goes hand in glove with the soul of the club and, added to the bravery of Lancashire Fusiliers who were so admired by their opponents, makes the "We are not English, we are Scouse" banner on the modern-day Kop all the more perverse. Allow me to stay with this for a brief moment and at the same time add the denial of Heysel to it.

One fan, Jay McKenna, was talking about LFC's Europa League Final in Basel, Switzerland in 2016. Jay was advising Reds on behaving sensibly when in Basel. He mentioned that local journalists and police had concerns about English hooligans bringing trouble to their town. Jay's response to the local police and journalists was this gem of denial and historical ignorance:

"English hooligans. They seem to be ignoring the idea we are not English."[19]

I do not want to disparage Jay, but he clearly has no idea about history of the club he supports and more significantly how hurtful his comments are to the memories of the men who died at the Battle of the Spion Kop.

Coming back to football, in one respect, we can say "well done, football" for paying respects to men who lost their lives fighting for their country, and as we have just seen, there is no doubting the British soldiers were really brave. On the other hand, I think we can safely say the Boer Wars and our occupation of southern Africa were not our finest hour as a civilised nation. For, as Foden points out, to many foreign observers, Britain at that time wore roughly the same mask as the United States today—the world's bully boy. The annexation of the Boer republics became both a liberal cause and a stick with which other European powers could beat John Bull and his evil empire.[20]

As Tabitha Jackson explains, " [...]the wave of virulent anti-British sentiment in the German and French press prompted a sharp reaction from their British equivalents".[21] The *Birmingham Mail* declared: "Stalwart Englishmen armed with good horsewhips should go to France and administer a severe castigation to the vulgar crowds. The Parisian, like a dog, barks loudest in his own kennel."[22]

Foden's comparison between our position just over a century ago and the USA today is, in my opinion, logical, considering we were in pursuit of diamonds and gold, and the Americans are often seen as chasing other people's oil.

I want to finish this part of the book by reinforcing the fact we are a violent nation and so an event like Heysel was always a possibility.

Not long after the Boer Wars, of course, the First World

War arrived. You may imagine that after those huge tragedies, we would have reflected and held back from becoming involved in further conflicts. In fact, as Cobain points out, between 1918 and 1939, British forces were fighting in Iraq, Sudan, Ireland, Palestine and Aden.[23] Now, you definitely would have thought that after the Second World War, we would have put our feet up, assessed the post-war make-up of the world and made decisions that did not include combat. No chance!

In the previous century, as Queen Victoria approached her diamond jubilee, she had rueful cause for satisfaction in her earlier warning to Prime Minister Gladstone that the nation had to be prepared for attacks and wars, somewhere or other, "continually".[24] Victoria's mantra of 'continually' being at war remained true for Britain after World War Two, and we have basically never stopped since. In the years after the Second World War, British servicemen were fighting in Eritrea, Palestine, French Indochina, Dutch East Indies, Malaya, Egypt, China and Oman. Between 1949 and 1970, the British initiated 34 foreign military interventions. Later came the Falklands, Iraq—four times—Bosnia, Kosovo, Sierra Leone, Afghanistan, Libya and, of course, Operation Banner, the British army's thirty-eight-year deployment to Northern Ireland.[25]

As Cobain noted in 2017, for more than a hundred years, not a single year has passed when Britain's armed forces have not been engaged in military operations somewhere in the world. The British are unique in this respect: the same could not be said of the Americans, the Russians, the French or any other nation. Only the British are perpetually at war.[26]

Not only are we perpetually at war, we are also capable of fighting any kind of warfare in any kind of conditions. As

Mallinson describes, before the US Army was drawn into the Balkans in the late 1990s, its generals would sometimes say, "We don't do mountains." When the Italian Army was asked if it might help with the intervention in Sierra Leone in 1999, its generals replied, "We do mountains and deserts, but not jungles." But in the last two decades of Victoria's reign, the British Army was doing mountains (Afghanistan), deserts (Egypt and Sudan) and jungles (Burma).[27]

I think it is clear our military past and our nature towards war leads one to the conclusion that the English Disease is hardly a coincidence. I will finish this chapter with a quote from Italian professor Alessandro Barbero, who described English soldiers during the Battle of Waterloo—incidentally, also in Belgium.

"However proletarian and semiliterate he may have been, the English soldier, well-nourished with meat and beer, stimulated with gin and convinced of his own racial superiority to the foreign rabble he had to face, was a magnificent combatant, as anyone who has ever seen hooligans in action at a soccer match can readily imagine."[28]

As I said, none of it is a coincidence.

PART TWO

A PERFECT STORM

SEVEN

ROME

When Liverpool met Juventus in Brussels, they were the defending European champions. A year earlier in Rome, the 'Red Machine' had gone into the lion's den and beaten the hosts, Roma, to lift their fourth European Cup. It was a staggering achievement, not only on the night, but over an eight-year period, the Reds had won the competition a mind-blowing four times. Coincidently, Liverpool had won their first European Cup in Rome in 1977.

One headline from an Italian magazine had cried at the time: "The Barbarians are Coming."[1] Yet when the Scouse army arrived, most Italians were delighted to find them happy, smiling and—on the whole—law-abiding. High-spirited, maybe, but generally not malicious.[2]

The local authorities, and British officials too, roundly applauded their supporters. Frank Docherty, a British Embassy spokesman in Rome, was full of praise for LFC fans:

"Liverpool supporters are behaving as we expected them to and are maintaining their good reputation."[3]

So whilst 1977 was a joyous experience on and off the

pitch for Liverpool fans, 1984 was different, and regrettably it is an element that played a major part in a perfect storm that led to the carnage 12 months later. A suspect who was arrested after Heysel told Merseyside Police: "When I was in Rome, I got beat up, so I just wanted to get my own back."[4]

So, what happened in the Eternal City that led to the inevitable in Belgium?

Well, it is clear that innocent Liverpool fans were attacked before and after the match, and the local police did not cover themselves in glory. Even the journey from the airport was alarming, as Tony Evans recalls:

"Carloads of youths in cloth-topped Fiats shadowed the coaches, pulling alongside while an occupant popped up through the roof to fire a flare or hurl a brick at the bus—all at motorway speed."[5]

Once in the city, life did not improve for Liverpool fans. Billy Merritt said:

"I remember the scene as we entered Rome of kids in a playground shouting abuse at us and hurling missiles at the coach. When we arrived, myself and a mate got on a tram to the Vatican and was told by a Roma fan that if they won the game we would be invited to the biggest party ever, if they lost he advised us to get out of Rome quickly or we would be seriously hurt."[6]

Billy goes on:

"After leaving the Vatican we went for a pint in a nearby bar, there appeared to be good banter with some Roma fans, but then armed police arrived and started pointing guns towards Liverpool fans, me and my mate gave it toes and hid in the bog inside the bar. After it went quiet, we headed towards the ground only to be chased by a large mob throwing bottles and stones at us, luckily we bumped into older Liverpool fans who helped us to safety."[7]

LFC supporter David Pye's memories of the match still linger. He says:

"You sensed immediately they [the police] were expecting trouble but seemed as fearful of their notorious home ground 'Tifosi' compatriots as they were of us, and whatever reputation we had gained. Common sense dictated that a group of us had already booked into the youth hostel that was part of the Olympic Stadium park, meaning we could pass under the radar of Roma fans patrolling the railway, bus and Metro stations."[8]

David continues:

"As we approached the ground, Liverpool fans were heavily searched, with any conceivable weapon confiscated —though significantly not ejected from the ground—which suggested there was a knife culture and that confiscation of fans' weapons was an accepted part of the game in Italy at the time. Again, this did not bode well. We could clearly see hordes of Roma fans pouring into other sections of the ground unchecked and unmolested. It was impossible to overstate the importance of this game to Italians—in their capital, with its history and traditions, in their most revered stadium, with a team of chequered history desperate to rekindle their own glory days, playing on their own ground. How could they lose? They dare not lose."[9]

Once inside the ground, the evidence of attacks by Italians on the English was clear to Tony Evans:

"There were people with bruised faces and patched-up shallow slash wounds that they dismissed as deep scratches; proof, if we needed it, that there was the potential for violence here on a scale to which we were unused."[10]

Despite winning the game, Liverpool supporters were

about to endure a nightmare on leaving the ground and, even whilst they were still celebrating in the ground, ITN was reporting: "Liverpool celebrate tonight and Roma commiserate, Italian police realise the next few hours will be crucial."[11]

For LFC supporters, those "next few hours" were an unbearable experience. On leaving the ground, Roma Ultras viciously attacked LFC supporters—and to make matters worse, it was reported, as we will see soon, that the organisations that were there to protect them were actually complicit in the assaults. The then *Daily Express* correspondent, John Keith, recalls:

"Outside the ground after the match, I saw first-hand violence. I saw English fans being attacked by Italian fans."[12]

He continues:

"I saw this truck coming down hurling missiles at anyone, anyone who was English, who they thought were Liverpool fans. And I dashed to the nearest hotel to file the *Daily Express* with some copy on it and it was a largely unreported event."[13]

Keith also understood the significance of the Rome attacks in relation to the following year's events. He remarks:

"But, I'm sure that the seeds of Heysel were sown that night. There was an animosity there which I had not experienced before."[14]

Livermore and Stuckey, who wrote an unpublished book on Heysel, also highlight the obstacles LFC fans had to face once outside the stadium:

"The Italians had not taken defeat lightly, and as they left the ground, Liverpool supporters were made to run the gauntlet of verbal and physical abuse. Roma fans sprang an ambush near the stadium coach park where they threw bottles and stones at the Liverpudlians. One man was stabbed with a stiletto that narrowly missed his lungs."[15]

Roy and Joan Gronow from the Wirral fell in the car park and were left trembling. Roy recalls:

"Joan was hysterical, so I shouted in Italian to three Roma lads getting into a Fiat. They hesitated, then one of them, a young law student, helped us both in and took us away from danger. We both felt we owed him our lives."[16]

Bob Davies, also from the Wirral, said:

"We all felt safer when the police arrived, but they immediately fired tear gas indiscriminately into the crowd. We all felt the effects. Our eyes were smarting, and it only made it more difficult for us to see where we were going."[17]

Tony Evans also remembers the behaviour of the police:

"Metal bins were set aflame and hurled down the steep grass verges, supplemented by bricks, bottles, and sticks. At street level, the Romans charged, a surge that seemed uncomfortably well-timed to coincide with tear gas the police shot into the rear of the Liverpool fans. As a contribution to crowd control, it was not the Carabinieri's finest hour."[18]

David Pye again:

"The Liverpool fans appeared to be set up by the police and Carabinieri in the immediate aftermath, being prevented from leaving the stadium until, it appeared, the Tifosi were ready for them. By now armed with baseball bats, clubs, chair legs, pool cues, chains and knives, a pitched battle ensued in the narrow streets of the ancient capital. Many English supporters and innocent tourists alike were trapped, beaten, brutalised and stabbed, for the most part in the buttocks—the ultimate slight, a trademark of Mussolini's Fascist vigilante mobs and Mafiosi enforcers."[19]

Even when Liverpool fans found relative safety on their coaches, the nightmare continued. Billy Merritt said:

"After the game we headed towards our coach, Roma fans were everywhere trying to pick off Liverpool supporters, I remember there was very little protection from the police. We boarded the coach and there was glass everywhere as most of the windows had been smashed. The coach driver advised us to lie on top of each other in the aisle to protect us from missiles being thrown through the broken windows as we left the city. Supporters told similar stories on the way home, some had been slashed on the arse, and had spent time in hospital."[20]

Billy's encounters in Rome certainly took away the shine of Liverpool's victory. He recalls:

"I had experienced some scary away days in the '80s but not on this scale, I wasn't arsed that we had won a European Cup, I just wanted to get home safe."[21]

It is clear from the picture David and Billy paint that the psyche of LFC fans changed after Rome. Tony Evans concurs; he also realised that problems in Brussels might lie ahead.

"Liverpool had won the cup, but it was not a day remembered with affection. Before the match, scooter gangs had stalked the travelling fans. After the game, Rome erupted in rage, and the bloody events around the Olympic Stadium left everyone who was there—and those who had only heard talk of what happened—determined not to suffer again at the hands of Italian ultras."[22]

Tony's final sentence and what he says next feed into the perfect storm.

"'The Italians won't do that to us again,' was a refrain

repeated in the weeks since the semi-final. It was not a matter of revenge. It was wariness, a fear that built itself up to an enormous rage that would spill out at the slightest perceived provocation. The anger was palpable, and not just toward Italians."[23]

THE DAY AFTER THE GAME, the Italian press let their feelings be known. *Il Messagero* claimed to have evidence of a premeditated campaign to "hunt down the English".[24] The paper added:

"The gravest aspect is that the English did nothing to provoke the violence. Yet once clear of the police cordon around the stadium they were set upon by the 'Romanisti' armed with broken bottles, sharpened sticks and lethal knives."[25]

Milan's *Corriere della Sera* claimed these Roman hooligans "did not demonstrate calm and self-control which are typical British characteristics."[26]

In 2015, Tony Evans once again echoed similar sentiments about the connections between Rome and Heysel:

"On going to Brussels, we'd all remembered what had happened to us the year before in Rome, where the Romans stabbed and slashed us and attacked us with a frenzy which we'd never seen before in Europe. And it kind of took away what innocence we had. So, when we went to Brussels we went with an attitude, a different attitude, a much more defensive attitude. It wasn't like, let's go and show the Italians, because we was as aware that Rome and Juventus were as far as say us and Chelsea, in terms of difference of attitudes and all that. But the prevailing mood in the Yankie [a bar in Liverpool] and the ordinary [a normal train, not a football special] was like no Italian will ever do that to me again. So, it was more tense, more of a hair-trigger feeling. It was less friendly perhaps than we'd ever been in Europe before."[27]

Tony's recollections really portray anxiousness and a stirring of aggression, which when combined with other factors, paint a clearer picture of why 39 people died.

LFC fan Peter Hooton also saw the possibilities for trouble after the events in Rome. He says:

"Liverpool fans didn't go out on that day to cause thirty-nine deaths. Of course they didn't, but, bearing in mind what had happened in Rome [...]"[28]

Livermore and Stuckey observe chillingly that once Liverpool knew they were to face Juventus in 1984 after the attacks in Rome the previous year:

"Liverpool fans, with long memories and fuelled with pride, were once again face to face with Italians. There were scores to settle and the battleground was Heysel."[29]

Further to the game in Rome in 1984, Liverpool actually played Juventus in the European Super Cup in Turin in January 1985, just a few months before Heysel. Once more, innocent LFC fans were attacked.

When trying to give context to Heysel, LFC supporter John Mackin recounts:

"Plus, the Super Cup Final in January that year. We were talking about an old mate of ours Jim Gardner. He was one of, I don't think very many Liverpool fans that went over for that and they were all attacked. They had to seek refuge on the team bus to get back to the airport away from the Communale [stadium] in Turin, and that was what four months before. So, on the grapevine there was all talk of the Italian football fans were, well Juventus fans were certainly capable of causing trouble, that Italian football fans generally given the terrible attacks on the Liverpool fans after the '84 final in Rome."[30]

John finished by, worryingly, stating: "It was no surprise that there was going to be some sort of disorder that night."[31]

For me now, the picture of what happened on 29 May 1985 is coming sharply into focus. After Rome, and to a lesser extent Turin, the spectre of violence and bedlam grew ever greater over Heysel.

EIGHT

LE BON'S BACK

In previous chapters we discussed ideas that are used to comprehend how individuals and groups behave in crowds. This may or may not come as a surprise to you, although it did to me, but those same theories—or should I say one main theory—dominate the training of police forces all over the world when they are considering how to supervise football crowds or other larger gatherings, e.g., political demonstrators. The principal method used by police forces is based on the theories of a Frenchman from the 19th century. Oh yes, you've guessed it—it is none other than Gustave Le Bon himself.

I would imagine now many people who went to matches in the 1980s are thinking, "Now it all makes sense." Because whilst hooligans were ubiquitous, so was a certain Frenchman within police ranks. In essence, the people who were controlling the crowd saw everyone within it as dangerous until proven otherwise.

I have made the point that what happened at Heysel is not complex; however, what we are about to see is that the communication and organisational structure between the

Belgian police and gendarmerie was far from straightforward, and it played a key role in the catastrophe.

Like in many capitals and big cities around the world, many different types of events are staged in Brussels. The police and the gendarmerie are used to agreeing how these should be handled and making arrangements as to how to deal with occasions, which can sometimes to be extremely violent.[1] With the final taking place in the Brussels District, it was the district commander, Major Keusier, plus his deputy, Captain Dekoninck, who prepared and carried out the mission in consultation with the chiefs of Brussels police.[2] On the day, communication between the two forces was provided by a liaison officer of the gendarmerie at the stadium and at the duty office in Rue Marche au Charbon. The job of the liaison officer was to communicate with his commander of the intelligence unit to convey information from the police.[3]

Returning to Le Bon, it must be pointed out that Belgian police and gendarmerie tried to put into place strategies that attempted, thankfully, to put Le Bon's influence on police crowd procedures on the back-burner—i.e., the Belgians considered the English crowd human beings. Pre-match, the Brussels police would have actually been praised by UK supporter groups because their actions would be seen as treating fans with respect, both for their approach in the city and then at the stadium in the evening.

The crowd control theory they attempted to implement in 1985 had yet to be termed academically. Today, as we saw earlier in a different context, that principle is known as Elaborated Social Identity Model.

For controlling football crowds, ESIM is based on low-profile policing and is seen as beneficial for the avoidance of fan violence and hopefully contributes to a festive atmosphere and to self-policing tendencies among fans.[4] For this to work, it is fundamental that police receive reliable information on the people who make up the fan base and that fans self-police one another. From a Belgian perspective, they believed they had all angles covered, as their interior minister, Nothomb, said: "The match was well prepared, and all measures had been taken considering what we knew."[5]

After the tragedy, the Belgians believed they had been sold a dummy by LFC officials in relation to the information given regarding their fans' previous behaviour. During the parliamentary inquiry in the aftermath, its inquiry chairman, Collignon, said: "The police could, to some extent, have been led astray by the management of Liverpool FC which on several occasions maintained that the Liverpool supporters were amongst the most peaceful in Britain."[6]

On self-policing, Tony Evans believes self-policing went out the window with the ale.[7]

On top of this, the Belgian police were unlucky enough to have come across the English Disease at its peak, and nobody deserved that. And as we will find out later, violence and repulsive behaviour began relatively early doors—think parts of central London before the Euro 2020 final. Xenophobia and racism were proudly on display too. This attitude was taken from the city centre to the stadium, plus many Reds turned up in their droves without tickets. As one LFC supporter says:

"Fifteen of us travelled together on the Monday afternoon [...] Out of the fifteen, three of us had tickets, yet everybody got into the 'game'."[8]

The repulsive xenophobic behaviour, leave me out; however, on the subject of entering without a ticket, I have to confess that I got into Wembley Stadium without paying during the mid-'80s. It was actually relatively easy to get into the national stadium, although you certainly would not attempt it at league grounds.

In 1984, when Everton played Watford in the FA Cup Final, I had a ticket, but like the fan above, many of my mates didn't and they all entered without any problems. How was this possible, especially considering there were two gates to pass through? Well, we simply cut out pieces of the *Liverpool Echo* or *Daily Mirror* and then wrapped a £1 note around the outside, so it looked like a wad of cash and you gave it as a bribe to the turnstile operator. Once you were inside, things were much easier because you just needed someone to pass you their ticket stub. Here two of your friends would pass through the second gate and then only one of them would come back out to the concourse, but of course he would be in possession of two stubs. This would continue until everyone was in. At the 1984 Charity Shield when it was a Merseyside Derby, we bunked into the stands, and we actually sat on the steps because we were in the seated area and of course we didn't have a seat. The '80s were a very different place, so I doubt that could ever happen again at Wembley—oh wait there...

IN THE NEXT CHAPTER, we will see how the police and gendarmerie acted on the day. However, first, it is important for us to discuss police training, through which we can discover the mindset of policing in general. We will also look at examples of best practice and not-so-best practice and contemplate the issues that can affect police performance. It is by looking at these elements that we can assess and reassess the role of the police and gendarmerie in Brussels.

As Hoggett and Stott's analysis suggests, a form of crowd theory associated with the work of Gustave Le Bon has become institutionalised within police training. This in turn leads to a potentially counter-productive reliance on the undifferentiated use of force when policing crowds. In addition, Hoggett and Stott say that such training outcomes not only are counter to the recent developments in evidence, theory and policy, but also undermine the police's ability to develop more efficient and effective approaches to policing crowds.

Along with Le Bon, Allport's concept of the dangers of the crowd is also prevalent in police training. As Hoggett and Stott argue, among the police in the UK, for example, these two classical theories combine in what has been termed the "agitator" model of crowd disorder. This model is based on the premise that crowds attract groups and individuals who seek to "stir-up" or agitate violence. They are then able to "hijack" crowds because of the inherent gullibility of the mass.[9] Put differently, a crowd is a situation whereby the bad can easily lead the mad. With this kind of thinking, police tactics can become arbitrary, counter-productive and can actually make situations worse.

An example of this kind of policing could be said to have been witnessed in Manchester city centre in 2008 during the Europa League Final between Glasgow Rangers and Zenit St Petersburg. An added problem in Manchester appears to be a lack of forward thinking by the city council. The reason this event is important for us is because this combination in Manchester of different official bodies seemingly making errors has echoes of Brussels.

Unlike Manchester, a great example of best practice in

policing football crowds was demonstrated during the Euros in Portugal in 2004, where the policing tactics were based on ESIM. In Portugal, this model of good practice emphasised the importance of maintaining fans' perceptions of the legitimacy of their collective relationship with the police. Where such legitimacy was perceived, it was predicted that fans would tend to enforce the maintenance of non-violent norms (i.e., they would "self-police"). Thus, instead of confronting fans, officers in normal police uniform would patrol areas where crowds were gathered and interact with fans in a friendly manner. Moreover, the success of the tournament in terms of the absence of collective disorder among fans is now widely acknowledged in policy circles throughout Europe.[10] Like I said previously, the Belgians sort of tried this at Heysel.

So, what happened in Manchester?

We know that police were attacked and property damaged in the hours of violence in the city centre. As the *Daily Record* reported, two officers—Mick Regan and John Goodwin—were caught by the mob, surrounded and battered. Police said that they had never encountered disorder of such "ferocity and intensity". All the defendants were captured after being identified through CCTV footage taken during the riots.[11] Passing sentence, Judge Andrew Blake compared the situation to the Blitz:

"The riot police were deployed in full riot gear and struggled to contain the trouble and restore order. What followed was the worst night of violence and destruction suffered by Manchester city centre since the Blitz. What came afterwards, the damage, the filth and litter was apparent to all who arrived in Manchester the following day. Many more than these 12 were involved. It had nothing to do with football rivalries but everything to do with drink. The anger of the mob was directed at the police doing their best to restore order."[12]

Later, the match commander for the game, Chief Superintendent Gerry Donnellan of Greater Manchester Police, observed:

"May 14, 2008, is a night when shameful violence marred what should have been a wonderful football showcase. All of these defendants took part in that violence and must share some responsibility for the disorder in our city. I must pay tribute to both the investigation team and to members of the public who helped us identify these people —without the great response of the Scottish public, we may not have found these hooligans."[13]

All sounds like a slam dunk. "The anger of the mob", as the judge said, just doing its thing. But wait...

It would be fair to comment that the city council and local police totally underestimated the number of Rangers supporters who would travel to Manchester. For the record, an estimated 175,000 Rangers fans, most without tickets for the game, were present. We mentioned before that the Belgians believed they were not given the correct intelligence regarding LFC conduct, an oversight which was fatal. In the Manchester case, it seems it might have been a lapse in forward-planning, but both situations have one thing in common in that once the information is incorrect, ESIM-style policing is built on shifting sand.

Millward makes the point that, for unknown reasons, neither Manchester City Council nor Greater Manchester Police appeared to realise that a UEFA Cup final just a few hours' drive from Glasgow would attract a huge number of ticketless supporters who wanted to take part in a 'fan party'. He goes on to say when this reality became clear, arrangements were made to accommodate supporters in three city-centre fan zones, which served food and (alcoholic and non-alcoholic) drink and intended to screen the football on giant TV screens. However, such plans were only announced on 8 May, six days before the final. This timescale was far too short to plan an event for over 100,000 people.[14]

Given these numbers, the facilities including fan zones were inadequate. As local resident Heather Parry said of the organisation:

"It's not just the accommodation that couldn't stand up to the demand: the lack of public toilets in the crowded areas meant that by Thursday morning, the whole area stunk (I don't need to tell you what of), and the sheer volume of people meant that simply getting from A to B was a logistical nightmare. Trams were stopped, streets were shut off, and for most Mancunians, it was just easier to stay in."[15]

I would like to add that thank goodness every Rangers fan based in Las Americas and Costa Adeje in Tenerife didn't attend, otherwise that figure would have trebled. Forgive the awful joke; however, it does highlight to me that officials in Manchester did not do their homework correctly, because even I could have told them how legendary it is for both Glasgow clubs to travel in numbers that even English clubs can't match.

Coming back to the context, in the fan zone at 7.40 p.m.—five minutes prior to the start of the match—the huge TV screen was still not switched on and the crowd audibly grew uncomfortable. At 7:45 p.m., a sign which said that there was a problem with the transmission came on to the screen, even though—according to fan reports—the TV had shown clips from past matches throughout the day. A loud collective groan was given by the fans, some of whom began to chant 'you're not fit to have the game'.

Once it was clear the match was not going to be transmitted, droves of restless fans began to hoard toward the exits to watch the match elsewhere. The numerical density —and possible alcohol-induced physical instability—of people in the arena meant many fans moved away from the exit in a 'domino effect'. This created visible collective panic in the arena.[16]

Inevitably, as Millward observes, this panic and the heavy alcohol consumption by an apparent great majority of people in the arena gave rise to a number of minor scuffles between supporters. As a limited amount of space appeared, fan gossip spread about a temporary metal gate panel that had been removed by fans where people could leave the arena. This meant that the crowd moved toward the supporters' self-made exit whilst other fans charged at the official exits and broke free, moving towards the public houses and betting shops in the area where they had the opportunity to view the match. As this happened, there were some minor altercations with police officers and security staff as fans hurriedly tried to flee the area.

Had many public houses in the vicinity been open at this point (they were closed because GMP had asked publicans to ensure that their businesses had extra safety provisions, such as stewards, which meant that some would have to spend an extra £3000 before the day of the match), it is likely that social disorder would not have spread beyond a minor level.[17]

Within minutes of these incidents, GMP's Tactical Support Group arrived on the scene, appearing to try to round up many fans and physically move them away from the area. It is in this next part where we see elements of Le

Bon-style strategies. Tactical Support Group officers rounded up some supporters; they physically knocked others to the ground. Not all of these supporters were young men but were of both genders and varying ages.

According to Millward, from his vantage point on a peripheral wall in Piccadilly Gardens, it appeared that some officers were hitting fans with their batons if they verbally questioned their approach. The policing style appeared to be adversarial, as greater numbers of intoxicated Rangers fans moved into the scene and threw bottles at Tactical Support Group officers. The growing number of fans meant that the Rangers supporters ceased to run away from Piccadilly Gardens, and some returned to seek vengeance. Resultantly, more Tactical Support Group officers appeared at the scene as the police officers and football supporters took turns in 'charging' at each other.[18]

Interestingly, there was a marked difference in the number of, and tactics used by, police officers during the day and evening of 14 May. In the day we had a great example of ESIM. For example, there were fewer visible police officers in and around the fan zones. Those officers that were present allowed the light-hearted fun to prosper, with reports that some even mildly joined in by having the tips of their noses painted blue (the colour of Rangers' shirts).

In contrast, during the evening, more draconian measures were adopted, especially by the Tactical Support Group officers who appeared to use unnecessarily heavy-handed methods. Indeed, the *Manchester Evening News* reported that by 3 June there had been 63 separate complaints against GMP, with 38 of those on the grounds of 'excessive force' (incidentally, almost as many as the 42 fan arrests on the evening of the match). The adopted approach appeared to inflame, rather than quell, social disorder, and this fits with O'Neil's argument when she suggested:

"The first thing that becomes apparent when a police officer speaks about football supporters in relation to the general public is that football supporters are not 'normal' people. They are often described as being 'tribal' or 'animal'. A few times I heard police officers say that football supporters are normal people outside the ground, but once they enter a 'red haze' comes over their eyes and they become a different person."[19]

Personally, I have always found the Manchester people I know to have a great perspective on life, so I'll finish with last observations from locals. As Millward says about one Mancunian: "At the train station, a local man, who had witnessed the turn of events, offered his opinion that Manchester City Council 'couldn't organise a piss up in a brewery'."[20]

Coming back to Heather Parry, she stated:

"However, the media is blaming a minority of Rangers hooligans for what we might call this 'mini riot', and completely missing the possibility that at least part of the fault in fact lies closer to home."[21]

She added: "We were expecting a disaster, and what we got was a mere debacle."[22]

WHILE SOME RANGERS FANS' experiences in 2008 were soured by organisational failures, the approach taken in Portugal at Euro 2004 led to an enjoyable time for many England supporters. It is common knowledge that fans of the national team have ruined one-off games and tournaments with their violence. However, at Euro 2004 their conduct was praised by UEFA. William Galliard, UEFA's director of communications, said:

"The English fans have been mixing with a lot of other fans, forming friendships. A lot of beer has been drunk together and lot of celebrating has been done together—it's a sea change."[23]

He added:

"We had a fan park near the stadium for the England v France game. Five thousand fans attended—two thirds English, one third French. Three thousand litres of beer were drunk but not one arrest made."[24]

In the run-up to 2004, it has to be said there were more than 2,000 banning orders to prevent known or suspected football hooligans from travelling to Portugal, but something just as significant was at play.

Before the tournament, Reicher et al. worked with the Portuguese Public Security Police (PSP) to produce a model of good practice in policing football matches. The model was implemented in all the areas under PSP control (which covered all the major cities in Portugal and seven of the ten tournament venues—the other three, in the south, were under the control of the Guarda Nacional Republicana (GNR). The core feature of the model lay in the notion of 'graded policing'. That is, four levels of policing intervention were developed with the aim of creating a positive and close relationship with crowd members, but also of monitoring incipient signs of disorder. This would then allow early appropriate and targeted interventions before conflict could escalate to a level where only draconian measures would suffice.[25]

The approach proved to be highly successful. Overall, the police maintained low visibility, and although there were large numbers of riot police around but out of sight, interventions by these units were very rare. This reflected a very low level of conflict. In only 0.2% of their observations was there any sign of violent behaviour, and even where there was violence, it involved very few people.

In tandem with this, there were a number of notable instances of 'self-policing' amongst fans at critical moments. For example, just prior to one of England's matches, as one group of England fans attempted to assault the police, other England fans confronted the group and actively prevented the attack from taking place.[26]

A spokesman for the FA said: "We are obviously delighted with the behaviour of England fans. The authorities have done an excellent job in keeping away trouble-makers but there's no room for complacency."[27]

This positive picture is corroborated by the official figures. There were no recorded instances of major collective disorder during Euro 2004 in the areas under PSP jurisdiction, and there was only one arrest of an England fan for a violence-related offence. This figure is in contrast to the 965 arrests of England fans during the earlier European championships held in Holland and Belgium in 2000. However, perhaps the most telling comparison would be with those areas under the control of the other Portuguese police force, the GNR, during Euro 2004. The GNR employed a more traditional 'high profile' approach to crowd policing. They either avoided close contact with the crowd or else intervened in force with full riot gear. This resulted in two major 'riots' during which 52 England fans were arrested.[28]

The success of the tournament in terms of the absence of collective disorder among fans is now widely acknowledged in policy circles throughout Europe. Moreover, research on the policing of and crowd psychology among fans attending the tournament largely confirmed the ESIM derived pre-tournament predictions.[29] We can see here how much effort went in to make Euro 2004 the accomplishment it was. As we'll see, that wasn't the case in Belgium, and I understand that was for different reasons, but the point I am making is one of best practice.

Despite the ESIM theory being a more civilised approach to policing crowds than the one based on Le Bon's theories, why do we still see so many incidents of police seemingly using the latter tactic over the former? Now, obviously there are times when the police are faced by a situation where hooligans have already done the damage before they can react or where a crowd is at its height of unruliness. Another reason might be because police logic and training still seem to be dominated by the likes of Le Bon; therefore, the mindset of officers in crowd conditions seems to be one of dealing with groups and then asking questions afterwards. We will now look at studies from different European countries which highlight this.

Starting in Italy, a study by Prati and Pietranoni assessed exposure to crowd conflict, adherence to classical views of crowd behaviour, public order policing methods and attributions of responsibility for crowd conflict among 352 Italian police officers.

Results showed that exposure to crowd conflict was related to adherence to classical views of crowd psychology, which in turn was related to 'bad practices' of public order policing. Police officers saw that both sports and demonstration crowds have a heterogeneous composition. Although crowds, especially the demonstration ones, were perceived as composed by a variety of people, police officers made a distinction between a majority and a minority. The minority is intentionally violent and capable of manipulating the mindless susceptible majority.[30] Broadly, this study supports the police perspective within the ESIM model and stresses the importance of implementing specific public order strategies and training programmes derived from recent empirical studies on the field of crowd psychology.

Coming back to the UK and the study we mentioned before by Hoggett and Stott in relation to Le Bon becoming institutionalised with police training. During their research, they observed that the idea of the inherent irrationality of the crowd was also reflected in discussions between trainers and students. For example, in the following extract taken from a debate between a training inspector and his students, the inspector asserts that crowds invariantly lead to a loss of individuality and rationality, which in turn leaves them open to casual social influence:

"Remember that once a crowd assembles, they lose their individuality. How many times have you heard a person at a football match say, 'I don't know what came over me.' Apparently, 75 per cent of the population can be influenced by the behaviour of others and can be made to conform."[31]

Students themselves then repeated this theoretical model of the crowd in their own discussions, even when trainers were not directly present. What was clear is that implicit in such discussion was the idea of the crowd's irrationality. As such, it was universally and explicitly accepted that "hooligans" (i.e. violent individuals or groups) could always become the primary factor governing the behaviour of the crowd as a whole. For example, during one exercise a student acting as a commander for the hypothetical policing operation specifically briefed the other students about the impact such minorities can have:

"If protagonists or ringleaders immerse themselves into the middle of a crowd, they can be the sort of brain or engine of that crowd driving them on."[32]

Furthermore, where hooligans were understood to be present, it was always the case that the crowd was described as a threat to public order and that there was therefore a necessary requirement to police all fans that were present. Thus, discussions of crowd dynamics sat neatly alongside judgements concerning how to react to sizeable crowds containing suspected hooligans.

It was evident to Hoggett and Stott that there is a relative absence of explicit theory in public order police training in England and Wales. In all the written police training materials they collected, there was only one explicit reference to a theory of the crowd. In line with classic theory, this single reference pointed unequivocally to the idea that in the crowd, individuals will collectively undergo a loss of rationality and be subject to contagion and impulsivity. This theoretical position is given added weight and credibility through the inaccurate assertion that this theoretical model of crowd dynamics and psychology is undisputed in the scientific literature.[33]

Hoggett and Stott concluded that there is, certainly within England and Wales, a lack of focus upon modern crowd theory within public order training.[34] It was their contention therefore that public order police training in England and Wales (and indeed internationally) must be updated to include the latest scientific knowledge so that officers can make these highly demanding decisions in the most informed way possible. Indeed, the evidence suggests strongly that where such knowledge is made available to senior commanders, there can be significant reductions in the overall levels of football-related disorder.[35]

I REMEMBER GOING to Nottingham to watch the Toffees play Notts County on 10 March 1984. We were at the front of the old-school police escort; when we looked back there were Evertonians everywhere, basically as far as the eye could see. At the time I remember thinking, "Oh my God, what a sight." I would have hated to have been a police officer that day, thinking, "Oh my God, there are Scousers everywhere." There was no trouble, but all the same, who'd be a police officer? Given what I've just explained, police officers must clearly have concern for their own safety in crowds, and who can blame them?

With this in mind, the fear and danger experienced by police officers, according to Prati and Pietranoni, has three major implications. First, if crowd members are all perceived to be potentially dangerous, then strict control and quick intervention against crowds was recommended in case of conflict. Second, if crowd danger is perceived as homogeneous, then there were tactical reasons for treating a crowd as a single unit. Finally, police officers tend to deny any possible responsibility for crowd conflict and to attribute it to outside forces. In other words, the violent and irrational nature of the crowd is a sufficient explanation for conflict, and there is no reason to address the role of the police tactics (e.g., use of coercion, undifferentiated intervention) in the dynamic.[36]

In the Britain, Drury et al. carried out a survey study involving 80 riot-trained officers from different United Kingdom forces, and their findings are similar. Drury et al. explored the validity and generalisability of the results about police perceptions and practices. Results showed that police officers view football and demonstration crowds as heterogeneous and, at the same time, comprising powerful minorities and changeable majorities [just like Prati and Pietranoni]. Consequently, police officers recommended strict control and quick intervention to prevent crowd conflict and did not see their own practices as responsible for the escalation of conflict.

And why does all of this matter, after I said the Belgians were trying to implement ESIM at Heysel? Well firstly, we are discussing best-practice, but more importantly for us when Italian supporters were fleeing the attack, some gendarmes actually beat them up with their truncheons. When you think of the last sentence, you think to yourself, "How the fuck could the gendarmes...?

Well, let's try and rationalise it, through research and the actual condition of the Belgian forces who were on duty. Research findings highlight that duty-related stressors among police officers are related to cynical and suspicious attitude towards people.[37] From a police officer's perspective, exposure to violence is a very negative job stressor and can contribute to depersonalisation and a negative, insensitive and cynical attitude towards the public or recipients.

Indeed, as Prati and Pietranoni claim, depersonalisation correlates strongly with more cynical attitudes towards the public and predicts more positive attitude towards the use of violence and actual violent behaviour during a police action.[38] They also argue that involvement in actual crowd conflict might be related to differences in adherence to an ideological view of crowds. Whereas personal experience of crowd events such as concert or sport events may be really pleasant, involvement in crowd conflict is a potentially traumatic event.[39]

According to the theory proposed by Niederhoffer, police officers come into the occupation with idealistic aspirations (e.g. serving the community), but quickly come to realise the hard realities of the world and of police work (in this case, involvement in violent crowd events). And as Prati and Pietranoni point out, over time, police officers then become increasingly stressed and may lose a sense of purpose.[40] These negative aspects can lead to officers becoming cynical.

This cynical attitude may be a way to cope with what is perceived to be an unfriendly and insecure world, providing a convenient explanation for constant disillusionment and a way of acting out anger and resentment. Cynicism as a coping method might be related to stress resulting from involvement in crowd conflict in that it poses a threat to the physical integrity of the self or others. In public-order policing, cynical reactions can take the form of adherence to an ideology that views crowd conflict as deriving from the pathology of the crowd itself or the form of approval of coercive and undifferentiated interventions. This happens because highly stressful experiences violate a person's expectations or well-established schematised knowledge of the self and the world, and can result in changes in one's beliefs and personal assumptions as a response.[41]

Moving away from the theoretical to the practicalities of everyday life, those on duty at Heysel were probably pre-occupied. One deputy in the Belgian Parliament stated: "I admire the courage of those poorly paid men."[42] Further to this, Belgian Interior Minister Nothomb explained in the aftermath that the staff of the Brussel's Gendarmerie had been overburdened with work since the beginning of the year—e.g. terrorism and the Pope's visit—and that they were permanently short staffed.[43] In addition, he pointed out that the amount of training given to officers had for years been reduced to a minimum because the whole force, including reserves, was fully deployed on normal day-to-day duties.[44]

Coming back to Prati and Pietranoni's view of officers "losing a sense of purpose". It would seem that on the night that many officers definitely displayed a loss in their sense of purpose.

NINE

THE GOLDEN RULE

As we saw before, two different organisations were in charge of security at Heysel: the Brussels Police and the gendarmerie. In a very simple way, the police were in charge in the city centre and they policed the Italian end at the stadium. The gendarmerie were at the Liverpool end, which of course included the so-called neutral Section Z where the tragedy occurred. You won't need telling here that there were problems within this two-pronged approach. More importantly, there were complications, particularly within the ranks of gendarmerie command.

On the subject of two heads being worse than one, Poels, from the City of Brussels Police, when giving evidence to the parliamentary committee, was asked if it would have been appropriate to give the entire task of maintaining public order to the gendarmerie. Poels disagreed with this assumption.[1] Next, a member of the committee asked Poels whether, despite sharing the work of crowd control so that police operated inside, and the gendarmerie operated outside, it would have been possible to have a uniformed command structure. Poels responded that there was a well-tried system of co-operation between the two forces.[2]

After the event, Lieutenant General Bernaert, overall head of the gendarmerie, admitted that although the structure was in accordance with custom and practice, tactically it was far from being the best solution. According to the *golden rule,* "unity of terrain means unity of command". Therefore, responsibility for the critical area constituted by the stadium should have been given to one force or the other."[3]

McGregor from British Transport Police, who we mentioned in Chapter One, saw things differently to Poels. He suggested that the deployment of a number of different police forces who apparently did not have compatible communications or centralised control made it difficult, if not impossible, to mount a co-ordinated response within the stadium when matters started to get out of hand.[4]

Interior Minister Nothomb agreed with Poels. He believed the police and the gendarmerie adapted their arrangements to fit the requirements outlined by the organisers during the many preparatory meetings, to fit the nature of the danger as it was perceived and the information supplied by Liverpool, acquired as a result of previous UEFA cup matches. He added the overall arrangements were adequate, until the precise moment when the tragedy took place.[5] We will stay this assertion, because available evidence would seem to counter this view.

We'll begin with the police because they most certainly did a better job than the gendarmes. The Belgian investigation concluded that police communications worked well and did what was necessary to maintain adequate liaison with the gendarmerie. At about 5:30 p.m. a senior police officer pointed out to an officer of the gendarmerie that the gangways between the sections should be occupied. Thirty police officers made themselves available to assist when the charge of Section Z was mounted. Dog handlers stationed behind the scoreboard warned the gendarmerie of what was happening in their sector.[6] The British had different conclusions.

De Pulford from British Transport Police stated there were an astonishing 19 separate independent police forces in Brussels (and these were supported on the day of the match by bodies of national police). He claimed the command structures on the day left a lot to be desired and the police operation, both inside and outside the stadium, appeared to have been neither effective nor co-ordinated. He added that there was no centralised control, nor were all communications compatible.[7]

De Pulford's colleague McGregor was introduced to Commissioner M. Wittam, the officer in charge of police operations at the stadium. McGregor remarked that Wittam was the most co-operative and industrious man, who used no support staff and was in fact a "one-man band". McGregor was unable to discuss Wittam's strategy or plans with him as he was running from one place to another. After the charges by Reds, McGregor actually left the stadium (he thought the match would be abandoned) and returned to Jette.

Whilst in Jette Police Station, he noted that there was no direct contact between that force and the stadium. Information was being gained from commercial radio and television and there appeared to be no appreciation of the seriousness of the situation. The lack of co-ordination was later highlighted to McGregor when he asked the local police commander to inform him how many fans were still at the ground to enable him to deploy his resources. This he was unable to do, as he had no radio contact with the ground, the information being obtained by sending an officer by car to make a physical check of the situation. According to McGregor, although the overall policing arrangements within the city of Brussels initially appeared adequate, the apparent inability to control the sale of alcohol and prevent heavy drinking was a major contributory factor to the disorder later experienced in the stadium.[8]

Next, we will turn to the gendarmerie.

At a meeting in Brussels on 26 April, there was agreement that there should be a barrier put up between Block Y and Block Z and another barrier between Block N and Block M. These were the sections between the supporters of the clubs playing and so-called neutral spectators, who were hopefully to have been mainly Belgians. The Belgian FA (RBFA) agreed with the authorities that there should be at least one gendarme on each of the steps of the segregation gangway between the supposedly neutral fans in Block Z and the English fans in Block Y.

After the disaster, Major Kensier, the Commander of the Gendarmerie for the District of Brussels, disputed this. The major stated that the Belgian FA had never submitted a precise list of demands. He explained that the gendarmes were stationed between the barrier and the English fans. This was so they could enter the crowd if necessary. There should have been 40 in that position, but there were only 12.[9] Captain Dekoninck, Kensier's deputy, took a different line to his boss. He believed that it was true that the gangway was to be occupied by gendarmes, but there was never any question of their undertaking to station a gendarme or two on every step.[10]

Commander of the gendarmerie Alpha Squadron,

Mahieu, who was in charge in the stadium on the night, claimed orders had been issued in writing the evening before and also verbally on the day. The written orders did not mention men being positioned between Sections Y and Z. He also said that after a tour inspection with the organisers at about 3 p.m. on the day of the match, it was decided that gangways should be kept permanently clear. 12 of the 34 men were stationed between the fences separating X and Y, on the Z side. Captain Mahieu went on to say that he had never been told about the alleged decision to place one man on every step. On the night, he noted too that there were Italians in Block Z but did not realise that they were in the majority. There were English fans there too; a few to begin with, but more arrived later as the film showed.[11]

In the light of the inconsistencies in their stories, Kensier, Mahieu and General Bernaert were called back for a second hearing by the parliamentary committee. Kensier stated that there had never been a request to put a gendarme on every step. It was the gendarmerie who decided to put men in the gangway, but never as many as one per step. Mahieu admitted that there had been a difference of opinion as to how the gangway was to have been dealt with. Should it be "festooned with gendarmerie" or kept clear? Bernaert changed his earlier statement in so far as he had said he knew that this had been requested by Roosens (from the RBFA).[12] Like I said earlier, Nothombs' claim of preparations being "adequate" seems a bit flimsy.

The gendarmerie took part in six preparation meetings before the day. It was later emphasised by the Belgian Parliamentary Committee of Enquiry that, aside from errors in the way in which these meetings were conducted, the fact that the interested parties were not always represented by the same people at these meetings undoubtedly led to decisions being taken which were not clear and, in some cases, positively ambiguous.[13] Furthermore, no members of the gendarmerie who participated in the preparatory meetings were present at Heysel on the day of the match.[14] Lastly, the problem of setting up a joint police/gendarmerie post had not been tackled at the preparatory meetings. This omission was a breach of orders.[15]

Moving on, equipment was shoddy. General Bernaert admitted that the walkie-talkies had rather old batteries or batteries which had been used.[16] Technicians were available at the stadium with recharged batteries in case there was any problem with the radio equipment, which of course there was. Added to this was that not enough attention was placed in checking whether the user was using the radio in the correct way.[17]

To make matters worse, some radio calls could not be heard, which could have been due to the levels of noise in the stadium.[18] Unfortunately, lack of resources had caused a delay in renewing equipment. This aside, the communication network had never been well organised.[19] It was hardly surprising that some equipment did not work, because in the aftermath, Interior Minister Nothomb revealed equipment budgets had been pared to the bone and the replacement equipment had not been provided when it should have been.[20] If we add this to the lack of moral we discussed in the previous chapter, we are hardly talking about the greatest police force ever to walk the beat.

The command structure of the gendarmerie left a lot to be desired on the day, too. Four hundred men had originally been detailed to attend; in the course of the evening 1900 additional officers joined. In all, 2,300 men (13 squadrons) had been called to the stadium.[21] Bernaert admitted the command structure was organised in such a way as to prevent the gendarmerie from reacting quickly enough to events. For one thing, the arrangements for circulating information on the state of the crowd were not good. An example of this was that Major Kensier, Commander of the Brussels District, did not know that tension was mounting in the stadium because he was only told about the situation at 7:25 p.m.[22]

Further, the arrangements for circulating orders as to the conduct of the operation were not effective. To expand on this from General Bernaert's answers to a series of questions about contact between the ministry of the interior, the gendarmes on the ground, the reserves and the gendarmerie HQ, it became clear that there were only two telephone lines available at the stadium and that the distance between the official box where the General was and the nearest telephone was about 100 metres; there were also quite a number of obstructions en route.[23] For all kinds of reasons, then, and also because some minor mistakes had been made, a really serious mistake was made. The effect of these minor mistakes was cumulative.

In its conclusions, the Parliamentary Committee of Enquiry believed the command structure within the gendarmerie was open to question.

They asked the question: "What is the relationship between HQ and the operational commander?" The reply given by the gendarmerie was that the operational commander was expected to know what the situation was and that it was not for HQ to intervene at this level. This assumed that the operational commander believed he had sufficient forces at his disposal to meet the situation, and that, should things have got out of hand, he would have taken the initiative in requesting additional manpower.

This is what should have occurred. Asked whether in this case HQ should have informed the operational commander of the situation since they had more information about it than he did, the gendarmerie replied in the negative. This was on the basis that at certain moments of crisis, they believed it necessary to avoid disturbing the commander by making too many telephone calls. The committee considered that if the HQ was aware that the situation was deteriorating then it had a duty to contact the command post rather than to wait passively for the operational commander to make contact.[24]

On the subject of liaison offices, the committee concluded that this was a cumbersome structure. It added, though, that perhaps this was the price that had to be paid for enabling two bodies to collaborate, whilst at the same time maintaining their independence.[25]

Gibson, the Commander of the Brussels Area Fire service, was questioned about his impression at the time the incident took place. He replied that the aggressive attitude of the fans had really worried him. He explained that in his opinion, the gendarmerie had reacted too slowly and added that this was not just an initial impression.[26] In addition, Bill Sergeant, a detective chief inspector at Merseyside police at the time and the man who led the UK investigation, said of the tragedy:

"I am confident that British police—without riot gear—could have done far better. Indeed, 20 Liverpool doormen would have stopped it in very little time."[27]

CAPTAIN MAHIEU, who as we have just seen was in charge in the stadium on the night, had a nightmare at Heysel. Everything that could go wrong did go wrong.

At a little after 7 p.m., Mahieu was outside the stadium. He was dealing with an incident which involved Reds stealing from a hot-dog stall. The parliamentary committee regretted the fact that the tasks of the Mahieu's Alpha Squadron were not clearly shared out between the commander and his assistant. At specific times, it was clear that the two officers were inside the stadium together and that at others; they were both outside. This situation was made worse by the fact that the radio communication system was defective.[28] Once outside, he had not been warned that the situation had changed inside. He had therefore not been able to do anything about it.

At 7:10 p.m. when Reds first charged, Mahieu saw nothing of it. He could have been reached by radio or message but received no communications. Mahieu was convinced that if he had been told the facts by senior officers, reinforcements would have been brought in. He went back into the stadium at 7:20 p.m. At that point, he tried to report what was happening to Kensier, who was at the command post at Rue de Louvain. The issue was that the major was in the process of sending messages to two other units. Mahieu was asked by the parliamentary committee what contact he had had with Major Kensier, who between 7 and 7:30 p.m. was at HQ. He said contact had been made several times.

Mahieu then gave an account of what happened when the English fans charged again at 7:20 p.m. He instructed the commandant of the third platoon, who were outside by the fencing, to come into the stadium with his men. Captain Mahieu made it clear that he himself could not call in reserves if things were not going according to plan. This had to be done through Major Kensier at the command post.[29]

We have just mentioned that the HQ was not in the stadium, but at Rue de Louvain. Bernaert suggested it was right to initially station the operational commander at Rue de Louvain; however, the investigation reported that he should have gone to the stadium as soon as it became clear that fans were arriving in much larger numbers than envisaged. Apparently, this was realised about 6–6:30 p.m.[30]

At his trial in 1989, it was said of Mahieu:

"He was always where he shouldn't be; he did not realise or pretended not to realise what was happening inside the stadium; not even a blind man would have missed that on that block a disaster was unfolding. Moreover, it's pointless for him to state that his orders were to stay outside the venue, because if there is an emergency, orders can be changed, and he should have used the radio to ask for backup."[31]

Mahieu took the rap for the whole operation. He received a nine-month suspended sentence for grave omissions of duty.[32] He was additionally fined several thousand pounds. On appeal, Mahieu's sentence was reduced to three months.[33]

TEN

TICKETS AND ARRANGEMENTS

The semi-finals were played on Wednesday 24 April. Defending champions Liverpool defeated Greek side Panathinaikos 5-0 on aggregate, whilst Juventus beat Bordeaux of France 3-2. Each of the two clubs in the final were to receive 25% of the available tickets.[1] Two days after the semis, LFC CEO Peter Robinson and Mr Kennefick, their travel liaison executive, went to Brussels for a meeting. Also present were: Albert Roosens of RBFA; Gendarmerie Captain De Koninck; Van Reusel, Von Volsom and Meura, all from Brussels City Police.[2] Robinson suggested that a joint meeting with Juventus would be useful, but this did not occur.[3]

During the meeting, it was agreed that the Brussels police were to be responsible for the area including Blocks O, N and M, and the gendarmerie for Blocks X, Y and Z. It was agreed Liverpool fans would be given Blocks X and Y of the terraces. In the stands, they were allocated U, V and W in one stand and A, F, B and D in another. Juventus were to be accommodated in Blocks O and N of the terraces, in Q, P and W in one stand, and in G, L, I and K in another.[4]

There was room for 12,100 people in Section M. 10,695 tickets were sold. In Sections N and O there were 12,200 places available, and 11,000 tickets were sold. For Section Z, 11,250 tickets were available; 10,688 were sold. For Sections X and Y, 11,950 were available; 11,000 were sold.[5] It was also agreed that each side would be issued with some 14,500 tickets, of which 11,000 were for the terraces.[6] The terrace tickets cost £4.50 each.[7]

Block Z and Block M would be allocated to neutral spectators, and the ticket arrangements would be overseen by the Belgian FA. Tickets for northern European countries —Norway, Denmark, Sweden, Holland and Germany— were for the areas next to the Liverpool fans. The RBFA decided to allocate tickets reserved for the southern European countries to areas next to the section set aside for the Italians. The other tickets were available to Belgians and were mainly distributed to Belgian travel agencies, and they went on general sale at the stadium.[8]

Robinson questioned the ticketing policy. He was uneasy about the decision to allow other spectators to stand between the Liverpool seating and standing area. He expressed grave concern in case tickets for this section should find their way into Italian hands. He emphasised that this could create a potentially explosive situation. The Belgian FA informed him that there were thousands of Belgian supporters who would want to see the game and they envisaged no problems as the tickets would be sold directly to Belgians.[9]

Robinson stressed the importance of ensuring that the tickets did not go on the "black market" as there were insufficient tickets to meet the demand from Liverpool and Juventus. Robinson and Kennefick asked how the balance of tickets was to be distributed. They were told that the remaining tickets would be sold through clubs affiliated with the Belgian FA, UEFA sponsors and also by general sale to the public. Robinson and Kennefick were worried about the general sale and asked what form it would take and what restrictions would be on the number of tickets available to each applicant. They were told that a maximum of five tickets per person would be allocated.[10] Roosens' ticketing list showed that for Block Z, Glasgow Celtic were allocated 24 tickets, The Scottish FA 24 and the Welsh FA 120.[11]

LFC said they were not given the opportunity at the 26 April meeting to advise nor was their opinion sought. Robinson also asked whether arrangements could be made for the English fans to be escorted continuously from the time they arrived. The police representatives explained that this would not be possible as arrivals were staggered over a long period. It was then proposed that representatives from Liverpool police should accompany the fans.[12]

It is worth noting that prior to Brussels the club had a history of excellent co-operation with both Merseyside and British Transport Police and had, for many years, had a large body of mature, police-briefed, well-disciplined stewards who travelled together with Liverpool-based BR travelling ticket inspectors and British Transport Police officers on football trains.[13]

According to Roosens from the RBFA, Desmet, his understudy, told him they had to do something for the Belgian public, because otherwise they would find it impossible to find any tickets. Desmet therefore proposed to organise a sale of tickets at the Heysel Stadium. As we just saw, when the tickets went on sale, a maximum of five tickets per person was allowed, at a price of 300 francs each.

On the first day of sales, they decided to sell 3000 tickets, believing that this would be enough, and would have meant that they could have started again the following morning if everything went off successfully.[14] Roosens said that because of the many Italian residents in Belgium and neighbouring countries, most of these 'neutral' tickets ended up in the hands of Italians. A certain amount were also sold on the black market.[15] This explains why Italian supporters were in Block Z, the sector next to English supporters. Added to this, Roosens believes there were more English supporters present than had been expected. The reason was a considerable number of English supporters came to Brussels without being in possession of a ticket. Consequently, they got their tickets on the black market. In addition, it appeared to be evident that a certain number of spectators succeeded in entering the stadium without tickets.[16] As for the locals, Roosens claimed the Belgian public was not so keen to come to the match since many were afraid.[17]

Baudoncq, a Belgian journalist, observed that most of those queuing for neutral tickets spoke French with an Italian accent.[18] He also saw someone carrying a whole reel of tickets; others in the queue were often getting more than five. Some people joined the queue again and again and sold a specific group of people tickets they had bought for 300 francs for 500 francs. Baudoncq met a Belgian travel agent, who reported to him that several of his colleagues, Italian travel agents, were in Brussels organising ticket purchases. A Neapolitan who specialised in black market ticket sales was also pointed out to him.[19]

When staff arrived the next day between 8:15 and 9:15 a.m., there was already a never-ending queue before the ticket offices even opened. The organisers asked the police to send someone over, two or three police officers were actually already present, and from that moment onwards, they proceeded with the sale. After one hour, Desmet telephoned Roosens, pointing out that things were not going well. He had noticed that there were more foreigners than Belgian citizens. He therefore felt that his objective had not been met and that the tickets were not going to the Belgians. He asked Roosens whether he should stop the sale. Roosens asked, "Have you still got a lot left?" He replied, "No, I've been to two or three ticket offices and there are 200 or 300 left." Roosens told Desmet to stop the sale, otherwise he believed that they'd have a revolution on their hands and there was a danger that there would be chaos.[20]

A person who was in the queue told Roosens:

"I can tell you that you really have been had. I found out that from someone in the queue that a certain company, the name of which I did not know, had come to Brussels by coach and 45 of their employees went to the ticket office one by one."[21]

Roosens now understood that all possible means were being used to obtain the maximum number of tickets. This is why they stopped the sales at Heysel. Roosens admitted that, like Baudoncq mentioned, some people left the stadium with whole rolls of tickets. One of the strangest stories includes a Mr Cools. Roosens said Cools, Manager of the Cercle de Bruges (Round Table of Bruges), had asked for 3000 tickets; Roosens told him this was out of the question, and they had an argument about this. Cools, did however, buy 1000 tickets. Roosens said he saw Cools again and asked him what he had done with the tickets. Cools told him that he had sold them to Boerenbond Insurance, who was sponsoring his club.[22]

AT 9 A.M. on 6 May, a meeting took place at the stadium. Interestingly, those responsible for the gendarmerie charged with following preparations had never before taken part in the meetings of co-ordination relative to the organisation of a football match at Heysel.[23]

A further meeting took place on 21 May. Serious concern continued to be felt at Liverpool, particularly when it became known that counterfeit tickets were in circulation in Italy and that there was also a black market in tickets; this meant tickets were likely to be available at the stadium on the day of the match. The situation was so crazy, with Peter Robinson claiming that Liverpool FC was offered tickets from agents who appeared to have a large number of black-market tickets to give to the club.[24] This concern was expressed by John Smith, chairman of Liverpool, to British Minister for Sport Neil MacFarlane. MacFarlane sent a telex message to the general secretary of UEFA on 28 May to request that UEFA's own rules be vigorously implemented. MacFarlane also warned of the danger of segregation being disrupted. Although the telex message requested comments, no reply was ever received.[25]

On 23 May there was a meeting at Tadworth, the British Transport Police training school. Various interested parties were there, including the Belgian Gendarmerie, Calais Police, Dutch Rail Police, Kent Police and the Department of Transport. The meeting first heard about the police operation from the European Cup Winners' Cup Final that had taken place in Rotterdam between Everton and Rapid Vienna the week before. Rotterdam was important for a couple reasons. First it gave the Belgians the opportunity to not just observe British fans taking over a continental city centre, but to scrutinise people from the same city. Second, the Belgians could see how the Dutch had handled fans in and around the stadium.

In Rotterdam, all police leave had been cancelled and 1200 men, including 70 members of the riot squad, were on duty, plus there were many police dogs. The presence of so many police may have impressed the visiting supporters, too. Interestingly, in Everton's case, British Transport Police believed the threat of being detained until 20 May for a serious misdemeanour undoubtedly had a salutary effect on Toffees, because few supporters would have risked missing the FA Cup Final against Manchester United three days later on the Saturday.[26]

According to British Transport Police, things passed off better than expected and Rotterdam police did a very good job.[27] An example of this is when it looked like tension was rising, the services of law and order organised a football match with supporters of Everton and Dutch policemen; the objective of inducing calm was achieved.[28] This is ESIM at its best.

There were a few problems in Rotterdam too. At least one bar was closed by 4 p.m. because beer glasses were being broken or stolen, and it was said, but not confirmed, that crates of beer were purloined from supermarkets.

When driving to the Feyenoord Stadium about 6:15 p.m. T. Sharp from British Transport Police passed many bars where Everton supporters, in the warm sunshine, were clearly intent on warding off the risk of dehydration.[29] Funnily enough, a friend of mine who was at the match recently told me that a guy behind him missed the game from start to finish because he needed 40 winks after having one or maybe possibly two too many. Five or six Everton supporters were detained for drunkenness and bottle-throwing, and a similar number of Austrians were also being held in custody. One Everton fan was taken to hospital for a hand injury caused by an Austrian.

In the stadium, the British and the Austrians were segregated in their respective blocks. The lack of this, as we know, was one of the major reasons for the problems in Brussels. Interestingly there were few or no police in the stadium; this surveillance fell on the private security people, which was ordered by the directors of the stadium.[30] This strategy was half followed at Heysel, in that there weren't many police in the stadium, but unfortunately, they didn't have the private security people required on duty. Roosens later explained why.

He disclosed the RBFA were finding it more and more difficult to find people who were prepared to do stewarding work, partly because they were often beaten up by impatient spectators at the turnstiles.[31] The company Securitas was employed at the stadium too. Roosens asked during one preparatory meeting whether Securitas guards could help with searches and undertake initial ticket checks in the area outside the perimeter fence that had been installed to create a neutral zone at the entrance to the stadium itself. The answer was that only the police could do this work. The Securitas guards therefore spread out around the main entrance itself to give a hand. To make matters worse—certainly from a communication perspective—Securitas employees kept in touch using walkie-talkies, but they were not allowed to use the wavelength reserved for the gendarmerie, and the police and therefore could not communicate with them.[32]

Staying with stewarding for a moment, in his case study during a match between Portsmouth and Southampton, Frosdick experienced stewards are more effective at 'policing' football crowds than inexperienced or aggressive police officers. He found that the stewards on the segregation line at Southampton dealt with the crowd surge more effectively than was seen in the aggressive police response.[33] This is important for Heysel because many gendarmes did not seem to be experienced enough to deal with the situation.

Coming back to Rotterdam, the Austrians, although fewer in number, made their presence felt with deafening sirens while the Everton supporters responded with Scouse tribal chants and flag waving. The Austrian supporters let off firecrackers, coloured smoke bombs and rockets during the match. No action was taken by the police. The Rapid fans also set fire to some flags. In contrast, there were no unpleasant incidents in the Everton half of the stadium.[34]

Van Reusal, Commissioner of the City Brussels Police, visited Rotterdam.[35] According to the Mayor (of Brussels) Brouhon[36] and Chief Commissioner of Police Poels, the gendarmerie declined the invitation.[37] Which, with hindsight, looks slack. Lieutenant General Bernaert alleged that one of the reasons the gendarmerie did not send an observer to Holland was they had been heavily involved with the Pope's trip to Belgium.[38]

The conference was also informed that, as a result of a request from the chief of Brussels City Police, the British Transport Police would be sending eight Liverpool-based police officers to Brussels. The officers would initially police trains from Liverpool in uniform, but on entering Belgium or boarding Belgian ships would change into plain clothes and have no police powers and act only as liaison officers. The next day in Liverpool, it was arranged that 12 senior stewards were to travel with the fans.[39]

On 24 May 1985, Robinson visited Brussels to collect complimentary tickets for officials. He saw Mr De Wint of the Belgian FA, who expressed concern about the counterfeit tickets. Robinson told him that, unknown to anyone, he had caused all the Liverpool allocation to be stamped on the back with the Liverpool crest. This would immediately enable the security men to identify the genuine tickets. From the evidence subsequently obtained, it does not appear that the Belgians made any use of that important information.[40]

On top of the genuine tickets that were sold on the black market, 2,500 counterfeit tickets had been printed and acquired by a travel agency in Milan.[41] On Friday 17 May, Roosens received a phone call relating to the forged tickets. The agent in Milan asked to come and show him some tickets which he thought were forgeries. The agent travelled from Milan with his lawyer and showed him a big suitcase containing 2,250 tickets. When Roosens examined them, he realised they were obviously forgeries. For Roosens, it was merely the feel of the paper. He then warned the agent and the lawyer that they could be in serious trouble. The Italian told Roosens that he had paid 5 million francs for the tickets. The agent was then questioned by the CID. Roosens phoned a higher authority but was told to call back on Monday. The Italian could not wait until Monday, so returned to Milan. Roosens advised him not to sell the tickets given he knew his identity. "Why not?" the agent said. "In Italy it happens all the time. The black market in tickets is more alive than the genuine one."[42]

In the end, the agency delivered 2,250 of these false tickets to the authorities. In order to avoid any possible risk resulting from the 250 counterfeit tickets which were still in circulation, the Belgian FA blocked 640 tickets which had not yet been sold so that these might possibly be exchanged against false tickets. 19 of these forged tickets were used.[43]

The ticketing fiasco had huge, fatal consequences. Amedeo Spolaore and Mario Ronchi booked their trip and bought their tickets from a travel agency in Treviso. Both ended up in block Z, and sadly, both were killed on the terraces of Heysel.[44] As Italian author Francesco Caremani tragically noted, Juventus fans that had purchased tickets for Block Z "paid more to die".[45]

From an English perspective, neutral (Spurs) fan Paul Fry actually purchased his ticket on the morning of the game at the box office. At the time, although he was at the game in a non-working capacity, Paul was working as a freelance journalist at the *Sporting Life*, the *Mail on Sunday* and the *Times*. He had reported on FA Cup Finals, World Cup qualifying matches in Australia and Scotland, plus a few European games for the *Times*, including a match in Belgium between Bruges and Nottingham Forest. Paul was travelling to Brussels for a few days to see his then Belgian girlfriend who worked as a translator for a Belgian bank. Paul picks up the story:

"I finished my shift at the old Mirror building in London around 9:30 p.m. Then took the train to Dover and the night boat over to Ostend in Belgium. The boat trip was a pleasant experience with people chatting and drinking."[46]

The following morning Paul took the journey into the heart of Brussels city centre, just a short walk from the Grand Place, the medieval square. His first task was to try and buy a ticket. He ventured up to the stadium, more in hope than expectation. Unsurprisingly, given what we know now, it was a very simple operation. He recounts:

"It was easy to get a ticket for the game, too easy in fact. There was a little hut just outside the stadium and I rocked up not expecting to get a ticket. I hadn't gone there with that in mind, but I thought I'd try my luck. There was a very small queue of about ten yards, and I bought a ticket for the equivalent of about £20."[47]

It turned out it was infamous Block Z. As Paul says:

"I was amazed. I didn't know what part of the ground I was going to be in. It transpired later that Block Z was where I was."[48]

With his ticket sorted, Paul was excited at the prospect of seeing two of Europe's giants. He recalls:

"I was really thrilled. I'd never seen a European Cup Final live."[49]

Little did he know.

The evening before the game, the RBFA made statements to the effect that the match had been perfectly well organised. At a later date, the Belgian authorities disagreed. They concluded that ticket sales got completely out of hand and that a large number of tickets to Section Z were sold to Italians who should not have been there.[50] They pointed out that both the RBFA and UEFA seemed more concerned with the financial and commercial considerations than safety precautions. Last, they noted that it was amazing that, knowing about the significance of the black market, the organisers did not warn the forces of law and order of the potential dangers.[51]

Alas, we will leave the last words to Albert Roosens. Sadly, he recollected:

"I had organised hundreds and hundreds of matches. This was to be the last because I have reached retirement age. I wanted it to be the crowning glory of my career: it has turned into a nightmare."[52]

At his trial, Judge Verlynde handed a suspended six-month jail sentence to Roosens for negligence and poor organisation.[53]

ELEVEN
"IT LOOKED LIKE A SCRAPYARD."

On 4 September 1984 Heysel was given hosting rights following a meeting on 31 August 1984. On 7 February 1985, UEFA delegates visited the stadium. Van Volsom from the Belgian police was present. He said the UEFA men looked at both the inside and outside of the stadium and made not the least comment or request for changes. Their trip lasted an hour and could be regarded as a formality. Van Volsom, who had known the stadium for well over 24 years, said it was rare for there to be any problems inside. Usually, the trouble was outside.[1]

On the 11 and 12 February, at the request of UEFA, another inspection was held at the stadium. Attending along with UEFA were representatives from the RBFA, the police, the press and Brussels city officials.[2] Wouters, Chairman of the RBFA, said he thinks that on this occasion 20 people took part in the visit. He noted that the entire stadium was inspected, as was the condition of the lockers, the changing rooms, and the sanitary and first aid facilities; access routes and parking facilities were also looked at. After the check, he said no adverse comments were made.[3]

Wouters claimed it should be recognised that from his experience of matches involving West Ham and Arsenal (where only minor incidents took place) this only reinforced his belief that the crowd safety arrangements at Heysel, if not perfect, were at least adequate.[4] Wouters did forget to mention Aston Villa's experience at the stadium. Villa had made an official complaint about arrangements at the stadium after their European Cup semi-final against Anderlecht produced a near riot in 1982. On that occasion, they wrote to UEFA complaining about inadequate segregation of supporters, casual sale of tickets on match day, lack of adequate police presence, and sale of alcohol in the vicinity of the ground. And in particular they pointed out that when trouble broke out behind one of the goals, Villa stewards (not the police) had to go into the crowd to intervene and keep rival fans apart.[5]

Coming back to the February checks, Resende from UEFA remarked that all the premises in the stadium were found to be in order.[6] From Brussels' point of view, Mayor Brouhon said that by choosing to play at the stadium, UEFA had shown in this case that the technical installations of the stadium presented the necessary guarantees which would enable the match to take place. He went on to say that he had never come across any remarks regarding its infrastructure, either from those in charge of clubs or from observers and organisers of international competitions.[7]

Despite the reassuring words above, Heysel Stadium was not fit for purpose and was a major contributor to the tragedy. The game—any game, in fact—should never have been played there. It was an insult to Liverpool and Juventus supporters to host the match in such a ramshackle football ground. In May 1985, the stadium was owned by the City of Brussels (VdB) and leased to the Belgian Football Association. This arrangement began in January 1978 and was to expire 31 December 1986.[8] The last inspection of the Heysel Stadium, by the Brussels Area Fire Service, had taken place in 1978.[9]

Heysel opened in 1930 and had been regularly used for football matches. It had played host to fifteen return matches, either for the European Cup, or those organised by the UEFA, and international matches were played there too. Just a few weeks before the European Cup Final, a match between Belgium and France was held there. It was attended by the same number of spectators as were present on 29 May, give or take three or four thousand. There was no criticism of the stadium on that occasion.[10] The stadium could house 62,000 spectators, although this was reduced for the final to around 58,000. An electronic scoreboard had been added in 1980, but seemingly nothing was done at that time to improve the terracing.[11]

Irish Red Kevin McFadden says of the ground: "It was a European Cup Final. I was in better grounds in the League of Ireland."[12]

Otello Lorentini, who lost his son, Roberto, during the attack, was shocked at the conditions: "A European Cup final between Liverpool and Juventus held in a stadium that was falling apart. I'd never seen anything like it."[13]

Liverpool's skipper on the night, Phil Neal, observed:

"My first thought was that it barely stood comparison with Wembley or Rome or other grounds where Liverpool had won the European Cup. The game would have sold out any stadium in Europe, yet instead of Barcelona or Madrid we got Heysel with its frail-looking fence."[14]

The inadequacy of the venue becomes clear on the day when one considers the words of Juventus president, Giampiero Boniperti, who recalled some years later:

"At noon we made the inspection of the ground, and we all tore our hair: it was old, decrepit and it looked like a scrapyard. There were wooden boards all over the place, they looked like cudgels."[15]

In Britain, once the full effects of the crowd disruption became known, the chair of the Public and Fire Brigade Committee authorised the deputy chief officer of the London Fire Brigade and the council's (Greater London Council) deputy structural engineer to visit Brussels immediately. They made this decision in light of the Council's recent moves to improve public safety in sports stadia and of the commitment to respond to the *Popplewell Report*.[16] The visit by London Fire Brigade was low-profile; this was in part because of the outrage felt over the activities of the British supporters. Consequently, this outrage led, to some extent, to a hampering of the UK inspection.[17]

A Liverpool City Council inspection took place on Wednesday 12 June and was carried out by Liverpool's city building surveyor. His task was to "seek and learn any immediate lessons for crowd safety following the tragedy which took place at the European Cup Final".[18] He had no remit to look at the causes of the tragedy. The London inspection, although hampered, did have more remit than the Liverpool investigation. Liverpool's surveyor was accompanied on the inspection of the stadium by the Brussels Fire Brigade Public Relations Officer, Mr F Boilean, and by the commander in charge of the emergency services at the time of the tragedy. As with the London trip, the surveyor's visit was low-profile due to the ongoing Belgian parliamentary enquiry into the tragedy; therefore, his report was private and confidential. Both reports were scathing.

We saw before, in passing, how chaotic entering the stadium was, and it is here we will begin when looking at the reports. Because of the lack of turnstile-controlled access points, the Liverpool report noted this situation had serious implications as to the manner in which the stadium authorities were able to ascertain with any accuracy the exact number of persons in any part of the ground, and thus prevent possible overcrowding.[19] In a previous chapter, we saw the consequences of overcrowding in stadiums. And the next part of the report could have been taken from any of the UK Government's reports we came across in Chapter Five.

"To make matters worse all the entrances were at the back meaning fans filed in in one direction, thus, all spectators on the terraces were in an enclosed space with only one means of egress. Therefore, there was no reasonable alternative means of escape available to cope with any emergency evacuation for whatever reason."[20]

During the parliamentary committee enquiry on 9 July, the commander of the Brussels Area Fire Service, Van Gompel, was asked about the limited number of means of egress. He admitted that the problem had never been raised, even though numerous errors could have been learned from the incident at Glasgow in 1971. He went on to say that the football authorities should have asked stadium officials to attend to this problem much sooner.[21] Furthermore, the toilets and refreshments were sited next to the entrance gates at the top of the terrace, and spectators requiring use of these facilities would cause more crowd movement than normally expected in a capacity crowd.[22] Also at the top of the terracing there was a portable timber shed which added to the chaos, for as the London report claimed:

"This was used to store crates of 'Coca-Cola'. Below this hut it was observed that there was a stock of 100 lengths of small-bore plastic pipes. It would seem clear from the number of pieces of plastic pipe scattered about the area and from viewing the footage of TV material, that these pieces of pipe had provided a convenient source of potentially dangerous material for use by the demonstrators."[23]

A suspect who was arrested by Merseyside Police after the disaster mentioned finding a piece of pipe on the floor.[24]

In terms of the terracing, the Liverpool report revealed that: "the surface of the terrace is compact earth of a shale-type appearance, with only the nosing of the step being formed in concrete. These concrete nosings had deterio-rated and crumbled over the years, exposing rusted exposed bars."[25] It described the general condition of the terracing as "poor".[26]

Of the crush barriers, deputy structural engineer Jan Korff, from Greater London Council, wrote:

"In my opinion the main killer was the crush barriers. Most people were killed on the terraces and the wall made an insignificant contribution."[27]

He also disclosed: "If the 55-year-old crush barriers had been replaced, then they could have survived the attack and deaths would have been very much limited."[28]

Staying with the crush barriers, *New Civil Engineer* magazine found exposed bars so corroded that as little as 50% of their original cross-sectional area remained sound. No repairs had ever been attempted to any of the crush barriers in the stadium.[29] The City of Belgium authorities (VdB) blamed cash shortages for the state of the crush barriers.[30]

In terms of crowd segregation between Y and Z, the LCC report stated that this composite construction, whilst forming a physical barrier, would not withstand a packed crowd on a terrace.[31] If it could not withstand a packed crowd, it is no surprise how easy it was for supporters to pull it down.

From a building perspective, in relation to the infamous wall, the London report highlighted that the wall had been constructed on top of a low, sloping, flat-topped concrete buttress which flanked and terminated the terrace steps. Neither the wall nor the brick piers were in any way 'keyed' into the concrete buttress, which in turn presented a structure which was totally unsuitable to take lateral pressure."[32] *NCE* concurred; they said the masonry wall along the side of Sector Z was tatty. The last five-metre run nearest the front of the terrace had tumbled over in the crush, splitting cleanly away from the plinths on which it sat. The wall had been built on top of the plinth with no attempt to bond to it. Additionally, the brick wall was inadequate, and its buttresses were built on the wrong side so they could not oppose the pressure of the crowd.[33]

In terms of the tragedy, the London report stated:

"In discussions with those directly involved in the rescue, it would appear that it was the pressure of the crowd which caused the collapse of the wall. Whilst no person was actually trapped under the wall, the crowd pressure caused many people to jump from the buttress down onto the debris from which only minor injuries resulted. However, the crowd movement caused many of the people, now funnelled and compressed into the angle between the lower terrace tiers and the wall, to stumble and have the remainder of the crowd trampled above them. Similar circumstances also resulted from the collapse of the perimeter fence and a number of people were also trapped underfoot. This appeared to be the main reasons for the high casualty section."[34]

In its summary, the LCC report declared:

"If the criterion of the Guide to the Safety of Sports Grounds (Football) Code were to be applied to this particular stadium, it is doubtful that the City Building surveyor would be able to recommend a grant of Safety Certificate issued pursuant to the Safety of Sports Grounds Act, 1975, to the appropriate Licensing Authority in this case."[35]

Responsibility for the stadium maintenance was with its owner, the municipal authority Ville de Bruxelles. But VdB did not carry out actual safety inspections. Freddy Thielemans, chief assistant to VdB burgomaster Herve Brouhon, said:

"The building is checked by the fire brigade. They have responsibility for all safety, including fire and structural aspects. It's a wide form of power. They check the stadium regularly, usually before each event, and it was done here."[36]

But the Brussels fire service flatly denied any responsibility for structural checks at the stadium. Operations chief Andre Ulkay responded by saying:

"The stadium owner normally guarantees safety. It's not a legal obligation but it is within the spirit of the law. We are asked for our view by the local authorities before they issue a building permit, but that only concerns the fire regulations."[37]

Like I said before, it would seem the last real inspection had taken place in 1978.

The absence of clear legal safety regulations and the subsequent confusion was further compounded. VdB controlled only the police, while the fire brigade was administrated by the city's other elected body, l'Agglomeration de Bruxelles, which had responsibility for all the city's technical functions.[38] Investigations by *NEC* showed complete confusion over who, if anybody, was responsible for checking structural safety at the Belgian stadium.[39] As we saw in the previous chapter and as the London report highlighted:

"The Deputy Chief Officer of the London Fire Brigade was, however, advised of a briefing meeting held the week before the match that was attended by a number of those responsible for the arrangements, to which the Fire Department do not appear to have been invited."[40]

It is clear that different organisations were negligent in relation to upkeep of the stadium. Taking everything into consideration, it begs the question: how on earth was the game ever played there?

TWELVE

"FOOTBALL WAS YESTERDAY'S SPORT."

1985 was an extremely violent year in Britain. The deaths in Brussels were, in the cruellest of ways, the end result of an amalgamation of issues. These issues had been building for years, not only in British football but British urban society at large. Alas, they came together that evening to produce a perfect storm, which wrought havoc on an unimaginable and bloody scale. The next few chapters will bring together some of those topics, concerns that left English football sinking more and more into the mire leading to Heysel, which left us in the gutter. Over decades, the perfect storm of Belgium had been gathering pace; 1985 saw the pedal hit the floor, and then nothing could stop what I believe was a self-fulfilling prophecy.

Added to the football was the Miners' Strike of 1984-85, and the scenes of chaos on the TV, seemingly most nights, from Northern Ireland. In Liverpool itself, like many places in northern England, unemployment was rampant. Then had the ignominious situation of seeing the national government bouncing Liverpool City Council all over the ring. If it were a boxing fight, it would have been stopped a lot sooner, considering the city was in no position to defend itself. Along with the hooliganism, only the latter point has any direct connection with Brussels in that it fell to the people who were fighting Thatcher to lead the reconciliation visit to Turin, and history records that that was a massive error of judgement.

A member of Margaret Thatcher's cabinet, Chelsea fan David Mellor, described the footballing times like this:

"Football looked like yesterday's sport, being attended by yesterday's people, a sort of sub-race of really unpleasant and unattractive individuals, who certainly in the eyes of people like Mrs Thatcher summed up everything that was awful about the English nation."[1]

What is crystal-clear is that football in England in 1985 was a million miles away from the family-friendly, all-seated stadiums we recognise today in the Premier League—although in an obstructed-view kind of way, Goodison has hardly changed. In the mid-'80s, violence was rising and attendances falling; the season before Brussels, Liverpool had won a treble, yet their average attendance was a mere 35,793, whilst Manchester United, England's biggest club, stood at just 42,534.[2] By comparison, during the 2016-17 season, Liverpool's average gate was 52,879 and Manchester United's was 75,290.[3]

Putting aside the game at Goodison Park we spoke about in Chapter Four, three games in particular stand out as part of a perfect storm. Over the next couple of chapters we will examine them.

Chelsea vs Sunderland. *Stamford Bridge, London, 5 March 1985.* When Chelsea played Sunderland in the second leg of the League Cup at Stamford Bridge, 40 fans were injured, 20 policemen were hurt and 104 supporters arrested in and outside the ground. Chelsea fans stormed the pitch after Sunderland's Clive Walker scored his and their second goal (the first was a beauty, by the way) and put the game beyond Chelsea. One Chelsea fan tried to attack Walker. Modestly, Walker played down the incident by saying Chelsea player Joey Jones "saved my bacon there".[4]

Chelsea supporters used seats as improvised missiles to throw at the police; one fan literally ran across the pitch carrying a chair (not a seat) to attack the Sunderland fans. The game was held up, and some Chelsea fans were trampled by police horses during the melee. When Colin West bagged Sunderland's third, there were police officers still on the pitch. Unsurprisingly, at the final whistle, the Sunderland players did not celebrate; instead they legged it down the tunnel.

Then football commentator for Tyne-Tees TV, Roger Tames, travelled down to the match on a coach with Sunderland fans. He gives an illuminating picture of how hazardous life could be for an away supporter, especially during the 1980s:

"It was basically frightening. Everybody who I was with did not enjoy the occasion. They'd gone down there obviously to see Sunderland win, but there was no celebration on the coach, they were just very pleased to get back on it. Certainly, I came out of the ground with one supporter and made a comment to him and he was literally too frightened to answer because he thought his Wearside accent would give him away and didn't want to face the consequences. In the stands in front of me somebody was attacked and most of the trouble was in the stands not on the terraces. All the tickets we had were through Sunderland Football Club officially bought and there was no segregation to be seen and Chelsea supporters in fact came in at half-time and were looking for trouble. The police came in, they did a good job

I thought, I was certainly pleased to see them. They came in and hauled a lot of them out. It was very very frightening, nobody enjoyed it and a lot of people would certainly not go back to Stamford Bridge again. If you want to know what drives people away from football, well that's it in a nutshell."[5]

FA Secretary Ted Croker, who was also at the game, commented:

"It's the clubs who we feel terribly sorry for because these people are calling themselves supporters of the clubs and yet they're the last people the clubs want inside. But we're interested in seeing the outcome of this too because I believe 104 people were arrested. We want to know what punishments are meted out to these people because this is one of the deterrents, I mean it's no good punishing the club."[6]

Croker's words are important to the whole question of hooliganism at the time because it seemed governments and clubs were going around in circles discussing whether the clubs should be held responsible or if it was fans that had to be held accountable for the disturbances. As we saw in a previous chapter, report after report was carefully filed away under the 'more use as a door wedge' section.

Before moving on to Chelsea's 'nuclear' solution to this riot, I would like to share two other examples from this game to demonstrate how mad and out of control English football was at the time. In 2008, Chelsea fans were reminiscing about the game on a fansite. One fan said the following:

"The sunderland fans got a much easier walk out of the stadium because the bulk of the real hooligans went straight to PG [Parsons Green] and wrecked the train carrying 200 or so ICF/U5's coming back from wimbledom."[7]

Several other fans on the site also recalled the incident. Essentially, it does not matter if there were "200 or so ICF"—what is really significant is the feeling that football hooliganism knew no boundaries. You have a situation where you might imagine Chelsea hooligans had had their fill for the night and would retire for a pint before last orders was called; instead, they went in search of further aggro.

The second event involves Ken Bates (the then Chelsea owner) and the TV rights to the match. Bates wanted £20,000 from Tyne-Tees TV to show two minutes of highlights. Tyne-Tees refused to pay, so the TV company obtained the pictures of the mayhem and goals from the company hired by Sunderland to record the match.[8] In addition, Bates went to the courts to try and obtain a high court injunction against Thames TV preventing them from showing the pictures of the riot. Bates failed and had to pay costs.[9] Today, you just could not conceive of the owner of a Premier League club running to the courts the day after a game and taking out injunctions over riots which had occurred in the stadium.

A few weeks after the Sunderland semi-final, Chelsea's solution to the problem was to install a twelve-volt, twelve-foot electric fence. During a TV interview, Bates was in a bullish mood and said he was prepared to fight the Greater London Council. The council argued that the fence was in breach of the Safety of Sports Ground Act, therefore the fence needed their consent. Bates believed he was following all accepted safety practices. He told the press:

"I really don't see what all the fuss is about quite frankly because if you just come here and watch a game, you sit in your seat and watch the game, you have no problem, and it doesn't affect you at all. The only person it's going to affect is someone who is a determined troublemaker. The local police have already indicated that if they do catch anybody, they'll throw the book at them under Section 5 of the Public Order Act."[10]

Bates then looked into the camera mischievously and remarked:

"Which carries a maximum penalty of six months and/or £1,000 fine. So, if anybody's daft enough to do it, they want a holiday at the government's expense, they should try."[11]

Thankfully, the electric fence was never switched on. To be fair to Bates, some of his ideas were visionary in comparison with other clubs. He at least tried to adhere to suggestions that had been recommended in various governmental reports down the years—I'm not talking about the fence of course. He was the first to introduce closed-circuit TV and family enclosures; he also proposed a national police task force on hooliganism and advocated constraints on convicted hooligans travelling abroad, long before such measures were introduced.[12]

For research purposes, I visited Stamford Bridge, and you are not going to be surprised to hear that it was impossible to compare that evening in March 1985 and the modern-day CFC. Even during the closed season, there's security searching you before you are near to the stadium itself. To me, it was clear that these days you would not be able to take your own chairs with you inside the stadium.

THIRTEEN

"IT WAS LIKE SOMETHING OUT OF ZULU"

***Luton vs Millwall**. Kenilworth Road, Luton, 13 March 1985.* The day before I visited Chelsea, I had visited Kenilworth Road. Unlike Chelsea, and despite the weather being much nicer in Luton than in London, it seemed to me that the stadium could not have changed much since the '80s. If I am being honest, I was shocked by the state of the ground —that's because it somehow made Goodison Park look like Las Vegas. And as anybody who has ever visited the Grand Old Lady in recent years will tell you, that takes some doing. What I could deduce by visiting was that the stadium on that night must have been terrifying for some locals, especially if they got caught in the narrowest of intimidating narrow alleyways that run along where the executive boxes are situated. Yes, you read that correctly, where the executive boxes are.

On the wall in the alleyway, Luton Council had a sign telling people fly-tipping was illegal and you could face a £400 fine or prosecution. Of course, that hadn't deterred some horrible people who had been tipping to their heart's content. And the narrowness of the alleyway had not deterred Huddersfield Town and Bristol City fans, because they had gone to the bother of placing their stickers on the fly-tipping sign.

Anyway, I digress, because if Heysel had not happened, this incident would probably have gone down in the archives as the worst football riot connected with an English club. It is, however, fair to say this was probably the most unpleasant football disturbance ever seen on English soil.

Just eight days after Stamford Bridge and only two months before Heysel, Luton faced Millwall in a FA Cup match. Thirty-one policemen were injured, sixteen other people were hurt, ten of which required hospital treatment, and unbelievably, Luton goalkeeper Les Sealey had a knife thrown at him. Thirty-one fans were arrested as hooligans went on the rampage before, during and after the game. Seven hundred seats were ripped from the stands and used as missiles. Outside the ground, houses and cars were smashed, and some residents were assaulted. For good measure, trains to and from London were destroyed. The FA said the violence was the main reason it was not chosen to host the European Championship in 1988. Ted Croker, the FA Secretary, stated:

"All the other statistics we were able to present, our overall presentation and the factors in our favour, would have indicated that we should have got the tournament."[1]

The signs for the mayhem to follow began in the afternoon at St Pancras Station in London. Roger Stott, MP for Wigan, informed Parliament the next day that:

"My honourable friend the member for Sheffield Central and I were at St. Pancras station at 4.10 p.m. yesterday, and that even at that early time there were at least 200 or 300 Millwall supporters, most of whom were drunk and many of whom were throwing beer over passengers, behaving in a loutish, hooligan fashion and terrorising most of the people on the platform. It was fairly obvious to those at St. Pancras last night that if that lot got on a train and were deposited at Luton there was bound to be trouble."[2]

Stott was most certainly correct with his assessment. Local woman Yvonne Fletcher recalled:

"By 3 p.m. the local radio was reporting that the Arndale Centre was shut because of trouble in the town centre, while before kick-off there were so many fights I said to my dad, 'This game is never going to happen'."[3]

ITN reported the first fans arrived on commuter trains as early as 4:30 p.m. (different to Yvonne—I would go with Yvonne's story, myself) and the bulk on football specials around 6 p.m. The trains were badly damaged, ceilings were torn off and the insides gutted; one alone was damaged to the tune of £45,000.[4] Around 6:30 p.m., there were huge numbers of fans waiting for the gates to open. Fifteen minutes later, supporters stormed one of the turnstiles and thousands swarmed in without paying. One Millwall fan blamed poor organisation. He said:

"First of all, trying to get into the ground was a complete and utter joke. And once in there, you've got eight thousand people packed in to where five thousand people capacity should be."[5]

Before kick-off, Millwall fans began climbing out of their section and into a stand occupied by home fans. Hundreds climbed out and started throwing bottles, nails and coins at Luton fans in the Oak Road end before violently appropriating the Bobbers' stand, ripping up seats and attacking home supporters. Incredibly, the game started on time. David Pleat, the then Luton manager, recounted:

"There were people being carried away on stretchers, fans on the edge of the pitch and players constantly looking up at their families because billiard balls were being thrown at the directors' box. I can't tell you much about the football because there was so much else going on. It was completely out of control."[6]

Fourteen minutes after the kick-off, referee David Hutchinson halted play as Millwall fans spilled onto the pitch. Helen Dunlop, who was taken to hospital, told the media from her hospital bed: "It was terrifying, just seeing them all charging down the field, it was like something out of *Zulu*."[7] She continued, "There was one policeman laying on the floor and a Millwall fan was putting the boot in his face. It was terrible."[8]

Referee Hutchinson pleaded with fans "to co-operate, enjoy yourselves and let us entertain you".[9] You can only admire his innocence and optimism. After twenty-five minutes of fighting, the game restarted; however, the threat of violence remained. Reporter Brian Swain recalls:

"The violence spilled everywhere. The police were trying to clear the main stand—getting us innocents to safety—and they asked us to leave the press box. But I was sat there with a bloody good story on my hands so I stayed on."[10]

At half-time, David Pleat spoke to the referee:

"He said, 'Look, don't worry, I'll make sure we'll finish it,' and he was magnificent. Somehow, he finished that game. By the end policemen who had survived the earlier fighting were standing on the touchline, so when a ball went out it literally bounced off them and came back into play. The whole evening was nasty, vicious and surreal."[11]

The worst violence erupted at the final whistle, when Millwall fans stayed behind and vandalised the seating and hoardings; they used the seats to throw at police. Three hundred fans attacked the police on the pitch, and during the chaos, one policeman was knocked to the ground and stopped breathing. A colleague who was trying to give help was punched and kicked; fortunately, he successfully got him breathing again.[12] In a reversal of Helen's "something out of *Zulu*", the police regrouped and counter-charged the supporters.

After the game, running battles continued outside the ground. Local resident Dennis Midwinter remarked:

"I went to the gate [next to the ground] to try and get assistance after the car windscreen had gone in; windows had gone in, in the street. And as I got to the gate I got hit on the head with an iron bar."[13]

Dennis received six stitches. One elderly resident pointed to her smashed-up house and said: "Fifty years I've been here and that's the first time."[14] Another resident added:

"They came tearing down the street, about 70-80 of them, and that bin up there, they used all the bricks as ammunition and just come along and belted through all the windows."[15]

Tommy Robinson, a member of Luton's hooligan crew known as the MIGs, believed it was not just Millwall fans that caused trouble that night, but several other London clubs too. He recalls:

"Normally that [the away end] would hold five to six thousand, that night there had to be in excess of eight or nine thousand people here trying to get into that ground. The tension for violence was in the air everywhere. There was a skip which we emptied on to them to hold them back where we could, as long as we could, until they appeared from that road down there as well. I know Crystal Palace were down here, we know guys who went to Chelsea that they were coming. We saw Arsenal at the bottom of the road. I even knew guys who came from Kent here. So, then we backed off to that corner, a group of ours jump up, we hear the words 'E,I,E Gooners who wants it.' You just think, 'Fucking hell, how much longer have we got to do today.'"[16]

Tommy went on:

"We still don't say 'Millwall overran us', we just say 'London and the south-east overran us that day.' When you're hearing stories about people having an ear bitten off, sirens in the background, ambulances, police not being very apparent, no control, it weren't great. It was horrible."[17]

Bob, a former Millwall hooligan, disputed Tommy's claim of other fans being involved. He was also scathing of the organisation. He said:

"It was Millwall supporters behaving bad, I suppose! It was the Luton club not being able to organise the match, it was the turnstile operators, it was the police not being able to control the situation and organise it. Millwall's got a lot of sleeping supporters that will only go to the big games and most of them are hooligans. They wait for the big games and they all turn up en masse. Then people turn and say 'it must be other things', it's not other things, it's just all our sleeping supporters come back. Really, if they knew there was going to be a disaster they should have called the game off and played it another time."[18]

On the way home to London, there was still time for one last brazen act of hooliganism. Supporters wrecked a train completely. British Rail workers who were used to seeing trains vandalised by football fans were astonished by what had happened. A BR spokesman said: "It looks as though a bomb had exploded inside some of the carriages."[19]

After the destruction of these trains, the authorities realised they needed more effective radio communication between British Transport Police and the ordinary police forces. The following season saw the installation of special radio sets that enabled British Transport Police and police forces to communicate with each other.[20]

ALONG WITH THE clear-up in Luton, the inquest started immediately. Tory MP Terry Dicks declared: "The culprits should be birched."[21] The police admitted they had not been prepared for the number of fans who turned up.

Bert Millichip, the FA Chairman, who was at the game, stated: "The scenes at Luton were the most disgraceful I have seen—and I have seen a lot."[22]

Maurice Woolf, who had reported on Millwall for twenty years, remarked:

"It absolutely sickened me last night. If I never see another soccer match after last night it wouldn't worry me, because a club like that doesn't deserve it. It's got such a magnificent chairman, wonderful manager, and terrific staff, it deserves much better. Instead of being a night to enjoy it became a night of horror."[23]

Former sports minister and then shadow sports minister, Dennis Howells, got the ball rolling by appearing on BBC Breakfast News at just after 7 a.m. the next morning. The presenter began with the eternal question of:

"What sort of precautions can we take against this happening again in the future?"[24]

Howells went on the attack against what he saw as the Thatcher government's lack of pro-activeness. He pointed out that under Labour governments, there had been enough legislation to combat hooliganism; however, it was the case that the present government wasn't implementing these policies. In relation to Luton-Millwall, Howells finished with: "Very depressing indeed."[25] Later in the day, he would attack the Thatcher government again, this time in Parliament.

The chairmen of Millwall and Luton were both called in for a meeting with Sports Minister Neil MacFarlane. He told them it was "time to end soccer violence"; they told him, "We wanted government action."[26]

During a TV interview, MacFarlane was keen on more reports. He said:

"We want to find out from the Football Association precisely what they intend to do about those clubs in the world of football who have an habitual record, whereby some of their followers are causing far too much violence which has become wholly unacceptable to people, which exasperates many, many people and yesterday was a classic example, so I want a report from them within a week about what their actions will be."[27]

As the day progressed, and with the Miners' Strike ended, football hooliganism was now top of the political agenda. Mrs Thatcher told MacFarlane "to pass on her annoyance to the FA".[28] She also ordered the FA to send a report to her within a week. Leon Britton, the Home Secretary, called for the police report. Thatcher also summoned the FA to a 'Soccer Summit' to be arranged at a later date; she wanted to stamp out the kind of violence witnessed at Luton and told them to look at ways of punishing clubs with a bad history of crowd trouble, which could include shutting the clubs down for a while. Moreover, she was demanding action for stiffer sentences for hooligans.

It would fall on FA Secretary Ted Croker the responsibility of presenting the report to Thatcher. In relation to disciplining clubs with a hooligan issue, he said:

"We are not suggesting for a moment that we don't have

a responsibility. We may take much greater sanctions against clubs, we may have to open up the rules to ensure that the sort of sanctions that take place in Europe, and you're probably familiar with those where we've seen that in the European Cups, Leeds United were banned for three years, Aston Villa, and West Ham played behind closed doors."[29]

On the unprecedented subject of shutting down clubs, he stated:

"I think at present our rules don't allow us to take that sanction, so we are limited to that extent. The only way we can take it is if we could prove conclusively the club is not taking precautions. That is not an ongoing situation and that could well change and that's all I'm saying is that's the area we've got to reconsider. And if we get it, it could work the other way if other clubs say they were just not going to play against let's say Millwall, we know that they are now a problem club, if other clubs say they are not going to play against Millwall, well that's the end of it, Millwall would have to come out of the league."[30]

In the House of Commons, Labour leader Neil Kinnock and Prime Minister Margaret Thatcher clashed over the way forward. Their debate was based around political considerations; Kinnock said he would support action against hooligans if measures were taken against the causes of hooliganism. Thatcher went with the discipline argument. Kinnock said:

"If the Right Honourable Lady is prepared to take action to get to the causes, I assure her, she'll have the full cooperation of the opposition in taking activities to provide the cures."[31]

Thatcher's response was to say there had been enough

enquiries into crime and hooliganism. She put the emphasis on bad parenting and the teaching profession:

"The causes will vary from the lack of parental discipline, lack of teacher discipline, background, everything. When one has said that [...] when one has said that it is not exactly easy to cure it."[32]

During the debate, John Carlisle, MP for Luton North was not about to take any prisoners. He expressed these thoughts:

"Is my honourable Friend aware that last night I attended the Luton-Millwall match and that consequently I was prevented from returning to the House to vote on a three-line Whip? I witnessed scenes which can only be described as terrifying. Is my honourable Friend aware that my constituents are very angry about the destruction of their homes, their shops, their town and their football club? They demand nothing less than revenge on those who inflicted that damage."[33]

Carlisle did not pull any punches with his next comments either. They were basically from the 18th century.

"On the question of harsher and stiffer penalties. Is he also aware that the only way to deal with these hooligans is to inflict upon them the physical pain which they last night so readily inflicted upon others? Does my honourable Friend appreciate that the time for talking, commissions and inquiries is over and that we must take action?"[34]

MacFarlane was diplomatic in his long reply. Moreover, he included this:

"As for individual assessment by the courts, my honourable Friend must not expect from me, from my department, to be responsible for the conduct of those sentencing policies. They are very much a matter for the magistrates."[35]

What the sports minister said in his reply to John Carlisle above is noteworthy because there appeared to have been no joined-up thinking between the government and the magistrates' courts when it came to prosecuting and sentencing football hooligans.

It seemed magistrates had a dilemma and could not pass the sentences politicians would have liked them too. For instance, in a typical case (not at football) of 'actual bodily harm', a sentence would be up to six months in prison. However, to get a conviction, the police would have needed a higher standard of detailed evidence about the offence, and in the mayhem of soccer violence, it was not always possible or practical for the police to attain this. Therefore, the police were more likely to bring the lesser charge of 'breach of the peace' because this did not need such high standards of evidence. The problem was there was no custodial sentence, but to be 'bound over for one year to keep the peace'.[36]

The debate in Parliament highlighted how much of a political topic football hooliganism was. In the press, Home Secretary Leon Britton attacked the savagery of football hooligans and warned that serious offenders could get life imprisonment. He went on to say youngsters "get caught up in mass lunacy".[37] He said some of these louts "believe they have a special licence to riot, well they haven't".[38] He told ITN News:

"I share the public sense of outrage. The police have adequate powers, they're usually able to deal with the problems, but not always. The courts certainly have adequate powers and I made clear just how great those powers are, in case of the more serious offences and also the sort of things that can be done. It's for the courts to decide how to use those powers in particular cases."[39]

Whilst politicians were speaking in Parliament, twenty-nine people appeared before Luton magistrates. One fan was sent to a detention centre for three months, another was given a suspended sentence plus a £750 fine, and another was fined £250 and received a three-month suspended sentence. As a sign of the times, two Millwall supporters who appeared asked for police protection when they left court because they had been met outside by about twelve Luton supporters; police led them out of court another way.[40]

After the sentencing, the political conversations turned to remedies. An alcohol ban in or near football grounds was proposed. A ban had already been in operation in Scotland for four years, and the Scottish FA felt things had improved since the legislation was implemented. Scotland also operated the sensible system of using local police forces to travel with local teams to away matches because they were in a position to spot troublemakers. A second idea was to force hooligans to attend detention centres on match days, and the contradictory solution of "tougher sentencing by magistrates" was also raised.[41]

Due to the chaos at Luton, Millwall's weekend visit to Brentford was called off, but this was because of a housing development being built at the visitors' end. This meant there would have been no segregation, and Brentford could not guarantee the safety of supporters in the ground.[42] Bournemouth also asked for their game against Millwall on 6 May to be postponed because they feared "Bank Holiday trouble".[43]

On Saturday's edition of *BBC Grandstand*, Tony Gubba interviewed the police chief in charge of the Luton game. The policeman's desk was littered with weapons from Wednesday's game. Tony began by asking him: "Tell us about the items on the desk, Bill?"

Bill replied, "They are just one or two examples of some of the things which were found at Luton football ground after the match. This for example is the knife which was thrown at the goalkeeper; fortunately, it didn't strike him, but it was picked up afterwards."

Tongue-in-cheek, the chief said, "We haven't yet traced the owner." After picking up a small retractable knife from his desk, he went on: "This was taken from a policeman's helmet, and it obviously had embedded itself in there and the helmet had served to protect him."

Tony then asks, "Had it been thrown or was it stuck in?"

Bill replies, "We can't tell, we were not aware of how it came to be in the policeman's helmet, it was found in the policeman's helmet, but on the outside."[44]

On April Fools' Day, Thatcher met with the FA and Football League and revealed a six-point plan that included the introduction of ID cards, better fencing and closed-circuit television.[45] The six-point plan also included a ban on alcohol in grounds, this suggestion led to the Control of Alcohol (Sports Ground) Bill going through parliament that summer. Despite having sympathy with the clubs that were barred from serving alcohol, the FA agreed with the government that alcohol was a contributing factor and to ban it within grounds, as had happened in Scotland with good results.[46]

Just staying with alcohol for a moment—the consequences of alcohol on football crowds is complex; however, it would very much seem that in Brussels 'self-policing' disappeared on the day because of alcohol. A Red said of the drunkenness: "While it cannot be denied that many

Liverpool supporters were in good humour, chatting with Juventus supporters, the vast majority were in a drunken stupor for most of the day, generally being obnoxious and terrorising the local residents."[47]

This is what the Belgian police had to face. Also, fans who were arrested mention the effects of alcohol on them. Pearson and Sale suggest in the UK there has long been an established correlation between alcohol consumption and violence and disorder. Many studies have noted the disproportionately high number of those who have been consuming alcohol among those arrested for disorder or admitted to accident and emergency departments with injuries gained from fighting.[48] Marsh and Kibby also point out that 50% of all offences of violence or disorder in the UK occurred at the traditional pub or club closing time on Friday and Saturday. Similarly, Hobbs et al. state how instances of crime and disorder rise with the numbers of licensed premises.[49]

I know there is an argument today to reintroduce alcohol back into football grounds (and not just on the concourse) like in other sports. Myself, I think it would be a mistake. The reason I say this is that I went to a match abroad, which went into extra time and penalties, and by the end of the game I was hammered. On top of this, I went to an Everton game relatively recently; we had been drinking early doors and had our hip flasks with us for during the game, and one of the lads, who was the worse for wear, left at half-time thinking it was full-time. He had it right, because we ended up conceding four goals in 12 second-half minutes. We are passive people, but given our country's track record with drink, the last thing we need is a tiny minority being pissed and causing mayhem.

Interestingly, once the shock of the tragedy had dissipated in Italy the Italian press moved to the social causes of the disaster and in particularly the effect that alcohol had on events.

Returning to the 1 April meeting, policing costs were also discussed. Jack Dunnett, chairman of the Football League, stated that if the government contributed more, it would be easier to provide sufficient police cover. The Prime Minister said she would undertake to look further at this. However, this was at odds with her Home Secretary, who just a few days earlier had it in mind to include a provision in guidelines under the Safety of Sports Grounds Act that clubs should accept and pay for a police presence in the numbers thought necessary by chief constables.[50]

Thatcher asked the FA to produce a report within six weeks on how to deal with hooliganism. A few days later, she wrote to the football authorities, saying: "The Home Secretary will be discussing with the police what improvements can be made to their effectiveness in dealing with football violence, particularly in obtaining evidence to bring more serious charges where appropriate."[51]

The police confirmed they would bring more serious charges whenever they had the evidence to do so. At the same time, they pointed out that when dealing with violent disorder involving large numbers of people, the immediate police priority must be to restore a degree of order (for example by clearing the pitch). The police believed it may be impractical or impossible to spare manpower to make arrests at that stage; arrests would follow as soon as the police felt they had the situation under a degree of control.[52]

The police regarded photography as important to assist them, both in identifying offenders and in obtaining evidence for use in court. There was, however, a 'slight' hitch with the well-meaning plan. The issue was that the equipment had been used in trials in Manchester, Birmingham, and Edinburgh, and it had not produced pictures of sufficient quality for use in identifying individuals.[53]

The government also wanted greater use by magistrates of their powers, under section 188 of the Licensing Act 1964. This meant licensed premises in areas where the presence of football supporters was likely to result in scenes of disorder and unruly behaviour could be closed. The police accepted that section 188 could be useful in some situations, and they would apply to the magistrates for an order accordingly when appropriate. However, the police saw some possible operational disadvantage if the closure of pubs near grounds led to the dispersal of potentially disorderly fans, who would thus become more difficult to control. They found it useful to know where supporters would meet (for example, at Queen's Park Rangers there are well known 'home' and 'away' pubs), and for this reason they did not foresee seeking to use section 188 except in extreme situations.[54]

Additionally, the Home Secretary considered it key to encourage football clubs to make submission to a search a condition of entry. The government intended to pursue this with the football authorities. The Metropolitan Police solicitor suggested clubs should put up notices to say that admission would be refused to any person who refused to be searched by the police.[55]

As we can see, the measures above were part of the ongoing football hooligan solutions merry-go-round that had been a constant conversation for decades. For the record, the FA later fined Millwall £7500 and ordered Luton to fence in all their fans.[56] Oh and by the way, Luton won 1–0 with a neat finish by Brian Stein, and goalkeeper Les Sealy, who had had the knife thrown at him, was clearly resilient, because he was out on the pitch the next morning having penalty practice.

Birmingham City vs. Leeds United. *St Andrews, Birmingham, 11th May 1985.* Only a few weeks before Brussels, a young fan was killed at Birmingham City's St Andrew's stadium. Due to crowd disturbances, a wall collapsed onto Ian Hambridge, a 15-year-old Leeds supporter. As the *Birmingham Mail* reported on that fateful day:

"Birmingham faced Leeds on the final day of the season knowing that victory could see them top the old Division Two table if Oxford lost. Both clubs had a history of crowd trouble and tensions had been high throughout the match. But no one could have envisaged the ugly scenes of violence that followed the final whistle."[57]

The *Mail* continued:

"In total 145 policemen were injured and 125 fans were arrested at Birmingham and at least 40 fans were treated at East Birmingham Hospital and about a dozen at Birmingham Accident Hospital."[58]

Justice Popplewell, during the Popplewell Committee investigation into football in 1985, described the Birmingham-Leeds game as more like "the Battle of Agincourt than a football match".[59]

Writing in his annual report for 1985, the West Midlands Chief Constable, Geoffrey Dear, described it as "possibly the worst crowd disorder ever seen at a football ground in this country."[60] He went on: "The trouble at the St Andrew's Ground led to a reappraisal of the scale of protective clothing for issue to officers in this Force together with other equipment to assist in dealing with severe public disorder, and the force is now much better prepared in this respect."[61]

Earlier, we had Millichip stating that "the scenes at Luton were the most disgraceful I have seen—and I have seen a lot." These two quotes are part of the reason I believe Heysel was inevitable.

Ian's death was overshadowed because on the same day, the Bradford Fire Disaster happened.

Bradford City vs. Lincoln City. *Valley Parade, Bradford, 11 May 1985.* As the BBC reported:

"The match began in an atmosphere of celebration as Bradford City, who had just been promoted to the second division, were about to play Lincoln City, watched by more than 11,000 fans. Just before kick-off Bradford City captain Peter Jackson was presented with the Third Division Championship trophy. Five minutes before half time at 3:40 p.m. a small fire was noticed three rows from the back of G block in the Valley Parade ground and fire-fighting equipment was requested. Within minutes flames were visible and police started to evacuate people in the stand. But the blaze spread very rapidly—within four minutes the whole of the roof and the wooden stands below were on fire and police struggled to save those who were too stunned or weak to escape."[62]

The fire cost the lives of fifty-six fans, and at least 265 others were injured.[63] Geoffrey Mitchell, a survivor, spoke of the horror that he witnessed:

"It spread like a flash. I've never seen anything like it. The smoke was choking. You could hardly breathe. There was panic as fans stampeded to an exit which was padlocked. Two or three burly men put their weight against it and smashed the gate open. Otherwise, I would not have been able to get out."[64]

Apart from being deadly, it was ironic that the exit Geoffrey mentions was padlocked. I say ironic because the reason it was locked was due to recommendations from the disaster we mentioned previously at Bolton Wanderers. After Bolton, one of the central recommendations of the subsequent inquiry was the locking of gates to prevent late and unauthorised entry.[65] The deaths at Bradford show how inept governments and football authorities had been in tackling problems within football; it seems the grounds were basically unregulated death-traps.

At the time, the fire seemed like a tragic accident. More recently, intrigue has been added to the story, which fits in with this awful period in English football history. As the *Daily Mirror* reported in April 2015, a new book looking into the stadium fire claimed a former chairman, Stafford Heginbotham, was connected to eight blazes before the fatal incident.[66] A book by fire survivor Martin Fletcher, *56: The Story of the Bradford Fire*, looks at a series of fires with alleged connections to Heginbotham that resulted in substantial insurance claims, the equivalent of millions in today's terms.[67]

FOURTEEN

THE LIGHTS WERE TURNED OUT

Today, Liverpool is a much different place in comparison with the '80s. It attracts people from all over the world; they come for the history, culture, sport, architecture, nightlife and, of course, because four lads shook the world. In the 1850s, the American consul, one Nathaniel Hawthorne, called Liverpool "the greatest commercial city in the world",[1] and in the 1960s, another American, writer Allen Ginsberg, said, "Liverpool is at the present moment the centre of the consciousness of the human universe."[2] Although I am sure I read somewhere he used to say that about everywhere he visited.

In 1985, the year of Heysel, the city was on its knees, and the lights were turned out for a period; it was a shockingly depressing time. It was basically impossible to get a job. The only thing I can compare it to is when Covid struck in the UK and many people, particularly in the prosperous south, realised for the first time that your life can be pulled from under your feet.

The decade had started horrendously with the riots in the Toxteth district of the city, and smaller copycat riots spread to other districts. Where I lived there was an incident where either police or residents' cars were set on fire next to the high-rise flats. Being curious, my mates and I went to have a look. As we were walking to the scene, lads from the estate began running towards us, hotly pursued by police officers—it was like a scene out of a movie. We had done absolutely nothing wrong, but of course we turned and ran. Ironically, a friend who was the quickest runner was unfortunately caught and nicked by the police. At the time, my friend and I were thick as thieves. Later that night, his mum knocked at our house, worried sick. She asked me if I had seen him. Of course, I knew he had been nicked (for nothing), but with my parents standing there, and being young and stupid, I informed his mum, "Sorry, I haven't seen him."

For the record, my poor mate was sentenced to something called "Scrubs", so he had to go to Mather Avenue Police Station in Allerton and clean the horse stables out every Saturday. From my perspective, it really was Robins and Cohen stuff. Anyway, I digress.

With the election of Margaret Thatcher in 1979, a blitzkrieg of inhuman economic policies were unleashed, which meant great swathes of the country were facing job closure after job closure. Margaret Thatcher's love for the likes of Milton Friedman and the Chicago school of economics, and economists such as Fredrick Hayek brought a maelstrom of despair, depression (both economically and mentally) and, as a consequence, violence to our shores. Thatcher's strategy of 'managed decline' in Liverpool decimated opportunities, pride, families and communities. At the time, the city was on the wrong side of geography, history and politics. This policy of 'managed decline' was a particularly cruel way of running an economy and an especially spiteful way to treat fellow citizens.

Official cabinet documents released in 2011 underlined the backhandedness and why Michael Hestletine is probably the most respected Conservative politician in the eyes of Liverpudlians like myself. After the 1981 summer riots, cabinet ministers and key advisers set down their thoughts in response to an impassioned plea by Heseltine, then environment secretary, for up to £100m to be invested in Merseyside to tackle urban decay and rampant unemployment. Although some of the Prime Minister's advisers and ministers thought the government should be "seen" to be doing something following the riots, they were concerned any additional spending would be "wasted".[3]

Geoffrey Howe, Chancellor of the Exchequer, argued that enough money had been spent on the city and they should not waste their energy "making water flow uphill".[4] Howe wrote to the Prime Minister warning her of the "need to be careful not to over-commit scarce resources to Liverpool".[5] Additionally, he commented:

"We do not want to find ourselves concentrating all the limited cash that may have to be made available into Liverpool and having nothing left for possibly more promising areas such as the West Midlands, or even the North East. It would be regrettable if some of the brighter ideas for renewing economic activity were to be sown only on relatively stony ground on the banks of the Mersey."[6]

Similar views were expressed by Keith Joseph, the industry secretary and a close ally of Mrs Thatcher. In response to Heseltine's regeneration proposal, he was minuted by a civil servant as querying whether the alternative should be a "managed rundown" of Liverpool and its surrounding area.[7] In another note, his private secretary asked for the minutes to be amended to remove reference to explicit economic regeneration as Joseph believed "it is by no means clear that any such strategy could lead to a viable economic entity".[8]

Like Keith Joseph, Howe also understood that if a city was left to 'managed decline', the consequences would be potentially embarrassing. He warned Mrs Thatcher that:

"This is not a term for use, even privately. It is much too negative."[9]

When this information came to light in 2011, Howe had temporary amnesia. He recalled: "I don't remember saying that at all, I have no comment to make on it."[10]

The importance of this in relation to Heysel and its aftermath cannot be underestimated. The city felt unfairly treated and abandoned, and as subsequent official papers revealed, this was certainly the case. The treatment by Thatcher's government led to a siege mentality—an outlook that was manna from heaven for deniers of Heysel.

Hindsight is a wonderful science, and looking back now, it is clear (and easy for me to say) that the city was crying out for a group of people who were connected enough (in Westminster) and politically savvy enough to have won the greatest game of political and economic poker in the city's recent history. Unluckily, that group did not exist. In saying that, in the light of the official papers, it seems connections might not have been enough to rescue the city. Derek Hatton was the most well-known of the city leaders. In 2014, Hatton told the BBC:

"There was a lot of anger around. Thatcher had come to power and was taking more money off the local authority. So, there was a mood in the city, which was saying, 'Hang on a minute! What's going on here?'"[11]

In 1983, Mrs Thatcher, savouring her victory in the

Falklands War the previous year, hammered Michael Foot in the General Election. In Liverpool, Labour won the city council elections on a socialist manifesto, the consequence being that two tribes went to war politically, but as the 2011 documents reveal, there was only ever going to be one winner.

The following year—and on a happier note—the city was basking in the footballing spotlight in an amazingly unique way. LFC won the European Cup, League Title, League Cup and, for good measure, the Reserve Title. EFC won the FA Cup and Youth Cup. The city was not only the capital of English football but European football too. In 1985 Everton won the League Title and European Cup Winners Cup, and Liverpool reached another European final again, making the city the centre of the footballing universe for another season. Just a few days before the final, the *Liverpool Echo* published an advisory article called "The Kopites Guide to Brussels". The piece hoped the city was on for a treble on the pitch after Everton's recent successes. The paper added: "[We are] hoping Liverpool repeats Everton's good-natured take-over of Rotterdam [...] so we can claim the title of the best supporters in Europe."[12]

As we will witness next, our city will never be able to "claim the title of the best supporters in Europe" again. Ever.

PART THREE
MATCH DAY

FIFTEEN

"THE TONE WAS SET."

On the most memorable occasion when Englishmen used Belgium as a battleground to confront continental rivals, novelist and playwright Francis Burney pleaded with an English officer for a passport to leave Brussels and avoid being caught between two armies. It was 17 June 1815, the eve of Waterloo, and the officer refused to let her escape, declaring:

"We want blood, Madame! What we want is blood!"[1]

A hundred and seventy years later, I went around to my mate's house to watch the game. With a few other lads, Blues and Reds, I would have imagined we were expecting a Liverpool victory because that was the way the world worked back then. When we arrived at my friend's, the tragedy had already taken place. It was as if we had been transported back in time to the battlefields of 19th century Europe, and instead of an officer of the realm, this time it was a group of men from our city masquerading as soldiers of the empire.

Apart from the blurred memories of Englishmen attacking Italian supporters, and then Juventus fans rioting at the other end of the stadium, I can only consciously remember one thing from the broadcast, and that was BBC host, Jimmy Hill, calling for the reintroduction of National Service. A second incident I thought I recalled was the image of a Juventus supporter in a standout white tracksuit top throwing objects—I now realise I had confused that with a Millwall fan in a white top throwing things at Kenilworth Road a few months earlier.

This part of the book is especially unpleasant reading. However, if nobody tells the story, I am not sure how our city will ever come to terms with the events. Then what are we left with? Well, we are left with the Rob Gutmanns of this world not knowing where culpability lies, and with Daniel Fieldsend types mounting their high horse and having a pop at Leicester City supporters.

Previously, we discussed the many components that were the basis of the perfect storm at Heysel. The scenes and the undercurrent caused by a sizable minority of LFC fans in Brussels city centre in the hours prior to kick-off were the last links that paved the way for the inevitability of the horrors which were to follow. As you can imagine, there are not copious stories about the daytime activities you would usually associate with such an event. Fans that were in attendance will never be whipping out and sharing the usual happy, silly photos that capture the niceties of the day. We will never hear supporters telling their family and friends, "That's me, Smigger, and Macca by the Manneken Pis enjoying the build-up."

Many Liverpool and Juve fans only experienced good behaviour and a friendly and relaxed ambiance in the city centre. Some supporters talk of a carnival atmosphere, with British and Italian fans mixing freely with each other, playing football, taking photographs, and exchanging mementoes. Some witnesses recall the police misreading the mood and that "far from the police standing by while something akin to a riot was taking place, the police were heavy handed, interfering with people who were merely singing and enjoying themselves and treating both sets of supporters to an excessive display of authority."[2]

As with many things in life, everything is about time and place, because there is also evidence emanating from the streets of Brussels that is full of obnoxiousness, extreme violence, revenge, xenophobia, excessive drunkenness and criminality. The image painted by some eyewitnesses is one of a European capital resembling a cesspit of hostility and primitive behaviour brought about by Englishmen unchained from the routines of everyday life.

ON 29 MAY 1985 Brussels woke up to glorious sunshine, and the day began calmly. Fans of both teams were mingling happily. *Observer* sports photographer Eamonn McCabe had driven from London to Belgium. With accommodation being full in the capital, he stayed at a hotel in Bruges. Being a football fan at heart—a Spurs fan, though through family connections Liverpool is his second team—he was really looking forward to the game. As he says:

"European finals in foreign countries then seemed exotic. They were wonderful occasions usually played in a great spirit."[3]

Once in Brussels, Eamonn parked up and went looking for fans to photograph around town. What Eamonn found was camaraderie between what he called: "Two magical European teams".[4]

On returning to the city centre after getting his ticket,

Paul Fry, briefly met up with his girlfriend and arranged to meet her later that evening. He came across a party mood; he says:

"The atmosphere was fantastic. There was a flower market, so it was very colourful against the backdrop of the timbered buildings. A wedding was taking place in the Guild Hall and this couple came out and fans from both teams serenaded them."[5]

As Paul joked: "It was like a European song contest."[6]

As we saw in Chapter One, Juventus supporter Simone Stenti recounts:

"I love so much those moments that come before an important match when there is the excitement, the build-up. There were lots of English people, I still have a Liverpool scarf I exchanged with an English supporter."[7]

During his duties with Belgian police, PC G. S. Laird from the British Transport Police also witnessed this cama-raderie. He observed from the window of his vehicle large groups of Juventus fans began to arrive at the square. He noticed that the Liverpool supporters mingled with their opponents and saw that football scarves and other favours were being readily exchanged. The mood of the rival sets of fans, he thought, seemed extremely friendly.[8]

LFC fan Paul Clark, who was a city councillor at the time, chairman of the Liverpool Liberal Party, and was part of the reconciliation delegation that visited Turin in the aftermath, agrees with the other descriptions of the mood in the city. Clark recalled the lunchtime atmosphere in the Grand Place was superb, with the Liverpool fans mixing in a friendly fashion with the Juventus fans. He witnessed much swapping of colours and photographs being taken of joint groups. Alas, he continued: "However, the drunken loutish element, as usual, were there as well."[9]

Bob Burns was the *Liverpool Echo* news reporter for the day in Brussels. He remembers an enjoyable atmosphere too:

"I remember going to the Grand Place and seeing all the festivities and it was one big party in the main square in Brussels. There just seemed to be a great atmosphere. I didn't really see any Juventus supporters around the Grand Place, if they were, they were low key, and there was no tension. The only thing I saw besides the Liverpool fans is Brussels is a big headquarters for the United Nations and what not, and the European Parliament. So, there were people there wearing really fancy outfits mingling with all these Liverpool supporters, it seemed kind of strange."[10]

So, it would seem the 30th European Cup was going to plan for both sets of supporters, UEFA, the local authorities, local people and local businesses.

Sadly, for the sake of history, not everyone possessed the party vibe. Tony Evans certainly didn't. Honestly, but ominously, he disclosed:

"Our train had just arrived at Jette station and a long column of Liverpool supporters set off downhill towards the centre of the city. I lingered and watched them, chequered flags flying, and thought it looked like a medieval army on the move. Above the narrow streets, the locals hung out of open windows and watched, half-grinning but nervous. As I set off for the Grand Place, I thought, 'We can do what we like today. No one can stop us.'"[11]

Tony's next insight into the ambiance of the day highlights what we discussed in relation to Rome having a bearing on events. He said:

"The mood in Brussels was complex. In the aftermath, most commentators would ignore the effect of the events in Rome the previous year and even those who alluded to

1984 saw Heysel in terms of 'hooligan gangs looking for revenge'. It was very different, much more complex and consequently more frightening. We were radiating aggression. The ultras had made us suffer once, but it would not happen again."[12]

The "radiating aggression" is taken to another level by what he saw next:

"We met a group of mates who had come by coach. A fellow passenger we all knew had leapt off as soon as they arrived and attacked two people, one an Italian, with an iron bar. That we'd long believed him to be psychotic did not lessen the shock."[13]

Here the word "psychotic" shows how some people can unfortunately 'thrive' in certain communities in Britain.

Tony Evans' next comments highlight the aggression shown on the day by some non-hooligan LFC supporters, such as himself:

"There were few direct attacks on opposition supporters, but there was an eagerness to take the upper hand in any potential conflict. No one wanted to be a victim. Minor misunderstandings quickly escalated into full-scale confrontation, much to the shock of the Italians. Turning into a narrow street in the centre of town, my brother and I saw about six Juventus fans in their twenties lounging outside a café, trying to look cool and tough at the same time. When one looked me straight in the eye, giving me a classic hard-case once-over, I snarled: 'Go on gobshite, say something'. They did not take up the offer. But the tone was set. And the drinking had not even started."[14]

Tony's words "the tone was set" plus his more than impolite attitude are again massive factors in understanding what took place. All the ingredients in those few words and his actions are again illustrations of why the deaths happened. By this, I mean Tony did not actually hit anybody, but he admits to snarling at Italians, so God only knows what level of aggression the LFCs fans that did attack Italians were operating at. Additionally, Tony, along with his brother, threatened six Italians; this attitude again has its origins in our country's empire mentality.

The British statesman and man of letters, Philip Stanhope, forth earl of Chesterfield, wrote in the 18th century: "That silly, sanguine notion, which is firmly entertained here, that one Englishman can beat three Frenchmen, encourages and has sometimes enabled one Englishman, in reality to beat two."[15]

Now of course Tony confronted Italians, not Frenchmen, but the principle remains the same, and that is that our history encourages us to either be stupid or brave when confrontations arise—sadly, it also means we are antagonistic.

In his previous comment, Tony finished by saying "And the drinking had not even started". It seems the drink was set to become the whisky chasers to history, empire, sociology and every psychological theory under the sun that involves hostility and intergroup behaviour. The consumption of alcohol, along with the theories and history we have discussed, meant, as Tony Evans said in one snappy sentence: "A large proportion of Liverpool fans seemed to have lost control."[16]

On a secondary note, Tony's words above also highlight how confused by Heysel some Liverpool fans have become. To repeat his words:

"When one looked me straight in the eye, giving me a classic hard-case once-over, I snarled: 'Go on gobshite, say something.' They did not take up the offer."

In a subsequent interview, Tony commented:

"Most [LFC fans] never meant any harm to anyone, most never even confronted a Juventus fan, most never even threatened them, I certainly didn't."[17]

To be to fair to Tony, he has come to terms with Heysel more than some others have; however, he is still a long way away from full acceptance because if "snarled" and "'Go on gobshite'" do not equate to "confront" and "threaten", it is time for me to get a refund on the dictionary I have. Plus, we will soon come across another incident where Tony "certainly didn't threaten any Italians".

SIXTEEN

CARRY ON

After an enjoyable introduction to the Belgian capital, Paul Fry observed that the atmosphere changed after lunch. He says:

"It was fine up until lunch and basically I had a vision in my head I could see Italians sitting at café tables eating a meal with the odd glass of beer. And yet I saw no end of people with shopping trolleys full of dumpies [small, bottled lager] and they were obviously the Liverpool fans."[1]

As Paul points out, that was just a thing at the time. He continues:

"It didn't help that it was a boiling hot day. They'd not eaten, and it had gone straight to their heads."[2]

On this theme, Liverpool fan Tom Johnston recalled:

"The town square in Brussels was ankle deep with broken bottles. One lad who couldn't have been older than 14 was so drunk his legs were not working. His mate had to carry him."[3]

PC Laird, who was based in Lime Street, Liverpool, went to the Grand Place at 2:45 p.m. He saw around 1500 football supporters, the majority dressed in Liverpool colours. He noticed immediately that most of the fans were in possession of bottles of alcohol. A number of these people appeared in a drunken condition and were singing and dancing. There was a small contingent of police officers in the square, and Laird was aware of other officers in nearby streets waiting in vehicles.[4]

His colleague Sergeant White, who like Laird was on patrol with the Belgian police, arrived about thirty minutes later. The Reds next to the Belgian police vehicle he was using were all very drunk, however, thankfully, not showing any signs of aggression at this stage. They were all singing and drinking from bottles. The drinks ranged from lager to hard spirits. Upon emptying the bottles, the fans were just dropping the empties onto the ground where they smashed, and as White states, they were singing their usual Munich anti-Manchester United songs.[5]

In a similar vein to his colleagues, PC S. Jones said that between 2:30 and 4 p.m. fans were singing, dancing and all appeared to be drinking. He heard large numbers of bottles smashing on the ground after having been emptied and could see that this was a regular habit, as the square was full of broken glass.[6] His colleague PC M. Jones recalled there were thousands of supporters, mostly from Liverpool, who had congregated and were drinking heavily. Everywhere you trod, you could not help but kick a bottle or can lying on the floor.[7]

One big attraction for Reds was an outside broadcast by Liverpool radio station Radio City from the Golden Boot Café in the square. A large group of fans, about 500, gathered underneath the window of the restaurant, singing and shouting towards the presenters. Two of the presenters stood at the window of the restaurant to encourage the group to sing loudly into the microphone. PC Laird realised that most of this group became very excited at these actions, and as a result he requested the commentators to refrain from this conduct. They did so immediately.[8] Likewise, Assistant Chief Constable McGregor was concerned by the Radio City outside broadcast. McGregor also told them to stop. Radio City told McGregor that ex-Liverpool captain Emlyn Hughes was going to appear soon. However, McGregor informed the police and radio crew that he should not and should enter and leave the premises by a rear door.[9] A few hours later, Hughes' world would collapse around him.

McGregor, who was accompanied by Department of Environment representatives, remarked that many supporters had crates or cartons of beer and at the time they were basically good humoured. However, he was still concerned. For him, it was obvious that the drinking would continue and the mood quickly change. Later in the day, McGregor pointed out that a minority of Reds were becoming aggressive, and he feared that some trouble could eventually take place.[10]

Whilst some Reds were still being good humoured, some under the influence were not. We highlighted in a previous chapter how Reds were "terrorising the local residents". They were terrorising Italians too. Journalist Ed Vulliamy witnessed the experience of two young Italian girls:

"They were admiring pictures of and reading about the Juventus team over a coffee in a bar. They were approached and prodded by three swaying Liverpool supporters, two in string vests and none exactly underweight—sung to in slurred tones at a distance of ten inches. Amazed, they smiled nervously and left the bar."[11]

Italian Alfio Tofanelli alleged of Kopites: "I saw three or

four hundred frenzied, drunk people with yellow-red scarves at the Grand Place breaking the shops and café windows facing the famous and elite city's square."[12]

One suspect's statement very much concurs with these testimonies on the consumption of alcohol. When he was arrested by Merseyside Police in June 1985, the suspect retold how he had arrived in Belgium and at the stadium. He informed the police that he started his journey by coach from Liverpool city centre about 10 p.m. the night before the game. Prior to boarding the coach, he and his friends bought six bottles of Pils each. When they arrived in Brussels around 2 p.m. the next day, they went straight to the pub and had three pints each. Afterwards they went to a shop and bought six more bottles of Pils each. When they finished them, they bought some more beer, but he couldn't remember how many.[13]

He then bought more cans. He said, "I'd say about six each. By this time, I was feeling quite drunk."[14]

Another suspect disclosed:

"I had been drinking bottles of lager before the match. It altered my mind, gave me Dutch courage. I've always had a temper but when I've had the ale, the aggression comes out and I'm like a different person."[15]

Tony Evans gives us an insight into why Kopites were so unbelievably drunk:

"The common belief was that Belgian beer was weaker than the booze at home. In the heat, young men used to drinking a gallon of weak mild were quaffing strong lagers and ales as if they were lemonade."[16]

The consequence of the strong booze and the environment it produced was demonstrated by the experiences of one embarrassed LFC fan who recalled her experiences in a McDonalds. She recalls:

"I was having a meal in a Brussels branch of McDonalds where the staff were threatened by half-naked supporters, one of whom was so drunk he had to crawl across."[17]

She continues:

"As I left, I told the manager how sorry I was and that we were not all like the people who had been in and left most of his young female staff in tears. As I was talking to the manager two people in Liverpool colours were relieving themselves against his front window."[18]

If this event had been a one-off that day, the supporter's story above might have had some comic value, in a *Carry On* sort of way. I can picture it now, Hattie Jakes apologising to a foreign restaurateur whilst a laughing Syd and Bernard are relieving themselves just before they succeed in chatting up two of the waitresses, despite not cleaning their hands. Like *Carry On*, the scene in Brussels would only have comic value to Brits and basically no other country on the planet. The scenes that occurred in Brussels during the afternoon could only happen in Britain on a Friday or Saturday night or in Benidorm, Magaluf and Kavos at any time of the day or night between May and August. Apologies to the locals of Benidorm, Magaluf and Kavos, but I am sure you are well aware I am not talking about you.

One foreign observer to the Britishness of the drinking on display was Dr Resende from UEFA. At lunchtime he was on his way to an official gathering at the town hall. Resende said he watched many screaming English supporters in the Grand Place and its surroundings. Inside the town hall were UEFA leaders, Belgian FA top brass and representatives from both clubs. Mayor Brouhon said he could hear the cries from the supporters, which reached up to the Gothique Room.[19] In reply to his talk, the President of the Belgian Union launched an appeal to the organisers of Liverpool and Juventus to use all their influence in order to ensure that the match took place under normal conditions.[20] Brouhon described the mayhem in the square as transforming from "student riots" in character to a more aggressive attitude with bottle throwing.[21]

As mayor of Brussels, Brouhon had reason to worry for his city because with the shenanigans happening outside he was also aware that the evening before a disturbance provoked by fans of both clubs took place in the city. There was theft, damaged caused and six people were arrested.[22]

After the reception, Resende went for a short walk where he was met by many youngsters, half nude and drunk, in possession of beer and wine bottles, with glassy eyes.[23] Ironically, one of themes at the lunch was violence in sport and of the efforts to fight this phenomenon in today's society.

In the disaster's aftermath, our peculiar relationship with alcohol was highlighted by one Red, who said: "The media and Italian people have slammed us for being drunkards but there were no more people drunk than on your average Friday or Saturday night in Liverpool city centre, and rowdy though it is, I cannot recall Ken Oxford [then Chief Constable of Merseyside] calling for the Paras to control them."[24]

The above observation is part of the problem that leads to cultural misunderstandings. For us as a nation, it is called 'having a good time on a Friday and Saturday night'; for foreigners, it is alien. As we saw in the introduction, Brussels café owner Daniel Deriviere expressed in shock the next day:

"What is wrong with you British? Have you become an angry tribe?"[25]

Daniel had been speaking to the *Daily Mirror*, who

reported: "[Daniel's café] was raped by marauding Liverpool fans."[26]

The "rape" included three hundred glasses being smashed, tables getting overturned and staff being attacked.[27]

BOB BURNS, the *Liverpool Echo* correspondent, mentioned earlier he had not seen Juventus fans in Brussels' main square, the Grand Place. We are about to see why not too many Italians would want to venture there. One LFC supporter recalled his experiences:

"Five minutes' walk from the cathedral is the picturesque Grand Place, a marvellous exhibit of Flemish architecture. On arriving within the vicinity, I noticed a horde of inebriated Liverpool fans. The majority appeared to be dragging around caseloads of ale. The square was completely covered with broken bottles. Any stray Italians venturing into the cauldron were subject to horrendous abuse. I personally hope they were not completely familiar with the English vernacular."[28]

It is absolutely no surprise that Italians stayed away. Never mind wandering through the Grand Place, some Juventus supporters had not even left their coaches before LFC fans were making their lives a nightmare. The LFC supporter continued his story:

"We progressed to the Manneken Pis statue nearby; simultaneously a coachload of Juventus fans arrived, only to be greeted by spitting on the side of the coach accompanied by antics expected of simple primates. Needless to say, their coachload consisted of women and children."[29]

A Juve supporter Edmondo Mastrilli, who arrived in

Brussels, unfortunately experienced the behaviour the Liverpool supporter is describing first-hand. Edmondo's coach was attacked by Reds with sticks and bottles as they arrived. There were horrible scenes, with women and children being kicked and trampled on.[30]

How upsetting does this all sound?

When you look at videos from the day, you can only cringe. There are fans with their tops off, others asleep on the pavements with cans of beer next to them, and one fan is exposing his backside to a camera.

In keeping with his day, Tony Evans' next story is also full of empire, criminality and bullying, topped off with a lack of common decency. He recounts:

"I went to find some beer, taking a red-and-white cap I'd found on the road to give some protection from the sun. Walking down a narrow street, I saw a crew of scallies laughing almost hysterically. Seeing my quizzical look, they pointed at a shop. It was a jeweller with no protective metal grating over the window. All you could do was laugh. Farther on, I saw a group of Juventus supporters, and one was wearing a black-and-white sun hat. It would give me more cover in the heat, so I swapped with him. Only he clearly did not want to part with his headwear. He had no choice. Sensing danger, he let me have it and looked in disgust at the flimsy, filthy thing I'd given him. This was not cultural exchange: this was bullying, an assertion of dominance. I remember strutting away, slowly, the body language letting them know how I felt."[31]

Like Tony mentioned earlier, he "certainly didn't threaten any Italians". And unfortunately for us, his story hasn't ended, he goes on:

"There was a supermarket by the bourse [stock exchange] and, at the entrance, there stood a Liverpool fan.

'You're Scouse?' he said. There was no need for an answer and he knew what I was there for. 'It's free to us today,' he said, handing me a tray of beer. The rule of law was over."[32]

Staying with the stock exchange for a moment, Belgian politician Vercaigne, who ventured past, said the steps of the stock exchange were invaded by hundreds of individuals who acted in an indescribable manner under the unconcerned eyes of two "good-old police officers".[33]

Coming back to Tony's words of "the rule of law was over", the next part of his 'search for beer' encapsulates better than anything what took place from lunchtime until around 7:30 p.m. that day:

"On the way back to the square, the group of Liverpool fans by the jeweller had been replaced by riot police. Glass was scattered all over the street, studded with empty display trays. There was hysteria—and pride—in my laughter. This was turning into an excellent day."[34]

Well, there's excellent and there's excellent.

Like Tony, Paul Fry was also in the vicinity of the jewellers. Paul says:

"It was down the side road. I saw the police there, but I didn't see what happened. I'd heard a jeweller's shop window had been broken and some stuff had been stolen in broad daylight."[35]

For Paul this is when he realised that something "naughty" was happening and therefore it was best to leave early for the stadium.

The thieves made off with approximately £125,000 of jewellery.[36] Sergeant White recalled the incident:

"The next call took us a few hundred yards down the road to a jeweller's shop. This had been attacked by a group of Liverpool youths and a quantity of jewellery had been stolen."

To make matters worse for White, while some of the officers were attending this incident, a radio call was received to the effect that there was trouble at the Grand Place. White returned and found a fight taking place among the Liverpool fans, with most of the aggression being directed at Belgian police. Bottles were being thrown about the square and towards the police officers. White was given a riot helmet for protection. The supporters were now very drunk, and it was some time before order was restored.

White then went to a shopping arcade, where he witnessed Reds roaming around, singing and pushing past people. Cars were passing by covered with beer, which had been splashed onto them. One or two had spittle on them. On a mobile patrol of surrounding streets, every bar White passed was full of drunken youths wearing LFC colours. Obscenities were shouted at the van as it passed. He came across one drunken supporter who was wearing a toy British police helmet. He was standing at a crossroads, directing the traffic, and causing a severe traffic obstruction. White removed him to the side of the road.[37]

PC S. Jones was also at the scene of the trouble in the Grand Place. He recalled about a dozen beer bottles were thrown at the vehicle and at the police in the area. Jones was on the receiving end of the bottles himself. With his Belgian counterparts, he moved towards the offenders, with one being arrested by two officers from their Mobile Support Group. As the officers took the offender from the main crowd towards their vehicle, Reds showered them with beer bottles, causing the offender to escape due to officers being hit by the bottles, which must have numbered in the hundreds.[38]

For the record, Tony Evans' jaunt around Brussels city

centre was still going strong. Here, he is talking about a friend:

"[John] was greeting Juventus fans in heavily Scouse-accented Italian. Naturally friendly, he is a man almost incapable of violence. A group wearing Liverpool shirts attacked him and beat him to the floor. 'I'm Scouse,' he was shouting. Few people have a stronger accent. 'No you're not, you Wop,' they said. It took a riot policeman to rescue him. We thought it was hilarious."[39]

Hardly surprisingly, Tony confesses: "My other brother was with me and was disgusted by how me and members of our group acted."[40]

Here we have Liverpool fans beating one another up, and we also have the racist language, although the part I cannot really get my head around is the "We thought it was hilarious". Unfortunately, this wouldn't be the last time LFC fans were fighting with one another.

Journalist Ed Vulliamy was a witness to the aftermath of the carnage in the Grand Place. He recalls: "We walked across the Brussels Grand Place, laid with a carpet of broken beer bottles, and up to the stadium with the English, waddling and bellowing, drunk on lager and the xeno-phobia of the day."[41]

The *Daily Mirror* also reported the xenophobia recounted by Vulliamy: "Words like 'Wop, wop, wop' were hurled at the easily aroused Italian crowd."[42]

A consequence of this rampant xenophobia was the stabbing of a LFC fan. The *Mirror* reported:

"Then a knife flashed. And Stephen Jackson fell wounded. This stabbing and the news flashed all the way back down the streets of Brussels. And anger was the outcome."[43]

The *Mirror* also sums up why Brussels city centre was a

standalone event: "In the Grand Place, a European show-piece of architecture where everything is normally civilised, delicate behaviour became rubble in Liverpool hands."[44]

Once Reds decided to leave the Grand Place for the stadium, they continued with their obnoxiousness and criminality. As PC K. Sutton witnessed at 4:25 p.m., in an area of one of the metro stations, Liverpool supporters had been dropping empty beer bottles off the top of a high flight of steps and causing a nuisance.[45] Around the same time, Inspector G.J. Fair, who was with two Belgian officers, was taken to various parts of the city. He attended three incidents involving Liverpool supporters who had been fighting. As he stated, it was fair to say that on each occasion, the supporters present were the worse for drink.[46]

In a similar vein, Sergeant White's final call was to attend Brussels Central Station. Here the supporters were joining the metro to travel to the stadium. When White arrived at the booking hall, he and Belgian colleagues found Reds were refusing to buy tickets and were jumping over the barriers. The station was full of commuters, and they were being pushed to one side. Again, the Liverpool youths were very drunk and carrying large amounts of beer. The situation was brought under control. The confiscation of alcohol caused quite a lot of dissent among the youths, who retaliated by using obscenities towards the police.[47]

Next, it was time for the stadium.

SEVENTEEN

CHINESE WHISPERS

Heysel Stadium is located in a leafy suburban neighbour-hood, and it is flanked by the iconic Atomium sculpture, the model of a reconstructed atom built for the 1958 World Fair. Despite its prime location and the prestige it was gaining from holding such a glamorous event, the stadium, as we already know, was not all it seemed. Eamonn McCabe was certainly not impressed:

"It wasn't a safe place. It was falling down."[1]

When I visited in late October 2021, I had a curious trip. When I came out of the metro station, also called Heysel, I looked directly to my left and thought, "That can't be it." It looked tiny and unimpressive; I thought it must be some sort of training facility in the shadow of the main ground. It wasn't. It was surrounded by a green fence, and it had those horrible, tall, uninviting turnstiles. I tried to walk round the stadium, but after about 20 metres there was a metal gate that prevented you from doing a continuous lap of the territory. There was also a piece of wasteland. I actually thought, "It's no wonder the fans were kicking off outside; the place is a dump."

However, things took a turn for the better. I went back on myself and headed towards the Atomium sculpture. It was certainly impressive. Once past the Atomium, you come across excellent municipal football pictures, a planetarium, the Belgian Paralympic Committee HQ and then an excellent athletics training complex. Opposite are a host of shops and cafés. You then find the front entrance to the stadium, and it looks fantastic with its gardens and statues. I thought, "This is more like it." Next to the stadium is a small football ground, and the terracing behind the goal looked like something straight out of the '80s. Eventually, I arrived at the metro station, Koning Boudewijn—King Baudouin to you and me; well, definitely to me—now the actual name of the new ground.

Ironically for the fans that arrived in the early afternoon, there was a pleasant atmosphere created by supporters of both sides. One fan said:

"When we first arrived at Heysel Stadium about 2 p.m., there was a carnival atmosphere—fans of both teams exchanging banter, souvenirs, etc, all in a good-natured way."[2]

Another commented: "The atmosphere was good humoured with the usual friendly banter between rival fans."[3]

At 2:30 p.m. Chief Inspector Griffin arrived at the stadium. Griffin had been allocated to Commissioner Wittam of 'A' Division, who was the officer in charge of the policing arrangements/operations both inside and outside the stadium and who we came across in a previous chapter . The weather was hot and sunny, and there were many thousands of supporters from Liverpool and Juventus very much in evidence. Large numbers were lying on the extensive grassed areas which surrounded the stadium. There was evidence of drinking alcohol, but there was, at the time, a lively atmosphere with many rival supporters exchanging their club favours.[4]

Paul Fry took a pleasant journey from the city centre to the ground. He got to the stadium early so he could see what the atmosphere was like and in turn get a good vantage point to watch the game. On arrival, it was clear to Paul that the stadium wasn't up there with the best in Europe. He says:

"It was clearly an old stadium, but that was more evident inside. It had breeze block walls, it had two skins basically apart from the main stand."[5]

Like many witnesses, he recalls: "At the end of the day it was an athletics stadium, with a football pitch in the middle."[6]

As with every other part of his day, Tony Evans' trip to the stadium was far from ordinary. He recounts:

"We boarded a tram to head north to the ground, slurring and swearing and exuding threatening, drunken boorishness. At our stop, we stood up to get off, and Robert [his friend] collapsed. The alcohol that had been nastily overriding a collective sense of decency was now severing the physical links between brain and body. We hauled him from the middle of the road towards the stadium, two of us with his arms over our shoulder while his feet dragged behind. He appeared unconscious."[7]

As we can see from Tony, he and hundreds more brought their obnoxiousness from the Grand Place to the suburbs. An LFC fan stated:

"On arriving at the Heysel Stadium, my wife and I went to a mobile [shop] outside the coach park that was selling soft drinks, hamburgers, etc. In the queue were drunken Liverpool fans who were using abusive language.

They were carrying six-packs of small-bottled lager. It seemed everyone was drinking beer and there was plenty of wine flowing."[8]

Tony Evans describes the scenes outside the stadium perfectly:

"At the ground there was madness. People were staggering, collapsing, throwing up."[9]

Along with the drunkenness, Ed Vulliamy also witnessed the English racism on display as LFC fans sang:

"We hate spiks, we hate spiks, ee-i-addio, we hate spiks."[10]

Vulliamy continues: "One fan jumped up and down in a frenzy, shrieking 'fucking spiks, fucking wops.'"[11] Tellingly, for all the deniers out there, he goes on: "There was not an Italian in sight. He was not distributing NF leaflets, he was not a 'cockney agitator', he was not being provoked—he was just drunk and looked proud to be representing what he saw as his team and his country."[12]

Bruno Guarini and his son Alberto had travelled to Brussels from Mesagne in Puglia. The trip to the final was a present for Alberto, who had recently passed his dentistry exams.[13] Bruno recalls:

"The English had their shirts off, lying on the grass with their beer, so we went straight inside."[14]

Heartbreakingly, Alberto did not survive Heysel.

Another Italian recalls the parade of flesh:

"At 5 p.m., the "reds" were camped all around the Heysel, lazily sunbathing as if they were lizards. Some of them had taken their shirts off; others were completely naked to consummate unspeakable obscenities."[15]

In contrast with the Italians, Tony Evans recalls with pride how "clustered around bars, we sang, bare-chested in the sun and, briefly, bonhomie abounded. It was almost idyllic."[16]

Reporter Peter Marshall, who was covering the game for BBC radio, picked up on the negativity and drunkenness around the stadium. He recalls that when he went outside, he saw the atmosphere had changed. It was after five by then. It was a very hot day, and as Marshall pointed out, it was clear the thing about no alcohol being on sale was complete nonsense. He witnessed drink everywhere; all around the ground there were kiosks and little bars, and they were full of Liverpool fans and things were sort of getting out of hand. By now there were police sirens being heard and fans were incredibly drunk. As Marshall observes, they were young lads who'd come over, it was a particularly hot day, and Belgian beer is strong. But things were out of hand and the atmosphere seemed to have changed. That was the first time Marshall realised that things might not be as they were supposed to be.[17]

On Marshall's point about there being no alcohol available: requests were made for this to be implemented, but that's all they were, because Belgian law did not allow the restriction.

Adding to the weird and intimidating atmosphere being created by Kopites outside the stadium was the spread of Chinese whispers. One fan remarked:

"Stories of Italians carrying and wielding knives were rife as we made our way to the game on our coach. I had seen none of these incidents."[18]

A fan, who was subsequently arrested, said of his earlier experiences in Brussels city centre:

"As we neared the railway station there was hundreds of supporters around and I passed a Juventus supporter. He pulled out a small axe. It was like an ornamental one, it was only small, a fancy one. He swung the axe at me and missed me by inches."[19]

He also told Merseyside Police:

"I've forgotten to mention that outside the ground I noticed that a lot of Juventus supporters were carrying knives and some of them were threatening other supporters, but I myself was not threatened."[20]

We are back to Rome again with Tony Evans' next comment:

"The rumours started spreading; normally you'd just dismiss them and go 'yeah, yeah, yeah', this always happens. You know whoever you were playing, they're attacking women and kids and all that. But after Rome and all the stabbings, so when you heard rumours of stabbings and there was even a mad one that a Liverpool fan was hung, they'd hung him from a tree. But you know there was a bit more nervousness about than normal."[21]

Tony continues:

"Normally things which you'd just write off and dismiss, 'oh behave yourself', you know. Or they'd always be a little dickhead who was running up and telling you that the Third World War had started, but after the year before in Rome there was a bit more belief in these rumours and so it was just, it was carnage outside. People were drunk and I think the normal restraints you get in a Liverpool crowd were kind of the brakes were off a little bit and it in that sense the mood was worse than I'd ever seen it."[22]

On top of the unruly behaviour and Chinese whispers, the Belgian organisers and UEFA's weak ticketing policy, which we read about previously, was clear to see outside the stadium. LFC fan Billy Graves recalls by looking at the touts and listening, it was obvious that they had the majority of these tickets and they were getting sold to Italian supporters.[23] Englishman Francis Burkert says in Brussels someone was clever enough to buy and re-sell tickets on the black market. Just before the game, he saw Juventus supporters buying tickets at up to £70 each. For Burkert, this explains why the Italians and the English ended up in contiguous sectors without police protection.[24]

These tickets Billy and Francis mention were for the so-called neutral section, Block Z. The ill-thought-out policy meant not only were fans separated by an ad-hoc dividing line, but some Liverpool fans actually shared Block Z with mainly Juventus fans. One LFC supporter, who was later arrested, told Merseyside Police he had a ticket for Block Z. He told them he went into the middle of Block Z and then, after realising it was full of Juventus fans, went over to where the Liverpool fans were.[25] After becoming anxious, he tried to get out of Block Z. He told the police:

"There was an English girl there, who could speak very good French. She was asking the policemen if he could let the fans out of the Z section."[26]

Merseyside Police asked him what the Belgian policeman had said. He replied: "He said, 'Go back, no way, no.'"[27]

They then asked him what happened next. He told them:

"Some Liverpool supporters went back, I think [name is blanked out] went back, I stayed there. So, this Italian fella came down and said something to the policeman. He said something like 'You'll have to let them go', and then the policeman opened the gate and let us out in groups." [28]

They moved the fans into Y section. Which, as we are about to see, made the overcrowding in that section even worse than it already was.

REGRETTABLY, entrances and security to the stadium were on par with the ticketing policy. Off-duty Manchester policeman and Red, Dunstan, recalled the police presence outside the stadium was minimal, and only four were inside the gateways through which 11,000 supporters had to pass. The four's sole purpose was to remove any poles from flags when it could quite clearly be seen that Italians at the opposite end of the stadium were waving flags.[29]

Dunstan added that the entrances were just two doorways, no turnstiles, which were manned by two elderly men at each. Shortly after he entered, the gates were closed on the fans outside as the gatemen could not cope. This incensed the fans outside, who were forced to climb over the walls to gain entry even though they were in possession of tickets.[30]

Councillor Paul Clark, who we came across earlier, realised how the chaos at the turnstiles could have serious consequences later in the evening. The first warning signs of possible problems appeared as soon as he saw the entrance to the ground. A thin mesh fence was being used to funnel people towards police officers, who were conducting searches. The mesh fence already had huge gaps in when he arrived at 6:30 p.m. Clark walked through one of the large gaps rather than join a massive queue to be searched. He then approached the turnstiles to find that there were none. There was just a gap with two officials taking a portion of the ticket. Numerous people were able to get into the ground with forgeries or even no ticket alone. Once in the ground, Clark was asked for his ticket by a drunken slob who was passing them back out of the ground to his friends. He successfully ignored him, but the slob was having no trouble in getting wads of tickets to pass out of the ground.[31]

With a fellow journalist, Steven Kelly attempted to enter Section X around 6:45 p.m. Kelly recollected:

"The police were turning fans away, claiming that the sector was full and that they should go to sector Y. This we dutifully did, only to discover that the entrance at sector Y was a mere door, the size of an ordinary household door with only one policeman taking tickets. Not surprisingly, within a few minutes a substantial crowd had gathered, all impatient to get into the ground and growing angrier by the moment at the slow process."[32]

Kelly continued:

"Some of the more impatient were already shinning up the wall to get in [...] policeman arrived on the spot and began lashing out at those half-way up the wall. 'Get that fucking policeman off the gate and let's get in', shouted someone from the back of the mob. The crowd surged forward and sideways so that I suddenly found myself heading for the walled corner and in danger of being trapped and crushed [...] Tickets were being passed back for anyone without one and the policeman, quite sensibly, had given up."[33]

What was the actual policy of the authorities at the entrance to the stadium? Well, the police and gendarmes intended to search fans near the outside fence with a view to confiscating sticks or other weaponry. It is perfectly clear from all the evidence that there were insufficient police or gendarmes to search all spectators. There is a great body of evidence that the searching was perfunctory; that because of the absence of turnstiles and the presence of holes in the perimeter wall, a large number of people got into the stadium without tickets; that those who had tickets inside were able to pass them back to those outside who did not.[34]

Roosens pointed out that only a superficial search had been viable. He added that to conduct a proper check would have taken about 30 seconds per person and would have taken 125 officers 4 hours to search all the spectators, and clearly this would not have been feasible.[35]

Weapons that had been confiscated earlier were retrieved. There were sticks used to carry flags, pieces of tree trunks, bottles and stones.[36] Roosens alleged that it was true that a number of Liverpool fans threw various items over the perimeter fencing to people already inside. Once inside, however, they went off to fetch sticks and all sorts of things which the others were throwing over the fence.[37] Additionally, it is clear that a number of spectators had had too much to drink. Bottles of drink were on sale at a number of stalls, thus providing more ammunition for the fans.[38] Other reports mentioned whole crates of beer being carried into the stadium by the Liverpool supporters.[39]

As we know from the London and Liverpool reports we discussed, once inside, the unsuitability of the venue became even more apparent.

EIGHTEEN

TWO-MATCH BAN

Paradoxically, and a fact lost in history due to Heysel being the Forgotten Tragedy, trouble first began at the Juventus end of the stadium. Some of the unrest was of a grave nature. The question is, would Juventus have been banned themselves if it weren't for the tragedy at the opposite end?

An Englishman wrote to Denis Howell, the ex-Labour sports minister, in the aftermath. The correspondent told Howell that a colleague told him that he had witnessed Juventus fans leaving Turin for Brussels being transported by 32 coaches under police escort. The fans were leaning out of the windows with scarves, knives and truncheons.[1] How accurate this statement is I don't know, but what I do know is if it is, we are about to meet the people the letter speaks of.

The first incident recorded in the Brussels Police Report took place at 3:55 p.m. when some of the temporary fencing, which had been erected all round the stadium, was knocked down by Juventus supporters.[2] It had been erected to enable the police to more easily search fans. It was about a kilometre long, comprising of fifty sections. Unfortunately, the fencing was not adequately supervised, despite the police services arriving in good time. They were unable to carry out complete frisking owing to a lack of numbers (40 police officers). Articles which were confiscated could not be taken away from the supporters owing to the fact that there were no containers. An attempt was made to make this situation good by using a van.[3]

With thirty or more sections of the fence already knocked down, the Italians broke through the no man's land and were in an imposing mass in front of the entrance doors of Blocks N and O. Thus, the control of tickets and the search operation had, consequently, been rendered very difficult at this place.[4]

By 4:05 p.m. calm had been restored. This was temporary, however. At 4:27 p.m., supporters arriving from the Avenue Impératrice Charlotte were breaking into the safety zone around the stadium. Thirty minutes later, there was fighting behind Stand 2 and bottles being thrown outside the stadium and from inside the safety zone.[5] At 5 p.m. when the gates opened, the Italian supporters flooded in and within half an hour their sections were full.[6] Chief Inspector M. Griffin said he was amazed that by 5.30 p.m. the Juventus end already seemed full. The Juventus fans were very noisy and waving their massive banners about; in contrast, the Liverpool end was sparsely populated.[7]

Two minutes after the gates opened, there was a request for assistance from sections M, N and O owing to the heavy influx of supporters. At the same time there were reports coming in of young people wearing leather jackets and carrying sticks being present in the area opposite the passage behind the Mell carpark.[8]

At 5:10 p.m. an ambulance was called to deal with a knife-wound victim.[9] At 5:25 p.m. some crowd disorder and other incidents were noted. A call came in for the Canine Brigade and mounted officers to come to the running track—an urgent request for support after a sudden flare-up amongst the Italians.[10] Reinforcements who had not been due to come on duty until 6 p.m. were called in.

At 5:35 p.m. general advice was issued not to allow supporters carrying sticks or long flag poles to enter the stadium. At 5.36 p.m. some Italians tried to get into Section O from Section M. At 5.39 p.m., CID intelligence reported that individuals carrying sticks were getting into Section M.

At 5:46 p.m. a decision was taken not to take sorties into the crowd, and only a defensive stance was to be taken. The justification for this was psychological—Italian supporters were beginning to direct anger at the police. At 5:55 p.m. there was general disorder in Section O. The supporters were becoming agitated, and two hundred of them were beginning to get worked up, hurling insults at the police in the segregation gangway.[11]

At 6 p.m. there was mass scaling of the walls of Section M by supporters because sections O and N were full. At the same time, some of the officers stationed inside the stadium were pelted with missiles by the Italians, who were attempting to use riot tactics by surging forward en masse and retreating. Meura, from the Brussels City Police, felt he had to make a choice between two possible courses of action: to resist the assault firmly or show flexibility. He believed it was always important to avoid provoking crowds. Since at the time the Italian supporters were going for the English supporters, what the police tried to avoid at all costs was a pitch invasion.[12]

At the same time, other Juventus fans were draping their banners in front of the advertising hoardings, and the commissioner instructed his officers to stop this from happening. This was done but was resented by the fans, who waved fists and shouted threateningly at the police.

One Juventus fan left the terraces and ran onto the pitch, carrying a carton containing white powder. He ran to the nearer goalmouth and sprinkled the powder in the goal. This brought tremendous roars of "Juva" from the Juventus fans. He then ran to the goal at the other end of the pitch and did exactly the same. On returning to the Juventus end, he sprinkled some powder in the centre circle. When he left the pitch, he was escorted along the running track by a uniformed officer. At that, the police were subjected to an attack of missile throwing from the Juventus fans. Large pieces of concrete were thrown in some quantity, as were litre bottles of water and orange juice, along with other less injurious articles. Eventually, the apprehended person was returned to the other Juventus supporters, and the situation calmed.[13]

PC Sutton from the British Transport Police arrived outside the stadium at 6:10 p.m. When he got there, he found some Juventus fans were fighting amongst themselves in the area of the turnstiles. Sutton and his Belgian colleagues returned to their vehicle about 15 minutes later. His Belgian hosts put on their riot helmets, as the Juventus fans had been attacking police with spikes and spears.[14] Inspector Fair, also from the British Transport Police, arrived about 20 minutes after Sutton. He went to the area behind the entrance to terracing area M. Here there was a great deal of confusion, with hundreds of people sporting Juventus colours trying to force their way towards the terracing entrance. There were several mounted Belgian police officers who were clearly having difficulty in controlling the crowd at this entrance.[15]

Inside the stadium the situation was becoming worse too. Fifty men were placed between Sections M, N and O, but they were forced to retreat at about 6:30 p.m. because of the aggression from the Italian supporters. The gangways were so structured that it was not possible to keep officers on the steps. The police could not prevent supporters from reaching the pitch when about 40 barriers intended to protect the pitch were knocked down. The fact that they were throwing lumps of concrete from the structure of the stadium and various metal objects caused enormous problems. Resende from UEFA witnessed these incidents and alleged that the fence surrounding the field of play and the fence separating the two sectors were demolished and that the fans entered onto the athletics track and threw missiles at the police forces.[16]

At around 7 p.m., the police in the gangway could not prevent five to six metres of the fencing from being torn down, then 30 metres of fencing was forced and trampled down so as to give direct access to the track, all this despite the use of shields and truncheons by the police, several of whom were injured. It should also be noted that stones and lumps of concrete and some beer bottles (20 in all) were raining down onto the track; some hooligans from amongst the supporters were even running up to the police with sticks and iron bars.[17]

At 7:06 p.m. requests were made for reinforcements in the gangway in Sections M and W, where the situation suddenly took a turn for the worse. During one of the interventions, a pair of handcuffs was pulled out of the hands of one officer. These were thrown around from one person to another.[18]

During the chaos, one fan was arrested (at a later date) for using a revolver. He was amongst a group of around 30 fans who were wearing face coverings to hide their identities. It was later reported that the suspect was beaten by Belgian prison officers after his arrest. He certainly got no sympathy from Deputy Peters, who told the Belgian Senate:

"People in this Assembly have complained because the Italian with the revolver got a few punches from the police later on. But he who sows shall also reap."[19]

What is less commonly known is the story of the same thing happening at the LFC end involving an LFC fan. Belgian police led investigations that a man in Liverpool colours was seen firing a gun at the stadium.[20] This sensational suggestion came from Louis Wouters, president of the Belgian Football Union, who said he would demand an autopsy 'for the first two victims, as it is unclear whether they were killed by knife stabs or by revolver shots.'[21] Belgian television also claimed that shots were heard before the outbreak of trouble.[22] The *Mail on Sunday* went with the headline: "Second gunman".[23]

The *Mail* reported that Belgian police confirmed on the Saturday evening that spent shells were found in the area. Commissioner Christian de Vroom, who was leading the police inquiries, declared:

"We are treating this evidence very seriously. We have already found two bullet cases on the terracing in Z block and our search is continuing."[24]

Paul Fry became a witness and actually did a line-up over the shots fired by the English fan. The line-up was a joke, because when they reeled the guys in to do the line-up, Paul had already met three of them in the reception because, unbelievably, they were policemen. So, as Paul said: "It definitely wasn't A, B or C."[25]

He didn't recognise D, E or F either.

In total, twenty-seven police officers were injured at the

Juventus end.[26] Meura, from the Brussels police, thought the apparent motivation of the Italians was hatred of the police. He stated it was an example of collective violence by young people with a desire to run wild. And that it was clear that some of those involved had an utter disrespect for authority, probably deriving from their attitude towards parental authority.[27]

On top of this, the Belgian reasoning was those involved were able to profit from the anonymity of the crowd which was a useful position from which to attack the police.[28] This comes back to the views of Festinger et al. and Zimbardo who we mentioned in Chapter Two.

To highlight how bad the rioting by Juventus fans was, the Belgian Parliamentary Committee observed the following comparison:

"Assurances were given to the effect that Liverpool was a club which caused virtually no difficulties. Indeed, apart from 7 minutes when the panic occurred, the Liverpool fans at the match caused fewer problems, generally speaking, than the Italians."[29]

In June during their disciplinary process, UEFA said of Juventus fans:

"Before the match, supporters of Juventus FC had shown a particular incorrect conduct tearing down the exterior fence outside the stadium, by setting off fireworks at regular intervals, by demolishing the fence surrounding the field of play and also the fence of the stadium separating the two sectors. In addition, missiles were thrown against the security forces and supporters of the club have entered onto the ground. After the tragic incident, which occurred at the other end of the stadium, they fought a battle with the security forces. A number of these supporters entered the ground and went practically across the whole length of the field of play in the direction of the sector occupied by the English supporters, without getting there."[30]

The punishment was this:

"The Juventus FC shall play its next 2 (two) home matches in the UEFA Club Competitions behind closed doors. In as far as this sanction is concerned, the Committee has taken into consideration the particularly serious previous disciplinary record of the club."[31]

If I were on the UEFA panel, I would have arrived at the same conclusions. It would have been impossible, given the tragic nature of Heysel, to have thrown them out. If, however, the tragedy had not happened, Juventus would not have been defending champions the following season.

NINETEEN

"A FOOTBALL TERRACING VERSION OF DANTE'S INFERNO."

When Liverpool players walked onto the pitch as part of their pre-match rituals, most things were as they should be. Bruce Grobbelaar went over to where the main bunch of Liverpool diehards were standing on the far side of the ground, and their humour was good. They even kicked a plastic ball down to the Liverpool players, and Grobbelaar and Sammy Lee joined in the fun and kicked it back to them.[1]

The fun was about to end. Not long afterwards, our nation was hearing this:

"This is war correspondent stuff here. Death, serious injury, violence, football has died, and the hooligans have won."[2]

The words above were spoken so vividly and hauntingly by respected BBC radio commentator, Peter Jones, just after LFC fans had attacked and killed innocent men, women, teenagers, and a young boy called Andrea Casula. In his essay, Fabio Chisari writes of Andrea:

"Eleven-year-old Andrea Casula loved football above anything else. He played in the youth team of Cagliari, his hometown club. And he loved Juventus. His father had promised after Juventus's defeat in the 1983 European Cup final that if Juve made the final again he would take him to the match. When his father kept the promise and secured tickets for the 1985 final Andrea went to school triumphantly, happy that he was to watch Platini and Boniek and his other idols in the flesh."[3]

When the emergency services took his body, Andrea was wrapped in the corpse of his father, who had attempted to shield him from the rampaging LFC fans.[4]

Where do you begin?

Like Jones said, it was "war correspondent stuff" and not the beautiful game. Jones also informed the audience back home:

"If you've just joined us, I should tell you of the awfulness and violence. The worst that I've ever seen has occurred here in the Heysel Stadium in Brussels. Liverpool supporters massed away to our left attacked Juventus supporters of which there was a small section on that same side. They charged into the Juventus supporters who fled in terror."[5]

Jones was joined in the commentary box by Mike Ingham, who was about to commentate on his first European Cup. Ingham recalls:

"Fathers and sons died in front of me—thirty-nine in all —and more than six hundred others were injured. I had prepared for a football commentary and found myself in a war zone."[6]

On air with Jones and Ingham that evening was ex-England and Liverpool captain and club legend Emlyn Hughes, who we spoke of earlier. A very emotional Hughes informed the British listeners:

"As we talk now, there's somebody else who's just been

pulled out down there wrapped in a brown blanket. It's a young girl, a young girl wrapped in a brown blanket."[7]

The serious trouble began around 7:15 p.m. and it was over with by around 7:30 p.m. That's how brief it was. Before the main fatal charge, there had been an exchange of missiles between mainly Juventus fans in Block Z and Liverpool supporters in Block Y.[8] Two previous attacks by Liverpool fans had also been repulsed. The third charge by Reds resulted in mass panic among the mainly Juventus spectators in Block Z. The Italian and neutral supporters, who were seeking to escape towards the perimeter, were squashed and suffocated by the press of large numbers.[9]

You see, no collapsed wall led to most of the deaths. The collapsed wall is a myth. An understandable one, given the crushing sound, but a myth, nonetheless.

We mentioned earlier about rival British fans 'taking ends', but instead of the usual "these charges looked really aggressive, in reality serious injuries seldom happened", here the consequences were beyond anything we thought humanly possible inside a football ground.

Journalists, Juve fans, Reds and neutrals point to different triggers for the instigation of the trouble. Some put it down to flares being fired. Others to flags and banners being burnt. Missiles of differing types is another. Some say it was down to LFC fans not having the space afforded to Italians. Spitting is another trigger, and from a Kopite perspective the assault on a young boy seems to be a popular story.

Journalist Paul Lacey of the *Guardian* said in a comment piece the next day: "The trouble started with a minority of Liverpool fans throwing missiles towards the Juventus supporters and drifting towards their part of the terraces."[10]

In an article also on the next day entitled "I saw our thugs start slaughter", a *London Evening Standard* reporter gave a first-hand account of what they saw: "I witnessed the cause of the tragedy at Heysel Stadium. And it was without doubt a large group of drunken hooligans from Merseyside."[11]

Whatever the cause, the assault left thirty-eight people dead on the night. The thirty-ninth victim, Luigi Pidone, who had been in a coma, died from head injuries on 14 August.[12] The majority who died were Italians; however, there were also four Belgians and two French people.

The only person from the British Isles to die was Oxford graduate Patrick Radcliffe, who had never been to a match before. Patrick worked as an archivist with the EEC in Brussels. His family watched the horror unfold on TV in Northern Ireland, never dreaming that he could be among the crowd. His cousin Kevin Sheehy responded to their loss the day after the game. Kevin disclosed that Patrick had never taken the slightest interest in football. Heart-wrenchingly, Kevin added that it was a tragedy that someone with so much to offer life should die in such a stupid way.[13]

The rest of the dead included two postmen, two cooks, three doctors, four students, a car mechanic, a soldier, a school janitor, a farmer, a taxi driver, several shopkeepers, a fashion photographer and a builder.[14] The list of the victims reflected the national and international nature of Juve's mass support. Only two of the dead were from Turin itself.[15] Somewhere between four hundred and six hundred fans (depending on which figures you use) were also injured.

As we all know, LFC fans were the primary cause of the deaths on the terraces, but how did the violence begin? Many Reds, Juventus followers, neutrals and journalists lay the blame squarely at the feet of the LFC supporters. Some Reds insist Juventus supporters instigated the disorder.

What is indeed crystal clear is that the charges and attacks were relatively all one way, from LFC supporters towards Juve fans, and it was these onslaughts that caused the deaths. That is the crux of the whole tragedy—if the charges had not occurred, nobody would have died.

One Red perfectly summed up the inhumanity that took place during those fifteen minutes of madness:

"It was a warm night, and the beer-garden atmosphere was insidiously transformed into a football terracing version of Dante's Inferno."[16]

WE KNOW NOW that trouble first began at the other side of the stadium. The first signs of unrest amongst the English were apparent during the youth match, which had been organised to keep the spectators occupied. This was towards the end of half-time. At about 6:15–6:30 p.m., Roosens from the RBFA saw the first example of the English throwing stones into Section Z. He recalled that he was all the more worried at the time because there seemed to be quite a few Italians on the English side, and also because he had requested a gendarme on each step, which had not happened. He sent someone to find the officers in charge of the gendarmerie so they could remedy this. The person he sent came back and told him:

"I can't find anyone. The gendarmes say that their chief is outside, and they can't get hold of him." [17]

Roosens decided to go himself. He fared no better than his deputy. Having given up hope of finding anyone who could deal with the matter, he was told that there was a command vehicle outside. On the way he met General Bernaert and asked him to alert the gendarmes.

Peter Robinson arrived around 6:30 p.m., and after leaving the dressing room, he went out and sat on a seat on the edge of the running track. He immediately observed that three-quarters of the standing area of the stadium was occupied by Juventus supporters.

At about 6:45 p.m. he saw Mr Aigner, an assistant secretary of UEFA. Robinson was angry that so many Juventus fans had been able to purchase tickets when assurances had been given that only 25% of the tickets would be allocated to the club. He protested vehemently about this and asked how such a state of affairs had arisen. He advised Aigner that if trouble followed, it would be the responsibility of UEFA for permitting this situation to occur. A short time later, Robinson saw Gunter Schneider of East Germany, a member of the UEFA Committee. He had a similar conversation, plus Robinson mentioned the lack of police bodies. Schneider did not comment as to this, and it may be that because of the noise in the stadium and Robinson's inability to speak German that his message was not fully comprehended.[18]

Albert Roosens personally edited the official match day programme. On the last page, he made a series of demands to the crowd: He appealed that "to ensure that the cup final proceeds in an atmosphere worthy of the occasion, spectators are kindly requested to:

- refrain from bringing bottles of any kind into the stadium.
- not throw any objects.
- not encroach upon the interior part of the

stadium under any circumstances either before, during or after the match.

- keep their expressions of joy or disappointment within the limits of normal good sporting behaviour.

- help the stadium security officials in carrying out their duties to prevent an unruly minority from spoiling the enjoyment of the majority who have come to see good football."[19]

As we are about to see, for one reason or another, all of Roosens' wishes were broken.

Like we said previously, some Reds blamed Italians for the initial problems, and probably the most common theory is the story of a young English boy being beaten up by Juventus supporters. Ian Walmsley from Bootle, David Carter from Maghull and Martin O'Shea from Garston all highlighted this in their accounts. Ian stated that the fighting started because a boy of only 10 or 12 was getting attacked by some Italians, so Liverpool supporters ran and the fence went.[20] David, one of the first to arrive back home at Liverpool Airport, claimed the boy was being kicked and punched by the Juventus mob. The Liverpool supporters retaliated and went after them.[21] Martin vividly remembered a small Liverpool lad, swathed in scarves, being repeatedly punched by two or three Juventus youths.[22] McGregor, from British Transport Police, picked up on this theme. He said that there were a number of descriptions of a young Liverpool youth receiving violent treatment from a number of Italian youths in Section Z. LFC's own documentation points out that it was not known what action the boy had taken to provoke this, but there was a suggestion from some witnesses that he had set fire to a Juventus flag.[23]

Some Reds pointed to their fans, and not just a young boy, being attacked in Block Z.

J. R. Hughes from Halewood saw a small number of Liverpool fans in Section Z were attacked by Juventus thugs who were "obviously looking for aggro".[24] Hughes added that this incensed the main group of Liverpool fans in Sections X and Y, and various missiles, including bottles and pieces of concrete, were thrown by Liverpool yobs at the Juventus yobs, who retaliated.[25]

Merseyside Police asked a Red, who was questioned in June 1985: "In your opinion, why did the Liverpool fans charge into the Italians?" His reply was: "To save their own supporters because they [Italians] were coming over attacking them, they had been looking at them menacingly earlier on."[26]

Patricia Myers, Jane Colley from Maghull, H. Harper from Sefton Park, John Standing from Rock Ferry and M. Johnson from St Helens believed Italians began the trouble by throwing various missiles. Johnson stated that all at once, a shower of bottles, tin cans and bricks came over from the Juventus side of the wire. At the time, Johnson didn't see them being thrown back, that was much later. He also saw the police over the fence hitting Liverpool supporters with their truncheons.[27]

Patricia Myers didn't see what happened but claimed Italians urinated in cans and threw them over the fence, drenching the Liverpool fans.[28] Colley remarked the atmosphere became very tense and then Italian fans started throwing bricks and bottles, to which Liverpool fans retaliated.[29] Harper witnessed Italians throwing coins at the Liverpool fans.[30] John Standing, who drove a coach to Heysel, said that at full-time of the youth friendly, the Juventus fans began to poke the pointed ends of their flag

poles through the rails at the Liverpool fans, including
Standing himself. Then they began throwing bottles over.
Standing says Liverpool fans responded by throwing back
bread rolls.[31]

The arrested Red we came across before who
mentioned that "lots of Juventus supporters were carrying
knives", also claimed that Italians began the trouble. He told
police:

"Once in the ground I was boiling with temper over the
Italian supporters. It was the way they behaved carrying
knives and that. After a short while the Italians started to
throw bricks and bottles at the Liverpool supporters. They
retaliated by throwing the same back at them. I myself did
not throw any, but I began to lose my temper."[32]

The next group of Reds saw things the other way
around. One alleged the missiles started flying mainly from
Liverpool fans in Y over to Z. Next minute, about 100
Liverpool fans went berserk. The fence and police stood no
chance, and the Liverpool fans poured across to Z.[33]

Another fan said:

"What then actually precipitated the assault on the
partition fences was difficult to say from where we stood,
but it was preceded by a hail of cans, bottles, and bricks
from people in Liverpool colours [...] This barrage of
missiles was returned by a few of the crowd who now withdrew a few yards back."[34]

A. McAlester from Tuebrook spoke of a Red battle unit
forming after the throwing:

"Bottles and lumps of concrete were being thrown at
the Juventus fans by this minority of Liverpool supporters
who had started to assemble into some form of battle
unit."[35]

S. Keeling from Woolton, Nicky Allt and Paul Bennett

put the cause down to Italian fans spitting, amongst other things. Paul from Anfield saw Italian supporters spitting through the fence. He went on to claim that these people were provoking Liverpool fans. Then he saw bricks, blocks of concrete and Coca Cola bottles being thrown at and over the fence into Block Y, where Liverpool supporters were situated.[36] Nicky Allt recounted that there was a bit of taunting, a few missiles thrown, and then the Italian fans started spitting. Nicky also said that in northern Europe "that's the lowest of the low, and only a coward is going to run away from that. That's when the charge started."[37]

Keeling, who was in Section Z, recalled:

"I made my way to the flimsy fence which separated both sets of supporters, hoping to be allowed into the Liverpool section. [...] At that time there were about 300 Liverpool fans standing alongside the fence and within the next ten minutes we were subjected to extreme provocation, not only were we jeered at, spat at, but a number of Juventus fans held up various offensive weapons including knives. [...] All of a sudden, missiles were thrown by both sets of supporters, and I turned around to face the Juventus fans and I was hit by a brick in the stomach."[38]

Eric Winters from Bootle saw it differently:

"Liverpool supporters draped their scarves and banners over the fence that was supposed to separate the crowd, as did the Juventus fans on the other side of the fence. [...] Then the Juventus fans removed Liverpool banners and started provoking Liverpool supporters. Liverpool supporters retaliated by spitting, throwing cans. I saw one Juventus fan scale the fence and call the Liverpool supporters to come in there, they spat and swore at them."[39]

Assistant Chief Constable McGregor re-entered the stadium at about 7 p.m. and went to the Liverpool end. The mood had become ugly. He noted that abuse was being exchanged between some Liverpool supporters in Section Y and Juventus fans in Z. There were a number of surges towards the dividing wire fence by both sets of fans, and he saw one Liverpool supporter climb the fence from Z into Y. He also witnessed objects being thrown in both directions, as well as towards the police on the perimeter track. McGregor himself was struck a glancing blow by a small piece of concrete thrown from the area occupied by Juventus fans. Whilst this was happening, he noticed that a small number of riot police had entered the ground and were ushering Liverpool fans through Z into Y.[40] Likewise Chief Inspector Griffin also noticed pieces of concrete being thrown indiscriminately from one sector to the other between rival fans.[41]

TWENTY

SPACE

Many Reds believe the firing of flares seemed to be the trigger. A. Anderson from Wigan stated there had been no trouble at all when suddenly a man of about 20, who was standing about five yards in front of him, set off a green flare. It shot high in the air over the Juventus fans and landed at the back of the stadium. About 30 seconds later, he set off another flare (a red one); this time it landed right in the middle of the Juventus supporters. It was at this point, according to Anderson, that all the hooligans attacked the Juventus crowd.[1]

Jeffery Morris from Norris Green recalled:

"I heard a whoosh from above and I looked up. There was a red flare heading into the Z section apparently from XY section to our left."[2]

S.A. Avann and his brother G.R. Avann said that after watching the youth game:

"Our attention was distracted by a 'distress type' flare which had been fired from our far left (somewhere near to where the terraces and the stands met) deep in the Liverpool section X. The flare landed deep among the Juventus fans congregated in the Z section. This sparked off a short period of missile throwing from both sides of the Y/Z partition."[3]

T. Johnston from Hough Green recounted that he couldn't be sure when the trouble started in the ground, but he agreed with most accounts that it was about 6:30 p.m. when the Liverpool fans started to throw stones and fire either rockets or flares in Section Z. Most people moved away from the fence. There was a period where things seemed to cool down, then as Johnston witnessed, the Liverpool fans started to push the fence down, without any provocation from the Italian fans.[4]

An Italian also believed the flares led to the trouble. Danilo Bartolozzi from Impruneta recalls:

"Everything started with rockets being fired. The fourth rocket went straight into a supporter. He was about 65 feet far from me. I saw him falling, his face covered in blood."[5]

These latter missiles were described in *Corriere della Sera* as the "powder magazine of the beasts from Liverpool".[6]

K. Martindale from Mossley Hill believes it started with a banner. He disclosed that he happened to see the very incident that started the whole invasion by Liverpool fans. For Martindale, Liverpool fans draped the intervening fence between themselves and the opposition supporters with numerous banners and flags. After the ritual burning of a Juventus banner, an Italian tried to place another banner on the fence. The Liverpool supporters then not only tried to remove the banner, but also the Juventus supporter. That was the time that many Liverpool supporters surged forward, bringing down the barrier and attacking anyone who appeared to be a Juventus follower, women and children included.[7]

Italians blamed the riot on Reds too. Simone Stenti recounted: "There was no provocation because in our section there were families."[8]

Eamonn McCabe made this point: "You've got tough football terrace people against people who are frightened."

Eamonn went on to speak about another incident he'd been involved in:

"I used to support Enfield Town, a small local team, and we were at Reading and they came after us, but you just knew what to do. There's no point arguing with these guys. And I remember at Reading, the old stadium, you had steps down and that could have got nasty."[9]

A Juve fan, Adriano Fronzaroli, declared to *La Nazione*:

"In block Z there were no Juve Ultras. We were all very quiet supporters."[10]

Adriano went on to say:

"No one reacted to the provocation. I don't know, I am not a violent person, but I got the impression that our submissive behaviour excited and spurred the others on."[11]

This "submissive behaviour" is backed up by a Liverpool fan, who recalled:

"Next thing I knew, the fighting broke out. There were no police at all to be seen. At first there were only about ten supporters involved but when the others saw the Italians were not fighting back, things just got out of control."[12]

On top of the provocation detailed, some witnesses put the space afforded to Juve fans in comparison with their rivals from Merseyside as a spark for fans pulling down the fence, which then led to the attacks. I put significant weight behind this idea myself. It is obvious that the Liverpool sections were overcrowded; witness after witness confirms this. I personally interviewed Paul Fry, who was in Block Z, and his story, despite all the madness associated with Heysel, has logic running all the way through it.

With Paul arriving early, the ground was sparsely populated:

"It wasn't crowded, but then it started building up and you could see that one of the problems was that Liverpool fans were crammed in. Some of the people were pressed up against the fence and they thought 'Hang on, they've got lots of room over there. Why can't we have that?' And also, 'we've come the shortest distance, they've got all three segments down the far end and why have we only got two?' [...] I think that was one trigger. There were so many triggers, it was nuanced. But beyond that, the initial thing that sparked it was I think overcrowding."[13]

He continues:

"My feeling at the time was they just want to come through the fence for space, that was my overriding feeling. And people started climbing the fence to come over; they didn't because it was a very high fence, but that was the overwhelming feeling that I had at the time. They were going to break that fence down whatever."[14]

And here's Paul's key point:

"So, it wasn't about attacking the Juventus fans; it was a claim for space. And then the Italians kind of backed away and backed away."[15]

When problems began, Paul went to the front of the terracing close to the pitch so he could get onto the pitch if he needed to escape. Paul didn't feel safe at the front, where the missile throwing had already begun, so he went to the back of the terracing to be close to the exits. In addition, Paul felt if Reds broke through the fence, he would be collateral damage, because he understood English fans would not be asking whether he was Italian or not, particularly as he wasn't wearing any club colours. His move to the back of the terrace was all about self-preservation.

Once there, Paul met an LFC fan who was only around 12 years of age; however, Paul claimed the boy was mature beyond his years. The boy was separated from his dad, but he wasn't too bothered as he knew they'd meet up later. It was clear to Paul that the lad had been all over Europe with Liverpool:

"Oh, my word did he know how the world worked and how football worked. And he was where he was [the back of the terrace] because he felt he'd be safer there."[16]

With Italians retreating and a hail of concrete coming over, it was at this point Paul sensed events were becoming even more dangerous, so he did the sensible thing and left the ground, but not before witnessing gore and death. With the stampede beginning, the young boy pointed out to Paul the sight of the first dead. This was before the actual charges. They were escaping the potential danger of being attacked, and they were running from the lumps of concrete coming over the fence, which caused the stampede.[17]

Regarding the police, Paul says that there was a police presence at the back of terrace, who were looking at the entrances. Unfortunately, they were passive, and they hadn't realised what had happened closer to the pitch, plus —and even worse—they looked like volunteers. It is here where Paul changed from a fan at a European Cup Final to a journalist, he remembers:

"When I realised people were dying, I thought I can't go into the office next week or tomorrow and say I was there, and I could never have put my hand up and said 'I've seen this'. So, I thought my job now as a neutral and a journalist is that I had to try and go and tell someone."[18]

Juve fan Roberto Verdelli also highlights the problems

over space. Roberto expressed the view that he did not believe that the English intended, at least not at the beginning, to attack the Juventus supporters; instead, he believed that their presence in Block Z was the result of Block X and Y not being large enough for them, given that they numbered at least 15,000 and there were still more pouring in. Block Z, by contrast, was not yet full, and offered an empty space or buffer zone formed between the sections. The open spaces within the Juventus section served as an invitation for the English fans restricted into such an inadequate space.[19]

Tony Evans too understood the significance of the perceived room provided to the Italians:

"Section Y, where we were standing, grew more and more crowded and, in front of us, a crush barrier buckled and collapsed. Next door, Section Z was supposedly a neutral area. It looked to be mainly Italian, with plenty of room available. We eyed the space with envy."[20]

It is worth staying with Tony's experience in the stadium for a moment because he allows us an insight into the dark atmosphere that was hovering over the occasion, including how out-of-control he was and how erratic events had become. He recounts:

"The rough treatment by police drew a response and most disappeared from the back of the section after skirmishes. Seeing a policeman beating a young lad who was attempting to climb over the wall and was caught in the barbed wire, I pushed the Belgian officer away. He turned to hit me with his baton, and I punched him—not hard—through his open visor. He ran away."[21]

He continues:

"With the police gone, groups of youths swarmed over a snack stand and looted it. I climbed on to the roof and was passed up trays of soft drinks to hand around. It felt like being on top of the world up there."[22]

Tony's language and involvement expose just how revolting people from our city behaved that day. On his striking of a policeman, there are three things. First, in Chapter Fifteen I said Tony didn't hit anybody, by this I clearly meant Juventus fans. Second, the punch he threw is classic Robins and Cohen from Chapter One. Third, the punch is a metaphor for Tony's imperialistic mentality, i.e., "I'm English and he's just Johnny Foreigner and I'll slap him if I want". Charles Glass, who we mentioned earlier, entitled his article about Brussels "Englishmen Aboard". I think by now we can safely say Tony's day in Brussels was the personification of Glass's title. Put simply, Tony was an Englishman abroad.

AS THE TROUBLE began and Reds started their initial forays toward Italians, the gendarmerie were conspicuous by their absence, and those who were on hand hardly covered themselves in glory. Manchester policeman Dunston recalled how the police, amazingly, turned and ran and at no time made any serious attempt to stop this relatively minor level of trouble, when they were adequately armed to do so with shields and large batons.[23]

The British policeman says of his Belgian peers that as the trouble escalated with Kopites tearing down the dividing fence, "the police backed away, showing embarrassing cowardice."[24] He continued:

"A now much larger group ran at the Italians causing widespread panic. Once again, the police were very slow in reacting [to] what was happening."[25]

One LFC fan, who would later walk out of the human body mountain with a broken foot, was unsure why it started, but was clear in who started it:

"Some Liverpool fans began punching the Italians on the terraces—I don't know why."[26]

He went on to say:

"The next thing I knew, the barrier came down and all the Juventus supporters panicked. Everyone collapsed in a heap and then a medic came along and dragged me away."[27]

Regrettably, this battle unit from our city was about to unleash the most sickening hooligan attack ever seen in European football. As one Juventus supporter recalls:

"I had never seen men behaving so furiously, I had never witnessed such unmotivated violence."[28]

And so, alas, the pandemonium began.

TWENTY-ONE

"DADDY, THEY'RE CRUSHING ME."

Photographer Eamonn McCabe arrived at the stadium "nice and early", so he could get accredited. Once inside, he was drawn to the Juventus end. He recalls:

"The first thing I really remember is the vivid fans of Juventus. Huge flares and flags, and for me, I had not seen them before. They had a wonderful team, very flamboyant. I was having a great time. I was shooting wide, tight. There were flags, flares and I was joshing with the fans."

The joshing was soon to be interrupted. Eamonn goes on:

"The way it started is I looked down the other end and I saw a red wave of fans going from right to left too quickly. They were on the run, and I thought 'Oh, I've got to go and do that now.'"[1]

The red wave set in motion a set of circumstances that no supporter should ever have to encounter for the sake of a football match. For those in Section Z, it came down to the basic human instinct of fight or flight. Paul Fry, as we saw earlier, spoke of self-preservation; he knew it was time to leave. Many of the fans didn't have Paul's experience. They were family units who hadn't expected to meet the English Disease, and once they had made their decision to stay, they certainly had no idea how to react to such a force. As the Belgian FA reported:

"It is clear that the public who were in the Block Z was principally composed of Italian fans who were obviously not in the habit of being placed on the terraces, but who had not been able to obtain sitting places due to high demand."[2]

The destructive scenes happened just after two schoolboy teams had put on an exhibition match as a curtain-raiser to the main event. During the confusion of the evening, it was even reported that among the victims were members of the Anderlecht youth team who had participated in the game.[3] A Dutch football fan, Rene Buitenkent from Den Bosch, was standing near the epicentre. At first, he witnessed just five or six people coming through a gap between the two sets of supporters. Then the rest saw the opening and followed:

"There was a panic. There was no way out."[4]

S. Culligan from Netherton recalled something similar to Rene. Culligan said at first there were only about ten supporters involved, but when the others saw that the Italians weren't fighting back, "things just got out of control."[5]

Journalist David Lacey witnessed something comparable from his vantage point in the press box. He recounts:

"There was a point by the wire fence where the police were concentrating. I looked at it through my binoculars and saw that there was a hole in the fence. The Liverpool fans were trying to get through and two or three police with dogs were trying to get at them. The fans reacted by saying 'come and get us' and 'if you don't come at us, we'll come at you', and started to widen the gap in the fence, flooded through and then the Italians almost like a shoal of mackerel, then beat a retreat."[6]

For the record, Belgian police received information that there were holes in the fence in X, Y and Z at 7:02 p.m.[7]

With anxiety ensuing, the occupants of Block Z, like Lacey said, tried to flee. Not all Juventus fans retreated, because there are many reports that witnessed some Juventus fans who stood and fought back. One Liverpool fan, Colin Wells, recounted that Italian fans charged towards the Liverpool section first and this was followed by Reds counter-charging.[8] There doesn't seem to be too much evidence to support Wells's account.

The gendarmerie attempted to intervene by hitting LFC fans with their batons. Simone Stenti then saw the reversal of the usual relationship between the police and hooligans:

"I saw a hooligan try to climb the fence, and a policeman went there with a truncheon and tried to stop him, but the hooligan took the truncheon and beat the policeman."[9]

G. Ireland from Woolton remarked that a small number of supporters reacted to the police, who immediately ran away and left.[10] Stenti and Ireland's accounts here support the point we discussed at the beginning of the book that respect for the police doesn't exist in some places in the UK.

It is at this juncture that the charges by Englishmen escalated to hundreds causing a deadly panic. We know from the previous chapters that the stadium was a death-trap in itself and, with it basically impossible to exit, once in you weren't getting out. Simone Stenti was with his father; he recounts:

"People were shocked by this attack and they panicked and ran away. The majority of people went towards the pitch to escape; we decided to go the opposite way, so we got squeezed like sardines against a wall. At that moment, I thought I was going to die. The worst thing was that the crowd was squeezing your chest, I couldn't breathe properly and when you can't breathe properly you can't think properly. You're surrounded by old people, women, kids, you're powerless. All you can think is 'you want to survive'."[11]

Simone's sanctuary came from the most unlikely of places:

"But then we found a solution, there was a toilet. It looked to us like a phone box, so we decided to get on top of it. I could only move my left arm and I pushed my father on top of this toilet and then he found the strength to pull me on to it, a strength I didn't know was possible. I could feel something gigantic was happening, but I couldn't figure out what it was and only later did I understand the magnitude of what happened. We found ourselves on the athletic track in the stadium. And then we saw the survivors, they were in shock, to me they looked like zombies with eyes of glass."[12]

Otello Lorentini, who we've met a few times before, has similar memories. Otello was at the final with his two nephews and his son Roberto. The normality of the start of Otello's story shows how normal routines in life can be interrupted by unexpected tragedy and chaos:

"I was relaxing, reading a newspaper, when I saw a single English hooligan. He jumped over a small fence and came charging towards us. Then, many more followed. They had lumps of terrace concrete, Coke bottles, beer bottles, rocks and even knives. Everyone panicked. There were seven or eight policemen standing on the pitch side of the fencing. We pleaded with them to call for reinforcements. But none came. I thought we would die. Everyone moved away from the charging Liverpool fans and, in the crush, the wall collapsed."[13]

The point regarding the wall saving lives was clear to Otello:

"This was actually lucky because otherwise thousands may have been killed."[14]

Horribly, Otello was about to meet the English Disease in person:

"I can still see the face of one hooligan who was about to strike me with an iron rod. I was fortunate, though, because he began hitting someone else. I turned to my son, but he and my nephews had disappeared, and now I thought to save myself. I escaped through a small door at the top of the terracing and eventually found myself on the field where people lay on the ground dead. There were still no police around. Many people were trapped and dying and there is one man I cannot forget—his face was covered in blood, and over these past 20 years I have dreamt about him many times. I waved Roberto's black-and-white Juventus scarf, so that he could see it and then I decided to return to look for my son among the corpses in Sector Z. It was then I met my nephew. He said: 'Come quickly, Roberto is not so good'."[15]

Otello's next memories are beyond sadness:

"He was lying on the ground, I put my head to his chest and could feel his heart beating. But then I realised he was dead. It was my temple that was beating not his heart. Then I was overcome with rage. [...] I was with my boy when an ambulance arrived, but I didn't know how I could take him home, I didn't know what I was going to tell his mother."[16]

Otello's son Roberto died in Sector Z. He died a hero. Roberto was a doctor and was gallantly trying to resuscitate a young girl. Tragically both of them, along with the girl's father, died at the hands of Reds. Posthumously, Roberto received a gold medal in Italy for Civil Valour (the equivalent to the George Cross in the UK) for his courage at Heysel.[17]

Bruno Guarini also painfully recounts losing his son on the terraces:

"Alberto had his Juventus bag to carry his binoculars and his packed lunch. The hooligans were at the other entrance, drinking and shouting. I said to Alberto, 'We'll go away from them—they might throw things.' So, we went towards the wall at the side. It was the worst thing I ever did because those near the English were the ones who survived. They came running at us through the fence. Alberto was caught against a barrier. His last words were 'Papa, mi stanno schiacciando'—Daddy, they're crushing me."[18]

Bruno lost consciousness. When he regained it, he insisted that the Red Cross join him to search for his son. They found Alberto; tragically, he was lifeless.[19]

With the commotion of death and mayhem all around, fans roamed aimlessly around the track and pitch. One bloodied Italian with tears rolling down his cheek mourned, "I've seen too much. I've seen death."[20]

He had seen death. When you look at images from the night you would have absolutely no idea that they were from inside a football stadium.

IN COMPARISON WITH SECTION Z, the perspective from Sections X and Y looked very different. One Red captures perfectly the aggression of one group and the sheer fright of another:

"Next the fence came down and fights developed in the initial wave. One could see fear and panic in the faces of

Juventus fans. This was exploited in the cacophony of hate as the crowd surged forward, now armed with broken bottles and sticks and stakes. The Italians, gripped with fear, panicked and the rest of the tragedy is now common knowledge."[21]

On the reaction of the security, the fan stated:

"No one in their ranks seemed to be able to take charge. Those of us who were in charge of our emotions screamed at the police to move. Unfortunately, we were drowned out by senseless people scattered around both blocks shouting the pathetic chant audible at home every fortnight, 'Scousers Aggro—Scousers Aggro'. We felt sick."[22]

Another Red also witnessed fellow Reds attacking Juventus fans. He recalls that it was bloody chaos. Liverpool supporters swarmed across the barrier into Section Z and then into the Italian fans. People were being indiscriminately attacked in the Italian areas. The fan continued:

"It was totally sickening. There was no restraint whatsoever. Usually, if there is trouble, people scuffle and break-off. Here it looked like murder." He added that people ran and ran at the Italian supporters, driving them into a small corner of the ground: "There was no escape—the morons then started throwing objects into the packed crowd of Italians to the right."[23]

Martin O'Shea witnessed many fights breaking out and Italians running. Wave after wave of Reds steamed over and bottles and stones flew overhead. After about half an hour, he could see the Italians all in the same corner and still people ran into them kicking and punching.[24]

Journalist Ed Vulliamy recalled:

"There were two charges by the Liverpool fans inside the ground. The first tore down the fence and several hundred young men lunged into the Italians, sending them fleeing under a barrage of iron rods, rocks, kicks and punches [...] During the pause that followed, and while some Italians fled onto the pitch, I saw the Liverpool fans enjoy their triumph, dancing and waving their flags. Then in concert they charged again, kicking and throwing anything they had, pushing and pushing the Juventus supporters to inevitable agony and death. A Nottingham publican who was the first to try and help the wounded told me he had seen the dead kicked, mutilated."[25]

Vulliamy's next recollection takes us to the depths of hell:

"I especially recall the Liverpool fans' whooping."[26]

It is clear when you watch footage of the attack many Brits are celebrating on the terraces. Whilst Juve fans and neutrals are trapped against the wall or fleeing for their lives onto the pitch, some Reds are revelling in their perceived gains. One supporter is standing on a crush barrier, arms aloft, as if what he is watching is the most natural thing in the world. Behind him and unknown to him, there are fellow Kopites attacking a Juve fan like a pack of wolves.

After the game, Vulliamy experienced two very different takes on the event. Back at his hotel one Red, when learning of the dead, remarked, "Good. They deserved it."[27] At the airport, another Red said, "I've been watching Liverpool for 25 years, now I'm through. I saw people kicking the bodies. There were bodies piled 10 deep and they were booting them. If that's football, I'm through with it."[28]

Many more English people were sickened by what they had been watching. Councillor Clark said:

"The majority of the Liverpool supporters were appalled. There were chants of 'Pack it in, pack it in, pack it in,' instead of the normal chant of 'Liverpool, Liverpool,

Liverpool.' The loudest chant directed at the louts being, 'You're the shit of Merseyside.'"[29]

R. Guy from Norris Green has similar memories:

"During all the fighting and charging the section of Liverpool supporters where we were now standing began singing 'Pack it in, pack it in' to which some of the rampaging yobbos turned and put up two fingers."[30]

Guy went on:

"We kept on pleading with them, but they kept on charging."[31]

TWENTY-TWO

THE WALL

The story of the infamous wall is the single biggest piece of misinformation connected with the disaster. It is now 'fact' the wall was the biggest killer on the night; only it wasn't. Tony Evans claims that no one has written more extensively on the subject of Heysel than him.[1] Given this, you would imagine his knowledge of the events is far superior to any other author, journalist or fan in the UK. However, on the same day he stated the above, he also wrote the following on a different platform:

"On that dreadful night 39 people, mainly Italian, were killed when a wall collapsed."[2]

At 7:27 p.m., the wall of Section Z collapsed,[3] and however dramatic it looked on TV, the wall was not responsible for the deaths. A stampede caused the deaths because fans were fleeing from an attack. Fans died from suffocation. In fact, the collapsing wall actually saved lives, because it released pressure and allowed fans trapped up against the wall to escape. Therefore, Tony is wrong.

Tony's confusion about the wall also underlines a previous point I made about not being allowed to discuss the subject. If we could deliberate on Heysel, the wall would become a less significant issue and not be seen as the reason why fans died. In addition, the fact he states "No one's written more extensively about the subject" than him, but clearly has no real knowledge about the deaths, demonstrates how poorly educated we are in the city and beyond.

During a BBC newscast during the match, newsreader John Humphries informed the nation:

"One eyewitness as quoted by Belgian Television a few minutes ago said many of the 'victims were trampled underfoot; they weren't actually crushed by that wall collapsing'."[4]

In addition, the next day, Commander Alan Gibson, the head of the Belgian emergency services, informed the world's press:

"Most of the people were killed when Liverpool supporters pushed forward and then people fell on top of each other and most of them died from suffocation. We gave oxygen to some people who had stopped breathing, but for some it was too late. Bodies piled on bodies on the perimeter fence."[5]

As we can see from the BBC report and Commander Gibson's statement above, there is no mention of the collapsed wall as the cause. Nevertheless, the collapsed wall did trigger mayhem and horrific injuries to those involved. After the wall collapsed, men, women and children trapped and being crushed by rubble screamed in agony, their arms stretched forward in appeals for help.[6]

Ken Taylor from Liverpool was caught in the middle when it collapsed; he recounted how he found himself fighting for his life. Ken fractured his arm and injured his wrist, but he almost got dragged under the bodies. As the crowd tightened around him, he couldn't move his arms and felt himself being lifted forward towards the pitch. Being reasonably strong, he managed to prise himself away but then fell down some steps where he injured his arm.[7]

Even after the wall collapsed, some Reds still attacked. One fan recalled:

"But still these sick so-called Reds carried on putting the boot in on fans who could not escape."[8]

Implausibly, as the Italians and neutrals retreated and then scrambled for their lives, hoping to scale over the perimeter fencing towards the pitch, the gendarmerie began forcing them back by clubbing them with their batons. This is a great example of Le Bon or Allport's influence on police training and possibly of the cynicism we spoke of. D. Jackson from Prenton witnessed the assaults:

"They [LFC fans] started attacking Italians who started pouring out onto the pitch. But the police who should have been helping them battened them and tried to force them back."[9]

With the Italians and neutrals dying, some Reds strolled back to their vantage points triumphantly. Their show of masculinity, some of it bare-chested, resulted in one fan roaming the terraces of Heysel, arms aloft jubilantly, as if he had just scored the winning goal in the match. One Italian fan's experience underlines the differing forms of 'masculinity' on show:

"I was right in the worst place on the terraces when the troubles broke out, I trod over some people too, I stepped over two people with wide-open eyes. I wondered, 'Am I a piece of dung or a man?'"[10]

When photographer Eamonn McCabe arrived at Block Z, he thought he was going to find a picture he had seen many a time down the years. He thought it would be a headline of 'Liverpool Skirmish' and thought it would be all over. He'd done it hundreds of times, throwing his pictures away when the game started because nothing came of it.

This time it was different. He says:

"I get there and all the Italians down that terrace are bunched up in the corner because they're frightened. Then all of a sudden, you've got a group of people who are not football fans caught up in a riot. I know if I get caught up in a riot I run, and the stadium is a gladiatorial stadium, so the natural inclination is to run up the back and hope you get out. They get to the top there's nowhere to go. They turn around and came down and sadly people fell, and people crushed them, and you can see it all in the pictures in terms of what happened. It was panic."[11]

Eamonn continues:

"So, I get to the wall and the camera gear I had was a long lens, a medium lens and then for the trophy pictures I had a little sure shot camera. I did it because when the trophy pictures run round, they're this close to you and you can't focus, you're falling over. If I was prepared for anything, I was prepared for a trophy picture at the end, but as I got there, they were all reaching out and the wall just crumbled in front of me."[12]

As it turned out, there would be no trophy pictures. Eamonn again:

"I got two snaps. One, two. If you look at them, they're all reaching out. Now, I've published that a few times, I do it because I know they all got out because they're on the wall. What I did then was get out the way and the Belgian Red Cross arrived."[13]

Eamonn stressed that many of the spectators in Block Z were still in their waiters' clothes. This clearly comes back to the ticketing arrangements, in that the local Italian community were able to purchase tickets easily because of the strong black market.

Eamonn points out that the people reaching out as the wall crumbled all got taken onto the pitch. Unfortunately, he had to witness some fans dying. He says: "The saddest thing for me is to see a human go blue."[14]

He did photograph dead bodies, but the *Observer* did not use the photos at the time. Eamonn emphasises that he had been sent there by his paper and the pressure was on him to record what he saw, even though he didn't know what was happening.

T. Johnston, who we came across before, heard a dull thud as the side wall gave way. However, many fans kept charging into the Italians; others danced up and down across the terraces. Only after this point did the police arrive in any number. However, they made little attempt to clear the area of Section Z still occupied by Liverpool fans. Next the mounted police came, and as Johnston remarked they "seemed to think they were giving a riding display as all they did was form lines and trot around the running track." [15] The thing that shocked him most was that as people were lying on the pitch dead or dying, a number of people started to play football in the goal mouth in front of him. With Rome in mind, Johnston added:

"There seemed to be some feeling that the Italians got what they deserved for what they did to us in Rome. I can't be 100% certain, but to the best of my knowledge these attacks were unprovoked, the Italians did not even fight back."[16]

Liam Griffiths and Justin Shanahan had had a great time before the match chatting with the Juventus fans and swapping scarves. Liam said it was one of the best crowds he'd seen. Unfortunately, that was about to change. For then

Liverpool fans started running and Italians panicked. Liam's seat was right by the wall, and he could see bits of plaster coming off from between the bricks. Then it went and he began to see the bodies. Liam had never seen a dead person before, but they were stacking them up near him under plastic sheets: "There was an old lady just by us and someone shouted; 'Hey up, she's dead.'"[17]

Liam's friend Justin disclosed:

"I saw a big fat guy, about 65, who'd fallen, and they were just using him as a mattress to jump on."[18]

Bruce Grobbelaar returned to the pitch. He told the *Sunday Mirror*:

"I felt totally helpless as I saw the Italian supporters squashed against the wall like sardines, and I knew something had to go. The wall went with a crack like thunder, and I could hear the screams as fans toppled on top of each other. [...] At that point I did not know anyone had died or was dying, but as the Italian supporters came past, they turned and spat at me."[19]

Chief Inspector Griffin was conferring outside the stadium with McGregor and Temporal when he heard a tremendous roar from within the ground at 7:25 p.m. Griffin had checked the time because the cheer was the type normally associated with the teams taking the field at the start of the match. He realised it couldn't be and thought the Juventus players must have walked onto the pitch for the traditional 'tread of the turf'.

Whilst standing at the gates, police sirens could be clearly heard and almost immediately a convoy of around thirty vehicles, all carrying police officers, poured through the gates. At this stage, Griffin and his colleagues were totally unaware of the reason for the police reinforcements. They made their way back to the entrance to the stadium, by which time fleets of ambulances were beginning to arrive and the police officers had left their vehicles, donned riot shields and helmets and gone into the ground.[20] On re-entering the stadium, McGregor found:

"Total pandemonium had broken out. People were running in all directions; many were injured, whilst many others were in a distressed and excited condition. I immediately realised that people were very severely injured and probably dead, but because of language difficulties, could not ascertain what had actually happened. We were in an Italian area in the main stand and although no violence was offered; it was obvious our presence was provocative and there was little we could do at the scene."[21]

Griffin recalls that on re-entering he could go no further than an eight-foot-high mesh fencing in front of the seated supporters. He says Italian fans were running alongside the fence in hysterical condition, trying to flee from the area. In their frenzy, they tore down one section of the mesh fencing and took their wrath out on the presentation stand, which had been erected to present the trophy at the end of the match. They were crying and tore down the presentation stand in frustration. They shouted obscenities at anyone remotely English, and at that stage Griffin was totally unaware of the reason for this. Griffin witnessed some Italians were being helped along by friends and looked to be suffering from varying degrees of shock/injury. In addition, the playing surface was a mass of people, police and fans.[22]

By now there were bodies everywhere. Plumber Giorgio Bianchi found his wife, Laura, alive under a pile of bodies. Giorgio, from Genoa, caught just a glimpse of her green cardigan and was able to drag her clear.[23] Fans with parts of their frames squashed stretched their arms out, screaming for help. Instead of medical assistance, the first help to arrive was armed police trying to quell the rioters. As Ian Hargreaves from the *Liverpool Echo* noted: "Neither police nor ground officials seemed to know what to do."[24]

Next, we are taken to new levels of depravity. We are entering Le Bon's "in a crowd, he is a barbarian—that is, a creature acting by instinct." For as the *Liverpool Echo* reported:

"...some of the drunken lunatics masquerading as supporters were actually kicking people as they lay dying on the ground."[25]

Modern crowd experts point to the weaknesses of Le Bon's theory, but for me it would be interesting to explain this fact without dismissing Le Bon.

Despite the madness, some Liverpool fans demonstrated great acts of humanity. Eight times, fan John Welsh risked his own life to rescue badly injured, trapped Italians. When John walked into the stadium, he and his friends found themselves in a riot. John threw away his flag and dived in the crowd to help. He managed to get one young girl onto the pitch and hand her over to a medic. He went back, and that's when the wall collapsed on top of him. People were trapped by rubble and dead bodies. From John's perspective nobody seemed to be doing anything, and one man thought his 14-year-old daughter had been killed. John was trying to pull people out, but fans were still pushing. He managed to get away and drag another man clear. The man was choking to death, and as John freed his tongue, the man almost bit his finger off.

John's most tragic moment came when he rescued a 19-year-old Italian girl. He went back into the crush, but people underneath him grabbed his legs and he got scared. He started going backwards towards the pitch and he realised he was trampling over the dead. John went in the ambulance to the hospital with the last girl he rescued. She was holding a thin wedding ring and trying to tell him something, but he couldn't understand. It was "the saddest moment of his life when she died".[26]

Ken Taylor, who we mentioned just before, went to the hospital like John. Ken recalled: "The scene at the hospital was bedlam and I had to wait several hours before I could be seen."[27]

One of the victims in the hospital was a 15-year-old Belgian boy called Philip Lambert. The teenager, limp and battered, was pulled unconscious from the macabre mound of bodies. He was thought to be dead. But rescuers detected a faint spark of life in his crumpled body.[28] For 24 hours, Philip clung to life in a coma. Then on Thursday night his eyes flicked open. Later, Philip said:

"I suppose I should be dead like the rest. The whole thing is a blank. I can't remember anything that happened, and I hope I never will."[29]

Philip also said that he would never go to a football game again. Dr Jean Van Greertruyden, who helped in the struggle to save Philip, commented: "It was touch and go, and he is lucky to be alive."[30]

THE RIOT SEEMED to end suddenly. At 7:29 p.m., the gendarmerie moved into the ground and took up position in Section Z, driving the English back towards Section X. At 7:37 p.m. the injured from all three sections began to be taken to Brugmann Hospital. At 7:38 p.m. the mayor requested ambulances at the main entrance as a matter of urgency. The situation became stable in Z at 7:41 p.m.[31]

The fire brigade and the Red Cross began to organise a

rescue operation. Grignet, head of the Red Cross, noted that apart from ambulance drivers, there were 102 medical and first aid staff of various kinds—doctors, ambulance crews, etc.—present at the match. In addition to the 102, there were people on standby in the surrounding districts. There were 54 people and about ten ambulances in reserve, and these reinforcements certainly proved useful. For a normal match, 50 staff would usually have been provided, but because of the level of risk, the figure was doubled.[32]

Van Gompel, Commander of the Brussels Area Fire Services, was at Heysel with 60 men. On the day in question, he said the resuscitation unit and other ambulances were stationed immediately next to the stadium. These vehicles arrived at the scene of the incident very rapidly. All five of the service's resuscitation units were used to attempt to revive victims. The use of these vehicles to take people to nearby hospitals allowed a much greater number of people to be saved than might otherwise have been the case.[33]

Eamonn McCabe thought the ambulance service did a pretty good job from what he could tell, but considering he was concentrating on his job, he says:

"I wouldn't know whether there were five ambulances there or one. [...] I saw loads—you can see in the photographs, the uniform, the green uniforms. So, they were there, they were on the terraces. They were as shocked as anyone. And they made stretchers out of barriers. That's the hardest picture I've got, where someone is running around with a crush barrier and they've used it as an improvised stretcher. So, they were using their loaf, they were really trying."[34]

A camp-hospital was arranged in front of the central stand and a tent mounted to shelter the corpses, and then a second one and then a third. Belgian TV made an emergency appeal for off-duty police, reservists and cadets to join the rescue operation. Half an hour after the attacks, with supporters now gone from Section Z, newspapers, magazines, shoes, trainers and broken crush barriers covered the terrace. The scoreboard to the left was still quoting the messages from the match programme. On the subject of shoes, Eamonn recalls:

"I can still remember people running on the terrace, panicking, turning around. I'll tell you, the strangest sight on the terrace was shoes. When people panic and when you run, wearing trainers, but the number of shoes on the terracing, just shoes and God knows where the people are. And I have one picture where one guy was shouting out 'Mario, Mario,' for his friend and that was one of the saddest things."[35]

Despite Section Z coming under control, at 7:41 p.m. there were fires in Section X where the Liverpool fans were. At 7:56 p.m., the Commissioner formally declared the situation a disaster and asked for maximum manpower. At 8:08 p.m. all the reinforcements from the city centre moved to the stadium; there was also an emergency call for taxis, doctors and blankets to cover the dead. At 8:17 p.m. the gendarmerie signalled that helicopters had taken off in the direction of the stadium.[36]

TWENTY-THREE

"WELL, WHAT AN UNHAPPY START?"

At 7:20 p.m., PC Sutton returned to the front of the stadium in a vehicle. He found a large-scale disturbance was taking place between rival supporters. Large amounts of police reinforcements were drafted into the area to deal with the matter. After the main influx of reinforcements arrived, the occasional minor fight broke out but was quickly stopped.[1] It was about this time that the driver of Sutton's vehicle informed him that a wall had collapsed in the ground and a number of supporters had been injured. Sutton saw injured people being carried out of the stadium and a fleet of ambulances and fire engines arrive.[2]

Soon bodies would lie uncovered on the ground, many without their shoes. One lady was wearing a black skirt which was hitched up revealing her ripped tights and filthy legs. Her arm was touching the exposed body of the man next to her.

By now, Paul Fry was outside, and he headed to the press box. The emergency services were in full flow, and just outside Block Z bodies were beginning to be laid out. The bodies were covered with an array of massive flags. To make matters worse, helicopters were arriving, so the flags were blown back, exposing the dead bodies.

Later, a senior doctor at the scene said: "As many as 50 may be dead. It's like a war zone."[3]

The dead, dying and injured were strewn across the precinct of the stadium as police strove to restore order and teams of paramedics administrated emergency treatment. Emergency volunteers helped, and friends and relatives walked crying and screaming among the stricken bodies. Canvas tents were set up as mortuaries outside the stadium, and one was turned into a makeshift chapel.[4] Corpses were carried there in green plastic shrouds.[5] A priest arrived to perform the last rites for those who had died.[6]

Guardian reporter Charles Burgess counted 28 bodies in a row in the lee of the stand where the violence had erupted. Burgess reported:

"They were almost lying on top of each other. Some were covered in blankets; others in black and white Juventus flags."[7]

Liverpool fan George Downey was a witness to the carnage outside. He was walking along the pavement outside the stadium with two friends when the nightmare began. He told the *Liverpool Echo*:

"A young Italian man came staggering towards us and collapsed on the floor in front of me. He was completely purple and his eyes were popping out of his head. I picked him up and put him in the back of a nearby van." [8]

During the terrible moments that followed—George estimated it was around twenty minutes—he rescued ten people, only to watch them die. But he helped dozens of injured to safety. Police cordoned off the area after the wall collapsed. But George and his friend Lennie Noble were dressed in casual clothes and had no Liverpool scarves, so no one moved them on. George recalled: "Neither of us stopped to think what we were doing; we just started to try and help the injured."[9]

Lennie said: "I watched a man crawl out of the gates very slowly. He had no trousers or shoes on, and he was streaming with blood." [10]

A medic grabbed hold of Lennie's arm and asked him for help. What Lennie recounts next is heartbreaking:

"I pointed to a young girl, but the medic gestured to say she was dead. She was only about 14 and she seemed far too young to be at a football match. Then her arm moved and I realised she wasn't dead. I cradled her head in my arms and stroked her face. She was very purple and like all other bodies, her eyes were sticking out like organ stops. But she grabbed my jacket and was trying to tell me something. Suddenly, she gasped and I felt her die. There were bodies all over the place. I lay her down and covered her face with a newspaper. I just pray I was able to give her some comfort before she died. I was just happy she did not die like a rag doll with no one around."[11]

Not all Reds were as heroic. As K. Martindale witnessed:

"The drunken Liverpool louts who were locked outside the stadium then proceeded to attack the ambulance men and Italian supporters."[12]

Attacking ambulance crews. But actually, it gets even worse. Martindale recalled Liverpool fans "pick-pocketing and kicking the corpses".[13]

We have to remember that the person who said this is a Red from the city. His journey home after the match once more underscores the madness of it all:

"I drove to Brussels and on the return trip decided at Zeebrugge to telephone home to ease relatives' fears. The lout in front of me dialled Liverpool just to find out how many were dead. He turned to me and said, 'We've killed forty' in a jubilant manner. I was speechless."[14]

Aren't we all?

WHEN PAUL FRY arrived at the press box, entering was as easy as any other part of the ground—i.e., no security. Paul remembers: "I was amazed I could get into the press box."[15]

Paul knew colleagues from the *Times* and the *Mail on Sunday* and so began chatting to Joe Melling, a journalist from the *Mail on Sunday*. A producer from the BBC overheard Paul speaking with Melling and invited him to be interviewed. Sitting next to him was Emlyn Hughes, who as Paul recalls: "Was in absolute bits. [...] Respect to the guy, he was cut-up for his club."[16]

On a positive note, Paul's interview meant his mum back home in Stevenage knew he was safe.

Less positively, after capturing the mayhem, Eamonn McCabe form the *Observer* signalled to the press box. He says:

"So, I'm taking these pictures, and sadly there are bodies on the pitch and ambulances driving through a gate, so I'm in and out from going to the ambulances; I'm going back onto the pitch. And the stadium is built in such a way that the press box is built on a cantilever over the pitch. It was leaning out over the pitch, and these guys—I remember Brian Glanville [a journalist] was there—and I'm going [Eamonn was gesturing with his hands about how many fans had died up to that point] and he's saying 'Eamonn, go on fuck off.' He couldn't see; they couldn't see."

Liverpool Echo journalist, Bob Burns, experienced the bedlam from the press box. He recalled:

"The press box was set way back, so you couldn't really see, but there was trouble. Somebody behind me, I think a BBC reporter said, 'There's casualties, people are dead' and I turned around to him and said, 'Please don't exaggerate, how do you know something like that?' And he said 'No, I can see on the monitor'. So, he had the monitor, the close-ups, and he was able to see stuff, so I thought I've got to get outside and see what's going on."[17]

Burns then recounted the turmoil that was occurring outside the stadium, as the enormity of the tragedy started to become apparent:

"I left my seat and walked into the leafy area outside the ground and was greeted by a scene straight out of a disaster movie. [...] I just couldn't believe what I was seeing. It was just like something you'd see on that big TV show Mash, where you'd see the helicopter scene, the hospital helicopters, helicopters in the sky and they didn't land near me. It was such a big concourse; it was a bit like the old Wembley. And then there were people just lying there, obviously people being brought out and people obviously dead. They were left alone. Right next to the stadium coming through the gates they were just being brought out to the concourse."[18]

The thousands of fans who had packed the area just minutes earlier had gone. Now, there were bodies strewn all over the place, covered in blankets. A helicopter landed and took away casualties, giving the scene "a bizarre war zone effect", in Burns' words. A priest began giving victims the last rites while the walking wounded, including several Liverpool fans, gasped for air. The survivors were taken to four main causality centres. One of the first waves arrived at the university hospital.

Burns finishes by stating: "Never will I forget the sight of body after body being carried out and placed near my feet and of the looks of utter devastation among the survivors."[19]

Whilst the written press were rewriting their stories from back-page news to front-page news and journalists such as Burns were searching out new stories, television companies had a decision to make: should they broadcast the game? Several of the 80 countries who were due to screen the match ended their coverage as Liverpool and Juventus walked onto the pitch. ZDF in West Germany, who expected 20 million viewers, said:

"We could not believe that after so many people had perished, they were going to carry on with the match."[20]

A spokesman claimed that the game only went ahead because UEFA stood to lose millions of pounds from TV stations all over the world if the match had been cancelled. [21] In neighbouring Austria, they ran repeated caption-flashes, saying:

"This is not a football broadcast but the report on prevention of another massacre."[22]

Switzerland stopped at half-time, as the scale of the death emerged.[23] At home, the BBC went ahead with showing the match. After coming under criticism, it defended its decision by stating:

"We continued to broadcast for the same reason that the national press gave the events so much coverage."[24]

It also went with the Austrian line. An official said:

"We weren't showing a football match in the end. We were covering a news story—tragic, but a major story."[25]

The evening's viewing was to become a truly surreal

experience. The BBC's coverage begins with a cringe-worthy handover from chat-show host Terry Wogan to Jimmy Hill. Hill is looking extremely uncomfortable because, of course, by this stage, he knows what happened, and to make matters worse for Hill, Wogan is cracking snide jokes about his famous chin. Hill retaliates by saying:

"You can come on my programme some time and I'll be kind to you, you lovely people. Thank you very much, Terry. It's the only time you've ever been shut up at this time of the night because it is some football match."[26]

Hill then introduces the programme by using the script that was written before the news came through: "Well indeed, it is some match with records galore hanging on the result of it. Can Liverpool retain the European Cup or will Juventus win it at last?"[27]

The famous *Match of the Day* music then kicks in with live images of (ironically) a calm-looking stadium, the Kop in full swing, goals from Liverpool's European triumphs and images of Juventus scoring a headed goal at the Holt End at Villa Park. Hill begins his announcement by remarking:

"Well, after a moment of hilarity with Terry Wogan and Bruce [Forsyth] there, I'm afraid the news is very bad from Brussels. Hooliganism has struck again and I'm afraid the scenes are as bad as anything we've seen for a long, long time."[28]

As Hill is speaking, British viewers receive their first images of the chaos that had descended on Brussels. Fans from Block Z are being carried out on crush barriers, which were being used as makeshift stretchers. The terrace is strewn with the possessions of the dead, the dying and the shocked survivors. The camera then pans to a young fan being attended to by medics. The dazed fan is grasping her forehead in absolute bewilderment. In the background, Juve fans from the other end of the ground are now attempting to exact revenge by trying to attack the LFC fans. Police with batons chase the Juve fans around the pitch, whilst the Brussels mounted police are organising their positions to prevent further bloodshed.

Hill then presents the panel of then Barcelona coach, Terry Venables, and ex-Liverpool captain and then Sampdoria player, Graeme Souness, by saying in a very understated British way:

"Well, what an unhappy start?"[29]

The two of them are clearly in shock. Hill is also traumatised because he states:

"We'll join John Motson [the BBC commentator]."[30]

In fact, the voice we hear is clearly that of Barry Davies not Motson. When Davies first begins speaking, the mounted police are now in situ on the track and pitch. It is clear the vast majority of both sets of fans have absolutely no idea of the seriousness of the riot that has taken place. Reds and Juventus fans are waving their scarves and flying their flags similarly to any other big final. One of the Liverpool banners reads "Watch out Brussels our Bruce is no sprout". Under normal circumstances this banner would have become part of Kopite folklore to go along with other famous banners from previous finals; instead, its joyful wordplay seems enormously out of place.

Davies sets the scene impeccably well; unfortunately, it has nothing to do with team news, football chants, funny banners or tactics. Instead, he says: "Well, for the last 50 minutes the Heysel Stadium in Brussels, the capital of Belgium, has been a sickening and bewildering sight."[31]

He continues: "For a while there were some scuffles between the rival supporters, a great deal of the sort of threatening animal hate-like behaviour which we have come all too accustomed to seeing at home."[32]

The shameful nature of the English Disease is transmitted through Davies' words. To make matters worse, he's sitting near the commentator for RAI, the Italian television company, who was surrounded by tearful, hugely animated Juventus supporters complaining to him about what had happened. As Davies is speaking, Juventus fans hold aloft a huge banner with the small town of "Casalpusterlengo" written across it, demonstrating the team's national importance.

Outside the ground, a big wheel is in motion, the sun is beating down, and with Juve fans gently swaying, it is impossible to comprehend what has recently happened.

Davies' co-commentator for the game is Bobby Charlton, possibly England's most famous ever footballer. After condemning the violence, Charlton says:

"They also had Joe Fagan who came out and tried to calm them down, to tell them to go back to their original positions in the ground and they've basically done that, up to a point."[33]

He then picks up on the inadequate segregation:

"I'm not trying to defend what happened, but certainly the section area that was supposed to divide the Juventus and Liverpool fans was really flimsy. It was so flimsy, it was ridiculous."[34]

Charlton then asks a rhetorical question:

"How do you explain it? I really, I don't know."[35]

Hopefully, the previous chapters have now explained it.

On Italian TV, an audience of nineteen million from all over the country tuned in expecting to see the players warming up. Bruno Pizzul had the difficult task of describing the scene live. He spoke of "clashes" earlier on

and outside the ground, and criticised the "complete inefficiency" of the Belgian police and authorities. Pizzul
expressed "strong doubts" that the game would go ahead.
Meanwhile, an appeal to relatives of Juventus fans to phone
the Foreign Ministry ran along the bottom of the screen.[36]

WITH CHAOS CONTINUING INSIDE and outside the
stadium, dignitaries in the VIP sector were initially
unaware of what was happening in Block Z, so as innocent
people were dying, they continued to enjoy the hospitality.
Their civilised evening of small talk, good food and drink,
followed by a European Cup Final, was soon to be interrupted as proceedings turned into full-scale turmoil.

Dr Resende from UEFA was in the Honorary Stand
when the decisive charge in Sector Z was launched. He
witnessed as suddenly a great number of excited and even
aggressive Italian fans appeared. Some of these supporters
were obviously in shock and they were injured. He asked
them what had happened. The reply was: "The English are
swines."[37]

At the same time, they accused the security services and
the organisers of inefficiency. Several of these fans were
desperately looking for family members and friends and
were asking for help. Subsequently, the fence separating the
Honorary Stand from the pitch was torn down and a wave
of spectators inundated the stand in the official reception
rooms below. Many of these spectators were injured, their
clothes were torn, they were without shoes, they screamed
and cried.[38]

With this happening, an impromptu and frenzied
meeting was about to commence. Amongst the people

deciding whether or not the match would go ahead were Herve Brouhon, the Mayor of Brussels; Robert Bernaert, the Belgian Gendarmerie Commander; the UEFA president; the UEFA general secretary; representatives of the clubs and both associations; the ambassadors of the two countries; and Gianni De Michelis, the Italian Government's minister of foreign affairs. Dr Resende from UEFA said once spectators were removed and taken care of in the entrance hall, the parties involved began to confer.[39] Not surprisingly, irritabilities amongst participants rose to the surface. De Michelis captures the breakdown in communication:

"Everybody was standing and shouting, trying to stick to his guns; there is a Babylon of languages: who speaks French, who speaks Italian. The point was: to play the match or to call it off? The discussion lasted almost one hour in a nightmare situation, because every one of us realised that the disaster was going on in the terraces—only then we were told that there were more than 30 people dead—but it may have been nothing in comparison to what could happen yet. We had to take the right decision. Now and again, somebody popped in to tell us that out there the tension was reaching a peak, that there were a lot of policemen, but they could not manage the situation."[40]

At this stage, Juventus did not want to play the game. De Michelis again:

"The Juventus party did not want to play. The Liverpool one said that they were available to play. In the meanwhile, the burgomaster kept talking about what had happened before, about what had caused the troubles, trying to justify the action by police and Gendarmerie. I interrupted him: 'Excuse me, we will talk later about what has happened before, would you please tell us whether you can guarantee a safe evacuation from the stadium?' He got upset: 'Who are you?' I replied: 'I am a member of the Italian Government.' 'Shut up, or I'll get you arrested!'"[41]

Brouhon was far from impressed with De Michelis. The mayor recalled:

"This minister had in no way any claim for being on the scene and was not only voicing his opinions in both a loud voice and in French, but was issuing instructions and orders, too. I pointed out to him he had no claim for being there, and that furthermore if he had any observations to formulate, he should take them up with the Minister for Foreign Affairs or any such Belgian official authority."[42]

The mayor continued:

"On the other hand, I added that due to his official rank in Italy; I saw no objection to his being at the meeting, on condition that he abstained from giving orders to people or to Belgian representatives of law and order. This "matter" was settled very quickly, amicably, as I understood the emotions that man was having to put up with what had happened, his pain being greater than mine."[43]

With tempers fraying inside, a second meeting, exclusively Belgian, took place outside the stadium in a command car. Sat inside the car were the Public Prosecutor; M. Roggen, the Governor of the Province; Bernaert of the Gendarmerie; Poels, Chief Commissioner for Brussels; a representative for the fire department; the director general of the Belgian Red Cross; and Roosens from the Belgian FA. The opinion of the Minister of the Interior was also sought by telephone.[44] The participants agreed that allowing 50,000 spectators to leave the stadium would have provoked riots which would have continued throughout the night and maybe even the next day and which would have perhaps caused the loss of human lives on a much greater scale than that which had already been caused.[45]

The conclusions of the second meeting were presented to the interested parties from the first meeting. UEFA, the Belgian FA and LFC agreed with the decision. Juventus were hesitant. De Michelis asked whether a guarantee could be given as to the safeguarding of Italians after the match. This assurance was given to him by General Bernaert and Brouhon.[46] The plan adopted to protect Italians was to surround the stadium with armour-plated gendarmerie vehicles to escort the cars of Italian fans, as well as providing a motorcycle police escort. When the guarantees were given, finally the president of Juventus gave his agreement for the continuation of the match.[47]

Gerhard Aigner, the former UEFA chief executive who was head of the competitions department in 1985, captures the continuing madness: "Two dazed supporters were in the room when the decision was made."[48]

With a resolution found, UEFA issued a statement which read: "a premature evacuation of the stadium would have presented an enormous risk that could have aggravated the number of casualties."[49] In response, Juventus released a statement to UEFA, which read:

"Juventus FC, notwithstanding the tragic situation which has arisen through causes attributable neither to this club or to its supporters, and which has caused the deaths of dozens of Italians, accept with discipline, even though with the heart full of anguish, the decision taken by UEFA, which has been communicated to our president, to play the match for reasons of public order."[50]

And so with that...

TWENTY-FOUR

"SOME HAD ALREADY TAKEN A SHOWER."

The VIP relatives of the Liverpool players came to realise their tickets were not the conventional VIP sort. Mark Lawrenson's stepfather, who went with a friend, spoke to Lawrenson later that night. His stepfather told him that they walked past a little avenue and there were just black body bags. Lawrenson, who only lasted a few minutes of the game because of a reoccurring shoulder injury, recalls:

"And they were thinking at the time; 'It was the IRA; it was whatever', it was just completely crazy."[1]

When Lawrenson said this, I thought the "IRA" bit seems a bit over the top. That's until I saw some pictures from the night that I hadn't previously seen. His stepfather's description was correct. Heysel looked similar to the aftermath of a bombing.

Paul Walsh's girlfriend, Mellissa Berry, said she was forced to watch the carnage. She recalled:

"I was grabbed by a Juventus fan who was in a rage. I was petrified. He led me to a window and told me to look at the dead bodies. I looked down and there was a pile of bodies heaped on top of each other. I saw one face clearly and I'll never forget it. I just went hysterical."[2]

Kenny Dalglish's wife, Marina, said:

"We had to sit through it all and we were scared stiff. We just held each other. It was just terrible. Some Juventus fans broke through a fence, got close to us and started spitting at us."[3]

It would seem the players, at least some, were aware that their relatives were facing a compromising situation. After witnessing the scenes at the wall, Bruce Grobbelaar went in search of his wife and his and her parents. He disclosed: "It was a harrowing experience for them."[4]

Grobbelaar's family arrived after the devastation, but saw the helicopters, ambulances and the bodies lined alongside the wall.[5]

WHILE THEIR RELATIVES experienced bedlam upstairs, the players should have been exchanging banter in the changing rooms, warming up on the pitch and listening to their final team talks. However, scenes of lunacy were about to unfold before their unbelieving eyes. The players seem to fall into two separate camps—those who watched in horror and others who have attempted to block out the insanity out of their minds. Both are natural reactions. It would also appear that senior Liverpool pros attempted to hide the enormity of the events from their younger teammates. Alan Kennedy, who was an injured squad member on the evening, recalls:

"Our changing room was next to sector Z. I wasn't fit at the time, and so at the first inclination of trouble the players asked me to investigate. Outside it was pandemonium. The wall had crumbled and people were struggling to get out."[6]

He adds:

"A UEFA official came into the dressing room to inform us that the kick-off would be delayed, and that four or five people had died. The more experienced players simply blocked it out. They said: 'Listen, we've got to concentrate on the game.' Others said that the match should not go ahead. In those circumstances playing the match must have been difficult for everyone."[7]

With the rescue operation under way, the Liverpool manager, Joe Fagan, told his players to stay in the dressing room. Fagan himself went outside to speak to the fans. He walked across the pitch, stripping off his jacket and shirt to reveal a red number 13—to identify himself to his team's supporters.[8] Fagan told the rioters:

"This is a football match. It is my last game as manager and you are spoiling it. Get back and be sensible."[9]

Centre-back Mark Lawrenson recounts:

"We heard this commotion, and our dressing room is really close to that end, where the wall collapsed. People realised it was a major problem and they stopped us from going out. And of course, they said 'the game's been delayed, a wall's collapsed.'"[10]

As there were amongst the fans earlier on, concerning possible violence outside the stadium, new rumours were spreading in the dressing room. Lawrenson again:

"It's like Chinese whispers. 'There's five dead, there's ten dead' and I'm going crikey. Then the Chief of Police for Brussels came into the dressing room, and he says, 'This game goes ahead' and we as a bunch of players say, 'No we don't want to play'. And he says, 'No-no, it's a safety issue and I've spoken to Juventus and it's a safety issue because now all of a sudden if I let everybody go with what's happened, I cannot be responsible for what happens.'"[11]

The player who replaced Mark Lawrenson, Gary Gillespie, falls into the 'when we all wake up this won't really have happened' group. He says of his experience:

"We were very much cocooned in that dressing room. We did not really know what the situation was outside. As we were getting changed in the dressing room there was the usual banter, obviously the usual nerves because it was such a big occasion, and then we got conflicting reports about what had happened."[12]

Liverpool goalkeeper Bruce Grobbelaar recalled:

"Many of the players were close to tears. Some went away into quiet corners, and I openly admit I cried for the dying. But we had to play, we knew that."[13]

Phil Neal has certainly not forgotten his memories from within the dressing room. He says:

"People were aware that the wall had gone down after a while in the dressing room. Bearing in mind Joe Fagan's already given his team talk, he was trying to keep us focused, but it was difficult with bodies being taken away. We just didn't know what to do with ourselves. The dressing room becomes a morgue. Players physically crying, tears dripping down."[14]

Jim Beglin, who was Alan Kennedy's replacement and the youngest member of the starting eleven, recounts the protective umbrella senior pros put around him:

"It was kind of kept from me. I wasn't informed as to the extent of what was happening. [...] So, I knew nothing about this when we took to the field."[15]

Another youngster that evening was Liverpool's reserve

goalkeeper, Chris Pile. Pile had never actually made an appearance for the first team and was only in the squad due to an injury to Bob Boulder. Of the trouble, he remarks:

"Each dressing room was situated in line with the edge of the 18-yard box. There was a huge crash at our end of the stadium. Rumours quickly started going around that 10, then 20, then 30, then 40 people had been killed. We didn't know what to believe. There was a suggestion that some kids had died. Then it was a case of 'What do we do now?'"[16]

And of the scenes in the dressing room, he recalls:

"The lads in the dressing room were doing different things to pass the time, such as playing cards or head tennis, the normal stuff. I don't remember too much discussion about whether the game would be abandoned. We didn't have a clue what was really going on outside. Phil Neal, the captain, disappeared a few times to talk to different people about what was happening. Then the lads walked out on to the pitch and the game kicked off."[17]

With Heysel being Heysel, it denied Pile the honour of becoming a pub quiz question.

As with the Liverpool changing room, the Juventus one was also one of madness. The Juventus manager, Francesco Morini, says:

"Some of the players were sitting with their heads in their hands, some were throwing up, some had already taken a shower and were dressed, ready to leave."[18]

The Juventus players had been on their way to the pitch for their pre-match warm-up when they were told of the troubles on the terraces. From the tunnel, they could see barefoot people in torn clothing roaming around the pitch, begging for help. These people tried to convey to the players what was happening, but they were too excitable, distressed and confused to provide a meaningful account.[19] Some Juventus fans converged on the changing room because they were looking for sanctuary from attacking Liverpool fans. As Juventus goalkeeper, Stefano Tacconi, recalls: "Our dressing room was like a casualty department."[20]

With rumours of the dead spreading and the stadium in chaos, the Juventus players decided to go onto the pitch to calm fans. Tacconi again: "When you're in the middle of a mob, even if they are your fans, you don't feel that safe. We were trying to get them to behave. You could hardly go out and tell the Ultras 30 people had died; it would have made them angrier. So, you try to persuade them, convince them it's not so bad. That fewer people are involved, they're injured not dead."[21]

Marco Tardelli, he of the famous 1982 World Cup cele-bration, discloses:

"On the night, I did not comprehend events fully because I was in the dressing room. The players did know that there had been trouble in the stadium but not that so many people had died. Looking back, I believe it was a big mistake of the Belgian police not to open the fences and let people escape the crush."[22]

———

BACK IN BRITAIN, ITV interrupted their evening schedule, which included Arthur C. Clarke's *World of Strange Powers* at 7 p.m. followed by *Coronation Street*, with a newsflash read by Sandy Gall. At this point 28 fans were thought have been killed. Sandy told viewers there would be a full report on *News at Ten*. At the same time, John Humphries was informing the BBC audience of the same news. He finished his announcement by stating:

"So clearly, it's the worst incident of its kind that's been seen in European football. Now back to Jimmy Hill."[23]

When we return to the studio, Hill is asking Souness and Venables whether the match should take place. While Venables is speaking, the violence is still happening behind the goal at the Juventus end. Supporters are taunting the police and throwing the crumbling stadium at them. On the halfway line, medics are carrying dead bodies out in the brown blankets Emlyn Hughes mentioned earlier. Hill then draws comparisons to the infamous Luton vs Millwall match we visited earlier.

Suddenly chants of "Juve, Juve" go up as Juventus players Cabrini and Brio try to calm their supporters down. The players are immediately surrounded by the Juventus fans. Cabrini and Brio are joined by more Juve players, including Scirea. It is clear some fans are trying to convey to the players what they believe to have happened at the opposite end of the ground, whilst at the same time some supporters are planting kisses on and hugging their heroes. The scrum around the players also includes the Red Cross medics and photographers. Irony of ironies, the opposite side of the ground is now sanguine in comparison. Up above, air ambulances are searching for places to land.

The fiasco of the security operation is now all too apparent as policemen use handcuffs to chain parts of the perimeter fencing to keep Juve fans from entering the pitch.

After a recording of the attacks is shown with a commentary by Barry Davies, Hill moves on to mentioning National Service, the one subject I remember from watching the game. With Venables managing Barcelona and Souness playing for Sampdoria, Hill uses Spain and

Italy as examples: "In Spain and Italy there's National Service, that is almost a must now."[24]

Souness mentions a teammate who has recently done National Service. Hill then asks Venables: "Terry, would you advocate that among other things?"[25]

Venables does not mince his words: "I have for a long time. I think that it does give you some sort of manners and responsibility and does knock you into shape."[26]

After the panel's conversation regarding National Service, Hill hands back over to Davies. At first the stadium is relatively quiet, but something triggers the Juventus fans, and a small group begins to make their way pitch-side. Some are carrying weapons, and they resemble a gang from the movie *The Warriors*. One fan in particular starts to goad the police by gesturing with a huge stick. From a police perspective, there is absolutely no intention of arresting any of the troublemakers.

Graeme Souness, who is really astute throughout, has to keep his council as Hill then goes on an unnecessary rant about Scottish fans. Souness is speaking about Liverpool and Juventus fans sharing their drinks and food in contrast to the chaos. Hill says:

"I always felt that about the England-Scotland game, because you know Scots are very welcome in England, a lot of them live here."[27]

Souness actually laughs at Hill's patronising manner. Hill continues:

"And I think there's a great affection for the Scots and what a lovely weekend that Wembley match could be if they came down in peace when they did come, I think Londoners would give them a warm welcome and, as you say share a glass of wine or a bottle of beer or something."[28]

Now Souness cannot believe his ears. Hill rants on:

"And make it a lovely sporting occasion. But I'm afraid we are well past that in the sort of things we've seen here today."[29]

Scottish people at home must have been raging at Hill's thoughts, considering it was English fans who had caused the trouble that night.

The panel are then interrupted by a news update. After Hill's needless verbal attack on Scottish fans, Scottish people rightly call up to complain. But Hill brazenly goes on the attack:

"I suppose you wouldn't believe it. People are ringing up from Scotland to say we are using the word 'British supporters' on a night like this. I don't think anybody is scoring national points for one country over another. English, they come from Liverpool, some of them may be Scots, some of them may be Welshmen, I don't know. I don't really think that point is significant, it just is so sad."[30]

Hill then asks the panel about the punishments for Liverpool and then, probably to infuriate Scots more, he mentions "British clubs" again.

Souness replies:

"They [UEFA] might use Liverpool [as an example] because Liverpool are the biggest name in European football. They might well say, 'Look you're an example to anyone else who steps out of line'. And I think although Liverpool have in the past had a tremendous record, what's happened tonight ruins all that and I think I'm inclined to agree with Terry; to say it's 'severe' is an understatement. I think they could quite easily turn around and ban all English clubs in Europe for however long they feel."[31]

With Davies describing the scenes around him, the camera pans to the press box. Some fans in the stand are waving and playing up for the cameras, demonstrating again how little some fans knew of the true situation. As Davies is speaking, more and more police are arriving at the stadium and taking up strategic positions. Although, it must be said, they do not look like a professional organisation. To be polite, some of the 'police' would not fill you with confidence.

The cameras move to the LFC end, and there are plenty of Union Jacks, one with 'Norris Green', which is a district of the city. One is supposed to be a funny jibe at Manchester United saying 'Atkinson fat head', and another hatefully says, 'Munich 58'. Whilst the fans are waiting, still more helicopters are circling the skies of Heysel.

Just before the match begins, one final episode sums up the unfairness and cruelty of that night. Juventus fans begin attacking one chap who was by himself. The guy attempts to defend himself, and the Juve supporters retreat and then, horribly, one Italian fan throws a piece of concrete, which strikes the guy on his head. He naturally turns to the police for protection, but instead of offering safety, one policeman proceeds to indiscriminately attack the poor man. Once more, the scene summed up perfectly Le Bon's influence on police training.

To give Souness credit, he understands the unreasonableness of the situation: "To be fair, he was the one getting the stick."[32]

Hill sees it differently: "He started it himself."[33]

AT 9:30 P.M., the two captains, Phil Neal and Gaetano Scirea, were asked to talk to the fans. Guido Dewindt escorted the Liverpool captain. By now the Liverpool end was calm, but some Juventus fans at the other end were still out of control. Dewindt recalls:

"I left the dressing room with the Liverpool captain. He didn't know anything, he hadn't seen anything, he'd been shut in all evening. We went outside, he was overwhelmed, he couldn't believe what he was seeing. It was a battlefield; he thought there was a war going on. He was so scared that he asked if he could hold my hand."[34]

Neal recounts:

"I was given a piece of paper by UEFA to say 'Read that to your fans'. I took one look and read through it and threw it back at them."[35]

The message Neal refused to read said:

"The match will be played in order to allow the police to carry out the evacuation from the stadium; do not reply to any provocation and keep calm. We are going to play for you."[36]

Neal believed it would be better if the message came from the heart:

"I can't remember until this day what I said, but I appealed to the fans because I was led to believe in going to announce that there's going to be a product, in other words, there's going to be a football game here."[37]

Part of Neal's announcement was: "The lads from both camps are sick and tired of waiting in the dressing room. We want to perform for you," and "Let's get on with it."[38] When you listen to Neal's announcement, you can hear the raw emotion in his voice, and whilst many fans cheered his speech and that of Scirea, the rioting was still in full swing at the Juve end. Neal returned to the dressing room with Dewindt and Liverpool FC's security man, Tony Chin. As they were returning to the dressing rooms, a Liverpool fan who had clearly been assaulted up by Juve Ultras had now been bandaged and was being escorted across the pitch by two Red Cross workers.

With the infamous 'Red Animals' banner by now unveiled by the Juventus fans, it was time to play the 30th European Cup Final.

TWENTY-FIVE

THE MATCH

When the teams finally walk onto the pitch, it is 9:45 p.m., (for the record kick-off was scheduled for 8:15 p.m.) and viewers around the world are about to watch possibly the most surreal game of football ever played in Europe. LFC squad member Alan Kennedy describes the lunacy:

"As you walked onto the pitch, you can't help but notice the wall that's down. You can't help but notice the stretchers, the ambulances that were still there."[1]

As the teams line up for the official photographs, there is still a stand-off between Juventus fans and the Belgian riot police at one of end the stadium, and fires are literally burning on the terraces. Kenny Dalglish is plainly grimacing, and his right leg seems to be moving uncontrollably; it certainly looks like football is the last thing on his mind.

For what it is worth, Liverpool lines up like this:

1. Grobbelaar
2. Neal
3. Beglin

4. Lawrenson
5. Nicol
6. Hansen
7. Dalglish
8. Whelan
9. Rush
10. Walsh
11. Wark

Juventus's starting eleven is:

1. Tacconi
2. Favero
3. Cabrini
4. Bonini
5. Brio
6. Scirea
7. Briaschi
8. Tardelli
9. Rossi
10. Platini
11. Boniek

The referee is Andre Daina from Switzerland, who himself was a former professional player and ex-international. As Daina is about to blow the whistle, Barry Davies utters words he never dreamt he would say before any kick-off:

"So, the match will begin with fires on the terraces, with policemen in riot gear poised to stop any problem before it starts."[2]

Next, he uses the classic commentator's line of: "And

Liverpool are defending the goal to our right."[3] The difference here is that, as he is speaking, goalkeeper Bruce
Grobbelaar is running towards the goal he will defend;
however, instead of witnessing the opposition fans in full
voice and waving flags, he is greeted by fires, policemen
manfully trying to put the said fires out with their feet, and
a Mexican stand-off between Juventus fans and the police.
When Grobbelaar arrives in his penalty area, he has to pick
up two flick-knives. To Grobbelaar's astonishment, when he
hands them to a policeman, the policeman just drops them
on the floor.[4] This could be a case of those "poorly paid
men".

As the game begins, an announcement repeats every ten
minutes on Belgian radio and TV to order all members of
the parliamentary state police to return to their units immediately to take up duty around the stadium to maintain
order when the game ends. Paratrooper units of the Belgian
army are also rushed to the stadium.[5]

As Ian Rush and Paul Walsh kick off, Davies remarks:
"Still fires to put out."[6]

Paul Walsh passes back to Kenny Dalglish, and it is
clear Dalglish does not want to be on the pitch. His pass to
Phil Neal basically says, 'Why are we playing this match?'

Neal feels the same way. He said, years later:

"It was all over bar the shouting, even tossing the coin;
heads, tails, let them have the choice. It was as simple as
that."[7]

After receiving the ball from Dalglish, Neal wins a
throw-in, and Barry Davies comments on the leadership
qualities of Neal.

Digressing from the match for a moment, Phil Neal has
since come in for some criticism regarding asking for money

for an interview with the *Guardian* in relation to Heysel. However, after carrying out lots of research, it is my opinion that he deserves much credit regarding his thoughts and anguish over the tragedy. He comes across as a man who was left totally devastated by the night's events.

ONCE THE GAME BEGAN, journalist Paul Fry sat on a set of steps in the press box because he didn't have an assigned seat. There was still an undercurrent of animosity; there were flares going off at both ends, particularly at the Italian end. Additionally, there was a feeling of 'will this flare up again during the game?' As the match continued Paul felt: "This is not a real game. You just felt like players were going through the motions. They clearly didn't want to play it."[8]

After only two minutes, Liverpool centre-back Mark Lawrenson suffered a shoulder injury and was replaced by Gary Gillespie. Lawrenson was struggling to play and fell after tackling Platini within a minute and ten seconds, dislocating his shoulder. He left the pitch and was taken to Saint-Luc University Hospital. His evening and morning were surreal to say the least.

The next morning, after his operation, Lawrenson agreed to speak with the press. In his words:

"The next thing is the world and his wife are in there and there were loads of Italians and they were very challenging. I'm lying in the bed half kind of awake and half not and they're given me all these questions and I couldn't really answer them. They were saying, 'Did you know people had died?' We were told people had died, but it wasn't Liverpool officials who told us. And in the end the surgeon said 'Look, we need to get you out of here'. I said 'Great, I can go back to the hotel.'"[9]

Lawrenson had a problem; he didn't have any normal clothes. The hospital contacted someone at the club, and coach Roy Evans and Lawrenson's then wife turned up with a Liverpool tracksuit. Given the circumstances, Lawrenson was surprised at the attire. And you can certainly understand his embarrassment at not wanting to wear anything with a connection to LFC. Wearing the tracksuit inside out, Lawrenson had to be sneaked out of the hospital through one of the service lifts. On this theme, at the airport, he and his teammates were spat on. On top of that, some people wrote all kinds of things on all the LFC skips containing their dirty kits, including about being killers.[10]

Dr Luc Corne said Lawrenson had apologised to medical staff for the violence at the game.[11] Medical teams who were battling to save lives of the injured were shocked by the extent of the carnage; they were appalled by the blackened, broken bodies of the dead. Dr Louis Tielemans, director of the AZ-VUB Hospital, said it was the worst he had seen in fifteen years in the profession:

"Where is it going to end? I think today must be the end of twenty years of this kind of trouble. We have to stop it now. This sort of crowd trouble is not the problem of Great Britain or Liverpool, but of a small number of violent people."[12]

He revealed his staff were battling to help five victims who were all in comas, including at least one who was thought to have suffered serious brain damage.

Among distraught spectators searching hospitals for missing friends was a group of thirty-five Maltese people. One told of their nightmare:

"The match had not begun, but supporters were throwing things, I could not see who was doing it. Then a group of Liverpool supporters came running and went through the barrier and came on us. We had to go running onto the pitch. Then the wall collapsed, with I think four or five of our Maltese people under it."[13]

He went on to say:

"The Liverpool supporters were terrible."[14]

While the game was being played, the dead were taken from the Red Cross tents just outside the stadium to the Military Hospital. There, two cordons of soldiers guarded the dead. The authorities feared that after the match, the news of the deaths would trigger more violence all over the city.[15] The commander who was in charge of the morgue recalled:

"We thought there was going to be rioting, tension was running high. We thought people would come to where the dead victims were and might become violent. We'd seen people dying in the stadium as a result of violence. We felt that those violent people might come here, anything was possible. That they would smash down doors, relatives would want to see the dead, that we wouldn't be able to stop them."[16]

After returning from the mortuary, Dr Corne commented:

"I did not see any identification, but I did see the bodies. Some were as young as 17 or 18."[17]

He said all the bodies were blackened, and most showed heavy injuries to the chest cavity, indicating death from asphyxiation.[18]

Martine Bollu was a social worker attached to the fire department and among the first to glimpse the devastation. She recalls:

"I was alone with all these bodies, and I was thinking only of the families who were waiting for information. I am a mother, and I know that I would have wanted to know if my child was dead or not. There was one man there, who had a big stomach, and he had a restaurant receipt in his pocket from only two hours earlier. I thought to myself, 'I hope he had a good time at the restaurant, because it was the last time for him.'"[19]

Returning to Dr Luc Corne. During investigations, it emerged that the concerns of local hospitals were ignored during preparations for the game and that medical services at the stadium had been woefully inadequate. Dr Corne said:

"There was only one physician. There were 100-150 people of the Red Cross, which are amateurs and that's all. I think maybe ten persons could have been saved if medical teams were present and if there was co-ordination between the different disciplines."[20]

BACK AT THE STADIUM, Davies perfectly sums up the beginning of the match:

"The feeling is understandably all a little unreal."[21]

Around the pitch we have the usual companies, such as McDonalds, Coca Cola, Philips and Canon dominating the hoardings—JVC, as a sign of the times, were advertising video machines. We can see Guinness and Cinzano displays and adverts for Camel, the cigarette brand, another indication of how life has changed. There is also an advert for Bull Computers, a French-owned company.

After 15 minutes, John Wark has the first real shot on

goal. A few moments later, Davies' commentary again travels into the unknown:

"I'm happy to report there is calm all around the ground. The riot police to the goal to our right have been able to withdraw and sit down and some of them at least are watching the match."[22]

A little later, Davies utters those well-worn commentators' words: "If you've joined us late..." Under normal circumstances, he would have said something along the lines of: "If you've joined us late, it has been a slow, cagey start. It is still o – o and the only chances of note have come from Liverpool players John Wark and Paul Walsh."

Davies actually said:

"If you've joined us late, the match kicked off very late because of problems in the crowd which resulted in, I'm sorry to say, in death and injury."[23]

JUVENTUS'S first real chance arrived in the thirtieth minute, when Grobbelaar produced a good save from Cabrini. Bobby Charlton later described Cabrini as the best left-back he had ever seen. Behind Grobbelaar's goal was the unusual sight of the massed ranks of Brussels' riot police. Five minutes later, Tacconi made an even better save than Grobbelaar from Ronnie Whelan.

The first half, just like the fires, fizzled out.

At half-time a list of missing persons was read out over the PA system.

For obvious reasons, the BBC's half-time coverage did not include the usual analysis you would expect; instead, it was dominated by BBC newsreader John Humphries relaying the carnage. Humphries then hands over to reporter Gary Lloyd at Downing Street. Lloyd informed the country:

"Number 10 Downing Street issued a statement tonight which said the Prime Minister had been following the reports on television. The statement said: 'She shared what would be the universal horror at the scenes which have been shown. Mrs Thatcher declared "those responsible have brought shame and disgrace to their country and to football"."[24]

Next, reporter Steve Graves interviewed the sports minister, Neil MacFarlane. MacFarlane was, for obvious reasons, a little emotional; however, that did not prevent him from displaying great diplomacy towards LFC fans. The broadcast returned to John Humphries, who informed the nation of the response of leading politicians of the day, such as David Owen, the SDP leader, and Roy Hattersley, deputy leader of the Labour Party. Humphries then handed back to Jimmy Hill. The panel in the studio tried to discuss the game, but of course it was really strained, and Graeme Souness looked like he had seen a ghost.

It wasn't only European networks sending reports back to their viewers. American network NBC went with the unfounded claim of the wall killing the majority and then told its audience:

"Most observers said this trouble was started by English fans who have earned a reputation for hooliganism both at home and at matches throughout Europe. Twenty thousand Liverpool supporters were in Brussels for their team's Championship match with Juventus Turin of Italy. Many of the British arrived drunk, others started brawls before the game began and some threw a table through a jewellery store window and stole the jewels."[25]

As you can imagine, half-time was no ordinary experience for the substitutes warming up. Substitute goalkeeper Chris Pile recalls:

"I remember doing a warm-up during half time and there were horse hoof prints on the turf. That emphasised to me some of the carnage that had gone on."[26]

———

WHEN THE SECOND half got under way, Australian Craig Johnston replaced Paul Walsh, who had been suffering from a stomach injury. In addition, Walsh had been hacked several times, and by today's standards Juventus would certainly be at least one-man light for the second half.

A few minutes in, Alan Hansen makes a run into the Juventus half. As he runs down the wing, you can hear half-hearted chants of "Liverpool, Liverpool." LFC fans then turn up the volume. Moments later, both sets of fans raise their voices. However, things are still far from normal.

Marcel Van Biesen, the head of the stadium, was stunned to find himself standing next to a Juventus fan who had fled from Block Z to the VIP stand. He was "barefoot and covered in blood, and yet he was cheering on his team."[27]

In the fifty-eighth minute, the defining moment of the match arrives. Ronnie Whelan loses the ball to Michel Platini on the edge of the Juventus box. Platini then hits a wonderful searching long ball towards Polish international Boniek; he nods the ball forward, and he is clipped by Gary Gillespie. Boniek drops to his knees in the penalty area whilst he is waiting for the referee's decision. The contact from Gillespie was certainly outside the box, but the referee points to the spot, and Boniek is then surrounded by jubilant teammates. Years later, Boniek recounted:

"I especially remember that night and it is for all the wrong reasons. Let me say it like this: if people go to watch the final of the European Cup it is absolutely ridiculous that they will never return home because they have been killed. I did not know the full extent of what had happened before the match began. But let me be clear—the players did not want to play. The authorities ordered us to. They believed that it would prevent a war between the fans. But the whole evening was absolutely dreadful. And stupid. I saw bodies being taken away from the stadium. It is not good to be to playing football when people are dying around you."[28]

Standing on the goal line, waiting for Platini's penalty, is Bruce Grobbelaar, who had been a penalty hero the year before in Rome. He recalls his thought process at that moment:

"I thought well this is it. They are trying to cheat us on a penalty, which was never a penalty and I'm going to do my best to stop this because that's just wrong. I got a rush of adrenalin wanting to save this penalty. When Platini, one of the best footballers in the world, steps up and wants to score a penalty against you, you want to do your best. It's him or you, and you can make a huge name for yourself by saving a penalty from Platini."[29]

Platini sends Grobbelaar the wrong way to score Juventus's first goal in a European Cup final. Platini peels away in celebration, his teammates join him, and the roars of "Juve, Juve" go up around the stadium.

Left-back Jim Beglin said of the penalty incident:

"The foul by Gary Gillespie on Bonieck, it was outside the box and afterwards that didn't matter, just as well they had a penalty and scored it. We didn't care."[30]

Twenty years after the game, commentator Barry Davies recalled:

"I spoke to Michel Platini later. He was very unhappy about the penalty. He didn't think it was legitimate and Juventus did not want to win that way. I said: 'Frankly, everyone in the media wanted the game over in 90 minutes. The last thing we wanted was extra time and the thought of a penalty shoot-out after that."[31]

Later in the second half, after a scramble in the Juventus box, Liverpool should also have had a penalty when Ronnie Whelan was clearly fouled by Bonini. Liverpool players surrounded the referee, but he waved away their appeals and instead he gave a throw-in. As Barry Davies said in commentary: "It was a very harsh challenge by Bonini and it was in the area."[32] Liverpool's Phil Neal later recounted the non-penalty award:

"I just remember Ronnie Whelan being brought down in a very similar manner and the referee saying no penalty. There's no way we're going to 1–1."[33]

Whelan himself said:

"I was a little upset I didn't get the penalty, but after the game, it's still not going to make a difference. And then you just feel empty. We've played a game for nothing. People have lost their lives, why? What's it all about? And I think that was the main question on all the players' lips: why?"[34]

After the penalty incident, Liverpool begins dominating the game and are unlucky not to equalise, but Whelan is again denied by another brilliant save from Stefano Tacconni. As Bobby Charlton noted:

"Fortunately for the Italians the goalkeeper Tacconni has had a particularly brilliant game and the two shots he had from Whelan were particularly outstanding saves."[35]

Tacconni recalls his performance that night:

"I was very angry, a coiled spring. Ironically, I played the game of my life maybe because I was so angry and focused. I wanted to prove something to the fans. To win for them. Clearly if you're going to play, you play to the death not for the cup itself, but for the fans who died so pointlessly. At least if they were up in heaven they would have seen the game."[36]

With just a few minutes to go, Juventus fans begin to celebrate as Liverpool search for an equaliser. But with this being no ordinary game, you can also hear the noise of police dogs barking all over the stadium. In one last, desperate attempt to equalise, Phil Neal sends the ball long; his attempt is well watched by Scirea, who heads the ball out for a throw. The final whistle is blown, and the most Pyrrhic victory in football history is won—although it does not look that way as players celebrate and fans storm onto the pitch to rejoice with them.

The Juventus fans behind Tacconni's goal were also revelling in the victory. Juventus players were criticised for their celebrations. Tacconni says of the merriment:

"It's as if we're all still under hypnosis, the fans too. If you'd interviewed them right then they'd have said 'we are the Champions of Europe, we've won the cup, we're the best'. Then the following day 'why did they play, they shouldn't have, why did they celebrate? They shouldn't have'. That's what football is all about, you go out and play and forget about everything but football for 90 minutes."[37]

So, after hours and hours, after thirty-eight people had died, Juventus had won 1–0. Barry Davies sums up the match by saying:

"Liverpool's run of success in European Cup finals comes to an end. Juventus create history by becoming the first side to win all three of the UEFA tournaments. One goal in this European Cup final scored by their Frenchman Michel Platini from a fine move which he ended by scoring from the penalty spot."[38]

The cup was not awarded on the field but handed over to Juventus in the dressing room in a wooden box ("as if it was in a coffin," goalkeeper Tacconi later said).[39] Once suited and booted, Platini was interviewed on French TV; he clearly did not look like a man who has just scored the winning goal in club football's biggest game. He told the reporter:

"After UEFA took the decision to let the match to go ahead, we didn't think of anything once it kicked off. So, you see, we were really happy that we'd won the match for the Italian supporters."[40]

He went on: "Football's a game that's in the heart but we took a big blow today."[41]

Francesco Morini draws a parallel with warfare: "In spite of the deaths and bloodshed, in the moment of victory you rejoice because it's like you've taken revenge on your enemy. Later you reflect on all those who've died, but right at the moment of victory, it's pure revenge. We were saying —we've beaten the English after they killed our fans. We've shown them that nothing can defeat us."[42]

Liverpool also received their medals. Chris Pile recounts: "Not that anybody wanted them, but we got our runners-up medals in the dressing room."[43]

With Juventus celebrating, the BBC then moved back to the studio in London, where Jimmy Hill asked for a response from Graeme Souness. Souness replied:

"It's a sad night, Jim, for everyone involved with English football. Sick for the lads, and sick for Joe [Fagan] because it was his last game."[44]

After the match Fagan told the press:

"It was a game of football in the end, but I don't think anyone's heart was in it. Mine was not."[45]

His predecessor, Bob Paisley, left shortly after kick-off. He said:

"I'm afraid I can't watch."[46]

Jimmy wrapped up the evening by saying:

"We leave you tonight with a feeling of deep sadness and our sympathy to those with relatives or friends who have suffered this evening. Thank you, Terry, and Graeme, and Barry, and Bobby Charlton in the stadium, for coping so well in such tragic circumstances on a night when Juventus won the European Cup. But football once more lost many friends. Good night."[47]

AFTER THE GAME, the full horror of the night began to hit home to the players. Chris Pile recounts:

"Craig Johnston and I were walking out of the stadium afterwards and took a wrong turn. We ended up in a gym where there were bodies being laid out. Armed guards stood nearby. We quickly turned around."[48]

Some Liverpool players visited Section Z. Jim Beglin remembers:

"It just looked as if carnage had taken place, which of course it did. I remember a handbag lying there, items of clothing and then it really began to hit us as to what happened."[49]

Ronnie Whelan says:

"You could see where the wall was down, shoes, bits of clothing, debris. It hits you and it hits you hard then."[50]

With the players boarding their coaches, Bruce Grobbelaar attempted to start the healing process. Marco Tardelli recounts:

"After the final, Bruce Grobbelaar came on to the Juventus team coach and apologised for the hooligans. But really, it was not the fault of either Liverpool or Juventus."[51]

Bruce Grobbelaar himself recalls:

"After the match, I went on to the Juventus bus and said: 'I am sorry for what happened.' I was not, though, saying sorry because it was our fault. I also wished them the very best in the future because they had beaten us one-nil. The players received it very well and though every football game matters, maybe it was fitting that Juventus won that match. As for the trophy itself, it should be donated, as a memorial to the dead."[52]

After the game, Paul Fry stayed in the press box to help with the editions. By the time he left the stadium, the vast majority of people had headed home. For Paul it was an eerie feeling; it was quiet on the metro, and an overwhelming feeling of guilt came over him. He was a Brit who was going back to stay in the house of a Belgian, and the Brits had brought all this shame and embarrassment on their country. He felt awful and was apologetic. His girlfriend tried to assuage his guilt by reminding him that he wasn't responsible, but Paul couldn't help but feel bad that British people had done this. As he says: "It wasn't the first time, and it wasn't the last time."[53]

Paul was asked to stay in Brussels for longer than expected and spent the rest of the week interviewing police officers and Italian families who were arriving at the airport to collect their dead relatives.

For Eamonn McCabe he recalls that as a sports photographer, he'd sat there for an hour and a half photographing a game that no one was interested in. Later that night, he was sitting in his hotel room, "trying to drink a beer just to calm down because every tissue in him was on fire".[54]

The Liverpool players and their wives were whisked away to a country club for what was supposed to be a celebration banquet.[55] Bruce Grobbelaar recounted:

"I sat quietly in a corner while my teammates tried to erase the memories with wine and a sing-song. But the songs were mingled with tears. [...] I couldn't join in. Different people react in different ways and it was simply not a moment for me to start singing. The other players, with a few exceptions, did not see what I saw, and if they had they would not have felt like singing."[56]

Not surprisingly after what he had witnessed, Grobbelaar was considering quitting Liverpool and football.[57]

While the players attempted to block out the incongruity, one Red kept the bizarreness of the day continuing after the final whistle. The fan, from Liverpool, was sentenced to three years and four months in jail for attacking two rival fans. The court heard that the Red was "fighting mad"[58] and that it took four policemen, three double-doses of Valium and a straight-jacket to restrain him.[59] Witnesses told the Brussels court that the fan had hidden the blood-stained weapon under a Union Jack.[60] One of the victims, an Italian hairdresser, spent fifty days in a coma and had to give up work because of partial paralysis resulting from head injuries. Judge Michele Berelymont said the sentence reflected the "climate of violence" at the stadium that night and the "dramatic consequences" of the attack.[61] Bert Millichip, the then FA chairman, welcomed the sentence:

"I hope this is going to be a lesson for others sentencing football hooligans to follow. I also hope people still with a mind to misbehave at football matches at home or abroad will take heed of this sentence. I am delighted because we must get rid of this scourge."[62]

All in all, between 7:30 p.m. and 11 p.m. 13 people were arrested at the stadium or in the immediate vicinity. They were all arrested for violent conduct, but none had been identified as having taken part in the charges.[63]

Whilst the match was still being played, the Committee for the Government Crisis gathered until 2 a.m. in the morning. Their activities included contact with the Italian and British authorities, preparation of a government communiqué, and replies to the press.[64] During this period, the Belgians were drawing up a precise list of the victims. The office was completely full of senior officials. They were checking whether they had the information the Italians had. Italian officials were in the office too. Both the Italian Embassy and journalists were ringing for information. At the same time, the officials were trying to establish exactly what had happened so that they could tell the Minister of the Interior and Prime Minister.[65]

The Public Prosecutions Office was asked to go to the ground. An official called Van Doren went. A report was made to him to request that the area where the events took place should not be touched. The examining magistrate asked for an expert to be appointed to investigate and gather the facts. Photographs were taken of the scene. The inspection finished around 1:30 a.m. Van Doren then went to the Military Hospital where teams of CID officers and hospital staff were making arrangements for formal identification of the bodies.[66]

To sum this part of the book up, I had to be dispassionate when writing it, or I would never have finished many of these paragraphs. What made these chapters even more difficult and frustrating was while I was researching and writing, I was forever seeing LFC fans on different platforms claiming to be "the best fans in the world". In the final part of the book we are going to see that Heysel played a huge part in the collapse of the Belgian Government. With this in mind, "the best fans in the world" line surely needs to end.

PART FOUR

THE IMMEDIATE AFTERMATH

The next morning, cities and towns from the Alps to Sicily flew flags at half-mast, and in the wide avenues of Turin, the city ensign was lowered everywhere.[1] Instead of waking up to celebratory headlines, Italians arose to "Massacre for a Cup",[2] and "Mass Murder in Brussels".[3] *La Gazzetta dello Sport* ran with a headline of "Juve Win a Cursed Cup".[4]

To the Italians, this was a latter-day invasion by Goths and Vandals.[5] Giuliano Zincone in *Corriere della Sera,* described evets as, "cannibal passions".[6] Editorial comment in the Italian newspapers was understandably bitter towards LFC fans. *Corriere della Sera* of Milan called Liverpool supporters "barbarians".[7] In Turin the local newspaper *La Stampa* called Kopites "authentic criminals".[8] If we return to our theories in Chapter Two, Paola Guzzanti, said of English fans that they were:

"Breaking the tenuous divide between man and beast."[9]

Much space in the newspapers and on TV was given to the harrowing accounts by Italian fans returning from Brussels of the scenes of violence and terror in the part of the stadium where the trouble erupted.[10] The stories made for horrid reading and included references to the robbing of the dead by British fans. Leonardo Coen and Mario Sconcerti from *La Repubblica,* said the English were also "pissing on the corpses"[11]. On this latter accusation, and despite this being reported in the Italian press, I find it hard to believe. Besides, whilst researching, I did not find any evidence of this in British or Belgian material. It was reported in Foreign Office documents, but they were quoting Italian newspapers.

Wide coverage was also given to statements by the UK Prime Minister and commentators on British TV deploring the violence, and to condolences offered to President Pertini, the Pope, Italian ministers and to the families of the victims.[12] Above all, however, the articles expressed shock and bewilderment at the senselessness of the violence and the fact that so many had lost their lives at what should have been a festive sporting occasion.[13]

The names of the dead were read out over early morning radio broadcasts, but many had only their birth places on their identity cards, and not their addresses, which added to an already confused situation.[14]

Grief-stricken Italians mourned their dead and poured out their hatred for LFC fans. Andrea Landini from Turin, whose father, Giovacchino, was amongst those killed, said:

"I want to get my hands round the neck of a Liverpool fan and show him how it feels to die."[15]

His sister Monica stated:

"No Englishman is ever going to set foot in here [their restaurant] again as long as I live. [...] All his life, my father worked a waiter and then a cook to make a living and raise us. When he had enough money he opened his own restaurant. Now those animals have ruined our lives."[16]

Giovacchino Landini was a Juventus supporter, but he

rarely went to matches. He preferred to watch the Sunday games on the television in his small trattoria. He was a popular man, and when Juventus reached the final, his friends tried to persuade him to go with them to the match. They had managed to get tickets for the stand. By the time he had made up his mind, all the seats had gone and he had to pay 50,000 lire (about £20) on the black market for one—five times the odds. The ticket was for the terraces of Section Z. According to his wife, when he left "he was as a happy as a child".[17] He was going to bring back the ticket stub for his son Andrea as a souvenir.

His wife was working at the trattoria when the news of the fighting came over the radio. As the television began to show pictures of the horror, customers tried to reassure her that Giovacchino would be safe. She rang the emergency number in Brussels that had been flashed on television, but it was constantly engaged. It was two hours before she got through and learned the news.[18] Outside the restaurant, the streets were beginning to fill with cheering crowds. It was reported in one English newspaper that Giovacchino was strangled to death.[19]

As we saw before, Giovanni Casula and his son Andrea also died in the massacre. Giovanni's brother, Vincazo, expressed his anger:

"Little Andrea was on a trip to Brussels for coming top of his form and now he is dead. We don't want anything to do with Britain or the British again."[20]

In Turin, gangs of youths found and burned Union Jacks. The British Trade Office and British Airways were attacked during the early hours of the morning. The trade office suffered a broken window, and both buildings were spray-painted with anti-British slogans. The British Airways manager in Rome instructed his Turin office staff to temporarily cover all BA signs and advised them not to wear their uniforms or BA insignia for the next few days.[21] The British consulate in Genoa requested both buildings receive extra police protection.[22] Anti-British graffiti was also daubed on the walls in Sardinia and elsewhere.[23]

British tourists were verbally and physically abused, and there were reports of English tourists being spat upon, and of bars and restaurants refusing to serve them.[24] Some of the most frightening reports came from Lido de Jessolo on the Venetian Rivera, where one hotel manager said he was warning Britons not to leave the hotel grounds for fear of violence. A mob also stoned British tourists in the Adriatic resort of Rimini.[25] Staying with Rimini, or should I say Riccione near Rimini, the European Police Amateur Football Competition was scheduled for 25–30 June. The chief constable of Leicestershire, who was the secretary of the UK Athletic Association, withdrew the British team from the event.[26]

In Milan, a bottle filled with petrol was thrown at the Cambridge Studies Institute,[27] and it was reported a Briton suffered a beating at the hands of a gang.[28] The tourist in Milan received minor injuries and was sent home after treatment at a local casualty ward.[29] The Consulate-General in Milan had to be evacuated after bomb threats were received.[30]

In Siena, an unlucky German was mistaken for an Englishman. The German required hospital treatment after being beaten up by an angry gang.

In the Italian Mediterranean resort of Diano Marina, a coach belonging to a Gloucestershire firm had its seats and tyres slashed and windows broken.[31] Daniel Campifi, who was only thirteen and whose mother was English, was beaten up and unfortunately ended up in a coma.[32]

Consulates were also well guarded, especially in Genoa, which represented the Turin area.[33] Also in Genoa, a Brit had her face slapped in the city.[34]

The police guard on the British Embassy in Rome was reinforced, and security was tightened at other potential targets.[35] The British Embassy in Rome was also bombarded with threatening phone calls.[36] Employees went to the ambassador and told him, "Oh God, it's just awful."[37] Embassy secretary Ann Ashford, who faced Roman traffic in her English-registered car, was insulted and spat upon.[38] Another embassy employee, who arrived at work shaken, reported that almost every passing motorist, seeing British stickers on her car, had shrieked: "Brussels, Liverpool, savages."[39]

The ambassador, Lord Bridges, then dictated a statement, which operators read to hysterical callers. Some callers listened; some hung up, swearing. His statement read:

"I was shocked and saddened by the appalling scenes of violence seen on TV from Brussels. I would like to express to the Italian people my deepest regret that British nationals should have been involved in such disgraceful events and I would also like to echo the words of Mrs Thatcher who expressed her horror over those responsible, who disgraced England."[40]

The ambassador took calls himself. He told BBC Radio 4 that some people were very angry, some insulting, some threatening and others calmly reproving. One call he said came very late at night from somebody who sounded as if he was a Catholic priest, and he said gently and calmly that what had happened was an insult to humanity.[41] Lord Bridges went on to say that British tourists should still travel to the peninsula, but they should keep a low profile. The interviewer, Peter Marshall, who as we saw before was at the game, asked him: "How do you keep a low profile on holiday?"[42]

Bridges replied with: "Well you don't go along the esplanade of a seaside resort singing 'God Save The Queen' and waving a Union Jack for example."[43]

The ambassador sent messages of sympathy to all the families of the deceased and wreathes were being sent to where they were advised they would be appropriate.[44]

Also in Rome, two female English teachers from the St George's International School had trouble over a two-day period. One had her car damaged and both suffered stone-throwing at their apartments. The local chief of police promised to provide some form of protection for the two teachers. In Florence the consul was spat at on arriving outside his office in the morning and later received bomb and assassination threats.[45]

The Italian press condemned the incidents of anti-British behaviour. They also directed criticism at the British tabloids for what they thought was sensational and exaggerated reporting of acts of intimidation against British people on the continent.[46] On 4 June *Corriere Della Sera* reported alarm in the Italian tourist industry at the potential fall in bookings from the UK that summer and quoted statements from local tourist authorities reassuring British holidaymakers that they had nothing to fear in Italy.[47]

ON THE EVENING of the game, Italian Prime Minister Bettino Craxi had been flying home from a visit to Moscow for a special meeting with his cabinet. Before he left, all he would say was: "The game should never have been played."[48]

It was later noted that Craxi was said to have telephoned from Moscow to have the game postponed.[49] Italy's sports-loving president, Sandro Pertini, refused to make any comment; a spokesman for his office in Rome said he was bitter and angry.[50] The next day, Craxi demanded a formal explanation from the British and Belgian Governments for rioting at the European Cup final. He said Britain was a country "submerged in disgrace by the criminal actions of violent and irresponsible groups".[51]

Italian Minister of the Interior Oscar Luigi Scalfaro said the British were responsible for the tragedy: "Their fans are for violence at any cost and in any case."[52]

But he also criticised the security arrangements of the Brussels police. He remarked:

"It is inconceivable that Belgian police in Brussels, which had six terrorist attempts in the past months, did not think of better preparations for such an event. Preparations were incredibly slipshod."[53]

A communiqué issued from the Prime Minister's office after the Italian cabinet met to discuss the tragedy said that security at the match was inadequate, and "weighed in a very serious way on the circumstances and their tragic consequences."[54] Mr Scalfaro, who was in charge of the Italian police, compared the police arrangements at Brussels to those of the final in Rome the year before:

"We had 3,000 police there. The Belgians had 240, from what I understand. We even banned fruit from Rome's Olympic Stadium. No cans, and no bottles."[55]

As we saw previously, LFC fans were attacked awfully in Rome, so while Scalfaro's comments are definitely understandable, they also ring a little hollow.

We mentioned earlier that Juventus had a national significance in Italy; with this came unfortunate consequences. Sick graffiti appeared on the walls of Juve's ground soon after the tragedy, and in Rome, some Roma fans were photographed, smiling, with Liverpool scarves behind a banner that read: "Brussels teaches us this: Juventus fans must die: Bruxelles insegna: i juventini devono morire".

Torino fans got their revenge for years of sick Superga chants, and 'Grazie Liverpool' appeared.[56] While Craxi and Scalfaro were expressing their feelings, the Minister for Relations with Parliament, Oscar Mammi, described the slogans that had appeared in Rome and elsewhere congratulating Liverpool fans on the deaths of the Juventus supporters as "incredible".[57]

Straight after the disaster, some opposition fans began mocking Juventus supporters inside grounds. Journalist Serafino Inguardia claims:

"The week after the game you had stadiums like the Bentegodi in Verona where the whole ground was singing 'Heysel' because they were happy about it, they were happy about what happened to Juventus fans."[58]

When the victorious Juventus team flew home to Turin, only a handful of supporters turned out to welcome them at the airport.[59] Some Juventus fans raced around in open cars flying the club's zebra flags after the match, and gangs from the rival club Torino paraded banners and slogans.[60] One placard read: "Aren't 35 dead enough for you?"[61]

Mayor of Turin Giorgio Cardetti went before the cameras, telling supporters:

"After seeing death and destruction before your eyes on TV, how can you do this? And also when half the city is in panic?"[62]

The largest Juventus fan club had been preparing wild

celebrations for the expected victory. Instead, it was turned into an emergency centre for families anxious for information about their relatives who had been at the match.[63] Juventus fan Ago Fabbri said:

"After many failures, we have finally won the European Cup, but now it is covered in blood."[64]

Italian fans returning from Brussels described Liverpool supporters as "wild animals".[65] Loredana Crema of Somma Lombardo was among those injured. Flown to Milan, she was in a wheelchair when interviewed about her ordeal. She said she had been in Section Z. "They threw stones at us," she said. "I was pushed all over the place. We retreated to a wall. Here, many people were overrun by the crowd. I fell and was stepped on by many. I was in a panic, I didn't know what was happening to me, then suddenly I was out of it. I saw a little girl with a glass bottle stuck in her tummy. There were corpses all around."[66]

The owner of Juventus, Giovanni Agnelli, flew home to Turin with his son Eduardo before the match began. Eduardo, who had watched the tragic scenes in the stadium, said: "It was an incredible sight of death, pain, and suffering, it was shocking."[67]

His father exclaimed:

"What incorrigible thugs! The only cure would be to forbid English people to go abroad to support their clubs."[68]

Agnelli was echoing the thoughts of many of his compatriots, who had no doubt that the LFC supporters were to blame and must therefore be punished.[69]

As Italians returned home the next day, Prime Minister Thatcher gave an interview on Italian TV. She spoke first of the outrage in Britain and of the setting up of the Disaster Fund. She was then quizzed on Britain's problems with soccer hooliganism. She pointed out that there was trouble at just a few particular clubs and that England was ready to introduce legislation that had been introduced successfully in Scotland. She also added there was an onus on supporters to give evidence against hooligans at their clubs.[70]

The next day, the Italian cabinet met, and Heysel was on the agenda. It was decided that an official approach should be made to the British and Belgian Governments seeking clarification of the discussions held and the precautions taken before the match by the relevant authorities to deal with any trouble. A further approach would be made to UEFA about their choice of stadium with "inadequate facilities" as the venue for such a match. Prime Minister Craxi was reported to have expressed his appreciation for the determination with which the British Government was tackling the problem and his indignation at the festivities organised by some Juventus supporters in Turin to celebrate the team's victory.[71]

ON A HOT, sunny morning, the relatives of the dead fans had the unenviable task of identifying, collecting and bringing home their loved ones. Some were wearing black and some wore the colourful summer clothes they'd had on when told of the tragedy. Dazed, but with dignity, the grieving families stood with their heads bowed in silence before the coffins. Others sobbed quietly, tears streaming down their faces. The twenty-five coffins, lined up in a bleak aircraft hangar in a Belgian military base, were a stark reminder of that terrible night.[72]

Among the two hundred mourners was Anna Casula, the wife of Giovanni and mother of eleven-year-old Andrea.

Sadly, she shook her head and whispered: "How could this happen?"[73]

Giovanni had been seen on television with a protective arm around his son. But they toppled to the ground as the crowd crushed them relentlessly. Anna had seen the tragedy on television but thought Giovanni and Andrea had seats in another part of the stadium. Later, when she rang the Italian Embassy in Brussels to double check, the sad news was broken to her. Now they lay in front of her—still side by side. Suddenly, Anna lost control of her emotions and burst into tears. Another member of the family also wept as he embraced her and tried to comfort her. Together they cried for the dead. Anna was led away by relatives who tried to console her.[74]

Giovacchino Landini's body was flown home and his coffin, alongside twenty-one other victims, was loaded into the hold of an Italian Air Force transport plane at Brussels military airport. His wife, Carolina, and daughter, Monica, were there to see him go. They had gathered in a hangar for a brief mourning ceremony with the rest of the relatives who had made the journey. The grieving was raw and open. Carolina and Monica huddled together weeping as they waited with other relatives of the dead for the ceremony to begin. Monica said:

"I hope that your young English fans are remembering us today."[75]

Signora Landini kept repeating:

"It's terrible, it's so terrible."[76]

The ceremony was held in a hangar at the edge of the tarmac. The coffins were lined up at the back, twenty-two draped in the Italian flag, two in the French tricolour and one in Belgian colours.[77] In the middle, in a small white coffin lay the body of Andrea Casula. Behind the coffins hung wreaths from the European Football Association, the city of Brussels, the French and Italian embassies. The British press pointed out that there was no sign of one from the British Embassy and moreover, for an initial church service in Turin, neither Liverpool nor the British Embassy managed a wreath. However, as we saw before the Embassy was aware of the sensitivities in relation to sending wreathes. The Belgian Prime Minister, Wilfried Martens, made a short and dignified speech. He told the bereaved families:

"Men and women who set off happily for a great festival of sport found violence and death waiting for them at the end of the road. The tragedy we witnessed at the Heysel Stadium will live on."[78]

He also remarked:

"We must all of us engage in reflection, on how to put an end to this mad race towards violence in sport and in our cities."[79]

Then, significantly, he switched from French to English and declared:

"We must all strive to give international events their original true meaning—that of a meeting between people from different horizons, not a confrontation between the sensitivities of different population groups."[80]

One mourner, distraught with grief, collapsed by her husband's coffin and had to be stretchered away for treatment.[81] There were prayers then, incongruously, a halting piano rendition of "Auld Lang Syne" came over the loudspeakers.

Prince Albert, the King of Belgium's brother, and his Italian-born wife, Princess Paola, began to move along the long rows of the bereaved, shaking hands and muttering words of condolences. By the time he came to Carolina and

Monica Landini, they were clutching each other and weeping. The prince stood by them for a few moments, touching them awkwardly on the shoulder, and then moved on, blowing his nose, close to tears.[82] The princess's lips quivered with emotion as she listened to the tragic stories the mourning families had to tell her. After the royalty left, the mourners surged forward to the coffins to say their farewells. One of them said:

"What the English fans did was horrible. They were like animals. Even worse—at least animals have dignity."[83]

But another woman replied:

"We cannot blame a whole nation for the actions of a few madmen."[84]

When the bodies arrived home, the Rome public prosecutor, Marco Boschi, ordered post-mortem examinations on the thirty-one Italian victims. He made the order under a judicial investigation opened by the Italian authorities, parallel to the one that had begun in Belgium. The order had the effect of stopping burial arrangements in several towns where the funeral services had already been held.[85] Boschi said:

"No one wishes to add to the problems already besetting the families of the poor victims. But it is our duty to ascertain precisely the motives for the death of each body."[86]

For some families, problems were most certainly added.

Doctors opened the coffins of two of the victims of the riot for post-mortem examination and found the wrong bodies. In Udine, the coffin identified as that of Nisio Fabbro, aged 51, was found to hold the body of a bearded young man. In Grotteria, in southern Italy, the family of Luciano Papaluca, aged 38, found the body of an unknown middle-aged man.[87]The Italian press on 2, 3 and 4 June carried detailed accounts of the arrival of the coffins of the Italian victims and of the funeral ceremonies in the victims' hometowns. The crowds of mourners were vast and ten thousand local people were said to have attended the funeral of one victim near Milan.[88]

In Italy, rage against the English quickly subsided, at least partly thanks to the clear admission of responsibility made by many in positions of authority in Britain.[89] Margaret Thatcher, the British Prime Minister, stated:

"British supporters are to be blamed. These hooligans are killing football."[90]

In addition, the sympathy towards the victims and their families exhibited by some in Britain also helped ease the rage in Italy. Pictures of a Liverpool fan trying desperately to pull as many people as possible out of the crush played an important role.[91]

Thus, after the initial anger at the behaviour of English hooligans, Italian and international public opinion began to point fingers at the Belgian police and gendarmerie, and at the Belgian Interior Minister, Charles-Ferdinand Nothomb.[92] The police were accused of mistakes in the deployment of forces in the crucial hours before the game, with a subsequent lack of communication among the units, and of poor professional behaviour in the face of the emergency. They were felt to have used both arrogant and unnecessary degrees of force, and sudden and undignified retreats when faced with real trouble.[93]

Despite the decrease in antagonism towards British people, British tourists were still reluctant to travel to Italy. Gill Saban and husband-to-be Ray Haines said they dared not risk the backlash of hate in Italy after the horror of the game. Gill said:

"We've heard so many stories of hatred shown by the

Italians against English holidaymakers that we are too scared to risk it."[94]

In Rome and Genoa, British Consular officials were quick to scotch reports that British tourists still faced hostility in Turin.[95] But journalist Mario Baudino, of the Turin daily paper *La Stampa*, commented:

"People are still scandalised and upset by what happened in Brussels. There is a small minority of Juventus who are very angry—just as there is a small minority of Liverpool fans who cause trouble."[96]

In mid-June, Italian Minister for Tourism Leon Lagorio was reported to be considering visiting Britain to allay fears of holidaymakers. The Italian Tourist Office in London said a meeting of top officials had taken place in Rome, and the British Government would be consulted about any visit. Mr Lagorio was quoted by American sources in Rome as saying that the problem of security for British tourists did not exist. However, a spokesman for the British Embassy, Gordon Pirie, said they were telling British tourists to keep a low profile.[97]

On 18 June the Italian Foreign Minister Giulio Andreotti wrote to Ambassador Bridges in reply to Bridges' letter sent the day after the tragedy. He informed Bridges that the Italian families who suffered at Heysel would have been comforted by the promptness and forcefulness of the public reactions of condemnation made by the very highest authorities in Britain, as well as by the spontaneous expression of solidarity shown by thousands of British people towards the families of the victims.[98] The letters exchanged by politicians and diplomats emphasise how important the swift responses of very senior UK politicians were in trying to mend bilateral relations.

IN AN UNBELIEVABLE TWIST OF FATE, Italy and England were scheduled to play each other at the Aztec Stadium in Mexico City just a week after the tragedy. To their credit, the Italian national team felt nothing could be gained from going home and that the match was essential if football was to have a future.[99] On the Friday, just two days after the killings, a full turn-out of players from both countries knelt in tribute to the dead at a Mass in Mexico City.[100] At the game, flags were flown at half-mast. There was a minute's silence, black armbands were worn and, most significantly, the teams entered the pitch as one group.[101] The England manager, Bobby Robson, said:

"The match will matter, but not as much as the spirit in which we hope to play."[102]

Robson went on to say:

"Enzo Bearzot, the Italian manger, agrees with me about this and we shall be getting amongst our players to stress the need for good behaviour and discipline. Football must win. Decent people will win. I'm sure of that."[103]

A statement issued by officials of both countries further indicated that the Italians were in a mood to forgive. The statement also highlighted the sheer class of the Italian nation. It read:

"Sgr de Gaudio and Enzo Bearzot greatly appreciate the gesture of friendship from England and stressed that English football remained for them a model of loyalty and sportsmanship."[104]

At the time, Italy was probably the world's leading football nation. They had won the World Cup in Spain in 1982 and in 1985, their league was the strongest in Europe. For me, the most memorable goal I have ever seen on TV was

Falcao's for Brazil against Italy in 1982. When I found out he played for Roma, it was clear Serie A attracted the best talent in the world. This talent included British players, such as midfielders Graeme Souness and Ray Wilkins, plus centre-forward Mark Hateley. Heysel, of course, brought these men a dilemma on a personal level. Souness's wife, Danielle, said:

"I'm sure the Italians will realise we are disgusted. I can't believe they will take it out on Graeme."[105]

Ray Wilkins, who was in the England squad in Mexico along with Mark Hateley, did not want his wife, Jackie, to return to Italy without him. Wilkins remarked: "If there's the slightest chance of trouble I would rather Jackie delayed going back."[106]

Beverley Hateley, Mark's wife, was staying at her parents' home in Nottingham during the close season. She vowed to return to Italy despite her fears. She said:

"I am worried but we have to return. I hope the Italians don't blame us. Italy is our home now. We have fallen in love with the country and its people. My heart goes out to the families who have lost their loved ones."[107]

Beverley continued:

"There may be some Italians who do not realise we feel just as badly about what happened as they do. I was sickened by what I saw on TV. It was totally mindless and I can't find words to express my disgust for these people."[108]

When all the bodies had been counted and all the relatives contacted, one mystery remained. Marco Manfredi, 40, a medical driver from Moncalieri near Turin, was still missing, and he was not amongst the victims. A search was set up in Belgium, and his wife, Rosita, flew to Brussels. There was no news for eight days. Then, on 5 June, a man was seen wandering around in the centre of Turin, near to a hospital. The police picked him up. His clothes were ripped and dirty, and he had a beard. Soon, they recognised him as Manfredi. He remembered nothing of the match. In his pockets were two fines he had received on French trains for travelling without a ticket. Marco remembered being in Nantes and other French cities. He had lived off "apples and cheese" until his money ran out, and somehow, he had got back to Turin. The *smemorato* of Heysel was not the fortieth victim.[109]

TWENTY-SEVEN

BELGIUM

Heysel sent shockwaves through Belgian society, and within a few months, it had begun a chain of events that would see the collapse of a western European government. Professor Jules Koninckx summed up perfectly the reaction within the country. Heysel "was a bomb that exploded in Belgium. It was a real drama at all levels".[1]

King Baudouin called President Pertini expressing his "consternation and solidarity". The King was said to have expressed his regret that the Belgium police failed in preventing the tragedy. Prime Minister Martens sent a telegram to Craxi and Scalfaro. He began by blaming British supporters for "an outburst of violence". He finished by saying the "Belgians [...] associate themselves with the grief of Italian families in mourning."[2]

Whilst Belgians felt a tremor the next morning, for Brits in Belgium there was an overwhelming feeling of shame. The *Daily Mirror*'s Paul Callan captured that embarrassment:

"However you stand, however you speak, however you behave, these quiet people will hate you. And it was worst to admit you come from Liverpool. Being British in the heart of the European Common Market today is no recommendation because the elegant city is still scarred with the merciless stupidity of Liverpool vandals. In short, the British stink in the nostrils of the people of Brussels."[3]

Just on this point, when I visited Brussels, probably because of all the research I have done, I had a true sense of shame travelling around the city.

Interestingly, or probably not, I went during Covid, and coming back in the departure lounge at the Eurostar station, most people didn't have their masks on because they were on their phones, eating or drinking. When I was looking around the lounge, I saw a guy with swept-back gelled hair, kept in place by more than the usual ultra-24-hour hold. To be fair to the guy, he was dressed immaculately, if a bit too over the top. Private jet, yes, but not Eurostar. He reminded me of the Harry Enfield character "Tory-boy". Anyway, when we started queuing up for the train, everyone now had their masks on, and I couldn't believe my eyes, because this guy was wearing an LFC one. It looked wrong on so many levels. I was thinking, 'I just couldn't wear that in Brussels,' and I am not talking about the fancy handkerchief in the top pocket of his blazer. But like said, my embarrassment was connected with my scrutiny of the subject.

Three days after the game, Brussels police defused a parcel bomb left outside a Marks and Spencer store, which police said could have caused a massacre.[4] A police spokesperson announced they couldn't discount the possibility that this was connected with the events on Wednesday."[5] British cars, holiday coaches and tourists were attacked in isolated incidents,[6] so whilst Brits in Belgium were keeping a low profile, the world's press wanted answers as to why so many people had died at a football match.

Belgian Interior Minister Nothomb believed the violence had been entirely due to an element of the Liverpool support:

"The Belgian people welcomed people coming here to play football, but they cannot understand that such violence can come from a civilised nation."[7]

Van Gompel from the Head of the Brussels Fire Service felt the same way. He informed the British press:

"You British football fans are murderers-and you can quote me on that."[8]

Coming back to Nothomb, emboldened by the British Government taking responsibility, he also added:

"Mrs Thatcher accepted the responsibility of the tragedy. We will take drastic measures against English football clubs and their supporters. The Belgian people are horrified by this tragic situation. We have nothing to reproach ourselves with, as far as security at the stadium is concerned. We cannot turn Belgium into a police state. On this occasion, every limit has been exceeded, as well as any reasonable forecast of troubles."[9]

Nothomb was asked whether there were too few police to segregate the two groups of supporters. He said that Liverpool had been made aware of the security arrangement well in advance, but when it came to the day, it had been impossible to cope with the ferocity of the British fans. He reacted with incredulity to suggestions that his government or his security organisation might have been responsible in any way for the disaster. He expressed the opinion that they had taken all the precautions, more than before any other football match, because they had feared violence from the British supporters.

In addition, he affirmed that the violence began before the match and most of the police force was outside to protect those coming in.[10] He confirmed that the Juventus players did not want to play the game after the riot, but to "avoid other violent incidents it was better that the match should be played."[11] He announced that there should be a public inquiry at the earliest opportunity.

The press also asked Nothomb if he would allow British teams to play in Belgium again. His response was:

"I should be very cautious before letting such groups come here, not to support a club, but to support violence in a stadium. We knew it was a danger, but we never knew that it could be so violent, so irrational, so brutal."[12]

Staying with Nothomb, during a parliamentary debate on 14 June, he began his speech by saying:

"I approach this debate in perfect equanimity. I realise that numbers of speakers will refer to or demand my resignation. [...] I also know that nobody really thinks that I am personally responsible for the deaths of the victims."[13]

He went on to claim that what had happened at Heysel was an international drama taking place in Belgium with the whole world looking on; aggression by a group of English supporters against a group of Italian supporters taking place at a private function organised by a Belgian organisation on behalf of a European federation. International political passions were also, therefore, unleashed. He suggested a collective responsibility fell upon English society, which tolerated this violence, trying to contain but not prevent it. Direct responsibility for the disaster, he believed, lay with the organisers. "It cannot be said often enough," he said, "that governments do not organise football matches, invite them to attend and make them pay for the privilege."[14]

During the same debate one Belgian politician remarked that it was clear that the English supporters were mainly responsible. He added that the English media that whipped them up was also to blame, as were those who'd failed to educate these young people properly. He finished by stating his nation should be grateful that in Belgium they have young people with some sense of what is decent.[15]

In the wake of a cabinet meeting, the Belgians imposed an immediate ban on visiting British football teams. The ban applied to all British soccer clubs, without exception. Amateur and professional sides were now firmly forbidden to play in Belgium, as were the British national teams. Even school sides were covered by the edict.[16] The justice minister, Jean Gol, who was also deputy prime minister, said it was not possible to make subtle distinctions between teams.

The Belgians advised other European countries to do the same, and the British Government believed some would accept the advice. Wilfried Martens, the Belgian Prime Minister, told reporters he expected his government's move to be followed by new crowd control and safety proposals from British clubs and UEFA. He declared:

"These measures are necessary if we are to change our decision. If they are not sufficient, we will maintain our position of a total ban."[17]

In announcing his decision to ban British teams from Belgium, Nothomb admitted to underestimating the English when he made his security preparations for the Liverpool-Juventus match. He told 150 journalists and 16 camera crews:

"Now we know it's possible for people to be so stupid. I think all the police in the world will take this foolishness into account."[18]

An English journalist assailed the minister with criticism made by Liverpool club officials that Belgian policing had been inadequate. Nothomb, who knew that thirty-eight corpses lay at that moment in a Belgian morgue, was barely able to conceal his rage.

"I will try to answer you peacefully, I think the criticism should not come from Liverpool, please."[19]

JUST AS THE last victims of the tragedy started their final journey home, British Foreign Secretary Geoffrey Howe arrived in Brussels for high-powered talks with his Belgian counterpart, Leo Tindemans. The UK government considered the idea of Howe visiting hospitals. However, with the hospitals thronged with Italians, many in a distraught state, there was the possibility of unpleasant and distressing incidents. With this in mind, the Belgians preferred to avoid such a risk.[20]

In the course of his brief visit to Belgium, Howe expressed once again Britain's horror at the tragic events just a few days earlier. He told Tindemans that Britain was now taking further steps to prevent a repetition of the events at Heysel, including new legislation in the UK. He informed Tindemans that Britain was ready to conclude a bilateral agreement with Belgium quickly on the repatriation of prisoners.[21] Howe, in reference to growing anti-British feeling, commented:

"I can quite understand the sense of shock in this country and there are two things that must happen. First, we must be sure that this kind of thing never again casts a shadow across our friendship, and, secondly, we must strengthen our friendship in the context of the European Community."[22]

Tindemans, who had been abroad at the time of the match, expressed understanding for the problems Britain faced and added that this should not be allowed to undermine bilateral relations. In addition, he said he would look into the position of the repatriation of prisoners. He went on to remark in confidence about the problems of management and coordination between the various Belgian police forces and the shortcomings in their control of the sale of tickets and in crowd management. Howe also informed Tindemans, as he told Nothomb, that British public opinion would understand if Belgian courts imposed severe sentences on convicted Britons. Howe added that he understood why the Belgians had imposed a ban on all British clubs.[23]

Ironically, one of the first victims of the ban was a police football team from Medway in Kent, who were not allowed to take part in an annual five-a-side competition. The tournament, organised by the Belgian police, was held in the small town of Zaventem, close to Heysel. The event consisted of eight police teams from five different nations. Kent Police asked the Belgian and British Governments for special dispensation so they could participate. The senior Belgian police officer arranging the competition, Captain Tempeles, said:

"It's only a week after the event of the Heysel Stadium and I don't know what your politicians will do."[24]

However, Captain Tempeles himself was more than happy for the British team to take part:

"They can come no problem, but they asked me to have written authorisation and I'm trying to get that."[25]

Unfortunately, the special exemption did not materialise. The Mayor of Zaventem complained to the Belgian Senate that the ban on British teams should not be applied to friendly matches like the police tournament. Chief Superintendent Alan Bourlet from Kent Police reacted to the five-a-side ban by saying:

"We've always fully understood the feelings of the Belgian authorities in this particular field, and we've supported it. But we had this invitation before this tragedy at Heysel and we've always said that if they weren't prepared to grant that dispensation, in the light of the ban on all clubs from this country, we fully understood it and we fully supported it."[26]

Despite not receiving the required authorisation to play, the five-a-side team from Medway still travelled to Belgium as a sign of goodwill towards their Belgian colleagues. Despite growing ill-feeling towards English people rising on the continent, Bourlet believed his men would not face a backlash from their Belgian counterparts:

"I'm sure they won't [face a backlash] because in fact the telex that we had today from the gendarmerie national, they did emphasise that we are very welcome, even though they knew we couldn't play football and we're not going to play football. There's no question of our officers participating as players or as officials, although they're not going to play football, they're very welcome to go as spectators."[27]

The police team returned to Rochester police station with an armful of cups and prizes even though they had never kicked a ball. They were given the awards as an act of kindness, and Eindhoven, the eventual champions, gave Kent the winner's trophy. Inspector Dave Cox, who arranged the trip for his colleagues, said:

"The team found it rather hard. They watched and one could see from their faces they were wishing they were on the pitch themselves."[28]

Cox went on to praise the attitude of other nations, despite the circumstances:

"It was absolutely marvellous; the hospitality was absolutely incredible."[29]

At the party to celebrate the competition, Captain Tempeles made a sporting speech, a talk that emphasised the significance of reconciliation. He told the guests:

"The gesture proves that a championship like this is not only important for the sport itself, but also for the human and professional relations which were made during this weekend."[30]

Despite not being allowed to enter the football tournament, the boys from Kent were allowed to enter the singing competition during the party, and thankfully, they won.

We mentioned a moment ago that the Mayor of Zaventem complained to the Belgian Senate. During a session of the Belgian Senate, Senator Vermeiren relayed his story of the football competition to his fellow members. During his speech, he first pointed out that it was a fundamental error in taking a decision immediately after the match to ban all English teams from playing in Belgium.[31] As for the tournament, he said he had come across the most pitiful situation. He said he saw a team of British police officers relegated to a corner as if they were criminals, in tears because, due to the minister's decision, they could not take part in the tournament. He apologised to the police officers himself.[32]

Coming back to the ban, he stated:

"I believe everyone approves of the Minister's decision to impose a temporary ban. The ban must, however, be more flexibly applied. I do not believe we can continue to allow the good relations we have always maintained with our neighbours on the other side of the channel to be damaged."[33]

Another deputy informed the house that members of the parliamentary football team had intended to invite their English counterparts to a match in Ostend. Unable to now do so, he stated:

"How can we have a unified Europe if we cannot even play football together?"[34]

During the same debate the political pressure on the government was ramping up. Senator Humblet said of the Prime Minister:

"I would ask the PM how he explains his failure to make a statement since the disaster? Should he not have seen it as his duty to address public opinion in this country and abroad and express our regrets?"[35]

Whilst Senator Debussere alleged:

"The authorities seem to have paid scant attention to the Belgians killed at Heysel and their relatives. They claim not to know anything about the funeral arrangements. They seem to have forgotten how bodies were eventually handed over and what happened over those funerals."[36]

Another early casualty was the world feather-weight world title fight between Barry McGuigan and Eusebio Pedroza on 8 June. With the fight taking place at Queen's Park Rangers football stadium the British Boxing Board of Control ordered that no alcohol would be sold.[37]

Meanwhile, fears were growing in Belgium of an Italian terrorist revenge attack against Belgian authorities, who had been blamed for allowing the disaster to happen. It was reported that the large Brussels-Italian community directed its hatred at any English-speaking visitor, but Belgians feared they might suffer the real backlash, especially if the Italian Government made high-level governmental protests about the organisation of the match. Fears escalated following non-stop criticism of the Brussels police over the way they had handled the match.[38]

When the Belgian official inquiry got under way, its inquiry investigating committee comprised of nine members of the House of Representatives, the lower house of the Belgian parliament.[39] One of its first tasks was to request copies of television film coverage of the rioting. Justice Minister Gol said that all the relevant evidence would be forwarded to England and Italy to help the authorities there identify and prosecute the rioters. He suggested it would be easier for those authorities to prosecute offenders in their own countries rather than to extradite them to Belgium.[40]

Gol's suggestion was definitely the opposite of the real situation under British law; therefore, any English supporter arrested in connection with the massacre had to be extradited to Belgium.

The Belgian Parliamentary Inquiry reported its findings on July 6, 1985. The thirty-four-page report underlined in its first paragraph that:

"British supporters who carried out the murderous charges [...] are principally responsible for the dramatic events."[41]

And:

"The violence was unprovoked by the Italian fans who were panicked by Liverpool attackers."[42]

Like the report, the chairman of the committee, Socialist politician Guy Collignon, had no doubt about the major cause of the disaster. He said:

"It is clear that those mainly responsible for the tragedy were the English supporters who made their murderous charge on Block Z."[43]

In addition, the report claimed, as we saw in a previous

chapter, that Belgian police believed they were misled by Liverpool FC about the danger posed by their fans. To repeat, Inquiry chairman Collignon said:

"The police could, to some extent, have been led astray by the management of Liverpool FC which on several occasions maintained that the Liverpool supporters were amongst the most peaceful in Britain."[44]

Collignon accused the organisers of preparing for the final with no more than routine caution. He also attacked the owners of the stadium for the poor condition of the terraces.[45] The ground was described as "dilapidated" with a crumbling concrete structure,[46] and Collignon said it was unacceptable that supporters should have been able to break off bits of concrete and use them as missiles.[47] The report described that UEFA only spent one hour inspecting the stadium and made no report about what they saw.[48]

The report sent a political earthquake through the Belgian Establishment. The mainly Socialist opposition was hoping to use it to drive the coalition of Christian Democrats and Liberals from office.[49] The government wanted an election in early December; however, those hopes were scattered to the four winds by the massacre. Six of the nine members of the all-party commission said that Nothomb should have had personal responsibility for the match arrangements. Five of the commission believed it was impossible to separate political and administrative responsibility, and with political tensions rising, the report led to calls for Nothomb to resign. This led to opposition parties tabling a motion of no-confidence in the four-party coalition government led by Wilfried Martens.[50]

There was some speculation in the Belgian press that the report may prompt the resignation of General Bernaert and even Nothomb, but neither had given any hint of contemplating such a step.[51] According to opinion polls, Nothomb's reputation had suffered significantly in the aftermath of the tragedy.[52]

A debate in parliament was arranged a week after the report was published. It was reported that, if unchecked, the political tension could lead to the collapse of the coalition.[53] It was predicted that if he was forced out of the government, his colleagues from the French-speaking Christian Democrats might also resign.[54] After the parliamentary debate, Nothomb refused to accept any responsibility or to resign and was supported by Prime Minister Martens. Years later, Nothomb would declare:

"I refused to resign because that would have meant that the government was accepting responsibility for the disaster. The government supported my decision not to resign."[55]

This is where things become really messy, and it is where the actions of the Englishmen begin to have an adverse effect on the internal politics of another European country. We not only left physical and psychological damage in our wake; additionally—and unbelievably—as we are about to see, we bequeathed political turmoil on the whole Belgian political system, a structure that was sensitive at the best of times due to its nationalistic make-up. The Francophone Liberals (PRL) at first joined opposition demands for the interior minister's resignation, but then suddenly reversed their position when they realised this could lead to the collapse of the government.[56] As Rudd argues:

"This blatant political manoeuvring by the PRL attracted condemnation from all sides."[57]

To recover some credibility for his party, Gol, the PRL Deputy Prime Minister and Justice Minister, resigned on 15 July and was soon followed by the five other PRL ministers. This left Martens no alternative but to tender the resignation of the entire government to King Baudouin. With no possibility of finding PRL either a new government or a new prime minister before elections had to take place, the king held the resignation 'en suspens'. The government therefore became a caretaker administration charged with expediting essential government business.[58]

This was, as Rudd points out, a somewhat undignified end for a government.[59]

TWENTY-EIGHT

LIVERPOOL

The city awoke in a confused and sorrowful state. It had expected to welcome home a celebratory cavalcade with adoring fans lining the streets. Instead, it awoke to one of the most shameful episodes in its long-interesting history. The town hall flag flew at half-mast, and council leader John Hamilton declared a day of mourning as the repercussions of football hooliganism shook the world. Derek Hatton, the deputy leader of the council, was horrified by what he had seen while sitting at home watching television the evening before. The next day, Hatton wrote in the *Echo*:

"As the pictures came on the screen it was hard to believe that they were actually happening in real life. It was almost as though the football had been cancelled and instead they were showing a sick film."[1]

Merseyside church leaders issued a joint statement. Roman Catholic Archbishop Derek Worlock, Anglican Bishop David Sheppard, and Free Church Moderator John Williamson said:

"We express our horror and deep distress at the tragic

reports from the European Cup Final. The picture is too confused to start allocating blame. We join with the vast majority of football supporters here, in unreserved condemnation at all such violence."[2]

Fans arriving back at Liverpool's main railway station, Lime Street, wept openly and could not bring themselves to talk about their night of horror.[3] Michael Selby from Aintree did speak. He described the scenes in a similar fashion to Derek Hatton:

"It was like a scene from a war movie. Bodies were being carried almost every second in blankets and on makeshift stretchers. Most of them seemed dead."[4]

Michael was still draped in a blood-spattered banner. He continued:

"I was hit on the forehead by a lump of concrete thrown from the Juventus end and never got to see the match. I am just thankful to be alive."[5]

In Dover, fellow Red Barry O'Hara, who we quoted in Chapter One, said:

"I will never travel with Liverpool again. The last time we went abroad we came back like heroes. This time we have come back in disgrace. I am absolutely ashamed of being a Liverpudlian."[6]

As we saw earlier, at Brussels Airport, LFC players were spat on. The skips that contained their dirty kits were scrawled with messages about being killers. Thankfully, the Belgians got the players out of the country ASAP.[7] Their flight turned out to be a silent journey.[8] When they arrived home, the Union Jack on the top of Liverpool Airport was at half-mast.[9]

At the airport, Steve Hamblett from Southport summed up the feelings of all the returning fans:

"It is unbelievable, everyone is just stunned. When the captain announced during the flight that 40 people had been killed the whole plane went silent. Until then we had only heard the rumours."[10]

From the players' perspective, Chris Pile recalls:

"When we landed there was a scrum of reporters and photographers. They all wanted to see Joe Fagan because he was leaving. There wasn't as much talk or questions of what had happened at the ground as you might have expected. I just got in a taxi and went home."[11]

Fagan himself was heartbroken. The widow of ex-Liverpool manager Bill Shankly, Nessie, could hardly bear to watch the barbaric scenes which preceded the final. Instead, she turned the television off and prayed for the families of the bereaved. Nessie said:

"Bill would have turned in his grave that is for sure. It was a very, very sad night for Liverpool. Bill was manager for 15 years and there was never scenes like those."[12]

The *Liverpool Echo* did an excellent job with their reporting, and its journalists must be afforded great credit. The reporters gave honest accounts of what they saw, how they felt, and the feeling of rawness was reflected in the language and the tone they used. They used words such as "murder" and "slaughter". The newspaper also apologised to Turin immediately. However, the *Echo*, through no fault of its own, printed the unsubstantiated stories about Chelsea and the NF given to them by Liverpool Football Club. It also handed oxygen—again, through no fault of its own—to some LFC fans who were more concerned about a football club's reputation than the thirty-eight who had lost their lives the evening before.

At the same time, the newspaper immediately set up an

appeal in collaboration with the now redundant Merseyside County Council. The plea for donations read:

"Merseyside County Council and the Liverpool Echo today launch an appeal to help the victims of last night's disaster. Hundreds of Italian and Belgian families have been ripped apart by the disaster and every penny raised in our appeal will go to help them rebuild their lives."[13]

The *Echo*'s main headline, which covered the whole front page, quoted former leader of Merseyside County Council Keva Coombes, who had asked the question: "How Many Deaths is One Soccer Match Worth?"[14]

The report summed up Heysel perfectly in just in 41 words:

"The safety of the stadium, the tactics of the riot-police, the ticket-sale arrangements were all called into question. But the world-wide TV audience and most spectators had no doubt that Liverpool fans started the fighting which led directly to the slaughter."[15]

The language used here, as I said before, is interesting because it calls the scenes on the terraces a "slaughter", and that is exactly what occurred.

The article also mentioned John Smith and his notion that "One theory was gathering strength—the National Front supporters from all over the country had gone to the match in Liverpool colours with the sole intention of causing trouble."[16]

It quoted LFC fans who blamed outsiders. A fan commented:

"They were speaking with Cockney and Glaswegian accents."[17]

The *Echo* comment was a brilliantly well-balanced piece. It tried to make sense of the enormity of the event and to cover so many angles in so few words. It declared:

"Through all the years, good and bad, the Liverpool supporters have never had to slink home in shame. Until today. For two decades, the Anfield Red Army has been able to look the football world in the eye. We were not Chelsea, or Leeds or Millwall. We were the Kop, the best-behaved supporters in the land. [...] Today, while Turin weeps for its dead, the decent men and women who wore their Red with pride, feel shame and helpless anger. The thugs who shared that colour have dragged their good name into the gutter. For two decades, the name of Liverpool has largely been associated with all that is good on and off the field."[18]

On the club's NF allegations, it advised caution:

"It has been suggested today that the National Front was behind last night's frenzy. That has yet to be proved. What should be admitted today is that last night thugs so terrified rival supporters that they fled in panic, fell and 38 of them were crushed or suffocated to death. And many of those thugs were from Merseyside. All the words in the world will not change that."[19]

The last part stated:

"So today we must address ourselves to a simple humble duty. To say to the grieving families in Turin how truly sorry we are for them in their bereavement. We have a lost a reputation, they have lost much, much more."[20]

The *Echo* apologising on the city's behalf the day after was truly correct and humane behaviour.

Ian Hargreaves, an *Echo* sports journalist, wrote a story headlined "A Night of Horror"[21] and its subheading was "The Battle of Brussels".[22] He began by calling the previous evening's events "the night European football died of shame".[23]

Despite the best efforts of Hargreaves, the *Echo* and

some Reds to provide a full and frank picture, for some fans the only important aspect of the story was how to save the name of the club, even before the bodies had been identified in the morgues of Brussels. One fan literally walked into the *Echo* offices to relay his experiences, which were based on the survival of a brand more than the reality of dead innocent people. The *Echo* reported the fan was broken-hearted and begged Europe's football overlords to clear the good name of his team's supporters. The "Reds' fanatic", as the *Echo* called him, was close to tears as he defended the club's magnificent reputation over years abroad.[24] The Red believed that the violence was not started by LFC fans, but "infiltrators". He was quoted as saying:

"Our reputation for the last 20 years has stood for nothing. But I can say with my hands on my heart that our supporters did not start the trouble."[25]

In the same vein, A.C. Ambrose from Allerton proclaimed:

"I did see some Liverpool fans throwing bottles, but who can say they were actually from Liverpool itself. You cannot tell me we Liverpool supporters waited 22 years just to start all this horror."[26]

Ambrose continued:

"So for God's sake clear our names. Find the scum who did it. They must be on video or photos, so please find them."[27]

Thankfully, they were on video or photos.

ON A MORE CONCILIATORY NOTE, plans were put in place for a Requiem Mass at the city's Catholic cathedral for the following evening. Several days later, 2,000 packed the city's Anglican cathedral. The service was officially entitled one of "Remembrance And Repentance Towards Reconciliation". Ordinary Merseysiders were joined by an international line-up of VIPs, which included MPs from all parties, Environmental Secretary Patrick Jenkin, Italian and Belgian diplomats, civic dignitaries and representatives from the Football Association, Liverpool FC and Everton FC.[28] The occasion began with the singing of the most famous football hymn, "Abide With Me". Two youngsters, nine-year-olds Elizabeth Lynan from Wavertree and Chris Sanchez from Childwall, lit a special candle for the dead. Italian ambassador Signor Andrea Cagiati said:

"I am very impressed by the ceremony which shows how very deeply this tragedy is felt by the British and especially by the Liverpool public."[29]

Steve Higginson from Childwall, Brian Daniels from Aintree and Jimmy Taylor from Everton laid a red and white wreath near the altar. It read:

"Our hearts are laden with grief. From the boys from the Kop."[30]

On a more practical level, travel agents in the city faced a stream of inquiries from frightened Merseysiders who had booked summer holidays in Italian sun-spots. Mike Golding from Horizon Travel Centre in Elliot Street stated:

"We are still waiting for full reports from our representatives in the resorts, but at the moment the word is to keep a low profile if you are British in Italy."[31]

It wasn't only holidaymakers who were nervous. On 31 May one local businessman wrote to the Prime Minister of the potential loss of business in Italy. He told the PM that after years of endeavouring to obtain good export business with an Italian company all their efforts had now been ruined by the events the previous Wednesday. On top of this, he claimed that when one of their directors spoke by telephone to an Italian, he was greeted with the words, "Hello Red Animal, what do you want?" and that he concluded the call by saying, "Goodbye to you and all Red Animals."[32]

TWENTY-NINE

TOO MUCH ON THEIR PLATES

Attempts at reconciliation began the very next day. Liverpool City Council contacted the British consulate in Genoa; however, the Mayor of Turin made it clear that he thought the time would not be right for such a visit until the feelings in Turin had cooled.[1] Liverpool Council repeated their proposal to the consulate again on 3 and 4 June suggesting the date of 17 June.[2]

Once the initial shock had turned to hard, cold reality, the city, through the council and local newspapers such as the *Liverpool Echo* and *Daily Post*, really tried to face up to the atrociousness of the situation. In behind-the-scenes moves, the city council wanted to include both city bishops, players from Everton and Liverpool, and opposition politicians in a civic delegation to Turin. The three- or four-day trip planned to leave Liverpool on 17 June and was to include a press entourage from Britain. At the same time, grieving Juventus officials were invited to Liverpool to hear for themselves the city's shame and regret about Reds fans' behaviour on that fatal evening.[3]

Derek Hatton, who was fundamental in attempting to find reconciliation, commented:

"The entire city now has responsibility to repair the damage done last Wednesday. We need to say sorry."[4]

Politically, not all the city was as convinced as Hatton. Opposition Tories on the council refused to join an all-party delegation, and Liberals warned the visit was dangerous and unwise. Conservative leader Chris Hallows was adamant in his rejection of the initiative. Hallows asserted:

"It is insensitive and too early. Labour are failing to recognise the enormity of the tragedy and the hatred towards the British public."[5]

Liberal leader Trevor Jones, who sought Foreign Office advice, said he did not wish to take part in the visit if the ruling Labour group was pressing it on the Turin authorities against their wishes.[6] He said he would join the mission if he was satisfied a proper welcome had been extended by Turin.[7]

Hatton hit back:

"The carping from the Liberals and Tories is obviously jealousy because we took this initiative. If we listened to them, we would never do anything. We must begin to repair bridges. If the Tories don't want to come, then so be it."[8]

After hearing of the consultations between officials of both cities, the other two political parties reassessed their positions. Geoffrey Brandwood, the deputy Conservative leader on the council, agreed to represent his Conservatives colleagues.[9]

The UK Foreign Office also had concerns. They were worried that the size of the suggested delegation and inclusion of a large posse of British press would cause practical and security problems for the Turin authorities at a time when the local feelings were still running high. In addition, they believed Turin would see a large press contingent with the official delegation as an attempt to seek publicity by the visitors for their own purposes. [10]

From an Italian perspective, it was thought that the Mayor of Turin would welcome a visit provided it was conducted in a sensitive and dignified manner.[11]

The day after Hatton's words, the traumatised city of Turin gave the green light for reconciliation with the people of Liverpool. Senior officials in Turin extended the hand of friendship by declaring:

"Liverpool leaders will be welcome in Turin. We shall be pleased to see them."[12]

Turin's mayor, Giorgio Cardetti, had been in touch with the British Consul in Genoa since the idea was first mooted.[13] He believed the goodwill visit should serve as a message to supporters throughout the world that football is not a form of war. He declared:

"We hope that out of this meeting will come the determination from both cities that nothing like the Brussels tragedy will ever happen again. We cannot let it become a festival. The dead will not allow that. It must take place in a serious dignified atmosphere."[14]

And he made it clear that: "Forgiveness must remain a personal thing for those who have lost a family member or who were injured themselves."[15]

But journalist Mario Baudino of the Turin daily paper *La Stampa* disagreed:

"People are still scandalised and upset by what happened in Brussels. There is a small minority of Juventus fans who are very angry—just as there is a small minority of Liverpool fans who cause trouble."[16]

Before leaving for Turin, a Turin-born Italian teacher

living in Merseyside, Rossana McKeane, wrote to the city civic peace mission:

"Do please accept my very best wishes for your visit to Turin. I am sure the goodwill shown on this occasion will help to restore good relations."[17]

Children at Mosspits School in Wavertree produced artwork and wanted to establish a friendly link with youngsters in Turin. Head Alan Mattews said it was difficult to think of something the children could do that would not be controversial.[18] One piece of work involved a collage of a bunch of flowers. Inside one of the blooms was the message: "Brussels—we send our apologies for the violence and the 38 dead. Above is the way we want it to be, our friendship for the world to see." Another read: "We are sorry innocent people died because of hooligans from our city."[19]

Before flying out, Derek Hatton told the people of Liverpool that during the visit that the delegation was going to condemn those people responsible for starting the trouble, including the fascist National Front. Further, the delegation was going to ascertain, jointly with Turin authorities, where the real responsibility for the tragedy lay, looking especially at the organisation and policing of the Brussels ground. Hatton said:

"We must be prepared to recommend international safety standards for all football stadia in Europe to ensure this type of tragedy never occurs again."[20]

There was another dimension to the visit too. Hatton wanted to establish links with Socialist parties and trade unionists in Turin, collectively to fight the root causes of hopelessness felt by many young people.[21]

When the delegation left Liverpool Airport, it included political, civil, church and Everton FC and Liverpool FC officials. At the airport eight pupils from St John Almond

High School in Garston displayed a colourful banner. The banner said in English "Give our Love and Prayers", and in Italian it read "Our prayers to the Italian people from St John Almond High School, England".[22]

Also on board the flight was *La Stampa* correspondent Enrico Singer, who wrote an eyewitness account of the flight under the headline "From Liverpool to Turin on the Jet of Peace".[23]

Singer's story began:

"At Liverpool, the jet rolled out on time on to the runway. In a moment, the port and the little brown houses of the suburbs disappeared behind the aircraft windows. The journey of reconciliation to Turin had begun."[24]

He went on to quote Derek Hatton as saying:

"We must try to rebuild peace. The violence of a group of thugs cannot be allowed to condemn a whole country."[25]

When the party arrived at Turin, airport crowds crammed to greet the twenty-eight-strong delegation. The tension of the two-hour flight melted in a welter of handshakes, hugs and kisses. Chaos also reigned at the airport as a pack of Italian photographers jostled for pictures of the Liverpool party, who were swiftly waved through immigration and customs to a private reception room.[26] Liverpool City Council chairman Hugh Dalton, who was taken aback by the warmth of the welcome, remarked:

"I was confident we would be welcome here, but I didn't expect anything like this."[27]

Most Italian newspapers commented favourably on the arrival of the delegation. *Corriere Della Sera*'s headline was "Peace Airbridge Between Liverpool and Turin". The Rome newspaper *Messaggero* said "The Day of Reconciliation".[28]

Also waiting at the airport was Liverpool fan John

Welsh, who we came across earlier, dubbed the hero of the Brussels tragedy after dragging Italian fans to safety amid the carnage at Heysel.[29] John had been flown to Italy by Italian television and he was given a free ten-day holiday in Rimini on the Adriatic coast. He told reporters:

"I am overwhelmed by the reception I've had here. Everyone has been coming up to me and shaking my hand and there is even talk of an audience with the Pope."[30]

One local newspaper said of John's heroics in the stadium:

"He is a symbol of what the English city of Liverpool wants to show to the world, its humanity, and its civilised qualities which have been besmirched, not for the first time, by the hordes of hooligans in Brussels."[31]

Juventus fan Giuseppe Gallegari wanted to meet his English saviour. He stated:

"We owe our lives to this Liverpool supporter. He is the one in the picture pulling an Italian to safety."[32]

Giuseppe continued:

"Immediately afterwards, he dragged me out when I was powerless to move and getting suffocated. I would so much like to meet him and thank him personally for saving my life."[33]

Giuseppe's story was told in sports paper *La Gazetta dello Sport*, under a huge headline: "English friend, we have spotted you."[34] The Prime Minister also sent John a letter praising his marvellous act in saving the life of Carla Gonnelli. Furthermore, she commended his compassion and humanitarianism.[35]

Among the Italians who joined in greeting Liverpool's civic leaders was airport worker Mario Abbatangelo, who had a special link with Merseyside. He had married a

Wallasey girl, Helen Smith. They now lived in Turin with their two children. Mario said:

"I feel sorry about it all—first of all because my wife is from Liverpool. The people of Liverpool don't deserve this type of stigma. I know the people of Liverpool well—they are warm and kind."[36]

He added:

"It's only a fistful who caused the trouble. I have been many times to Liverpool—at home I have a Liverpool football scarf—and I share the shame of Liverpool today."[37]

The Liverpool delegation was welcomed to Turin's splendid city council chamber in the 17th century Palazzo Civico.[38] More than a hundred people had gathered to greet the twenty-eight members of the goodwill group from Liverpool, while millions of Italians saw events inside the packed chamber live on television. The event was held under tight security, with civil and military police on duty in force and a special pass system for admittance to the chamber. The Socialist mayor, Giorgio Cardetti, paid tribute to the Liverpool delegation's "act of courage and humility" in coming to Italy, and presented a gold medal to John Welsh for his heroism.[39]

Liverpool City Council chairman Hugh Dalton met widow Carolina Landini, who we met in a previous chapter. Dalton later disclosed:

"I am aware that no words can express the sadness that Signora Landini feels at this moment. But if our visit can achieve anything, then perhaps we can extend the hand of friendship."[40]

Archbishop Worlock said after meeting with Carolina that the most eloquent testimony of the tragedy was her tears.[41] Anglican Bishop David Sheppard probably summed up the mission best:

"Today's meeting was like a visit when there's been a bereavement. It doesn't matter too much what words you say. It matters that you come."[42]

During the ceremony, Councillor Dalton stood next to Turin mayor Cardetti and read a prepared speech. Then, dramatically, he put his prepared text aside to speak emotionally. Facing a battery of television cameras and photographers, he told the audience:

"We ask you, on behalf of the people of Liverpool, to accept this expression of our heartfelt sorrow and sadness at the many deaths caused in the Heysel Stadium at Brussels, when Liverpool went to meet Juventus. I believe this is a time for something from the heart. Liverpool as a city, in its two football clubs, has a wonderful record of sportsmanship for 20 years. The tragedy is that one terrible evening the whole reputation of that wonderful 20 years of sport was destroyed by mindless individuals. It is our hope that those responsible for this tragedy will eventually be brought to trial. And plans and procedures are going ahead with that aim at the present time."[43]

Mayor Cardetti made an emotional reply:

"Our meeting here must produce a condemnation of all violence. The massacre at the Heysel Stadium was a triumph of stupidity that destroyed the meaning of sport as the affirmation of skill and beauty, elegance and style."[44]

The mayor ended his speech by stating:

"There has been no war between Liverpool and Turin, so it makes no sense to say that we are here to make peace. This act of reconciliation on your part is an act of courage and humility that we especially welcome. Let us work together to ensure that there will be no more absurd tragedies like Heysel."[45]

In a wonderful show of dignity, Signor Catella, who we

met in the Introduction, the regional head of the Olympic Committee, told the Liverpool delegation:

"The whole world of sport in Italy and Turin believes in sport. Juventus and Torino, Liverpool and Everton, will continue to meet in great rivalry and friendship."[46]

Earlier, vice-chairman of Liverpool FC Bill Corkish, supported by Everton director David Newton had crossed the council chamber to shake hands with Juventus vice-president Rayno Giordanetti.[47] Giordanetti said:

"The negative behaviour of a few must not influence relationships between our two cities. We must avoid turning such events into tragedies."[48]

During their visit to Juventus's stadium, the Liverpool delegation presented framed pictures of the city of Liverpool to Juventus officials, Gianpiero Boniperti and Eduardo Agnelli. The possibility of a charity football match between Juventus and Liverpool to raise money for the families of the dead was mooted. The idea had been put forward by Derek Hatton, and when the matter was raised with Eduardo Agnelli, he admitted it was a possibility, but he said the decision would have to come from the Juventus team.[49]

A special Mass, led by Archbishop Worlock, was held in an ancient church in the heart of the city, and there was scarcely a dry eye to be seen. Italian mothers stood, eyes brimming with tears, as emotion built up during the highly charged service in memory of the thirty-eight people who had died.

Hundreds of people unable to get into the shrine of Our Lady of Consolation applauded as the Liverpool delegation arrived. A special round of applause was reserved for John Welsh. Inside the beautiful thousand-year-old Byzantine basilica, four youngsters dressed in Juventus tracksuits carried a Juventus banner to the magnificent silver-and-gold altar, which was decorated with flowers in the red and white of Liverpool. Sermons given by Bishop Sheppard and Archbishop Worlock were clapped by the congregation.[50] Sheppard and Worlock were supported by Cardinal Anastasio Ballastrero and twenty other clerics, who preached a message of reconciliation between the two communities.

Inside the church, the atmosphere was heavy. Sombre organ music was played under dim lights. When the worshippers were eventually asked to exchange a sign of peace with their neighbours, locals stepped forward to shake hands with British pressmen. Many could only murmur "God Bless".[51]

COVERAGE of the delegation's visit was extensive, with front page reports in practically every paper in Italy. A ninety-minute national television programme reported the entire visit.[52] Reports of the delegation's activity in Turin were almost wholly positive. The British Embassy in Rome reported on 19 June that the Italian press and TV saw the visit as highly successful.[53] The visit to Turin should have meant reconciliation was within touching distance, and Hugh Dalton proclaimed:

"This is just the start of a bridge-building exercise between Liverpool and Turin."[54]

In addition, Dalton wrote to the British Consulate in Genoa on 20 June. He started by thanking the consulate for their help and then stating that the trip had been well received by the media and hoped that it had gone some way to helping the healing process.[55] Regrettably, this could not have been further from the truth.

When I was researching this book and I came across the positive headlines from the *Daily Post* and *Liverpool Echo* about the reconciliation trip, it made me even more curious about why this trip did not lead to something continual and concrete. The answer was simple in the end: the trip turned into a bit of a PR disaster, and if I had been a Turin official, I would have been left scratching my head at some of the contradictory behaviour of a few of the Liverpool representatives, and there would be no way I would invite them back in a hurry.

You see, the *Post* and the *Echo* had these huge encouraging headlines—for example, "The Sign of Peace,"[56] and "Hugs and Kisses as Peace Mission Arrives in Turin".[57]

However, they were often accompanied by smaller, more discreet stories with no headline, which were reporting in essence 'How not to conduct a reconciliation trip'.

Some national British newspapers picked up on the clumsy and embarrassing attempts at reconciliation, as did *Messaggero*, which talked of a cold ceremony and a failed embrace.[58] Let me make it clear, I am not criticising anybody who went to Turin on a peace mission—you deserve much praise and I applaud you. I recognise that June 1985 was a very different place in comparison with today when we have most of the facts to hand. Nevertheless, grave errors were made, and the Liberals and Tories who believed the visit was too soon have been proved correct by history.

The difficulties began as early as Turin Airport, in what was probably a misunderstanding. Nonetheless, it led to ill-feeling from the start between the Liverpool party and some parts of the Italian press. The Liverpool delegation had been angered by the attitude of the Italian press after they had declined to give a press conference, saying that anything which needed to be said would be said the next day. The result was Italian dailies accusing the Liverpool delegation of "running scared" and of showing more concern about getting to the luxury of their hotel than answering questions.[59] The Liverpool party, however, expressed praise for *La Stampa*, whose correspondent had joined the trip from Speke Airport.[60]

Let us say that *La Stampa* did indeed deserve credit; however, by giving it acclaim, the delegation was probably— if unintentionally—alienating further other members of the Italian press. Added to this, the Italian press did report that there were arguments during the flight between members of the Liverpool party. Opposition councillors are said to have accused the Labour members of manipulating the mission for political purposes.[61]

However, even if the airport scene was just a mere mix-up, subsequent blunders were made by the Liverpool city delegation. For example, during a speech, Mayor Cardetti put the blame squarely at the feet of "Liverpool hooligans drunk on beer".[62] He added:

"Behind such fanaticism there always lies situations of social disconnect and ignorance. That does not justify hooliganism or vandalism but imposes on all of us the moral duty to remove such cause. [...] It is a sad thing for societies to claim to be advanced if we need football matches to cope with phenomena deriving from under-development and social deprivation."[63]

The events in Brussels, Cardetti said, were like some ancient sacrificial rite. This massacre preceded the match with the disturbing message that war may well take the place of play.[64] He also said:

"It is the fanaticism of the supporters that increasingly

risks becoming the mortal sickness of a society which, having lost faith in its ideologies, seems to desire both bread and circuses at any cost—exactly like a millennium ago."[65]

The Turin mayor's speech makes it crystal clear that he believed blame for the deaths lay with sheer hooliganism by Reds on the day. The delegation from Liverpool should have accepted this. Even if some of them did not agree with it, people from our city had caused enough damage to Turin. However, during his speech, following Mayor Cardetti's, Hugh Dalton went down the road of 'we take responsibility, but...'. Dalton spoke of the sense of shock and sorrow that had penetrated Liverpool. He said:

"We have prayed and wept together; words could not express what was felt."[66]

He went on to tell the audience that in no way did Liverpool condone what happened and he fervently hoped that those responsible would be brought to trial. Dalton continued by saying Liverpool, like many cities, had its problems, and no greater problem was that of its unemployed youth. Dalton said that social factors such as unemployment did not in any way excuse what happened in Brussels, but the tragedy had been used as a vehicle by various people "to denounce the city as a whole".[67] He went on to say:

"The city is suffering as a result of the tragedy; I am sure this will make the city of Liverpool more determined than ever to put pressure on the government to change its policies. The top priority must be the dignity of work."[68]

What Hugh Dalton was saying was correct, but he was telling the wrong audience. He was speaking in Turin, not Liverpool, and the subject was the deaths of football fans in a football stadium, not a conference on job creation. His speech seems very insensitive. This was picked up by journalist Alan Copps from the *Telegraph*, who pointed out that the atmosphere in the 17th-century city hall was "charged" and sometimes there was an "embarrassing exchange of messages".[69] Copps also pointed out that the hosts "listened uneasily" when Dalton spoke about unemployment.[70] After Dalton's speech, Cardetti was firm in his reply:

"The massacre at Heysel Stadium was a triumph of vulgarity and stupidity in a situation that destroyed every atom of the meaning of sport and the affirmation of skill, duty, elegance and style."[71]

And whilst the mayor accepted that the ground and the policing were inadequate, he said the causes went deeper: "the new barbarism, or the new civilisation".[72]

Later in the day at a press conference, more differences between the two delegations emerged. It was reported that Derek Hatton insisted that UEFA would have to bear a large measure of responsibility. He presented Cardetti with a report by the Liverpool building inspector we saw earlier condemning Heysel as a "third-rate stadium".[73] One Italian reporter challenged him:

"Is this the latest attempt to shift responsibility onto others for what happened?"[74]

Hatton replied:

"Had that match taken place on any first division ground in Britain, or the Juventus ground, that tragedy would not have happened. It only happened as a result of the appalling state of that ground."[75]

Cardetti said he would not be signing the report. He added: "It isn't for us to judge who was responsible."[76]

The Foreign Office noted that Cardetti and other members of the Turin delegation were aware of these awkward edges, although they weren't prominent in the reporting of the Italian press and TV reporting. It would seem that the awkwardness was smoothed over mainly due to the evident determination on the Italian side to make the visit a success, and the presence of the two Liverpool bishops.[77]

Returning to Derek Hatton's comment. As I have said throughout the book, the stadium played its part. However, have you ever seen a football stadium running across a terrace attacking people? Have you ever come across a stadium drinking ale all day? Do you know a stadium that participates in intergroup behaviour? Can you name me a stadium that once ruled the world and, as a result, commits mayhem when some of its football fans and holidaymakers travel abroad?

As we saw before, during the visit to the Juventus stadium, the visiting delegation presented the hosts with pictures of the city of Liverpool; I think that was a miscalculation. Could you imagine going to Paris on holiday with friends or family and one of your party is murdered, never mind thirty-nine, and two weeks later, when everything is still so raw, the city of Paris sends you a picture of the Eiffel Tower as a way of apologising? The picture is only going in one place, and it is not on top of the telly.

As a city, our attempts at reconciliation have been embarrassing, and in Book Two, we will return to this subject and look at ways of hopefully reversing this situation.

Just one final thought on the visit to Turin, and that is related to the chaos in our city which I spoke of earlier. When the delegation left, they were leaving behind a city still anxious after the Labour-controlled city council's approval of a deficit budget in defiance of the new law and the government. The joint shop stewards' committee was trying to hire a large stadium, possibly Everton or Liverpool grounds, for a meeting of the council's whole workforce. The meeting would be followed by individual union branch meetings to seek mandates for strike action should Liverpool councillors be taken to court.[78] With this in mind, it is highly likely that some of the delegation who were on the trip had more than enough on their plates at home, even before having the tremendous responsibility of achieving reconciliation.

THIRTY

"THE RUBICON HAD BEEN CROSSED."

Whatever the upper echelons of the British Government had planned for the morning of Thursday 30 May evaporated the evening before on the terraces of Heysel. At this point, the government had been informed by Belgian police that 42 fans had died and that there were 275 wounded in various Brussel hospitals. The government understood that the Belgian media put the blame squarely on the British supporters, but that the tone was on the whole sorrowful rather than angry. In addition, they were made aware that the overwhelming impression left with the Belgian public was of scenes, shown repeatedly on TV, of Liverpool supporters throwing missiles and scenes of the dead and injured.[1]

A message from Margaret Thatcher was sent to the Italian Prime Minister Craxi. It started with:

"No words can adequately express the horror and revulsion which I and millions of British people felt at the scenes of violence which we witnessed at last night's European Cup Final in Brussels."[2]

It ended by saying:

"I am immediately making available £250,000 as an initial contribution."[3]

Thatcher held an emergency meeting at 10 Downing Street with Sports Minister Neil MacFarlane, Home Office Minister of State Giles Shaw and Foreign Office Minister of State Richard Luce. During the meeting, Thatcher was anxious that the police should co-operate fully with their Belgium counterparts, and it was mentioned that Kent and Merseyside had already offered assistance. The Prime Minister also hoped the police would make full use of the television film available to try to identify the instigators of the incidents.

She was particularly concerned about the claims from John Smith, the Chairman of Liverpool FC, that the National Front had been responsible for the trouble.[4] It was agreed that the National Front's possible involvement in soccer violence should be investigated further.[5]

Merseyside Police had a video of the TV transmissions, which was being viewed by a number of officers who were regularly on duty at Liverpool and Everton FC. The BBC, ITV and the Belgian authorities were also supplying TV film. Special Branch and officers at Chelsea, in light of John Smith's claims, were also examining footage.[6] It was noted that to date Special Branch had no evidence of central co-ordination by the National Front, either at Brussels or in previous matches. At the same time, they did not discount the possibility that individual NF members, or small groups, may have been involved.[7]

After the meeting, Shaw spoke to Chief Constable of Merseyside, Ken Oxford. Regarding NF infiltration, Oxford thought this was an "old potato" and there was no hard (or soft) evidence to back the allegations.[8]

The Prime Minister said that she had already received a detailed eyewitness account from Peter Bottomley, a government minister who was present at the match.[9] Bottomley visited several hospitals in Brussels and gave a TV interview echoing the Prime Minister's comments. Additionally, the Prime Minister hoped to speak to a number of sports journalists who were present. She had requested that the Home Secretary, Leon Brittan, should write to the Belgian minister of the interior expressing sympathy and assuring him of our co-operation in any inquiry he might hold.[10]

The meeting then turned to football legislation and football authorities. The Prime Minister asked that the Home Office bring forward legislation along the line of the Scottish legislation ASAP. Thatcher suggested that the provisions about alcohol in sports grounds, which were to be incorporated into a bill in the next session on public order, should be put into a self-standing bill to be introduced in the current session. It was agreed that this would be investigated as a matter of urgency. Drafting would need to be accelerated and the proposals cleared through House of Commons and Lords committees.[11]

The discussion then moved on to whether withdrawal of passports could serve as a way to prevent hooligans from reaching overseas fixtures. Shaw pointed out that passports could be withdrawn only in very specific circumstances, none of which seemed relevant to the problem. In any case, the existence of the British Visitor's Passport limited the effectiveness of such a measure.[12]

The Prime Minister said that, ultimately, it was essential for those perpetrating acts of violence at football matches to be apprehended and charged, and for appropriately severe sentences to be issued. She feared there might be a tendency on the part of prosecuting authorities and courts abroad to take a lenient line, preferring to send offenders back to Britain at the earliest opportunity. It was noted that prosecutions could be brought for offences committed abroad only in exceptional cases such as murder. Authorities might have been more ready to prosecute if there was an understanding that those found guilty could be returned to Britain to serve any sentences. It was agreed that this should be investigated.[13]

MacFarlane told the meeting that UEFA were certain to carry out their own investigation of the previous night's events, which would probably show that the arrangements made by the Belgian authorities were deficient in many respects.[14] Nevertheless, it was also likely that they would decide on strong action against English clubs, probably including a lengthy ban on English participation in European competition.

The meeting was also told that UEFA were not terribly well organised and so this would be a lengthy business. The Prime Minister noted that in these circumstances, it might be best for the Football Association itself to volunteer to withdraw English participation until such time as adequate measures had been taken to ensure that there was no possibility of a repetition of the scenes in Brussels. MacFarlane said that senior officials of the Football Association were in Mexico for England's summer tour, and a message should be sent to them suggesting their immediate return to consider what action the Football Association should take. That message should make it clear that public outrage required action from the Football Association.[15]

On behalf of MacFarlane, a message of condolences was sent to the Italian Minister of Sport, the Mayor of Turin and the President of Juventus FC. It started with a bit of copy and paste about it:

"No words can adequately express the horror and revulsion which I and millions of British people felt at the scenes of violence which we witnessed at last night's European Cup Final in Brussels."

Well, at least it ended differently to the Prime Minister's message. It read:

"All countries must work together to ensure that such horrific events do not occur again."[16]

After the meeting, the Prime Minister gave an impromptu press conference in Downing Street. She began firstly by giving a statement for the gathered media. She informed them that the first thing she did was send a message to the Prime Minister of Belgium, Martens, stressing the country's horror and revulsion and declaring her intention to make an immediate initial contribution of £250,000 to a disaster fund.[17] Cheques were sent to the bereaved families on 12 July.[18] Each family received £5000.

On the subject of the Football Association, she announced:

"I had arranged a meeting with the Football Association on 21 June to discuss their responses to our previous meeting and suggestions and to decide precisely what should be done before the next season. I think that meeting must be brought forward now so that we can get things into action, as many of them before the next season and therefore, I'm asking them if they'll bring it forward."[19]

On John Smith's claims of outside involvement, she said:

"I have asked if I could see John Smith. I think that he might wish immediately to get back to Liverpool with his team but at the moment he can. I would like to see him myself and of course we can get him down here quickly."[20]

She then took questions. The last was: "How serious a blow has this been for Britain's reputation abroad?"[21]

Her response was:

"A very serious blow indeed. And our people feel it. Everyone feels it. And this might make it easier to get through any changes that we need, or I hope if there's any evidence against particular people that people will come forward with that evidence because it's the thugs that are destroying football. It's not the families who want to go. The families are afraid to go with the thugs there. It's the thugs. And if anyone has any evidence, I hope they will come forward."[22]

ON THE CONTINENT, UEFA officials in no uncertain terms blamed LFC fans immediately. They contemplated the possibility of banning English clubs from European matches. A three-man commission was set up to investigate the riot in the stadium and it promised to report before 4 July. The date was significant because it was the day of the draw for European competitions for the 1985–86 season. The three-man commission was composed of Gunter Schneider of West Germany, Erik Hyldstrup of Denmark, and Dr Da Silva Resende of Portugal.

Schneider, who had been the official UEFA observer at Heysel, stated:

"Only the English fans were responsible. Of that there is no doubt."[23]

Jacques Georges, the UEFA president declared:

"The committee will have to judge and they must be decisive. This is not a matter of football but humanity. We cannot tolerate the continuation of this appalling behaviour."[24]

The UEFA secretary, Hans Bangerter, told the press:

"My personal view is that having written so often about this problem, having warned for so long, the only consequence now can be to suspend, definitely, the club involved. Whether there will be an extension I don't know. Theoretically, it could go as far as suspending the national team from European competitions. We have reached the stage now where football is at the crossroads. We cannot and are not willing to let this game be killed by irresponsible elements who have no place in football stadiums."[25]

What Bangerter forgot to mention was a telex message he had received the weekend before the match from UK Sport Minister Neil MacFarlane. As we saw, alarmed by reports that segregation at the match might prove to be inadequate, MacFarlane had sent a telex message to Bangerter in Berne.[26] He said he would welcome Bangerter's assurance that UEFA's rules and provisions on crowd segregation, drawn up by the Council of Europe in 1984, would be vigorously implemented. No assurance—or reply of any kind—was received.

AS the earlier emergency meeting revealed, FA Chairman Bert Millichip and Ted Croker, FA Secretary, were in Mexico with the national team. They had first heard of the disaster whilst sitting in the transit lounge in Miami. Croker's name came over the tannoy, which he found strange because few people knew he was there. When he answered the telephone, a voice told him:

"I'm from the BBC in London. Can I have your

comments on the deaths at the European Cup Final in Brussels tonight?"[27]

Croker replied that he didn't even know that there had been trouble. Millichip and Croker continued their journey to Mexico City, but they had already resolved themselves to catching the next plane back to Britain. When they arrived at the Camino Real Hotel in Mexico City, they received a call from a member of staff at the British Embassy saying that the Prime Minister was insisting that they return to London immediately.[28] They did not have time to speak to England manager Bobby Robson, who was asleep. However, by chance they did have time to speak to midfielder Glenn Hoddle, and he had not yet heard of the disaster.

The urgency of Mrs Thatcher's summons was clear from the way she sent the British ambassador in Mexico City to interrupt Mr Millichip's trip.[29] The ambassador passed on a letter from the sports minister, which read:

"I am sure that you appreciate the enormity of last night's events, the horror which everyone in the United Kingdom feels, and the strength of the demand for swift and decisive action. I know that you and the whole FA will share these feelings. I am sure that you and perhaps one or two other colleagues will wish to return immediately to the United Kingdom to consider these matters."[30]

It continued:

"I understand that UEFA will be considering the future of English clubs' participation in European football and I am sure that you and your colleagues will yourself wish to review the actions that the FA should take. I believe that you will also agree with the Prime Minister that the meeting planned for 21 June must now be brought forward because measures to combat football hooliganism before the start of next season have taken on an added urgency. The Prime Minister has asked that we find a much earlier date, and I am sure that you will wish to review immediately, in preparation for that meeting, your responses to some of the suggestions that were put to you."[31]

Millichip left for London immediately. Before boarding the aircraft, he remarked:

"We must consider taking action before anyone else does. And that could mean action at any level."[32]

Conservative MP David Mellor highlighted the seriousness of the previous evening's event:

"Everyone knew that a Rubicon had been crossed. This was much worse, so much more public, and happening on a European stage and made the humiliation that much more intense."[33]

Mellor also gave an insight into Thatcher's inner thoughts on the national game:

"I think Mrs Thatcher would have banned football if she thought she could. She regarded what was happening in football as a cancerous growth that spread out through the rest of society."[34]

There were alternative opinions to Mrs Thatcher's, for, as David continued, "The English FA thought what was happening in the rest of society was polluting football."[35]

Thatcher had no time for compromise with the FA. As we have just seen, she summoned Millichip and Croker to Downing Street, and as Mellor points out, their response did not impress her:

"There was a famous incident, which has never faded from the memories of those who heard it, when Ted Croker, the then Secretary of the FA, was prepared to voice the feelings that a lot of his colleagues had but they never expressed in her presence: 'That football was the victim of wider trend in society', and he said, 'Prime Minister, we want you to take your hooligans out of our game.' I thought she was going to kill him."[36]

One of the seven journalists Thatcher invited to Downing Street was Jeff Powell. Powell recounted:

"The fact that they [the government] were immediately drawing in people to deal with this meant this had gone to the very top of the agenda. It was almost on the level of 'here's a national emergency and it's going to have to be dealt with'."[37]

Taking into consideration the global reach of the Premier League today, what Powell says next shows how football was teetering on the brink during the aftermath of Brussels. He described Thatcher's mood and the meeting in the following way:

"She came in pretty distressed and upset about what had happened. We raised the fact that football was in peril. I was feeling pretty passionate about the whole thing, also angry, and wanting something done. There were no holds barred in the conversation. There was a serious sense of urgency and a serious will to get things done. There was a real sense whatever decisions had to be made, no matter how difficult or unpopular they were going to be, they were going to be taken and they'd be taken quickly."[38]

Thatcher had no interest in the culpability of the stadium and the Belgian authorities and was about to take a radical step that would alter English football.

Jeff Powell recalled Thatcher saying:

"You're going to have to deal with this. You're going to have to come up with proposals. Here are some of the things I've been hearing; you tell me what you're going to do."[39]

Under pressure from Thatcher, Millichip and Croker faced the prospect of taking English clubs out of Europe.

Millichip told a press conference: "She seems intent on the solution and indeed the future of football in this country will depend upon us finding solutions and answers."

Those solutions and answers were to have serious repercussions for a sport already looking over the precipice.

THIRTY-ONE

BANNED

On Friday 31 May, on the steps of Downing Street, the FA announced its decision to withdraw English clubs from playing in Europe in a self-imposed one-year ban.[1]

Bert Millichip and Ted Croker had earlier in the day been ushered into the cabinet room to meet Mrs Thatcher, Home Secretary Leon Britton, the number two at the Foreign Office, Giles Shaw, and Minister for Sport Neil MacFarlane. Thatcher left the FA in no doubt that she was firmly in charge and she was very upset not only at what happened in Brussels, but at the incidents both in Luton and Bradford. Croker said that Thatcher was in a bullish, almost hectoring fashion giving the impression she thought football was responsible for these tragic events through its negligence. She seemed to have no feeling for the game and did not seem to appreciate that it brought great pleasure to millions of players and watchers every week for 40 or more weeks a year. Croker said he was left with the feeling that she would not have thought it a loss to the social scene if football was stopped altogether.[2]

Both the Prime Minister and Neil MacFarlane regarded

the one-year ban as inadequate. MacFarlane told the *Sunday Times* that English football was on probation and that a one-year ban on European visits was unrealistic. He commented:

"It should be in excess of two to three seasons, which will take us into 1988."[3]

With legislation on the way, he went on to say:

"Now we have to see how quickly football authorities react to our package and the effect that has upon the football world and the cancerous violence."[4]

Hans Bangerter also dismissed the one-year ban as an "inadequate gesture". He stated: "There was practically no limit to the sanctions that might be imposed."[5]

The Football League, which was not consulted, was opposed to the decision. Bert Millichip from the FA admitted the ban was a pre-emptive move and that UEFA would have implemented it anyway.[6] He said:

"It was very important that the FA took positive action and immediately."[7]

Millichip also confessed it was the toughest decision he had ever taken.

Ted Croker believed that if the FA hadn't announced its withdrawal then the punishment meted out by UEFA would have been much more severe. He went on to say:

"It is now up to English football to put its house in order."[8]

David Mellor believed the FA's decision to pull out of Europe was a choice they did not want to make:

"I don't think on their own they would have made these decisions. These decisions were forced upon them. But I think they recognised that the rear-guard action that they'd been fighting against the government, and what was to a significant degree an irrational detestation of the game Mrs Thatcher had. After Heysel the game was up."[9]

The FA's decision to withdraw made front-page headlines in all the Italian newspapers on 1 June. The Italian newspapers reported the meetings held between the Prime Minister and various organisations involved were welcomed, and were given prominent coverage, as was the potential financial loss of British clubs.[10]

Before the FA made its announcement, Liverpool had already decided to pull out of the UEFA Cup for the following season.[11] The teams affected by the ban for the following season, along with Liverpool, were Everton, Manchester United, Norwich, Southampton and Spurs.

Football League president Jack Dunnett stated:

"It's hard on the clubs concerned, but you have to weigh that against the loss of life and the damage caused by our supporters in Europe."[12]

He added:

"Really there is no argument. If the Prime Minister orders you to do something you have to do it. The League is subject to the jurisdiction of the FA, and the FA are responsible."[13]

The clubs who had qualified saw events differently. Norwich City club chairman Sir Arthur South accused the FA of a "silly and absurd" reaction aimed simply at impressing the Prime Minister.[14] Sir Arthur said:

"We have suffered because a number of hideous people have gone abroad deliberately to cause trouble."[15]

As the *Daily Mail* reported, Everton faced the heaviest penalty of any English club, and the irony was that their army of some 25,000 followers behaved superbly throughout their club's European Cup Winners Cup campaign, in Ireland, Czechoslovakia, Holland and West

Germany. After the final win over Rapid Vienna, the authorities in Rotterdam and UEFA officials praised them.[16] Jim Greenwood, of Everton, believed the FA should have waited for detailed reports on the riot before taking action. He stated: "They have been pressurised into what could be an irrational decision."[17]

Manchester United's chairman, Martin Edwards, said he was "hurt and surprised" by the voluntary ban.[18]

In an opinion poll in the *Times*, respondents were asked: "Do you approve or disapprove of the FA's decision to withdraw English teams from European competition for the next year at least?" The result was pretty conclusive:

Approve 68%

Disapprove 25%

Don't know 7%[19]

On the same day the FA announced the ban, Margaret Thatcher gave a TV interview to the BBC. The first question was "How do you feel about the decision to pull English clubs out of European football?"

She replied:

"I believe the Football Association took absolutely the right decision and I believe that it will make it clear for all those people on the Continent who like us saw those terrible scenes that we are taking this with the utmost gravity, and it is the kind of decision which the situation itself called for."[20]

With no room for compromise, the national game had hit a low point, but it was about to sink to its lowest ebb ever. Two days later, and much earlier than first expected, UEFA banned English clubs from playing in Europe indefinitely.[21] Soon after, the world governing body, FIFA, also banned English teams. The announcement came after an emergency session of soccer chiefs in Switzerland and could not be appealed.[22] Jacques Georges said:

"I like England. But unfortunately, every time we have big trouble, it involves English fans."[23]

He told the media: "The barbarism in Brussels required the stiffest penalty."[24]

Although UEFA had banned individual teams in the past for misdemeanours, it had never expelled an entire national association before. Georges added it would be decided at a later meeting whether the English national team would be allowed to compete in the next European Championship. He also said the federation planned to introduce additional measures to increase security in and around stadiums during matches.[25]

Georges' colleague, Hans Bangerter criticised the Thatcher government. He remarked:

"Organised football alone can't solve the problem. As long as the British Government doesn't step in to make sure, there's little chance for change in fan attitude."[26]

In relation to the ban, Bangerter declared:

"One, two, three, four, five or even more years. Nobody can tell. Clubs may petition for reinstatement one by one; it's a good bet that Liverpool will be last."

Scotland, Wales and Northern Ireland were exempt from the ban, and further disciplinary action against Liverpool FC was being considered. A British representative on UEFA's eleven-strong executive committee said he had unsuccessfully tried to push for the ban to be limited to a set period. But David Will, president of the Scottish FA, disclosed: "The feeling in UEFA is very, very strong."[27]

Reacting to the decision, Football League president Jack Dunnett, whose views seemed to have changed over the subsequent few days, commented: "It is unfair to punish clubs which had nothing to do with the Brussels tragedy."

But the move was welcomed by other leading figures in English football. Ted Croker said: "There are many of us who don't want to see us back in Europe until we have got our own house in order."

He added:

"The ban could be one or ten years. I don't want to see English clubs in Europe until their fans behave."

Bert Millichip declared:

"You can't measure financial loss against the loss of life."

AT 3:30 p.m. on Monday 3 June, Margaret Thatcher stood up in the House of Commons and opened a debate on the carnage of five days earlier. The discussion included lots of British regret and sorrow. The considerations, just like after the Luton game, went along party lines, with Labour looking for solutions to the causes and the Conservatives wanting immediate action and retribution. On top of this, Luton MP John Carlisle was still obsessing over more painful measures.

Thatcher began by sending profound sympathy to the victims. She then moved on to outlining new legislation to tackle football's ills. What she said next demonstrated the precarious position football had found itself in:

"I recognise that such measures would mean a radical change in the way in which football is conducted in this country, but radical change is needed if football is to survive as a spectator sport and if English clubs are once more to be acceptable abroad."[28]

Next to speak was the leader of the opposition, Neil

Kinnock. He started by condemning the hooligans and by offering his deepest condolences. He attacked the government's proposals by stating that the suggestions do not begin to match the scale of the crisis in British football, both in and near to British football grounds.

Next to speak was MP Eric Heffer, whose constituency included both Everton and Liverpool FC. Heffer asked the PM if she was aware that there was a deep feeling of grief among the people of Liverpool. He went on to say that the people of Liverpool were crying for the dead and for their families; they were crying for the city, because they never expected, with their record, that such an event could occur; they were crying for football both in Britain and internationally. Heffer then touched upon the possibility of outside political interference in the tragedy, the role of UEFA and the Belgian authorities. He asked of Thatcher: "[...] not to become involved in a cover-up of the terrible events."

His speech is of the day, because with hindsight, Heffer would have found it impossible to substantiate the claims of outside interference.

After the PM replied, next up was John Carlisle, who carried on where he left off after the Luton debate. Liverpool Labour MP, Eddie Loyden, asked for "the fullest and most comprehensive inquiry". The Prime Minister avoided committing the government to an inquiry. This was a huge error by the Thatcher administration, because we are left with a situation, even today, where the population of the UK has no real understanding of what took place.

ON 7 JUNE, the Football League began their annual meeting in an atmosphere of near despair following FIFA's imposition of a worldwide ban on English professional sides playing abroad. For once, almost all were united in their belief that the world's governing body had overreacted by imposing such a blanket punishment that effectively turned English clubs into football outcasts. League president Jack Dunnett called the move "totally unreasonable", FA secretary Graham Kelly said it was a "panic measure", and Liverpool CEO Peter Robinson felt it was "most unfair on the many English clubs who have never been in trouble".[29]

What annoyed League representatives most was that this was the first time FIFA had acted in such a drastic manner, even though examples of violence and hooliganism had become increasingly common. Eight people had died in an outburst of violence in Mexico City less than a year earlier, yet nothing had been done and there were no moves to stop games going ahead.[30] Ironically, the ban only applied to club sides, when the national team's fans were the worst consistent offenders.

With a ban in place, the English clubs banned from participating in European competition, except for Tottenham, began legal proceedings against the FA, UEFA and FIFA. The clubs and the Professional Footballers Association (PFA) believed that the actions of the FA, UEFA and FIFA were illegal. Manchester United director Maurice Watkins announced that lawyers acting for the four clubs and the PFA would lodge the application. Speaking for Manchester United and the other clubs, Watkins said they had decided to commence proceedings to mitigate the extremely serious consequences for football clubs and professional footballers in England that would undoubtedly flow from the cumulative effect of the actions of the FA, UEFA and FIFA. He said those actions had been taken without any consultation with either the clubs or the PFA.[31]

Tottenham were originally grouped with the other four clubs in the action, but the London club decided against the move. Tottenham defended their actions to opt out of the High Court bid. Their secretary, Peter Day, remarked:

"We discussed the situation in detail with other clubs. The fact that we are out of Europe next season could prove costly and we realise a good run in the UEFA Cup could have netted us up to £500,000. But we felt it would be unwise to go against the wishes of the government and the public."[32]

The High Court application sought orders requiring:

- The FA to nominate the clubs for entry to European club competitions next season.
- UEFA to accept the nominations and enter the clubs into the draws for each competition.
- FIFA to lift its ban to compete in those competitions, and to take part in other matches against non-English clubs.[33]

The banned clubs' grievances received support in the House of Commons during a debate on 'soccer violence'. The debate opened at the extremely late hour of 11:58 p.m. with an impassioned plea by Bob Parry, the MP for Liverpool Riverside:

"UEFA's decision to ban English teams from competing in European competitions was a panic decision, but FIFA's decision to ban all English teams from playing in foreign countries was a shattering blow to most sane football fans, including the Football League."[34]

Parry went on:

"The Dutch police made it quite clear that they felt that the Everton fans were the best supporters they had ever seen. Everton football club went to Wembley not once or twice but four times last year, and there was no trouble whatever among Everton fans at any of those games. Therefore, a team such as Everton and its fans should not be penalised."[35]

Parry was swimming against the tide. Ted Croker believed the four English clubs attempting legal action in order to lift the ban on playing in Europe were "chasing a lost cause".[36] Croker also hit out at the proposed action by stating: "I'm just surprised that clubs have forgotten so quickly the full implications of the tragedy in Brussels."[37]

Croker did not believe any action against UEFA could succeed. He added:

"As I understand it any action against UEFA would have to go through the Swiss courts, who traditionally uphold the rules of the sporting organisation. Apart from that, UEFA do have the right to reject any clubs applying for entry into their competitions and have done so in the past, a notable case being that of Leeds United in the 1970s."[38]

He went on:

"As a member of UEFA's disciplinary commission, I knew we had been on a knife edge for quite a little while and that any serious incident could cause English clubs to be banned. And it was apparent even without the terrible aftermath which saw people killed that the trouble in Brussels would have brought a ban."[39]

Using a political catchphrase from the times, he declared:

"The ban will not be a short, sharp shock. It will be a long, sharp shock and I just hope it makes them finally realise that their terrible behaviour is just not acceptable."[40]

In the second week of June, Thatcher met with the football authorities in a follow-up from the 1 April meeting. By now there was an urgent need to take stock of the progress which had been made since the last meeting and to identify what further measures needed to be taken.[41]

She told the meeting (as we have heard several times now) that the government proposed to introduce—if possible, this session—legislation similar to that contained in the Criminal Justice (Scotland) Act 1980. The proposals on assemblies in the open air would permit the police to impose limits on the numbers of people attending football matches if they anticipated disorder. The police already had full powers to take the necessary steps to deal with criminal activity inside grounds. Popplewell would continue with his inquiry into the events at Bradford City and Birmingham football grounds on 11 May. He would also take into account any lessons to be learned from the events in Brussels on 29 May. The Prime Minister hoped to receive his interim report before the end of July.

The meeting also heard that the government had been working with the police to consider measures that would improve their effectiveness in dealing with football violence. The police had confirmed they would bring serious charges whenever the evidence was available. The police would discuss with the government and the Football Trust the outcome of the CCTV experiment; in particular, they would see if more sophisticated equipment could be provided, capable of taking pictures that could be used to collect evidence as well as for crowd control. Two more hooligan vans would be purchased. The Association of Chief Police Officers had agreed that the British Transport Police should be provided with multi-channel radio sets to give them access to police radio communications. The police aimed to introduce for next season new arrangements for collecting and disseminating information about behaviour at matches. They would be discussing arrangements with the football authorities to ensure that they were able to search people entering grounds as a condition of entry.

With the continent in mind, the government would continue to co-operate in developing international measures to deal with hooliganism. The sports ministers from the Council of Europe would be reconvening at a meeting on 27 June. The hope was that the existing Council of Europe recommendation on reducing violence at football matches could be strengthened into a binding convention. Furthermore, an agreement with UEFA would be sought to require that the arrangements for international matches should comply with certain conditions. The drafting of the convention would need to be considered carefully.

Millichip accepted the need to clarify the application of the UEFA and FIFA bans, but his particular concern was the danger that the first match played by the England national team in Europe would lead to an outburst of violence, which could well result in the England team being banned from the World Cup, for which the draw would take place in May 1986.

With the government realising the difficulties of preventing supporters from the UK being able to buy tickets on the day at matches abroad should not be underestimated, MacFarlane noted that this was why there was a need for a European initiative, such as was currently under way.

The Football Association and the League said they remained concerned about organised hooliganism, particularly at matches overseas. They had already pursued arrangements whereby no tickets were made available to UK supporters for these matches. But it was difficult, if not impossible, to prevent fans travelling on their own initiative. The Prime Minister noted that in the case of Mexico, it had been suggested to the government there that visas should be obtained in advance. The government was pursuing this. This, again, emphasised the need for proper controls on overseas matches through the appropriate international forum.

The FA and the League said that identifying the hard core of those responsible for inciting others to hooliganism was difficult. Though the Association and the clubs had much information, it could not be used to pin down the culprits because there was no central co-ordinating point. The Home Secretary noted that the new police arrangements for collecting and disseminating such information would help. He also agreed that the police should nominate a specific department to whom all such evidence could be referred. This would enable a data bank of information to be developed cumulatively. He would consider further with the police how this might best be arranged.

The football authorities agreed that safety at grounds needed to be considered. For instance, in the case of perimeter fences, it was important to ensure an easy and quick exit from stands was available. In a similar vein to the police, the Football Association would continue its discussions with the Football Trust to encourage the introduction of CCTV as widely as possible, and special attention needed to be paid to picture quality.

Ted Croker said that a new offence should be created for unauthorised access to the pitch. The Home Secretary believed the simplification and modernisation of the legislation on public order would encourage the police to bring charges of, for example, threatening behaviour where this was called for following an invasion of the pitch by fans. He agreed, however, to consider the idea of a specific new offence in consultation with the police. On Jack Dunnett's suggestion, the Home Secretary also agreed to consider the possibility that clubs should be provided with the names of those who had been convicted of offences relating to football hooliganism to help them keep out those with a record of violence.

The Prime Minister then turned to the action the FA and the League were now proposing to take on the points identified at the earlier meeting as falling within their area of responsibility. She took the view that improving control over access to football grounds was essential. The troublemakers had to be isolated and dealt with. Membership cards were a feasible way of doing this. Some clubs were already experimenting with them.

She accepted the difficulties of introducing a national scheme immediately, but it was important that any systems that the clubs set up should not only be effective in controlling access to all parts of the ground but should also be compatible between one club and another. Unless the systems were compatible, clubs could spend large sums and access to away matches could still prove impossible to control. The Football Association and the League agreed urgently to consider jointly with the government, in a working group under the chairmanship of the minister for sport, the details of a scheme of membership cards, initially at club level but bearing in mind the need for compatibility, and to offer advice accordingly to the clubs as soon as possible.

On travel arrangements for supporters, it was noted that the recent decision by British Rail not to offer cheap fares on football trains might increase the use of private transport. This could make it more difficult to control consumption of alcohol en route to matches. The FA pointed out that there was generally less trouble at matches where stations were close to grounds, and they confirmed that this would be a factor in their consideration of which grounds should be used for certain matches. The FA and the League agreed to continue their discussions with the minister for sport on these matters, and on the arrangements for issuing tickets.

The FA would also continue their discussions with the Football Trust about improving the arrangements for seating in grounds and introducing family enclosures. The Prime Minister noted that controlling the issue of tickets both at home and away matches would be considerably more effective as a control if membership cards needed to be presented before tickets could be bought. In conclusion, the FA and the League agreed that they would keep in close touch with the government on all these matters.

Summing up, the Prime Minister noted that, ultimately, clubs were responsible for the safety of those using their ground. That was a responsibility which could not be evaded. The clubs, the Association and the League therefore had to set actions in place that would protect those who wished to attend matches to watch the game, and to forestall those who went to cause trouble. The alternative was the collapse of football as a spectator sport.

After the FA and the League representatives had left the meeting, it was agreed that the Home Secretary would consider the possibility of taking powers to close clubs whose supporters had a poor record of violence. This might have been required if the football authorities proved unwilling to take the radical steps to combat hooliganism that were now required. The FA already had such a power but had proved unwilling to use it or to amend its rules to enable it to be deployed more effectively.[42]

ON 29 JUNE the Prime Minister's plans for a national soccer membership scheme met with increased resistance from football authorities. League officials were preparing a report to Mrs Thatcher backing the FA's belief that the card system was unworkable. Ted Croker said:

"Many of us feel the membership card scheme is a red herring that has been thrown across the trail by the government."[43]

Croker, talking after the FA-League joint liaison meeting in Bournemouth, added:

"We are not prepared to make cosmetic changes. That's why we are strongly against a membership card scheme. I submitted a report to the PM stating that a national scheme was totally impossible. We have still had pressure put back on us by the government, who I suggest don't know much about this subject. The Football League have agreed they are now going to put a report in as well. I'd be surprised if it didn't totally conform with ours, and ours is in conformity with the Association of Chief Police Officers."[44]

The conformity with the police Croker referred to was in relation to a deterrent the FA had tried to implement in the past, but as he said of the restriction:

"It became a farce. Supporters very soon learned that if they went to matches in any great numbers the police let them in because it was easier to control them inside."[45]

On 3 July, Football League chairmen met to discuss issues that could make or break the future of the game. They were considering a six-page dossier, prepared by their management committee, setting out the League's feelings towards ground safety and crowd control.[46] The report had been prepared after meetings with the Prime Minister and the minister of sport, and the League made it clear that it could not accept "total responsibility for anti-social behaviour" and clubs.[47]

Also on the agenda for the London soccer summit was the thorny question of the new television contract.[48] For those who have only grown up with Sky TV's wall-to-wall football coverage, in 1985 there was a live football blackout.

First, chairmen thrashed out the hooligan issue in the wake of the Brussels tragedy and the domestic disgraces at Chelsea and Luton.[49] They also discussed the issue of membership schemes, which they were not in favour of. Rather than reject them out of hand, they proposed meetings with the Football Trust and the Sports Council to compare various schemes. What was certain was that there would be more all-ticket matches and an increase in morning kick-offs during the following season.[50]

On 9 August, before the start of the new season, MacFarlane wrote to all MPs to give them information about the package of measures agreed between the government and the football authorities. First, he informed them of the Sporting Events (Control of Alcohol, etc.) Act, which had received royal assent on 25 July. The designation order came into effect on 9 August—the day before the FA Charity Shield match at Wembley between Everton and Manchester United.

Next, he told them the government had published the interim report on the inquiry into safety and control at sports grounds under Popplewell's chairmanship. The inquiry made a number of important recommendations for crowd control and "anti-hooliganism" measures.[51] The Association of Chief Police Officers introduced a new system for exchanging information about the conduct of fans, to assist in anticipating and preventing trouble. There would now be three Home Office photographic vehicles available for deployment at football matches, together with two experimental high-definition cameras. The police role would be further strengthened by the proposed public order legislation to be introduced next session (this was connected with the problems of sentencing we spoke about in an earlier chapter). In addition, MacFarlane mentioned discussions that had started with UEFA on introducing more binding requirements for matches held under their auspices. Talks were also being held with the Mexican Government on possible ways of controlling travel to the World Cup Finals in 1986. The measures being taken by the football authorities and clubs included:

- Increased fines for disciplinary offences by players.
- Banning known hooligans from grounds.
- Revised ground regulations posted around stadia, including a clause making "police searches" a condition of entry.
- CCTV installed quickly at as many grounds as possible.
- More all-ticket and morning matches.
- Identifying matches likely to have violence so that effective precautions could be taken.

Extra measures were still being considered. In particular, the government was assisting the football authorities in the urgent development of a membership card scheme. The football authorities and the clubs recognised the importance of positive publicity to encourage fresh modes of behaviour in the new season. Various national and local schemes looked likely to be developed.[52]

MacFarlane finished his letter by stating:

"I hope that Members will give such initiatives every support and encouragement. We all share a concern to restore the good name of football, locally and nationally, and of course of our country abroad."[53]

Despite the parliamentary debates and the apparent show of concern and urgency, Ed Vulliamy correctly noted in 2015:

"The atmosphere back in England was astonishing, though in retrospect to be expected, and I doubt it would be any different now: an orgy of denial, excuses, and a search for rotten apples in an otherwise healthy sport and proud nation."[54]

Of LFC, Vulliamy remarked:

"After Heysel, I hoped for some gesture by Liverpool, or unilaterally from the Kop, towards their victims and Juventus—but there was none."[55]

In relation to his then employer, he recalled:

"Even my employer, Granada, based in the north-west, eagerly deployed the hack excuses about the ground, the ticket sales policy—as if these alone were murderous."[56]

In the end, after meetings and more meetings, English clubs missed out on European club competition for five seasons; and as we saw before Liverpool faced an additional year's ban. By the time we returned, European football was light-years ahead of the English game. After dominating European club competitions for so long, it was not until 1999 that an English club won the European Cup again.

If you had said at 6:14 p.m. (UK time) on 29 May 1985 —just moments before LFC fans unleashed their fifteen minutes of madness—that an English club would not win the biggest trophy in European club football for another fourteen years, you would have been laughed at.

Considering the nadir in Brussels and all the previous misdemeanours of English fans abroad, the ban was the correct cause of action. Even as a teenager, at the time I instinctively knew the ban was correct (forget the politics and possible ulterior motives of the decision—people died) and my viewpoint remains the same today. For the clubs disturbed by the sanction, it was certainly a missed opportunity to taste the pleasures of European football: a short break abroad and possibly eternal glory for the clubs, players and fans. The clubs who missed out during the ban were:

1985-86: Everton, Manchester United, Norwich, Southampton and Spurs.

1986-87: Everton, Manchester United, Oxford United, Sheffield Wednesday and West Ham.

1987-88: Arsenal, Coventry, Everton, Norwich City and Spurs.

1988-89: Everton, Luton Town, Manchester United, Nottingham Forest and Wimbledon.

1989-90: Arsenal, Derby, Norwich City, Nottingham Forest and Spurs.

Despite these clubs missing out, we can never compare this to just one life that was lost, never mind thirty-nine.

THIRTY-TWO

CUSTARD CREAMS

Immediately after the tragedy, John Smith, Liverpool's chairman, committed one of the biggest errors in the club's history. With no concrete evidence, he accused "Chelsea's NF fans" of causing the mayhem on the terraces.[1] Not only was this insulting to Chelsea, it has also allowed some LFC fans the opportunity to hide behind this untruth for years after. On a secondary note, it shows you how crazy this situation is, because we are left with a situation where the NF leadership was thinking, "Shall we sue?"

The day after the game, Smith toured the stadium and told the press that he believed the troublemakers were National Front supporters, probably from the London area. But, as the *Liverpool Echo* reported, when asked to comment in greater detail, he said that any comments would be revealed in his report on the disaster to the Prime Minister, Margaret Thatcher.[2] On his return to Liverpool, after inspecting the debris, the devastation and the disaster of Heysel Stadium, Smith repeated his claims of outside involvement:

"The trouble was started by Chelsea's National Front fans. Six of them, and I have the proof."[3]

He added that the six NF supporters were "delighted with the death and destruction of Heysel".[4] To support this, Liverpool officials had consistently said they had seen or been confronted by NF supporters at Heysel. Smith also alleged:

"They were boasting they had caused the trouble that evening and seemed pleased with their actions."[5]

Chelsea chairman Ken Bates was incensed at suggestions that the brutality and bereavements were the work of Chelsea fans. He responded to Smith by saying:

"Allegations of that sort against Chelsea supporters are not just untrue, they are totally irresponsible. [...] This is a time for dignity, for mourning, for common sense. Every genuine Chelsea fan wanted, was willing for, Liverpool to win the European Cup. If they had retained the trophy, Chelsea would have qualified for Europe next season in the UEFA Cup."[6]

Bates went on to criticise the Liverpool chairman personally:

"Liverpool chairman John Smith has now reached a big stage rather late in life. He is no longer merely a club chairman but is chairman of the Sports Council and a member of the Football League Management Committee. He really ought to be more careful. Six drunken yobs with southern accents are not Chelsea supporters."[7]

In his own inimitable style, Bates continued:

"Mr Smith says they approached him and frightened him as he was boarding the Liverpool team coach. He had twenty super fit athletes in that coach. The Liverpool team. Why didn't he have them out of the coach to apprehend those yobs and hand them over to the Brussels police?"[8]

The NF chairman, Ian Anderson, said he had been contacting all his regional organisers to try to establish whether they knew of any members who went to Brussels. "None did. I've checked everyone and got the same reply."[9]

He added:

"Mr John Smith is blaming the National Front to cover up his own inadequacies in being unable to gain assurances of crowd safety at Brussels."[10]

We will examine the police investigation in Book Two, but at this stage it is worth commenting that John Smith's allegations against various groups were later found to be baseless and they were known to be unfounded within a few days of the tragedy. In light of Smith's accusations, Home Office documents show that the authorities were taking his claims seriously. As we saw earlier, one memo dated 31 May revealed:

"To date the Special Branch have no evidence of central co-ordination of football violence by the National Front, either at Brussels, or even in previous matches. [...] But they do not discount the possibility that individual NF members, or small groups may have been involved."

With this in mind, Special Branch officers and police officers in London examined film material looking for "Chelsea's NF fans"; they did not find any. Liverpool policeman Bill Sergeant, who led the probe into Heysel, says of the NF links put forward by Smith:

"My investigations never indicated any evidence of extreme right-wing instigation or co-ordination of events that night. The then Liverpool chairman, John Smith, had been quoted suggesting this. I interviewed him and he claimed he had been misquoted."[11]

Misquoted?

I can fully understand why LFC officials conducted

themselves in such a manner in the days during the immediate aftermath. However, what I cannot rationalise is how
they behaved in the weeks, months, years and even decades
after the disaster. With the fans, it is quite easy to understand their behaviour because we have lots of psychological
research at our disposal that explains their attitudes to a tee.
With the club, I have struggled to match psychological theories to their deeds because their behaviour really is so
uncaring and baffling. For me, it is a kind of entrenchment.
Therefore, I believe the reason for the club's attitude is not
to be found in psychology, but in history, a theme we will
discuss in the next chapter.

Like I said a little earlier, fans have also hidden behind
the Chelsea accusation. One fan, Chris Rowland, wrote:

"Not quite as unfeasible as it may sound; Chelsea stood
to gain from a Liverpool victory-or a Liverpool ban-as they
themselves would then qualify for European football the
following season. Besides, a European Cup Final in Brussels would make an attractive, possibilities-packed Bank
Holiday week alternative for a Londoner, just a hop across
the water and barely further than Brighton, Southend or
Margate."[12]

There's denial and there's denial. And there are theories
and there are theories.

Just to stay with Chris for a moment. In 2015, he
appeared on a podcast produced by the *Anfield Wrap*
fansite. To be fair to the *Anfield Wrap* they produced lots of
great material on the disaster, some of which I have referenced. However, there was a huge Achilles heel to their
work in that some of their guests, like Chris, are still very
much in denial.

Added to this, the host of the podcast, Neil Atkinson,
interviews Italian author Francesco Caremani. During the

interview Francesco tells him that the behaviour of Reds in the Grand Place in the afternoon, as we saw earlier, was of a hooligan nature. This didn't prevent Neil later in the podcast making the insinuation that the trouble in the Grand Place might be "confirmation bias after the event". Plus, in a written article he says he read all sorts of materials on Heysel. Therefore, I can't understand why he's bringing up the subject of confirmation bias. Well, actually I can, it's denial. To make matters worse Neil posed the "confirmation bias" question to Chris.

AFTER THE DISASTER, LFC fan and local youth worker Peter Hooton was busy building bridges. He recalls:

"Straight after the game I'd already been organising a youth trip, a youth exchange. I was a youth worker in Cantril Farm [a district of Liverpool] and I'd already been organising with Mauro, who was a Juventus fan, a youth exchange. We turned it into a reconciliation trip, grass roots, got a bit of backing from the John Moores Foundation. We organised trips to Anfield and Goodison, so this was in August of '85, so it was only a few months afterwards."[13]

The continuation of Peter's story demonstrates a form of behaviour that has you scratching your head:

"I must say that even though they gave us a guided tour around the ground, it wasn't the greatest, it was a cold reception we got and I was embarrassed. Granada Reports and BBC North West were trying to say 'Come on, come on camera and talk about it'. No, I won't do that, because I felt a bit ashamed, the way the club was treating them. What they were expecting, maybe the chair, maybe the manager to come out and you know it was great for me, I hadn't seen him play, but Billy Liddell [one of Liverpool's greatest ever players], he was the tour and he gave them a cup of coffee and a couple of custard creams and I just felt embarrassed and it was as if this was just a normal. [...] It's not the fact that these are twenty Juventus fans."[14]

The tale gets worse. He continued:

"So, I felt from this very early stage that Liverpool were trying to go 'this is something we don't really want to acknowledge'. I never talked on Granada Reports, but I think after thirty years I'm justified in saying it now. In the end, we had to plead with some of the hierarchy to come down and meet them, they did in the end. Obviously, they didn't know who Bill Liddell was, they wanted and they were thinking they were getting to meet the first team players and it just never happened. And they were even told vigorously 'to keep off the grass'."[15]

Like I said before, I can understand the attitude of John Smith and other LFC officials in the days following the deaths; the enormity of the situation must have been overwhelming and judging people in such circumstances is unfair to say the least. Nevertheless, Peter's visit to Anfield with the kids from Turin was further down the line and, therefore, shines a spotlight on the club's attitude. "Keep off the grass", for goodness' sake.

What is also interesting is that Peter, unsurprisingly, said, "it was a cold cold reception we got and I was embarrassed." I think it is fair to say any human would side with him; however, what makes this even more startling is that Peter said this about the causes of the thirty-nine deaths:

"The reason that disaster happened is simple, it's because of the inadequacies of the authorities."[16]

Additionally, a Rob Steen article, when mentioning the enduring denial of Heysel by the *Liverpool Echo*, noted

"Prominent, as ever, were the views of Peter Hooton."[17] During an interview with the newspaper in 2015, Peter had commented:

"There was no attempt at saying sorry because we didn't feel any guilt. That might look bad in black and white, but we'd been having a laugh with Juventus fans all through the day of the match."[18]

Two aspects stand out about Peter. First, his line about "we didn't feel any guilt" on the surface sounds strange; I feel guilt over Heysel because people from my city killed innocent spectators. But Peter's 'lack of guilt' is actually easily explained through psychological research, as we will see in Book Two. Second, and more significantly, Peter's views get to the root cause of understanding the club's approach to Heysel. You see, even Peter, whose language would suggest is clearly in denial, is criticising Liverpool FC. That is how awfully the club have behaved.

Coming back to the club's questionable conduct, LFC fan Kevin Sampson says:

"Over the next few weeks, my friend Peter Hooton called on all his contacts in the city to arrange a friendship trip for a group of Juventus fans, led by Mauro. John Peel DJ'd an exuberant gig on the Royal Iris ferry boat but, while the clubs, hotels and restaurants of Liverpool threw open their doors, it was only Everton that invited the young Italians to their ground."[19]

Kevin's statement above demonstrates how coldly the club acted. Many residents of the city were trying to take the correct cause of action, as were organisations, with the noticeable exception of one.

Unfortunately, some of the players' conduct has come into question too. A Juventus supporter claims that whilst he and his party were driving, the day after Heysel, they came across the Liverpool team coach and he became outraged because: "[Ian] Rush and some of his mates responded to us with laughter."[20]

Now of course, only Ian Rush and the Juventus fans know for sure what took place in 1985. In Rush's defence, there is an image from the 2005 game when the clubs faced one another for the first time since 1985.[21] Phil Neal, Michel Platini and Ian Rush are holding up a plaque to signify the importance of the game. Neal seems to be in agony, with the painful memories written all over his face; Platini is solemn, whilst Rush, and I'm embellishing of course for effect, has the smile of a double rollover lottery winner. It is as if he does not understand the context of his environment. So far, I am hardly defending him, and I doubt he will be paying me a retainer anytime soon to be his lawyer—however, let me explain.

Several years ago, I worked for a company, and a small part of my duties entailed driving foreign people (in a minibus, a very long one) to various places of interest. One of these trips took me to Bath in the south-west. A colleague suggested a car park near the Hilton. He clearly did not like me, or he was a demon parker. To call it a "car park" is being ultra-flexible with the language—it was clearly constructed when the Luftwaffe dropped bombs on Bath during the war. To make matters worse, it was on a slope; there were no proper parking bays, plus I cannot park a Fiat Cinquecento, never mind a minibus.

On our return, I attempted to leave the car park, which meant reversing the minibus. One of the foreign guys offered to guide me, so he jumped out and began gesturing with his hands. I could see a smile on his face, so I assumed I could continue backing out—next moment, *bam!* I had hit a car. The issue was, I noticed over the following few days (whilst I was cursing him), that the chap in question had a permanent smile on his face. Looking at the picture from 2005, this could be the reason Juventus fans assumed Rush was laughing at them—Rush may simply be a person with a fixed expression. (Apologies to the person whose car I hit because I did the cowardly thing and disappeared sharpish, but thankfully there was no real damage. Well, not to the minibus anyway.)

On 24 June, UEFA wrote to Liverpool informing them of their punishment. The letter read:

"The supporters of Liverpool FC have shown an undisciplined, aggressive and extremely violent conduct towards spectators, who in their great majority were of Italian origin and also towards the security forces. Furthermore, they had demolished the fence separating the two sectors. In particular, they threw missiles (bottles etc.) and fired rockets against spectators in the other sector. Approximately one hour before the official kick-off of the match, they launched repeated attacks against the spectators concerned, causing ultimately to the death of 38 people and injuries to 300 to 400 spectators, some remaining in a critical state."[22]

With the above in mind, UEFA decided to suspend Liverpool FC for three seasons from all UEFA Club Competitions for which the club would qualify. The suspension was to begin once other English clubs were readmitted.[23]

On 8 August, Liverpool appealed the ban. The club spoke about its fans' record in its four previous European Cup Finals. It stated: "No serious problems before, during or after the matches were experienced."[24] I would beg to differ after Paris. They then moved on to their punishment. They claimed that although there was abundant evidence of gross negligence on the part of the organising authorities,

Liverpool had received the most severe punishment. They believed the punishment was unfair because it imposed a sanction which had no time limit.

For them, this meant it destroyed incentive and motivation. They believed it could lead to the demise of Liverpool as a major European sporting institution, whilst its competitive future remained uncertain.[25]

The club thought their suspension should be reduced for five main reasons.

First, they claimed it was "Inappropriate". Under this heading Liverpool said that the deaths were not a direct cause of the violence, but a consequence of the inadequate stadium, poor policing, and improper ticket sales. Next was: "Too Severe". Here the club mentioned that an indefinite ban could make recruitment of new players more difficult.

Third was "Unjust". They pointed out that the "Exemplary Punishment" was in contrary to all principals of natural justice. Next was "Uneven". The club suggested that it could be fairly said that the behaviour of the Italians throughout was far more violent than the action of Liverpool followers, which lasted for a very short time.

They ended with "Appearance of Justice". Here, they highlighted the role of UEFA. They said that UEFA themselves should bear responsibility for their choice of stadium and failure to supervise ticket and segregation arrangements. They suggested that UEFA should not be seen to be imposing excessive punishments on others, which might be thought to draw attention away from their own involvement.[26]

Liverpool concluded that they could not be considered either morally or in law at fault for this accident.

Accident?

They also requested that their suspension should end

when English clubs were once again considered fit to be admitted back to European competition.[27] So no punishment then.

For me, as I said previously, I can understand club officials' behaviour in the days after the disaster, but this report was sent months later. I would be surprised if any football club on the planet has ever sent such an insensitive document. In truth it is an embarrassment to good taste and decency. In my opinion it seems to put the loss of life a long way behind the importance of a game and a club that plays that game. The document LFC sent to UEFA was sixty pages long; unfortunately, page one of the document is now missing. I really hope that missing page showed bucketloads of contrition.

As we saw before, Peter Hooton and Kevin Sampson's memories of LFC's behaviour from 1985 certainly make for uncomfortable reading. So, what happened as we approached nearly a decade after Heysel? Was there a thawing in attitude? LFC supporter John Mackin had meetings with the club in 1994 hoping to pay respect to the dead. He recalled:

"Liverpool didn't want to know for quite a while afterwards. I'd been speaking to people at the club about it. I knew there was a memorial stone somewhere in a corridor inside Anfield. And it was round about when the Kop was getting rebuilt, so that would be, what, '94? We said, 'Can we move it into the Kop so ordinary supporters can pay their respects?' I knew a lot of people who'd been at the game who again had felt like this general burden of shame, embarrassment. So, we wanted to do something public, and the club refused and said 'No, because it would get vandalised', which I found gob smacking. I mean it would be inside the ground and only available for vandalising during a match day when there would be stewards around and other supporters who were going to stop it, so I think they just wanted to sweep it under the carpet."[28]

John's recollections highlight two things. First, the heart of the club seems as hard as concrete. Second, it tells you all you need to know about the contempt the hierarchy had for the fans.

Just before the tenth anniversary, John had another meeting with the club officials. He said:

"The tenth anniversary again we played Blackburn the last game of the season, when Blackburn won the title, we approached them about doing something official then and got completely no response. The local paper again didn't really want to know about it and we had to use fanzines and leafleting. We had what you could call a Juventus flag day, Peter Carney was instrumental in helping me doing this, and Billy Merrit. The only way that got any sort of mention in the press that weekend was that people thought there were Liverpool fans on the Kop with Blackburn colours on because they weren't in red and white and it was black and white, and black and white scarves, and it was just assumed they were in Blackburn colours because they didn't want Man United to win the league. So, I think for a good decade after the game nobody wanted to know."[29]

At least some fans were trying to show respect, if not the club and the local paper. The *Echo*'s role at the beginning in the coverage of Heysel was balanced and some journalists wrote some insightful and heartfelt articles. Unfortunately, this approach was not adhered to in the following years.

THIRTY-THREE

OUR CILLA AND THE PRODDY-DOGS

As I said in the previous chapter, the very fact Liverpool FC were appealing against their ban a few months after the disaster, and not only that, but the content of their appeal, informs me that their attitude is to be explained by history and not psychology. For me, this stems from the origins of the club. I could be totally wrong, and I am more than willing to listen to other theories, but for now I am happy enough to share my thoughts and stand by my take on the situation.

One reason I am so convinced is that the club's behaviour in 2011–12 during the Luis Suarez-Patrice Evra racial incident was a case of history, not psychology repeating itself. To stress again my concept could be way off the mark. Now with crowd theories I could dip into previous research to support my opinions, here however, there is no precedent. But, I think we can agree that there might just be a connection between the attitude in 1985 and the defence of Suarez. For now, stay with me, because my theory needs a lot of explaining.

When I was growing up, there was no religious, political

or geographical divide between Blues and Reds in the city. To emphasise the fact, many families were, and still are, split right down the middle in their football allegiance, probably more than in any other British city that has two teams. Politically, basically everybody in our district was a Labour supporter. In terms of religion, of all the lads I knew growing up, not one of them was religious, despite many of them attending religious schools—yes, I do see the irony. However, thinking about the origins of those schools now, they are clearly connected to the city's history when life was very different. Amongst ourselves we never thought about it —they were just schools.

In the city itself, I can never remember talking to anyone about an overlap between football and religion. Nonetheless, I can recall two conversations about the city's football and religious allegiances in the other parts of the country. The first was in a bar in London with a Blackburn Rovers fan. When I told him I was a Blue, he said I was "a good Catholic boy". I remember being surprised by his comment. The second exchange was in the West Country with a colleague. The lady in question was the last person on the planet I would have expected to have a footie chat with, but she did say, once, "Everton's the Catholic club in Liverpool." Again, I was stunned that people thought there was a religious divide between Liverpool's two main teams, and I told her, "It's an urban myth."

Happy to report that she did take a very faint passing interest in the Toffees due to my support. Maybe it was the pictures of Dixie Dean, Alan Ball and Tim Cahill on my desk. Coming back to the comments, for me, it seemed like a lazy analogy—two cities, Liverpool and Glasgow (famous for its footballing sectarian issues), with an Irish influence, they must be the same. Nevertheless, it appears they were both on to something, and it was me who had been ignorant all these years.

My curiosity increased around this theme when during my research for Chapter One, Robins and Cohen, who we mentioned in terms of working-class male violence, kept referring to LFC as a sectarian (Protestant) club. Further to this was a bunch of quotes that put a sectarian twist on the histories of the clubs. Academic John Williams recalls:

"People 'dressed' their houses to advertise Cup Final footballing allegiances, though my Mum would never allow my brother's Evertonian blue to go up in case neighbours or passers-by mistakenly took us for Catholics."[1]

Liverpool author John Woods remembers: "It was strange in the 1930s for a Catholic to support Liverpool."[2]

Historian James Handley wrote: "Everton Football Club, like Celtic Football Club, owed its success to immigrant support, the Irish in Liverpool rallying wholeheartedly round it."[3]

Even Cilla Black got in on the act—yes, exactly, Cilla. She claimed:

"In Liverpool, even in the two-ups and two-downs, most Protestants were Conservative and most Catholics were Labour, just as Everton was the Catholic team and Liverpool the Proddy-Dog one."[4]

Now I would hate to be relying on 'our Cilla' as a credible reference; however, one of Liverpool FC's most famous players and captains, Tommy Smith, recalled LFC's perceived sectarianism:

"Being a Roman Catholic school, religion played a large part in our school life. Pop Moran even tried to turn me off football at Anfield—Catholics were traditionally Everton supporters and players, Liverpool were the Protestant team.

Pop honestly thought that being a Catholic I wouldn't be happy at Anfield."[5]

In addition, in August 2018, an Everton fansite called *Toffeeweb* published an article called "Is Everton Protestant or Catholic?"[6] The author, Bob Waterhouse, had twenty-one references in his piece—twenty-one references on a football fansite. When do you ever see that? Basically never. Despite his research, he was still criticised by many respondents just because he was writing about the subject. However, these fans had no evidence whatsoever to prove Bob was wrong; their replies were basically 'let sleeping dogs lie'.

Well, I think it is a mistake to let sleeping dogs lie, because for me this question explains the reason LFC reacted the way they did in 1985. To understand this, we need to venture back to the 19th and early 20th century to the unique environment of north Liverpool, where both Everton FC and Liverpool FC were formed. You see, this distinctive setting was a battlefield of political and religious intrigue and, most often, not in a good way. For any readers, who are not aware, LFC came into existence due to a boardroom fallout within EFC. Basically, without EFC there is no LFC, certainly not the one we recognise today.

This means LFC was born in a boardroom and does not have the historical origins of a normal English football club. LFC did not come from an ironworks like West Ham United, a church like Everton, or a connection with teachers like Sunderland. And for me that is why no contrition was shown in 1985. I understand people may even laugh at what I have just said, and that's cool. But, like said, there is no precedent.

I THINK TODAY, most people in the UK are aware that Liverpool is a left-leaning city. Indeed, the idea that the Conservatives could be electorally successful in Liverpool is so implausible that following the city's 2012 mayoral election, *BBC Radio 5 Live* reported that the Conservative candidate was defeated by a rival dressed as a polar bear.[7] However, this is a relatively recent phenomenon. Historically, the city was in many respects a Tory town. The Conservative Party was the dominant political force from the mid-eighteenth century and remained so until the middle of the 20th century.[8]

As proof that there has always been strong Conservative support in Liverpool, here are a few basic facts. At one time the Liverpool Working Men's Conservative Organisation was the country's strongest, and the Liverpool Conservatives agency was the largest in the country. The Working Men's Conservative Organisation founded in 1868, had twelve flourishing branches by 1872 with representation on all committees of the Constitutional Association. Its importance was such that Liverpool politics have to be seen through this lens.[9]

In 1914, the Labour Party occupied only seven of a possible 140 seats on the city council, and it was only in 1955 that Labour achieved its first municipal majority in the city.[10] Despite Labour's victory in the mid-1950s, the Conservatives averaged 49.8% of votes cast in local elections in that decade and 51.1% in the 1960s.[11] Let me repeat that: in the swinging '60s whilst one Scouser was doing his bed love-in in Amsterdam, another 51.1% of Scousers voted Tory. And it was only in 1972, a mere thirteen years before Heysel, that the Conservatives lost control for the final time.[12]

So whilst in the 19th and 20th centuries many working-class people around the country were fighting for workers' rights and trying to form trade unions and laying the foundations for what would eventually become the Labour Party, many working-class people in our city dutifully voted Tory.

So why was this the case? Well, it was down to the city being a port city and not a manufacturing town, and down to its geography meaning there was huge immigration of Irish workers. And as Dunleavy points out, although anti-Irishness was a prominent feature of life in British society throughout the 19th and much of the 20th century, it was exhibited in extraordinary dimensions in Liverpool as it moulded the popular Conservatism and Labour Party to a degree unseen anywhere else in England.

In truth Liverpool was politically backward in comparison with other English cities and it is a legacy we are still struggling with even today.

It is common knowledge how significant the Irish famine of the 1840s was to Irish history. The famine was also an immense influence in shaping the future political, religious and cultural landscape of Liverpool. It acted as a catalyst for huge amounts of Catholic Irish immigration into the city—at one point in the city's history, twenty-five per cent of the population was Irish-born—and most of those who stayed in Liverpool were either too poor or unskilled to make a life elsewhere.[13]

Thus—and stating the obvious—some parts of the city became very Irish. As we have just said, the Irish migrants were mostly Catholic but as Dunleavy notes with them was a Protestant section who brought with them an aggressive Orangeism that served to activate latent British anti-Catholicism.[14]

Given this, it was no coincidence the city also became

the centre of Orange Lodge activity in England during this period.[15] And as Alexei Sayle, in a three-part series on the city in 2008, suggested, "Liverpool is the only city in England where somebody can ask you if you are 'Orange' and not be talking about your mobile phone network."[16]

Whilst in other cities, the Lodge declined over time, in Liverpool it actually grew. For example, in 1881, Liverpool held 127 Orange warrants, in Manchester it was 143, and in the North-East of England (Yorkshire up to the River Tees), forty-two.[17] By 1915, Liverpool's warrants had increased to 197, whilst Manchester's fell to just thirty-six and the North-East to only three.[18]

So, whilst the Lodge became less relevant in other parts of England and then irrelevant, in Liverpool, as a consequence of the mass Irish immigration and the increase in Orange activity, the city became split along religious lines.

In the 19th century and early 20th century, rioting was frequently juxtaposed with ostentatious religious celebrations in sectarian Liverpool. The main 'Green' and 'Orange' congregational days were St Patrick's Day and the Twelfth of July respectively. These days were often marred by sectarian violence. With a cited average 'Twelfth' turnout of 40–50,000 people by the 1870s, and with Liverpool by the 1890s being the largest Roman Catholic diocese in England with over 400,000 people—about one fifth of the country's total Catholic population[19]—religion and sectarianism had become prominent in the city by the turn of the century.[20]

An obvious example of this was the election of the Irish nationalist T. P. O'Connor. O'Connor as MP for Galway from 31 March 1880 to 24 November 1885 and then MP for Liverpool Scotland from 24 November 1885 to 18 November 1929.[21] The election of O'Connor highlights the craziness of the political scene in Liverpool, where we had an Irish nationalist MP being elected in an English city with a constituency called Scotland—you could not make it up.

During one general election, O'Connor's opponent was a radical Conservative called Vesey Fitzgerald,[22] so even the names, never mind the storylines, were straight out of central casting.

As with the majority of immigrant communities in Britain, the Irish in Liverpool resided in the same districts, and so as MacRaild observes, Catholicism, as it progressed among the urban Irish poor, developed a culture that, among consistent professors of the faith, was a "whole way of life"—a culture that bound people together through a collective psychology and shared social circumstances.

Outwards from the priest and church, there emanated a network of things that Catholics could do or feel, a series of structures that carried emotional weight as well as material certainty. Schools were planted, clubs were formed and benefit societies grew from the collectivist religious consciousness of those who shared the faith. Migration merely increased reliance upon, and commitment to, the support networks that were so important to people travelling away from cultural roots.[23] Liverpool made fertile ground for this Irish invasion.

At the same time, the Irish community in Liverpool also had to face the Orange Lodge and the political might of the Conservative Party. Although Orangeism was a movement comprising mostly of working-class people, it has generally been viewed by historians as a movement against class.[24] In doctrinal terms, Orangemen sought to uphold the common Protestant desire for independence of thought and action through Bible Christianity. In common with other critics of Catholicism, Orangemen lambasted priests and the roles ascribed to them in Catholic liturgy as mediators between the people and God. Their age-old desire was that Catholics should be granted no concession—not even mere social and political parity—and for Ireland to remain within the Union.[25]

Catholics were to be denied equal rights, and the United Kingdom was to remain at the centre of Empire. Given that this was the case, we might be surprised—as Orangemen themselves were often surprised—that their appeals to an imagined common cause against 'Popery' were met mostly with indifference, and sometimes hostility, from Britons. The Order's Loyalism may have had a particularly acute meaning in the countryside of Ulster, or in the growing sectarian redoubt of Belfast, but it did not transfer fully to new locations.[26]

However, it did in Liverpool. As MacRaild argues, just as Irish Catholics and other migrants held firm to the belief that their church was the focus of their community, so did Irish Orangemen look to shared spirituality and the sociability of their lodges to cement their own notions of community.[27]

During its growth in the 19th century, Liverpool lacked the large manufacturing plants in which employer paternalism was to flourish best. Liverpool, a freeman borough, possessed a pattern of liberties and endowments that sustained the Tory allegiance of riverside artisan trades, exemplifying, as Belchem states, "the autonomy of the political".[28] As a consequence of this, Liverpool did not have an orthodox working-class culture in comparison with other English cities, for example in terms of trade union protection. When allied to ethnicity, Protestant sectarianism provided a solid base for popular Tory support, addressing workers' fears, not of Rome or reform, but of Irish immigration.[29]

With the above in mind, Liverpool, as David Jeffery proposes, is perhaps unique amongst the great English cities in the extent to which religion has played a role in its development. As such, party political support in Liverpool in the 19th and early 20th century was based on the religious divide between Protestants and Catholics, not class,[30] and it was within this environment that the city's two major clubs arose.

In general, Catholics supported the Liberals, Catholic parties and, eventually and much later than other cities, the Labour Party. Amid ethnic and religious disunity, the Orange Order became attractive to the Protestant working class, which desired an organisation that offered its own welfare schemes and mutual fellowship, comparable to what their Irish counterparts found in the Roman Catholic Church.[31] This meant also that working-class Protestants voted Tory. Thus, sectarianism in Liverpool engulfed religious, political, and economic spheres.

As Neal argues, "The [Protestant] Clergy genuinely believed that Catholicism was evil, the Tories wanted to use it [sectarianism] for political power at voting time, and the working-class resented all these paddies and wanted a punch up."[32]

Dunleavy makes the point, "this 'exceptionalism' of Liverpool politics would hinder the evolution of the Liverpool Labour Party as it was unable to combat the primacy of ethnic politics until 1955, a generation after equivalent triumphs in other major British conurbations."[33]

Joan Smith, in her hugely influential article *Labour Tradition in Glasgow and Liverpool*, suggests that, in Liverpool, the "common-sense" of Tory Democracy and

Irish Nationalism presented a barrier that only the most ardent socialists could cross. She argues that because of sectarian "common-sense" the socialists were left isolated from their communities and shut off from the life of the town, culminating in a weak, often opportunistic—and always divided—labour movement. Throughout the period, the Labour movement appeared totally unprepared or unwilling to understand this common-sense. Their annual report in 1907 illustrates the prevailing attitude:

"[...] during the coming year, we hope to [...] educate more and more of those workers to abandon old prejudices, to forget side issues and ancient shibboleths and to turn their faces to the sun in the full realisation that the only freedom they can hope to win must come from their own ranks."[34]

Some historians have argued that the ferocity of the hostility between Irish Catholics in Liverpool and the 'native' British Protestant and Irish Protestant communities surpassed the sectarian divide in the west of Scotland and only stands in close comparison with the experience of towns in Northern Ireland.[35]

One historian writes:

"Liverpool—sister of Belfast, rough, big-hearted, Protestant and Unionist."[36]

Baxter also supports this view. Baxter observed that religion in Liverpool "has dominated its political life and distorted it in a way that was unknown even in Glasgow—only Belfast can offer a comparison".[37] The modern perspective, especially today with so much revisionist history being spouted, is often to call Liverpool an "Irish city" and not in the Belfast sense. But as Kennedy claims, during the period stretching between the mid-19th century and mid-20th century, it would be more accurate to describe Liverpool as an Orange city.[38]

As we have now seen, Liverpool was, unfortunately, England's most sectarian city. The question is "Did this influence the origins and the hearts of the city's two sides?" and "Did this affect LFC's attitude in the immediate aftermath of Brussels"?

I THINK we can safely say that Everton versus Liverpool is one of the most well-known and prevailing rivalries in British sport. The first derby was at Goodison Park on 13 October 1894. The result was a 3–0 to the Toffees.

When it comes to the split within the Everton boardroom and the forming of LFC, the orthodox view is that it was down to some Everton members not wanting to pay extra ground rent to its then president, John Houlding. On top of this was the matter of Houlding being a brewer and many of Everton's members being of the more temperance persuasion.

Punching holes through this accepted tale is the work of historian David Kennedy, who more than any other writer has researched the finer details of the split. Kennedy argues the split was primarily a governance issue—as he calls it, the final act of a drawn-out power struggle over many years between competing factions amongst the Everton membership attempting to impose conflicting corporate strategies for the development of the club.

In effect, Kennedy believes that the two factions offered rival models of the function of a successful football club in late Victorian England. The faction that found its champions in men such as George Mahon, William Clayton and

James Clement Baxter sought to ensure membership involvement in the control (and the eventual ownership) of the club—to establish a democratic governance structure reflecting the views of the broad membership. Club president John

Houlding, on the other hand, sought a modern corporate solution that would put the club on a sound financial basis. This, however, was to be a solution whereby Houlding would take control and run the organisation with the administrative help of a handful of committee members owing personal loyalty to him alone.[39]

To understand how we reached the point of no return within the EFC board in 1892, it is imperative that we return to the 1870s and the formation of the club itself.

The story begins, unbelievably, with a Yorkshireman and cricket. Yorkshireman Reverend Ben Chambers came to Liverpool in 1877 to become Minister of St Domingo New Connexional Methodist Chapel. He joined the chapel's temperance group, Band of Hope, and began a Bible reading class for the younger members of his congregation. It is believed that around the same time he also set up a cricket team to gainfully occupy the time, while inspiring a team spirit in the young men of the parish during the summertime. They played in a field off Oakfield Road in Anfield. The outcome must have been successful, as it was then decided to organise a football team to keep the same young men happily occupied while keeping fit during the winter months. In 1878 the St Domingo team played their first football match in the south-east corner of Stanley Park. The team soon became established, as the sport grew rapidly in popularity, and with more and more players and supporters joining from other local parish teams, it was decided to call the team

Everton Football Club to be more inclusive to the local area.[40]

As we can see St Domingo/Everton was set up to be a community club at heart, and despite the overwhelming wealth and financial craziness of the modern-day football, there is (usually) still a beating heart of goodwill within the club's actions today. The reason I am mentioning this is that when I was growing up, and you still hear it today, many Reds would say their club "exists to win trophies". Even as a youngster I always found it odd (and not just because Everton rarely win anything), but of course when I was young I did not have the rational thought to understand why it sounded strange to me. Today, because of the research I have done, I understand that it is almost literal. For as we are about to find out, LFC was set up to win trophies.

Coming back to the 19th century, Everton soon became the most significant football club in north Liverpool, a situation that did not go unnoticed in the world of business and politics. As Kennedy highlights, it would appear that this appeal attracted the patronage of local political and business figures. Men of both local and national prominence became patrons of the club in its earliest days. David MacIver, the co-founder of the Cunard Shipping Line and a Conservative MP in his time for both Birkenhead and Liverpool Kirkdale; Sir Edward Whitley, the Conservative MP for Everton; and Lord Sandon, another Liverpool Conservative MP, were patrons of the club in the 1880s.[41]

This appeal also attracted John Houlding, the man at the epicentre of the separation and the founder of Liverpool FC. As Mason notes, by the end of the 1880s he was a well-known figure in local political circles, frequently referred to in the press as King John of Everton. He was chairman of the Everton Conservative Association and of the West Derby Board of Guardians, and from 1884 he was a member of the City Council for Everton and Kirkdale Ward. He became an alderman in 1895 and, after a certain amount of unsavoury politicking inside his own party, mayor in 1897. He was also a Freemason and Orangeman.[42]

Besides the civic importance Houlding would have attached to his association with the club, as a businessman, he would no doubt have seen the possibility of profiting from it. Already having his Sandon Hotel near to the club's Anfield Road ground and acting as its headquarters and, no doubt, attracting extra custom through the connection.

Houlding also sought from the club an exclusive arrangement to provide refreshments within the confines of the ground on match days. This led to a situation where many members of the club perceived an undue and increasing commercial influence upon club affairs. Therefore, according to Kennedy, the governance of Everton became a seriously contested issue among a membership who viewed their organisation, the 'Good Old Club', as a standard-bearer for communal pride and identity at least as much as they saw it as an organisation to collect trophies, and certainly as more than its capacity to generate profits for those investing money for its development.[43]

For all of Houlding's financial commitment to Everton, control of the club still rested decidedly with the club's committee. It would appear, therefore, that his ability to determine the destiny of Everton in an autocratic manner was limited.[44] However, as president, Houlding could elevate to the committee one club member to supplement the officers of the club—many of whom, in any case, were business or political associates of Houlding and who appeared to have faced little opposition in gaining their posts. For example, the list of officers of the club from the mid-1880s through to the split in 1892 reveals a cluster of Houlding loyalists, men who would later side with the president in the club split of 1891–2 and help set up Liverpool FC thereafter.[45]

Whilst the split was taking place the biggest issue of the day in north Liverpool was that of Home Rule, the movement that campaigned for an independent Ireland, a subject that also emphasised the differing nature of Liverpool's two major football clubs.

In terms of the timeline: LFC was formed in March 1892 and the general election took place in July 1892, and Home Rule played a massive part in the campaign. The constituency of Everton was Liverpool's 'premier' seat,[46] and at one point it was believed Houlding would stand. As Jeffery explains, those against Home Rule tended to vote for the Conservatives, whilst those in favour voted for the Irish Nationalist Party (in its various guises),[47] and the Liberal Party too. One clarion for the 1892 General Election was sounded by the new Conservative candidate for Liverpool, Houston: the granting of Home Rule, he said, "would mean civil war in Ireland".[48] The Liverpool Orangemen, "that very important and powerful body", in Houston's opinion, would not "stand quietly by and see their kinsmen and the loyalists of Ulster massacred and slaughtered".[49]

A stone's throw from Anfield and Goodison is the district of Bootle. The MP for Bootle at the time was Colonel Sandys (I did say you could not make the names up). Colonel Sandys announced that "Ruling Ireland was like controlling a savage dog."[50] Remembering the Indian Mutiny, when he had slept with a revolver to discourage murderous sepoys, Sandys gave his Liverpool audience a recipe for disciplining an inferior animal. Some reported

Sandys as having said that the "Irish were like savage dogs, and ought to be muzzled", but what was significant was that Sandys was among the most popular of the regional MPs. As Waller notes, Sandys' Protestant backbone was rigid. He had refused all dealings with a Catholic home secretary, and now he warned against Jesuit influences in the press and "Romanising" in Anglican institutions. Sandys believed in "a great Romish conspiracy to trample down the liberties of Britain".[51]

Along with politicians, there were many public statements made by prominent club representatives of both Everton and Liverpool concerning the issues of religion, ethnicity and the all-pervasive matter of Irish Home Rule—statements that would have driven home their differences for any interested outside audience. For example, Irish Everton director Dr William Whitford—described in the local press as 'an ardent Home-Ruler'—made an impassioned speech during the municipal election campaign of 1892 against the blocking of Irish Home Rule by Ulster unionists.[52] He announced:

"Ulstermen do not desire to govern Ireland according to the wishes of the people of Ireland, but according to the narrow prejudices of the so-called 'loyal minority'."[53]

Another Everton director, Liberal councillor Alfred Gates (a name which was "as a red rag to a furious bull" to the Conservative-Unionist Party, according to the *Liverpool Daily Post*), was, according to Kennedy, a "strenuous advocate of Home Rule" and keen to show that "the Orange Tory Party were losing ground in Liverpool".[54] Speaking to a Liberal-Nationalist audience, Gates suggested that "if Liberalism had a little of the enthusiasm and spirit of the Irish it would be in a better position today."[55]

If Houlding was the most obvious connection between Orangeism and Liverpool FC, perhaps Dr James Clement Baxter, a director, later chairman, and a prominent Liberal Catholic, who financed much of the building of Goodison Park, was the most identifiable link between Everton and Irish Catholicism. In contrast to Liverpool FC's Protestant constituents, "frequent press reports of directors James Clement Baxter and Alfred Wade attending Irish National-ist League meetings would have underlined for the public a sense of the general sectarian tone of the men inhabiting the Everton boardroom." [56] Though George Mahon was a "staunch Methodist and organist at St Domingo parish church", he was also an advocate of Irish home-rule. Although born in Liverpool, he was brought up and educated in Ireland.[57]

The political rhetoric of EFC officials was the polar opposite of their counterparts across the park. As Kennedy highlights, from figures amongst the Liverpool FC hierar-chy, on the other hand, there was an equally strident and public outpouring of feeling toward the Protestant-Unionist cause.[58] Founder and chairman of Liverpool FC John Houlding quite obviously found it difficult to contain his religious leanings as a Conservative-Unionist and an Orangeman whilst carrying out his duties as a guardian at the West Derby Poor Law Union. Guardians were elected to their positions by rate payers and were responsible for the administration of poor relief in their area—in this instance, a huge swathe of land that encompassed the whole of the north end districts of Liverpool and beyond to neighbouring towns, such as Bootle, Seaforth, Waterloo and Crosby, making it the biggest Poor Law Union in the country.[59]

As Kennedy suggests, Houlding held huge power, and he pointedly refused to grant Catholic priests any payment for ministering to Catholic inmates of workhouses within his jurisdiction, whilst allowing such payment to Church of England and Nonconformist ministers.[60] In a letter published in the *Liverpool Courier*, Houlding set out his opposition to a motion put before the Poor Law Union to also allow payment to Catholic priests as an act of justice and common fairness:

"I defy any member of the Board or any judge in the land to show me an Act of Parliament which expressly stated that they should pay Roman Catholics for services performed in workhouses. If English Unions did appoint a Roman Catholic priest it is only done by a clear evasion of the law, and often perhaps for the sake of quietness."[61]

Another director, Edwin Berry, the successor to John Houlding as club chairman, made plain his opposition to the re-emergence of an influential Roman Catholic Church in British society. Addressing an audience of the National Protestant Union in 1898, an Evangelical Anglican body committed to helping "sound Protestant" candidates at elections, Berry offered his support to "the repression of lawlessness and Romanising influence", declaring himself to be a "loyal Churchman with every desire to further the principles of the Church of England in accordance with the Reformation".[62]

Along with Houlding and Berry, there was also Sir James Willox, Conservative MP and President of the National Protestant Union. Willox was not a club director but was an influential large shareholder in Liverpool Football Club, using a 'proxy' on the board to advance his interests in the club. Willox publicly backed the decision to set up Liverpool out of the remnants of the staff left behind at Anfield in the wake of the 1892 split. A firebrand in the defence of British dominion over Ireland, Willox, speaking to a meeting in his parliamentary division, attacked Liberal policy on Ireland:

"To conciliate four million people in Ireland, are we going to sacrifice one million and a half of loyal Protestants and faithful lieges of the Queen?"[63]

When the split came within Everton, the substantial Conservative presence at Liverpool is especially noteworthy, with eleven of the twenty-one directors and administrators of the club between 1892 and 1902 actively involved in Conservative politics.[64] The level and nature of the Liverpool hierarchy's involvement in Conservative politics is of particular interest. Six directors—Benjamin E. Bailey, Edwin Berry, John Houlding, William Houlding, Simon Jude and John McKenna—were members of the Constitutional Association, the ruling body of Liverpool Conservatism. The Constitutional Association exercised complete control over district Conservative associations in Liverpool, and affiliated societies and organisations such as the Orange Lodge.[65]

With the above in mind, it is not surprising, as Belchem notes, that Liverpool FC were criticised in the socialist press for not allowing a pre-match collection in aid of the striking (and starving) Dublin transport workers.[66]

With this going on during the development stage of both clubs, how could supporters not be influenced?

As Roberts observes, the origins of Everton's Catholic support lie in the late 19th century when Dr Baxter [who we mentioned earlier], a prominent Catholic doctor and a leading light in the Catholic community, joined the Everton board. He brought with him the thousands of Irish Catholic families from the Scotland Road area who duly became Everton supporters.[67]

The Catholic dimension was maintained in various

ways at Everton, not least in the 1950s when the core of the Everton team hailed from the Republic of Ireland. Everton forged connections with clubs in Ireland such as Dundalk and Dublin teams Shamrock Rovers and Shelbourne.[68]

Ex-player Tommy Eglington emphasised Everton's connection with Éire in recalling his playing days: "Back in the fifties, Everton was the team in Ireland. We had a number of Irish players then and the boats would be full of fans coming over every Friday night to watch us."[69]

A consequence of this was Everton were the first English club to have a supporters' association set up in Ireland, becoming the first example of a club with a large 'overseas' support as hundreds of Irishmen travelled to Liverpool for Everton games.[70] This led the Labour MP for Walton, the late Eric Heffer, to explain in his biography *Never a Yes Man* that he was obliged to lean towards Everton because, as the Catholic team, it was closer to his own High Anglicanism than the more Orange-tinged Protestantism of Liverpool FC.[71]

Corbett said that "Everton possessed so many Irish players in the mid-1950s that there was a contemporaneous joke that twenty minutes could pass without a Protestant touching the ball."[72] Added to this is the common knowledge that there were always Catholic priests in the stands at Goodison in the 1950s.

By contrast, as Kennedy describes, Ireland was a virtually untapped market for Liverpool FC until the end of the 20th century.[73] Throughout this project I forever saw Irish Reds claiming they support the club because of the history of the club and city. Not sure how that one works to be honest. Everton yes, Liverpool no. Belfast yes, Dublin no.

Emphasising this point, modern-day Orange Lodge Grand Master Ron Bather says:

"Primarily Liverpool was a very Protestant football club. The initial teams [...] when it was formed, you had to be a Protestant to be a player. Virtually all the initial team that played for Liverpool were all Scottish Presbyterian religion. If you go back to the 1920s and 30s Liverpool was considered the Protestant team and Everton the Catholic."[74]

In addition to Bather, Lodge Master and Liverpool fan, Dave Hughes, suggests that: "The Orange connection between the Orange Institution and Liverpool Football Club was very, very firm at one time."[75]

Today, there is and has not been any sectarianism between Liverpool's big two for decades. However, and it's only a theory, I believe the seeds of the denial of Heysel were formed in the make-up of the original board. The report sent to UEFA in 1985 was basically the Orange rallying cry of "No Surrender" wrapped up in a document. And the treatment of Patrice Evra in 2011-12 by LFC management and huge numbers of their fanbase only cements my belief further. Roots will always be roots and LFC's will always be Orange.

One final thought, it would be brilliant if others could add to the debate on the *Forgotten Tragedy*.

EPILOGUE

PAUL FRY

On 29 May each year, Paul reflects that it was an important day in his life. He had witnessed something historic that was possibly the start of a turning point in the game he was brought up with and loved. He still feels firm in his belief of what he's been convinced of all along: that it was Liverpool fans that kicked it off, but the Juventus fans down the other end didn't need any encouragement at all. In terms of guilt, he thinks it should be spread between the fans, the police and the people who organised it, because there were warnings not to play it at that stadium. He's certain the Belgian FA should have said sorry.

EAMONN MCCABE

The hardest thing I did—I was on Alan Green on the BBC, and he was doing a 30th anniversary. And he got me on and I'm talking about it quite dispassionately, and then suddenly, I heard the soundtrack and then I was in tears. I was right back, and I think I dealt with it over the years, because when you are distanced through a lens, you are distanced from it. It was the soundtrack, the irony of me being a photographer. It was the soundtrack which brought it all up. That's where all the emotion really came out. I know it's daft that 30-odd years later, but it's funny what triggers these things. And I've looked at the pictures over the years and they're on the screen, and in the *Britain in Focus* [a BBC documentary] they used some quite hard-hitting pictures, but they're a bit grainy and out of focus, but it still works.

I won news photographer of the year for that. I wish I never had. I like winning awards, but... Looking back on my career, that was '85, and I left the *Observer* in '88 after the Seoul Olympics, but I thought 'if that's football you can have it'. It's the highlight and lowlight of my life. It's where I went for one of the biggest nights of sport. I went as a sports photographer and came home as a news photographer, and that was really sad.

MYSELF

This project was all about getting something off my chest. I have to admit, I feel better for it. I just hope for anyone who has taken the time to read this, you have learnt something about the disaster that you didn't know before. Next for me is to write a follow-up, which will cover the themes I mentioned in the introduction. Wherever you are in the world, I'd just like to take this opportunity to thank you for reading. Just one final thing. I know that at this stage I could and maybe should print a list of the people who died in Brussels, but to be honest I don't think I have earned the right to do that at this stage. Basically, nobody in our city has.

BIBLIOGRAPHY

Archives

Eric Heffer Papers. Heysel Stadium Tragedy 1985-1989. Manchester People's Museum.

National Archives. Kew Gardens London.

Papers of the Popplewell Inquiry into Crowd Safety at Sports Grounds. Bradford University.

Newspapers, Magazines and Periodicals

Daily Express
Daily Mail
Daily Mirror
Daily Post
Daily Telegraph
Financial Times
The Guardian
The Independent
The International Herald Tribune
Liverpool Echo
London Evening Standard
Mail on Sunday

Newsweek
New Civil Engineer
New Society
New Statesman
Soccer & Society
The Spectator
Sport in Society
Sports Illustrated
Sunday Mirror
The Sunday Times
Today
Tribune
The Washington Post

Reports

Committee of Inquiry into Crowd Safety and Control at Sports Grounds Final Report. 1986.

Heysel Stadium Brussels, European Cup Final, Wednesday, 29th May 1985 General Appraisal of Ground Conditions. Report of the City [Liverpool] Building Surveyor.

Parliamentary Committee of Enquiry. House of Representatives 1984–85 Session.

Safety at Sports Grounds Preliminary Report from [London] Officers Visiting the Heysel Stadium in Brussels.

Books and Articles

Adang, Otto M.J. "International police co-operation around football matches: Euro 2000 case study." (2009).

Apostolos, Kalafatis. "Assessing the Football Banning Orders in the light of s.14A(2) Football Spectators Act 1989." (Date Unknown).

Benkwitz, Adam A. & Gyozo Molnar. "Interpreting and

exploring football fan rivalries: an overview." Soccer & Society. (2012).

Billig, Michael. "Henri Tajfel's 'Cognitive aspects of prejudice' and the psychology of bigotry." British Journal of Social Psychology, Vol 41, (2002): 171-188.

Brechbühl, Alain, Annemarie Schumacher Dimech, Oliver N. Schmid, & Roland Seiler. Escalation vs. non-escalation of fan violence in football? Narratives from ultra-fans, police officers and security employees. Sport in Society. (2016).

Caremani, Francesco. Heysel: The Truth. Turin: Bradipolibi Editore, 2015.

Challenger, Rose, Chris W. Clegg, Mark A. Robinson, & Mark Leigh. Understanding Crowd Behaviours Volume 1 – Practical Guidance and Lessons. The Stationery Office, 2010.

Challenger, Rose, Chris W. Clegg, Mark A. Robinson, & Mark Leigh. Understanding Crowd Behaviours Volume 2 – Supporting Theory and Evidence. The Stationery Office, 2010.

Cleland, Jamie & Ellis Cashmore. "Football Fans' Views of Violence in British Football: Evidence of a Sanitized and Gentrified Culture." Journal of Sport and Social Issues Vol. 40(2) (2016): 124–142.

Cocking, Chris. "Crowd Flight in Response to Police Dispersal Techniques: A Momentary Lapse of Reason?" Journal of Investigative Psychology and Offender Profiling. (2013).

Croker, Ted. The First Voice You Will Hear Is.... London: Collins, 1987.

Dart, Jon. "Confessional tales from former football hooligans: a nostalgic, narcissistic, wallow in football violence." Soccer & Society (Jan 2008): 42–55.

De Vries, Peter, Mirjam Galetzka, & Jan M Gutteling. "Persuasion in the wild: Communication, technology, and event safety." (2014).

Drury, John & Clifford Stott. "Contextualising the crowd in contemporary social science." Contemporary Social Science 6, no. 3 (2011): 275-288.

Drury, John, Stephen Reicher & Clifford Stott. "The Psychology of Collective Action: Crowds and Change." To appear in In Culture and Social Change: Transforming Society through the Power of Ideas, Edited by Brady Wagoner, Eric Jensen, Julian A. Oldmeadow. (2009).

Drury, John. "Crowd psychology". In T. Teo (Ed.), Encyclopaedia of Critical Psychology (2014): 341-344.

Drury, John. "Collective Resilience in Mass Emergencies and Disasters: A Social Identity Model." Psychology Press. (2012).

Drury, John, Chris Cocking, & Stephen Reicher. "Every man for himself - or for the group? How crowd solidarity can arise in an emergency: An interview study of disaster survivors." (Date Unknown).

Drury, John & Chris Cocking. The mass psychology of disasters and emergency evacuations: A research report and implications for practice. (2007).

Drury, John & Stephen Reicher. "Collective Psychological Empowerment as a Model of Social Change: Researching Crowds and Power." Journal of Social Issues, Vol. 65, No. 4, (2009): 707—725.

Drury, John, Stephen Reicher, & Clifford Stott. "The psychology of collective action: Crowds and Change Culture and social change: Transforming society through the power of ideas." Edited by Brady Wagoner, Eric Jensen and Julian Oldmeadow. (2009).

Drury, John, Stephen Reicher, & Clifford Stott. "The

Psychology of Collective Action: Crowds and Change in Culture and social change: Transforming society through the power of ideas." Edited by Brady Wagoner, Eric Jensen and Julian Oldmeadow. (2009).

Drury, John & Stephen Reicher. "Collective Psychological Empowerment as a Model of Social Change: Researching Crowds and Power." Journal of Social Issues, Vol. 65, No. 4, (2009): 707—725.

Dunleavy, Cameron. "How did the Development of Religious Sectarianism and Irish Nationalism Shape Liverpool's Political Environment from 1836 to 1939?" (Date Unknown).

Dunning, Eric, Joseph Maguire, Patrick J. Murphy & John P. Williams. "The social roots of football hooligan violence." Leisure Studies 1, no. 2 (1982): 139–156.

Dunning, Eric. "Towards a Sociological Understanding of Football Hooliganism as a World Phenomenon." European Journal on Criminal Policy and Research 8, (2000): 141–162.

Evans, R & M. Rowe "For Club and Country: Taking Football Disorder. Abroad." Soccer & Society, 3:1, (2002): 37-53.

Festinger, Leon, Albert Pepitone and Theodore Mead Newcomb. "Some consequences of deindividuation in a group." Journal of abnormal psychology 47 (1952): 382–9.

Finucane, Patrick. A case study of football hooliganism in Belgium. (2016).

Foot, John. Calcio: A History of Italian Football. London: Harper Perennial, 2007.

Fremont-Barnes, Gregory. The Boer War 1899-1902. Oxford: Osprey Publishing, 2003.

Freud, Sigmund. Group Psychology and the Analysis of

the Ego. Vienna: Internationaler Psychoanalytischer Verlag, 1921.

Frosdick, Steve. Organisational Structure, Culture and Attitudes to Risk in the British Stadia Safety Industry. Basil Blackwell Ltd, 1995.

Frosdick, Steve. "Pompey v Saints: A Case Study in Crowd Segregation." International Journal of Police Science & Management 7, no. 3 (2005): 149–159.

Frosdick, Steve & Robert Newton. "The Nature and Extent of Football Hooliganism in England and Wales." Soccer and Society Vol. 7, No. 4, (December 2006): 403–422.

Gibbons, Tom, Kevin Dixon, & Stuart Braye. "The way it was' an account of soccer violence in the 1980s.'" Soccer & Society Vol. 9, No. 1, (2008): 28–41.

Giulianotti, Richard. "Supporters. Followers, Fans, and Flaneurs: A Taxonomy of Spectator Identities in Football." Journal of Sport & Social Issues, Volume 26, No. 1, (2002): 25-46.

Hadler, Theodore. "The Crowd Science. Understanding the Socio-Psychological Behaviour Pattern of Individuals in a Group." (Date Unknown).

Harrison, Michael & Jane Adlard: "Intra-police communication in public order police management." Policing and Society. (2016).

Hogg, Michael A, & Graham M. Vaughan. Social Psychology (Sixth Edition). London: Pearson Education Limited, 2011.

Hoggett, James & Clifford Stott. "Crowd psychology, public order police training and the policing of football crowds." Policing-an International Journal of Police Strategies & Management 33, no. 2 (2010): 218-235.

Hoggett, J & Clifford Stott. "The role of crowd theory in

determining the use of force in public order policing." Policing and Society. (2010).

James, Mark. & Geoff Pearson. "30 Years of Hurt: The Evolution of Civil Preventive Orders, Hybrid Law, and the Emergence of the Super-Football Banning Order." Public Law, No. 1: (2018): 44-61.

James, Mark and Geoff Pearson. "Public order and the rebalancing of football fans' rights: Legal problems with pre-emptive policing strategies and banning orders." Public Law. (2015): 458-475.

Jeffery, David. "The Strange Death of Tory Liverpool: Conservative electoral decline in Liverpool, 1945-1996." British Politics 12 (2017): 386–407.

Johnes, Martin. "'Heads in the Sand': Football, Politics and Crowd Disasters in Twentieth Century Britain." Soccer & Society 5, no. 2 (2004): 134–151.

Kennedy, David. "Introduction." Soccer & Society, 12:4, (2011): 471-473.

Kennedy, David. "In the beginning God created Everton." Soccer & Society, 12:4, (2011): 481-490.

Kennedy, David. "Houlding and the rise of factionalism." Soccer & Society, 12:4, (2011): 491-496.

Kennedy, David. "1892: the coup de grace against Houlding." Soccer & Society, 12:4, (2011): 497-509.

Kennedy, David. "Moonbeams and baying dogs: football and Liverpool politics." Soccer & Society, 12:4, (2011): 510-522.

Kennedy, David. "And then there were two: Everton and Liverpool football clubs, 1892–1902." Soccer & Society, 12:4, (2011): 523-537.

Kennedy, David. "Everton and Liverpool in the post-Houlding era." Soccer & Society, 12:4, (2011): 538-551.

Kennedy, David. "Red and blue and orange and green?"

Soccer & Society, 12:4, (2011): 552-564.

Kennedy, David. "Conclusion." Soccer & Society, 12:4, (2011): 565-567.

Kennedy, David. Merseyside's Old Firm? The Sectarian Roots of Everton and Liverpool Football Clubs. Independently published, 2017.

King, Anthony. Violent pasts: collective memory and football hooliganism. The Editorial Board of The Sociological Review. (2001).

Le Bon, Gustave. The Crowd: A Study of the Popular Mind. 1896.

MacRaild, Donald M. Faith, Fraternity & Fighting: The Orange Order and Irish Migrants In Northern England, C.1850-1920. Liverpool: Liverpool University Press, 2009.

Mallinson, Allan. The Making of the British Army. London: Bantam, 2009.

Marsh, Peter, Kerry Fox, G. Carnibella, J. McCann & J. Marsh. Football Violence in Europe: A Report to the Amsterdam Group. Social Issues Research Centre, 1996.

Mason, Tony. "The Blues and Reds: A History of Liverpool and Everton Football Clubs." The History Society of Lancashire and Cheshire 13 (1985): 107– 128.

McDougall, William. The Group Mind. Cambridge: Cambridge University Press, 1921.

Millward, Peter. "Glasgow Rangers Supporters in the City of Manchester: The Degeneration of a 'Fan Party' into a 'Hooligan Riot'." International Review for the Sociology of Sport 44, no. 4 (2009): 381–398.

Neville, Fergus & Stephen Reicher. "Contemporary Social Science: The experience of collective participation: shared identity, relatedness and emotionality." (2011).

Ostrowsky, Michael K. "Sports Fans, Alcohol Use, and Violent Behavior: A Sociological Review." (2016).

Pearson, Geoff. The researcher as hooligan: where 'participant' observation means breaking the law. International Journal of Social Research Methodology Vol. 12, No. 3, (2009): 243–255.

Pearson, Geoff & Arianna Sale. "'On the Lash' – revisiting the effectiveness of alcohol controls at football matches." Policing and Society 21, no. 1 (2011): 150–166.

Pearson, Geoff. "An ethnography of English football fans Cans, cops and carnival." Manchester University Press. (2012).

Pearson, Geoff, in Alexender Schwell, Nina Szogs, Malgorzata Kowalska, and Michal Buchowski, (editors). New Ethnographies of Football in Europe. People, Passions, Politics. Palgrave MacMillan. (2015).

Pearson, Geoff & Clifford Stott."Farewell to the Hooligan? Modern Developments in Football Crowd Management." Critical Issues in Global Sport Management. Routledge. (2016).

Pearson, Geoffrey. Hooligan: A history of respectable fears. The MacMillan Press Limited, 1983.

Poulton, Emma. "English Media Representation of Football-related Disorder: 'Brutal, Short-hand and Simplifying'?" Sport in Society: Cultures, Commerce, Media, Politics. (2005).

Prati, Gabriele & Luca Pietrantoni. "Elaborating the police perspective: The role of perceptions and experience in the explanation of crowd conflict." *European Journal of Social Psychology* 39, no. 6 (2009): 991-1001.

Ransford, Oliver. The Battle of Spion Kop. London: John Murray, 1971.

Raineri, Aldo. "Crowd science – A planning approach to safety at mass gatherings and events." (2016).

Redhead, Steve. Hit and Tell: A Review Essay on the

Soccer Hooligan Memoir. Soccer and Society, vol. 5, No. 3 (2004): 392–403.

Redhead, Steve and Geoff Pearson. "A commentary on 'Little Hooliganz: The Inside Story of Glamouros lads, Football Hooligans and Post-Subculturalism'." Entertainment and sports Law Journal 8(2) (2010).

Reicher, Stephen, Clifford Stott, John Drury, Otto Adang, Patrick D. J. Cronin & Andrew G. Livingstone. "Knowledge-based public order policing: Principles and Practice." Policing-an International Journal of Police Strategies and Management 1, no. 4 (2007): 403–415.

Roberts, Keith. "The rise and fall of Liverpool sectarianism: An investigation into the decline of sectarian antagonism on Merseyside." PhD diss., University of Liverpool, 2015.

Robins, Dave and Philip Cohen. Knuckle Sandwich: Growing Up in the Working-Class City. London: Penguin, 1978.

Rowland, Chris. From Where I was Standing. GPFR Publishing, 2009.

Rudd, Chris. "The aftermath of Heysel: The 1985 Belgian election." West European Politics 9, no. 2 (1986): 282–288.

Spaaij, Ramón. Understanding Football: A Comparison of Six European Football Clubs. Amsterdam University Press, (2006).

Spaaij, Ramón. "Men Like Us, Boys Like Them Violence, Masculinity, and Collective Identity in Football Hooliganism." Journal of Sport & Social Issues Volume 32 Number 4 (2008): 369-392.

Stott, Clifford, Paul Hutchison & John Drury. "'Hooligans' abroad? Inter-group dynamics, social identity, and participation in collective 'disorder' at the 1998 World Cup

Finals." The British journal of social psychology 40, no. 3 (2001): 359–84.

Stott, Clifford, Otto Adang, Andrew Livingstone, & Martina Schreiber. "Tackling Football Hooliganism." A Quantitative Study of Public Order, Policing and Crowd Psychology. Psychology, Public Policy, and Law Vol. 14, No. 2, (2008): 115–141.

Stott, Clifford, James Hoggett & Geoff Pearson. "Keeping the Peace' Social Identity, Procedural Justice and the Policing of Football Crowds. Brit. J. Criminol. 52, (2012): 381–399.

Suttles, Gerald D. The Social Order of the Slum. Chicago: University of Chicago Press, 1970.

Tajfel, Henri, M. G. Billig, R. P. Bundy & Claude Flament. "Social Categorisation and Intergroup Behaviour." European Journal of Social Psychology 1, no. 2 (1971): 149–178.

Tajfel, Henri. "Social Psychology of Intergroup Relations." Annual Review of Psychology 33 (1982): 1–39.

Taylor, Ian. "Putting the Boot into a Working-Class Sport: British Soccer After Bradford and Brussels." Sociology of Sport Journal. (1987): 171-191.

Waller, P. J. Democracy & Sectarianism: A political and social history of Liverpool 1868–1939. Liverpool: Liverpool University Press, 1981.

Wannel, Gary. "Football, crowd behaviour and the press." Media, Culture and Society (1979): 327-342.

Williams, John. "Fans: Consumers, Hooligans and Activists." In Steen, R, Novick, J & H. Richards. (eds). The Cambridge Companion to Football. (2013): 198-212.

Young, Kevin. "The Killing Field": Themes in Mass Media Responses to the Heysel Stadium Riot.'" International Review for the Sociology of Sport. (1986).

INDEX

NOTES

Introduction

1. Tom Mullen, "Heysel disaster: English football's forgotten tragedy?" *BBC News*, May 29, 2019. http://www.bbc.com/news/uk-england-merseyside-32898612.

2. Nick Miller. "Vox in the Box: Tony Evans," *The Set Pieces*, 2016. https://thesetpieces.com/interviews/vox-in-the-box-tony-evans/.

3. Papers re Heysel Football Disaster, 1985–1989, GB 394 ESH, LP/ESH/08, Papers of Eric Heffer, Labour History Archive and Study Centre, Manchester (hereafter cited as Heysel, Papers of Eric Heffer).

4. Heysel, Papers of Eric Heffer.

5. Chris Tyrrell, (@tizzthered), tweet, Jan 6, 2018, https://twitter.com/tizzthered/status/949737766547542017.

6. Dan Fieldsend, "Witnessing Liverpool's Reclamation of Shankly's Vision – A front-row view," *Football Paradise*, June 4, 2018. https://www.footballparadise.com/liverpool-scouse-republic/.

7. Stephen Walmsley, "Liverpool In Kiev: There Are Places I'll Remember All My Life," *The Anfield Wrap*, June 1, 2018. https://www.theanfieldwrap.com/2018/06/liverpool-kiev-places-ill-remember-life/.

8. Rob Gutmann, "Us and them – time to pull up the drawbridge," *The Anfield Wrap*, February 14, 2012, *Internet Archive*, https://web.archive.org/web/20130222091755/https://www.theanfieldwrap.com/2012/02/us-and-them-time-to-pull-up-the-drawbridge/.

9. Gutmann, "Us and them."

10. Gutmann, "Us and them."

11. S. Montague, "Shoddy Stadium behind riot death toll," *New Civil Engineer*, June 6, 1985.

12. Montague, "Shoddy Stadium."

13. Jamie Jackson, "Heysel: The Witnesses' Stories," *The Guardian*, April 3, 2005, https://www.theguardian.com/football/2005/apr/03/newsstory.sport.

14. The Anfield Wrap, "Heysel 30 Years: Oh God, what have we done," *The Anfield Wrap*, May 28, 2015. https://www.theanfieldwrap.com/2015/05/heysel-30-years-oh-god-what-have-we-done/.

15. Paul Callen, "Shame," *Daily Mirror*, May 30, 1985.

16. Dennis Newson, *Britain to hand over soccer thugs*, 25 April 1986, HO 291/2060, Prisons and Prisoners Repatriation and Deportation Football Hooliganism, National Archives, London.

17. Francesco Caremani, *Heysel: The Truth* (Turin: Bradipolibi Editore, 2015).

18. Off the Ball, ""Heysel is never ever mentioned". Mark Lawrenson recalls night of the 1985 stadium disaster," April 15, 2021, YouTube video, https://www.youtube.com/watch?v=YXZfMJEmN_g.

19. Off the Ball, "Heysel is never ever mentioned."

20. Rob Steen, "Interwoven tragedies: Hillsborough, Heysel and Denial," *Sport in Society* 19, no. 2 (2016).

1. A Shared Upbringing

1. *The Explosive 80s: How Heysel Changed Football*, Channel 4, May 23, 2005, television broadcast.

2. John Keith, host "A-Z of Merseyside Football," *Radio City Talk* (podcast), June 15, 2017, https://audioboom.com/posts/6018685-a-to-z-of-merseyside-football-d-part-03.

3. Fabio Chisari, "'The Cursed Cup': Italian Responses to the 1985 Heysel Disaster," *Soccer & Society* 5, no. 2 (2007).

4. "Witness: The Heysel Stadium Disaster," *BBC World Service*, May 29, 2015, http://www.bbc.co.uk/programmes/p02ryjg5.

5. Peter Gruner and Emma Lee-Potter, "I'm ashamed to be from Liverpool," *London Evening Standard*, May 30, 1985.

6. "Witness: The Heysel Stadium Disaster."

7. Neil Atkinson and Gareth Roberts, hosts, "Podcast: Heysel 30 Years," *The Anfield Wrap*, May 28, 2015, https://www.theanfieldwrap.com/2015/05/podcast-heysel-30-years/.

8. Atkinson and Roberts, "Podcast: Heysel 30 Years."

9. Atkinson and Roberts, "Podcast: Heysel 30 Years."

10. Atkinson and Roberts, "Podcast: Heysel 30 Years."

11. Eric Dunning, J.A Maguire, P.J. Murphy, & John Williams. "The Social Roots of Football Hooligan Violence." *Leisure Studies*, 1:2, (1982): 139-156.

12. Dave Robins and Philip Cohen, *Knuckle Sandwich: Growing Up in the Working-Class City* (London: Penguin, 1978).

13. W.I. McGregor, *European Cup Final*, British Transport Police, May 5, 1985.

14. Gerald D. Suttles, *The Social Order of the Slum* (Chicago: University of Chicago Press, 1970).

15. Robins and Cohen, *Knuckle Sandwich*.

2. Us and Them

1. Gustave Le Bon, *The Crowd: A Study of the Popular Mind* (1896).
2. "Oh God forgive me for what have I have done," *Liverpool Echo*, June 11, 1985.
3. *Liverpool Echo*, "Oh God forgive me."
4. Le Bon, *The Crowd*.
5. Gary Slutkin, "Gary Slutkin: rioting is a disease spread from person to person – the key is to stop the infection," *The Guardian*, 14 August, 2011, https://www.theguardian.com/uk/2011/aug/14/rioting-disease-spread-from-person-to-person.
6. Slutkin, "Rioting is a disease."
7. The Anfield Wrap, "Oh God, what have we done."
8. Le Bon, *The Crowd*.
9. Sigmund Freud, *Group Psychology and the Analysis of the Ego* (Vienna: Internationaler Psychoanalytischer Verlag, 1921).
10. Michael A. Hogg and Graham M. Vaughan, *Social Psychology* (*Sixth Edition*) (London: Pearson Education Limited, 2011).
11. *Liverpool Echo*, "Oh God forgive me."
12. The Anfield Wrap, "Oh God, what have we done."
13. Hogg and Vaughan, *Social Psychology*.
14. The Anfield Wrap, "Oh God, what have we done."
15. The Anfield Wrap, "Oh God, what have we done."
16. The Anfield Wrap, "Oh God, what have we done."
17. The Anfield Wrap, "Oh God, what have we done."
18. The Anfield Wrap, "Oh God, what have we done."
19. William McDougall, *The Group Mind* (Cambridge: Cambridge University Press, 1921).
20. "Was a match worth it?" *Liverpool Echo*. May 30, 1985.
21. Leon Festinger, Albert Pepitone and Theodore Mead Newcomb, "Some consequences of deindividuation in a group," *Journal of abnormal psychology* 47 (Jan 1952).
22. Rose Shepherd, Christopher Clegg and Mark Robinson, *Understanding Crowd Behaviours, Volume 2: Supporting Theory and Evidence* (Norwich: The Stationery Office, 2010).
23. Stephen Reicher et al., "Knowledge-based public order policing: Principles and Practice," *Policing-an International Journal of Police Strategies and Management* 1, no. 4 (2007).
24. Atkinson and Roberts, "Podcast: Heysel 30 Years."
25. "London," *The Real Football Factories*, created by Peter Day, Bravo, May 6, 2006, television broadcast.
26. Henri Tajfel, "Social Psychology of Intergroup Relations," *Annual Review of Psychology* 33 (1982).
27. Tajfel, "Intergroup Relations."
28. Hogg and Vaughan, *Social Psychology*.

29. David Shariatmadari, "A real-life Lord of the Flies: The troubling legacy of the Robbers Cave experiment," *The Guardian*, April 16, 2018, https://www.theguardian.com/science/2018/apr/16/a-real-life-lord-of-the-flies-the-troubling-legacy-of-the-robbers-cave-experiment.

30. Hogg and Vaughan, *Social Psychology*.

31. Martin Randall, "From the first provocation," *Daily Post*, June 17 1985.

3. Klee vs Kandinsky

1. Henri Tajfel et al., "Social Categorisation and Intergroup Behaviour," *European Journal of Social Psychology* 1, no. 2 (1971).

2. Tajfel et al., "Social Categorisation."

3. Tajfel et al., "Social Categorisation."

4. Tajfel et al., "Social Categorisation."

5. Tajfel, "Intergroup Relations."

6. Hogg and Vaughan, *Social Psychology*.

7. Michael Billig, *Henri Tajfel's 'Cognitive aspects of prejudice' and the psychology bigotry,"* in British Journal of Social Psychology, Vol 41 (2002): 171-188.

8. Reicher et al., "Knowledge-Based Public Order Policing."

9. Reicher et al., "Knowledge-Based Public Order Policing."

10. John Drury and Clifford Stott, "Contextualising the crowd in contemporary social science," *Contemporary Social Science* 6, no. 3 (2011).

11. Drury and Stott, "Contextualising the crowd."

12. John Drury, Stephen D. Reicher and Clifford Stott, "The Psychology of Collective Action: Crowds and Change," To appear in *Culture and Social Change: Transforming Society through the Power of Ideas*, ed. Brady Wagoner, Eric Jensen, Julian A. Oldmeadow (2009).

13. Clifford Stott, Paul Hutchison and John Drury, "'Hooligans' abroad? Inter-group dynamics, social identity, and participation in collective 'disorder' at the 1998 World Cup Finals," *The British journal of social psychology* 40, no. 3 (2001).

14. Tom Rostance, "England v Tunisia: The story of the trouble at France 98," *BBC News*, June 17, 2018, https://www.bbc.com/sport/football/43217083.

15. Rostance, "England v Tunisia."

16. Rostance, "England v Tunisia."

17. Stott, Hutchison and Drury, "'Hooligans' abroad?"

18. Stott, Hutchison and Drury, "'Hooligans' abroad?"

4. "We Have Come To Expect It from English People."

1. Dunning et al., "Football hooligan violence."
2. Dunning et al., "Football hooligan violence."
3. Marsh et al., *Football Violence in Europe.*
4. Marsh et al., *Football Violence in Europe.*
5. Marsh et al., *Football Violence in Europe.*
6. Rob Steen, "Sensationalists United? Football hooliganism and the English press," *Sport in Society* 19, no. 2 (2016).
7. Steen, "Sensationalists United?"
8. Steen, "Sensationalists United?"
9. Steen, "Sensationalists United?"
10. "Blackpool FC terrace murder victim remembered," *BBC News,* August 23, 2014, https://www.bbc.com/news/uk-england-lancashire-28888465.
11. *BBC,* "Terrace murder victim remembered."
12. Steen, "Sensationalists United?"
13. Steen, "Sensationalists United?"
14. Dunning et al., "Football hooligan violence."
15. Marsh et al., *Football Violence in Europe.*
16. comegetsome, "Tottenham Hooligans rioting against Feyenoord," May 28, 2010, YouTube video, https://www.youtube.com/watch?v=_8nZuW9EM7w.
17. comegetsome, "Tottenham Hooligans."
18. comegetsome, "Tottenham Hooligans."
19. Steen, "Sensationalists United?"
20. Austin Dawkins, "Shame of Paris – 1975 Revisited," *The Scratching Shed,* May 28, 2015, http://www.thescratchingshed.com/2015/05/shame-of-paris-1975-revisited/.
21. Dawkins, "Shame of Paris."
22. WOODDDDDDDDYALUFC, "Duncan McKenzie On 1975 European Cup Final Robbery," February 9, 2010, YouTube video, https://www.youtube.com/watch?v=g9G6_kJYh6o.
23. Ted Croker, *The First Voice You Will Hear Is...* (London: Collins, 1987).
24. Croker, *The First Voice.*
25. "England fans rampage in Luxembourg," *BBC On This Day,* http://news.bbc.co.uk/onthisday/hi/dates/stories/november/16/newsid_2540000/2540025.stm.
26. Terrace Retro 3, "Football Hooligans – Luxembourg v England," November 25, 2014, YouTube video, https://www.youtube.com/watch?v=4Y_S1IJvBlc.
27. *BBC On This Day,* "England fans rampage."

28. Terrace Retro 3, "Football Hooligans."
29. Terrace Retro 3, "Football Hooligans."
30. "Echo Comment," *Liverpool Echo*, May 30, 1985.
31. Brian Roberts, "Rioting Reds Fans Banned by Hotels," *Liverpool Echo*, May 26, 1981.
32. Roberts, "Rioting Reds."
33. Roberts, "Rioting Reds."
34. Roberts, "Rioting Reds."
35. Roberts, "Rioting Reds."
36. Roberts, "Rioting Reds."
37. Roberts, "Rioting Reds."
38. Roberts, "Rioting Reds."
39. Roberts, "Rioting Reds."
40. Ian Herbert, "Liverpool and Manchester United: A feud too far," *The Independent*, September 22, 2012, http://www.independent.co.uk/ sport/football/premier-league/liverpool-and-manchester-united-a-feud-too-far-8163756.html.
41. Herbert, "Liverpool and Manchester United."
42. Tony. Evans, "End of the Innocence," *Well Red*, December 24, 2010, https://issuu.com/robbohuyton/docs/wellredmagazine3/37
43. The Anfield Wrap, "The streets around Goodison were like a war zone. *that* FA Cup semi-final in 1985,", October 2017.
44. Evans, "End of the Innocence."

5. Wasted Opportunities

1. Lewis @lewispringle, tweet, March 7, 2018, 9:29 p.m., https://twitter. com/lewispringle/status/971135690741374977.
2. Lewis @lewispringle, tweet.
3. Martin Johnes, "'Heads in the Sand': Football, Politics and Crowd Disasters in Twentieth Century Britain," *Soccer & Society* 5, no. 2 (2004).
4. Johnes, "'Heads in the Sand'."
5. Oliver Popplewell, *Committee of Inquiry into Crowd Safety and Control at Sports Grounds Final Report* (London: Her Majesty's Stationery Office, 1986).
6. Johnes, "'Heads in the Sand'."
7. Johnes, "'Heads in the Sand'."
8. Popplewell, *Inquiry into Crowd Safety.*
9. Thomas Molloy and Seamus McDonnell, "Burnden Park Disaster: The FA Cup game that continued with 33 people dead at the side of the pitch," *Manchester Evening News*, March 9, 2021, https://www. manchestereveningnews.co.uk/news/burnden-park-disaster-fa-cup-19990589.

10. Johnes, "'Heads in the Sand'."
11. Molloy and McDonnell, "Burnden Park Disaster."
12. Molloy and McDonnell, "Burnden Park Disaster."
13. Popplewell, *Inquiry into Crowd Safety.*
14. Popplewell, *Inquiry into Crowd Safety.*
15. Popplewell, *Inquiry into Crowd Safety.*
16. Popplewell, *Inquiry into Crowd Safety.*
17. Popplewell, *Inquiry into Crowd Safety.*
18. Popplewell, *Inquiry into Crowd Safety.*
19. Popplewell, *Inquiry into Crowd Safety.*
20. Popplewell, *Inquiry into Crowd Safety.*
21. Popplewell, *Inquiry into Crowd Safety.*
22. Popplewell, *Inquiry into Crowd Safety.*
23. Popplewell, *Inquiry into Crowd Safety.*
24. Popplewell, *Inquiry into Crowd Safety.*
25. Popplewell, *Inquiry into Crowd Safety.*
26. Popplewell, *Inquiry into Crowd Safety.*
27. Popplewell, *Inquiry into Crowd Safety.*
28. Popplewell, *Inquiry into Crowd Safety.*
29. Record of proceedings of a session of the full senate, June 14, 1985.
30. Popplewell, *Inquiry into Crowd Safety.*
31. Popplewell, *Inquiry into Crowd Safety.*
32. Popplewell, *Inquiry into Crowd Safety.*
33. "F Troop, Treatment and the Half-Way Line," *Panorama*, directed by Mike Catherwood, BBC1, November 14, 1977, television broadcast.
34. "F Troop, Treatment and the Half-Way Line."
35. "F Troop, Treatment and the Half-Way Line."
36. Record of proceedings of a session of the full senate, June 14, 1985.

6. A Violent Nation

1. Charles Glass, "Englishmen Abroad," *The Spectator*, June 8, 1985.
2. Allan Mallinson, *The Making of the British Army* (London: Bantam, 2009).
3. Glass, "Englishmen Abroad."
4. Rogan Taylor, "The Empire Strikes Back," *Time Magazine*, June 19, 2000, http://content.time.com/time/world/article/0,8599,2051233,00.html.
5. Taylor, "The Empire Strikes Back."
6. Taylor, "The Empire Strikes Back."
7. Heysel, Papers of Eric Heffer.
8. The PakoAyestaran Fanclub, post to "They call us murderers ...a blog," *Red and White Kop*, December 11, 2006, https://www.redandwhitekop.com/forum/index.php?topic=143565.80.

9. Patrick Wintour, "Straw Blames the empire," *The Guardian*, July 17, 2000, https://www.theguardian.com/politics/2000/jul/17/uk.race.

10. Gregory Fremont-Barnes, *The Boer War 1899-1902* (Oxford: Osprey Publishing, 2003).

11. Fremont-Barnes, *The Boer War*.

12. Fremont-Barnes, *The Boer War*.

13. Fransjohan Pretorious, "The Boer War," *BBC History*, last updated March 29, 2011, https://www.bbc.co.uk/history/british/victorians/boer_wars_01.shtml.

14. Fremont-Barnes, *The Boer War*.

15. The British Newspaper Archive.

16. The British Newspaper Archive.

17. Oliver Ransford, *The Battle of Spion Kop* (London: John Murray, 1971).

18. Ransford, *Spion Kop*.

19. Jay McKenna, *"A great change of pace,"* The Anfield Wrap. May 12, 2016.

20. Giles Foden, "Bringing it all back home," *The Guardian*, September 4, 1999, https://www.theguardian.com/books/1999/sep/04/books.guardianreview?CMP=share_btn_link.

21. Foden, "Bringing it all back home."

22. Foden, "Bringing it all back home."

23. Ian Cobain, "Secret Wars," *The Guardian,* September 8, 2016, https://www.theguardian.com/uk-news/2016/sep/08/britains-secret-wars-oman.

24. Mallinson, *The British Army*.

25. Cobain, "Secret Wars."

26. Cobain, "Secret Wars."

27. Mallinson, *The British Army*.

28. Mallinson, *The British Army*.

7. Rome

1. The Anfield Wrap, "Heysel 30 Years: When in Rome," *The Anfield Wrap,* May 28, 2015, https://www.theanfieldwrap.com/2015/05/heysel-30-years-when-in-rome/.

2. The Anfield Wrap, "When in Rome."

3. Atkinson and Roberts, "Podcast: Heysel 30 Years."

4. The Anfield Wrap, "Oh God, what have we done."

5. Evans, "End of the Innocence."

6. Billy Merritt, comment on "Oliver Kay: What About Justice for Heysel?" *The Anfield Wrap*, May 30, 2016, https://www.theanfieldwrap.com/2013/05/what-about-justice-for-heysel/.

7. Merritt, "Justice for Heysel."

8. Rob Steen, "Interwoven tragedies: Hillsborough, Heysel and Denial," *Sport in Society* 19, no. 2 (2016).

9. Steen, "Interwoven tragedies."

10. Evans, "End of the Innocence."

11. *Football's Fight Club*, directed by Gareth Williams, Channel 4, April 4, 2002, television broadcast.

12. *Football's Fight Club*.

13. *Football's Fight Club*.

14. *Football's Fight Club*.

15. The Anfield Wrap, "When in Rome."

16. The Anfield Wrap, "When in Rome."

17. The Anfield Wrap, "When in Rome."

18. Evans, "End of the Innocence."

19. Steen, "Interwoven tragedies."

20. Merritt, "Justice for Heysel."

21. Merritt, "Justice for Heysel."

22. Tony Evans, "Our Day of Shame," *The Times*, April 5, 2005.

23. Evans, "Our Day of Shame."

24. The Anfield Wrap, "When in Rome."

25. The Anfield Wrap, "When in Rome."

26. The Anfield Wrap, "When in Rome."

27. Atkinson and Roberts, "Podcast: Heysel 30 Years."

28. Atkinson and Roberts, "Podcast: Heysel 30 Years."

29. The Anfield Wrap, "When in Rome."

30. Atkinson and Roberts, "Podcast: Heysel 30 Years."

31. Atkinson and Roberts, "Podcast: Heysel 30 Years."

8. Le Bon's Back

1. Events at Heysel, Reports to the Internal Commission.

2. Gendarmerie Commander Lieutenant General Bernaert, *Submission to the Minister of Interior*, 4 June 1985.

3. Captain Dekoninck. The Parliamentary Committee of Enquiry, July 9, 1985.

4. James Hoggett and Clifford Stott, "Crowd psychology, public order police training and the policing of football crowds," *Policing-an International Journal of Police Strategies & Management* 33, no. 2 (2010).

5. "Inquiry on Soccer Riot Hears Reports of Errors," *The Associated Press*, 1985.

6. "Belgians blast Liverpool FC," *Liverpool Echo*, 1985.

7. Atkinson and Roberts, "Podcast: Heysel 30 Years."

8. Heysel, Papers of Eric Heffer.

9. Hoggett and Stott, "The policing of football crowds."

10. Hoggett and Stott, "The policing of football crowds."
11. The Daily Record, "Football thugs who rioted in Manchester during Rangers' UEFA Cup final appearance are jailed for 16 years," July 1, 2012, https://www.dailyrecord.co.uk/news/scottish-news/football-thugs-who-rioted-in-manchester-1068999
12. Press Association, "Hooligans jailed after Rangers' Uefa Cup final riot in Manchester," *The Guardian*, September 3, 2010, https://www.theguardian.com/football/2010/sep/03/rangers-hooligans-manchester-riot.
13. The Daily Record, "Football thugs."
14. Peter Millward, "Glasgow Rangers Supporters in the City of Manchester: The Degeneration of a 'Fan Party' into a 'Hooligan Riot'," *International Review for the Sociology of Sport* 44, no. 4 (2009).
15. Heather Parry, "The Glasgow Rangers Riots: Was Manchester to Blame?" *Bleacher* Report, May 16, 2008, https://bleacherreport.com/articles/23619-the-glasgow-rangers-riots-was-manchester-to-blame.
16. Millward, "Glasgow Rangers."
17. Millward, "Glasgow Rangers."
18. Millward, "Glasgow Rangers."
19. Millward, "Glasgow Rangers."
20. Millward, "Glasgow Rangers."
21. Parry, "The Glasgow Rangers Riots."
22. Parry, "The Glasgow Rangers Riots."
23. Vivek Chaudhary, "England fans shockingly well behaved," *The Guardian*, June 30, 2004, https://www.theguardian.com/uk/2004/jun/30/football.euro2004.
24. Chaudhary, "England fans."
25. Reicher et al., "Knowledge-Based Public Order Policing."
26. Reicher et al., "Knowledge-Based Public Order Policing."
27. Chaudhary, "England fans."
28. Reicher et al., "Knowledge-Based Public Order Policing."
29. Hoggett and Stott, "The policing of football crowds."
30. Gabriele Prati and Luca Pietrantoni, "Elaborating the police perspective: The role of perceptions and experience in the explanation of crowd conflict," *European Journal of Social Psychology* 39 (2009).
31. Hoggett and Stott, "The policing of football crowds."
32. Hoggett and Stott, "The policing of football crowds."
33. Hoggett and Stott, "The policing of football crowds."
34. Hoggett and Stott, "The policing of football crowds."
35. Hoggett and Stott, "The policing of football crowds."
36. Prati and Pietrantoni, "Elaborating the police perspective."
37. Prati and Pietrantoni, "Elaborating the police perspective."
38. Prati and Pietrantoni, "Elaborating the police perspective."
39. Prati and Pietrantoni, "Elaborating the police perspective."
40. Prati and Pietrantoni, "Elaborating the police perspective."

41. Prati and Pietrantoni, "Elaborating the police perspective."
42. Record of proceedings, Papers of the Popplewell Inquiry.
43. Gendarmerie Commander Lieutenant General Bernaert.
44. Nothomb, June 14, 1985.

9. The Golden Rule

1. Chief of Police for the City of Brussels Poels, *The Parliamentary Committee of Enquiry*, July 9, 1985.
2. Poels, *The Parliamentary Committee of Enquiry*.
3. Bernaert, *Submission to the Minister of the Interior*. June 4, 1985.
4. McGregor, *European Cup Final*.
5. Nothomb, June 14, 1985.
6. The Parliamentary Committee of Enquiry, *Conclusions*, July 9, 1985.
7. M.H.S. De Pulford, Brussels: Report by the British transport Police, August 1, 1985.
8. McGregor, *European Cup Final*.
9. Major Kensier, *The Parliamentary Committee of Enquiry*, July 9, 1985.
10. Captain Dekoninck, *The Parliamentary Committee of Enquiry*, July 9, 1985.
11. Commander of Alpha Squadron Mahieu, *The Parliamentary Committee of Enquiry*, July 9, 1985.
12. Gendarmerie Commander Lieutenant General Bernaert, *The Parliamentary Committee of Enquiry*, July 9, 1985.
13. The Parliamentary Committee of Enquiry, *Conclusions*.
14. *Supplementary Report RE: Final Tie of the European Champion Clubs' Cup Liverpool FC versus Juventus Torino of 29.05.1985 at the Heysel Stadium in Brussels.*
15. Bernaert, *Submission to the Minister of Interior*.
16. Bernaert, *The Parliamentary Committee of Enquiry*.
17. *Supplementary Report RE: Final Tie*.
18. Bernaert, *The Parliamentary Committee of Enquiry*.
19. Mahieu, *The Parliamentary Committee of Enquiry*.
20. Nothomb, *The Parliamentary Committee of Enquiry*.
21. Bernaert, *The Parliamentary Committee of Enquiry*.
22. Bernaert, *The Parliamentary Committee of Enquiry*.
23. Bernaert, *The Parliamentary Committee of Enquiry*.
24. The Parliamentary Committee of Enquiry, *Conclusions*.
25. *Supplementary Report RE: Final Tie*.
26. Commander of the Brussels Area Fire Service Gibson, *The Parliamentary Committee of Enquiry*, July 9, 1985.
27. Jackson, "Heysel."
28. *Supplementary Report RE: Final Tie*.
29. Mahieu, *The Parliamentary Committee of Enquiry*.

30. Bernaert, *Submission to the Minister of Interior*.
31. Caremani, *Heysel*.
32. "14 Britons Sentenced to 3 Years for Roles in 1985 Belgian Soccer Riot That Killed 39", *Los Angeles Times*, 28 April 1989.
33. Caremani, *Heysel*.

10. Tickets and Arrangements

1. Deputy Prime Minister, Minster for the Interior and Civil Service, June 6, 1985.
2. Brussels City Council, Central Department Office of the Chief of Police, June 4, 1985.
3. LFC, Liverpool Football Club Documents Annexed to Submissions to UEFA Appeal, August 8, 1985.
4. Popplewell, *Inquiry into Crowd Safety*.
5. Albert Roosens, *Evidence of Mr Roosens RBFA*, The Parliamentary Committee of Enquiry, House of Representatives, July 9, 1985.
6. Popplewell, *Inquiry into Crowd Safety*.
7. LFC, Documents Annexed to Submissions to UEFA Appeal.
8. Roosens, *Evidence of Mr Roosens*.
9. LFC, Documents Annexed to Submissions to UEFA Appeal.
10. LFC, Documents Annexed to Submissions to UEFA Appeal.
11. Brussels City Council Sports and Arts Department, Notes of the meeting held on 23 May at the Heysel Stadium, May 24, 1985.
12. Brussels City Council, Central Department Office of the Chief of Police, June 4, 1985.
13. McGregor, *European Cup Final*.
14. Roosens, *Evidence of Mr Roosens*.
15. Commission of investigation concerning the tragic incidents at the Final Tie of the European Champion Clubs' Cup Liverpool FC versus Juventus FC of 29.05.1985 at the Heysel Stadium in Brussels, 1985.
16. Commission of investigation.
17. Roosens, *Evidence of Mr Roosens*.
18. Baudoncq, *The Parliamentary Committee of Enquiry*, July 9, 1985.
19. Baudoncq, *The Parliamentary Committee of Enquiry*.
20. Roosens, *Evidence of Mr Roosens*.
21. Roosens, *Evidence of Mr Roosens*.
22. Roosens, *Evidence of Mr Roosens*.
23. URBSFA, Measures arising from the directive of the UEFA.
24. Liverpool Echo, "Former Liverpool FC chief executive Peter Robinson says Heysel was an accident waiting to happen," *Liverpool Echo*, May 25, 2013, https://www.liverpoolecho.co.uk/news/liverpool-news/former-liverpool-fc-chief-executive-3424056.
25. LFC, Documents Annexed to Submissions to UEFA Appeal.

26. T. Sharp, British Transport Police, May 17, 1985.
27. Sharp, British Transport Police.
28. G. Poels, The Chief Commissioner of Police, June 4, 1985.
29. Sharp, British Transport Police.
30. Poels, The Chief Commissioner of Police.
31. Roosens, *Evidence of Mr Roosens.*
32. Roosens, *Evidence of Mr Roosens.*
33. Steve Frosdick, "Pompey v Saints: A Case Study in Crowd Segregation," *International Journal of Police Science & Management* 7, no. 3 (2005).
34. Sharp, British Transport Police.
35. Commissioner of the City Brussels Police Van Reusal, *The Parliamentary Committee of Enquiry*, July 9, 1985.
36. Herve Brouhon, *General Report relating to the football match at the Heysel Stadium*, Cabinet of the Burgomaster, June 5, 1985.
37. Poels, The Chief Commissioner of Police.
38. Bernaert, *Submission to the Minister of Interior.*
39. McGregor, *European Cup Final.*
40. LFC, Documents Annexed to Submissions to UEFA Appeal.
41. Commission of investigation.
42. Roosens, *Evidence of Mr Roosens.*
43. Commission of investigation.
44. Caremani, *Heysel.*
45. Atkinson and Roberts, "Podcast: Heysel 30 Years."
46. Paul Fry, Face-to-face interview with the author, May 18, 2021.
47. Fry, interview.
48. Fry, interview.
49. Fry, interview.
50. *The Parliamentary Committee of Enquiry*, July 9, 1985.
51. *The Parliamentary Committee of Enquiry*, July 9, 1985.
52. Roosens, *Evidence of Mr Roosens.*
53. *Los Angeles Times*, "14 Britons Sentenced."

11. "It Looked Like a Scrapyard."

1. Van Volsom, *The Parliamentary Committee of Enquiry*, July 9, 1985.
2. URBSFA, Measures arising from the directives of UEFA.
3. Wouters, Chairman of the RBFA, *The Parliamentary Committee of Enquiry*, July 9, 1985.
4. Wouters, *The Parliamentary Committee of Enquiry.*
5. I. Hargraves, "Tragedy Disaster Warning," *Liverpool Echo*, 1985.
6. Resende, *Personal Observation of Dr Resende*, Commission of investigation concerning the tragic incidents at the Final Tie of the European

Champion Clubs' Cup Liverpool FC versus Juventus FC of 29.05. 1985 at the Heysel Stadium in Brussels, 1985.

7. Brouhon, *General Report*.

8. Brouhon, *General Report*.

9. Commander of the Brussels Area Fire Service Van Gompel, *The Parliamentary Committee of Enquiry*, July 9, 1985.

10. Wouters, *The Parliamentary Committee of Enquiry*.

11. The Anfield Wrap, "Why did no one see it coming," *The Anfield Wrap*, May 28, 2015,

12. Chris McNulty, "'For me, the night football died' – Donegal man recalls Heysel disaster," *Donegal Daily*, May 29, 2020, https://www. donegaldaily.com/2020/05/29/for-me-the-night-football-died-donegal-man-recalls-heysel-disaster/.

13. *The Explosive 80s*.

14. Paul Wilson, "Heysel was the worst thing imaginable, says Phil Neal," *The Guardian*, May 28, 2010, https://www.theguardian.com/football/blog/2010/may/28/heysel-disaster-25th-anniversary.

15. Chisari, "'The Cursed Cup'."

16. *Safety at Sports Grounds Preliminary Report from [London] Officers Visiting the Heysel Stadium in Brussels*.

17. *Safety at Sports Grounds Preliminary Report*.

18. *Heysel Stadium Brussels, European Cup Final, Wednesday, 29th May 1985 General Appraisal of Ground Conditions. Report of the City [Liverpool] Building Surveyor*.

19. *Report of the City Building Surveyor*.

20. *Report of the City Building Surveyor*.

21. Van Gompel, *Evidence given by Mr Van Gompel, Commander of the Brussels Area Fire Service*. Parliamentary Committee of Enquiry. House of Representatives 1984–85 Session, July 9, 1985.

22. *Report of the City Building Surveyor*.

23. *Safety at Sports Grounds Preliminary Report*.

24. The Anfield Wrap, "Oh God, what have we done."

25. *Report of the City Building Surveyor*.

26. *Report of the City Building Surveyor*.

27. Montague, "Shoddy Stadium."

28. Montague, "Shoddy Stadium."

29. Montague, "Shoddy Stadium."

30. Montague, "Shoddy Stadium."

31. *Report of the City Building Surveyor*.

32. *Safety at Sports Grounds Preliminary Report*.

33. Montague, "Shoddy Stadium."

34. *Safety at Sports Grounds Preliminary Report*.

35. *Report of the City Building Surveyor*.

36. Montague, "Shoddy Stadium."

37. Montague, "Shoddy Stadium."

38. Montague, "Shoddy Stadium."
39. Montague, "Shoddy Stadium."
40. *Safety at Sports Grounds Preliminary Report.*

12. "Football Was Yesterday's Sport."

1. *The Explosive 80s.*
2. Herbert, "Liverpool and Manchester United."
3. The Daily Express, "Premier League Average Attendance 2016/17," *The Daily Express*, January 20, 2017, https://www.express.co.uk/pictures/sport/8371/Premier-League-average-attendances-2016-17 League
4. mack1969, "Chelsea V Sunderland Milk Cup Semi Final," February 21, 2009, YouTube video, https://www.youtube.com/watch?v=tXsUJ6wQihM.
5. mack1969, "Chelsea V Sunderland."
6. mack1969, "Chelsea V Sunderland."
7. "Chelsea vs. Sunderland, Milk Cup Semi-Final 1985," *CFCnet*, September 15, 2008, *Internet Archive*, https://web.archive.org/web/20160127023015/http://forums.cfcnet.co.uk/topic/38994-chelsea-vs-sunderland-milk-cup-semi-final-1985/
8. mack1969, "Chelsea V Sunderland."
9. mack1969, "Chelsea V Sunderland."
10. Thames News, "Chelsea Football club | Install Electric Fence | Shocking Fans! | Football |TN-85-062-007," October 9, 2015, YouTube video, https://www.youtube.com/watch?v=AfwdbULERHY.
11. Thames News, "Chelsea Football club."
12. Steen, "Interwoven tragedies."

13. "It Was Like Something Out of Zulu"

1. STHLDN, "Luton vs Millwall FA Cup tie 1985. News footage Part 3," March 17, 2011, YouTube video, https://www.youtube.com/watch?v=dEoGMK7FVPc.
2. HC Deb, March 14, 1985, vol 75 cc439–43.
3. Sean Ingle, "Luton Town v Millwall 1985 – the night football died a slow death," *The Guardian*, February 15, 2013, https://www.theguardian.com/football/blog/2013/feb/15/luton-millwall-1985-fa-cup.
4. STHLDN, "Luton vs Millwall FA Cup tie 1985. News footage part 2," March 17, 2011, YouTube video, https://www.youtube.com/watch?v=WYqNmCv8Ag4.

5. STHLDN, "News footage part 2."
6. Ingle, "Luton Town v Millwall."
7. STHLDN, "News footage part 2."
8. STHLDN, "News footage part 2."
9. Ingle, "Luton Town v Millwall."
10. Ingle, "Luton Town v Millwall."
11. Ingle, "Luton Town v Millwall."
12. STHLDN, "News footage part 2."
13. STHLDN, "News footage part 2."
14. *The Real Football Factories,* "London."
15. STHLDN, "News footage part 2."
16. *The Real Football Factories,* "London."
17. *The Real Football Factories,* "London."
18. *The Real Football Factories,* "London."
19. STHLDN, "News footage part 2."
20. Home Office C4 Division, *Prisons and Prisoners Repatriation and Deportation Football Hooliganism,* HO291/2060, 1985.
21. STHLDN, "Luton vs Millwall FA Cup tie. 1985. UK news footage Part 1," March 17, 2011, YouTube video, https://www.youtube.com/watch?v=Fx1UgBzuJZ8.
22. Ingle, "Luton Town v Millwall."
23. STHLDN, "News footage part 2."
24. STHLDN, "UK news footage Part 1."
25. STHLDN, "UK news footage Part 1."
26. STHLDN, "News footage part 2."
27. STHLDN, "News footage Part 3."
28. Home Office, *Football Hooliganism: Police Aspects,* Home Office Document. May 23, 1985.
29. STHLDN, "News footage Part 3."
30. STHLDN, "News footage Part 3."
31. STHLDN, "News footage part 2."
32. STHLDN, "News footage part 2."
33. HC Deb, March 14, 1985, vol 75 cc439–43.
34. HC Deb, March 14, 1985, vol 75 cc439–43.
35. HC Deb, March 14, 1985, vol 75 cc439–43.
36. *BBC News.*
37. STHLDN, "News footage Part 3."
38. STHLDN, "News footage Part 3."
39. STHLDN, "News footage Part 3."
40. STHLDN, "News footage Part 3."
41. STHLDN, "News footage Part 3."
42. STHLDN, "News footage Part 3."
43. STHLDN, "News footage Part 3."

44. STHLDN, "Luton vs Millwall FA Cup tie 1985. News footage Part 4 – Final," March 17, 2011, YouTube video, https://www.youtube.com/watch?v=L7uxCAIqBoA.

45. Richard Edwards, R. "The worst five months in English football: Thatcher, fighting and fatalities in 1985," *FourFourTwo*, January 14, 2015, https://www.fourfourtwo.com/features/worst-five-months-english-football-thatcher-fighting-and-fatalities-1985.

46. Croker, *The First Voice*.

47. K. Martindale, "It all started with a banner," *Liverpool Echo*, June 11, 1985.

48. Geoff Pearson and Arianna Sale, "'On the Lash' – revisiting the effectiveness of alcohol controls at football matches," *Policing and Society* 21, no. 1 (2011).

49. Pearson and Sale, "'On the Lash'."

50. Home Office C4 Division, *Prisons and Prisoners*.

51. Home Office, *Football Hooliganism*.

52. Home Office, *Football Hooliganism*.

53. Home Office, *Football Hooliganism*.

54. Home Office, *Football Hooliganism*.

55. Home Office, *Football Hooliganism*.

56. Croker, *The First Voice*.

57. Birmingham Live, "From the Archives: Football violence led to fan's tragic death," *Birmingham Mail*, April 19, 2013, http://www.birminghammail.co.uk/news/local-news/archives-football-violence-led-fans-158156 .

58. Birmingham Live, "From the Archives."

59. Popplewell, *Inquiry into Crowd Safety*.

60. Birmingham Live, "From the Archives."

61. Birmingham Live, "From the Archives."

62. "1985: Fans killed in Bradford stadium fire," *BBC On This Day*, http://news.bbc.co.uk/onthisday/hi/dates/stories/may/11/newsid_2523000/2523561.stm.

63. *BBC On This Day*, "Bradford stadium fire."

64. *BBC On This Day*, "Bradford stadium fire."

65. Ian Taylor, "Putting the Boot into a Working-Class Sport: British Soccer After Bradford and Brussels," *Sociology of Sport Journal* 4, no. 2 (1987).

66. Sam Rkaina, "Bradford City stadium fire: New book claims former club chairman connected to eight blazes before fatal 1985 incident," *Daily Mirror*, April 15, 2015, http://www.mirror.co.uk/news/uk-news/bradford-city-stadium-fire-new-5524368.

67. Rkaina, "Bradford City stadium fire."

14. The Lights Were Turned Out

1. Clive Gammon, "A Day of Horror and Shame," *Sports Illustrated*, June 10, 1985, https://www.si.com/vault/1985/06/10/620867/a-day-of-horror-and-shame.

2. Gammon, "Horror and Shame."

3. S. Gainsbury, J. Pickard and A. Bounds, "Tories debated letting Liverpool 'decline'," *Financial Times*, 2011.

4. Home Office, *Football Hooliganism*.

5. Duncan Gardham, "1981 files: Margaret Thatcher secretly advised to abandon Liverpool by advisers," *The Telegraph*, December 30, 2011.

6. Gardham, "1981 files."

7. Gainsbury, Pickard and Bounds, "Tories debated letting Liverpool 'decline'."

8. Gainsbury, Pickard and Bounds, "Tories debated letting Liverpool 'decline'."

9. Gardham, "1981 files."

10. Gardham, "1981 files."

11. Helen Grady, "The English city that wanted to 'break away' from the UK," *BBC News*, November 8, 2014, http://www.bbc.com/news/magazine-29953611.

12. "The Kopites guide to Brussels," *Liverpool Echo*, May 25, 1985.

15. "The Tone Was Set."

1. Glass, "Englishmen Abroad."

2. Popplewell, *Inquiry into Crowd Safety*.

3. Eamonn McCabe, Face-to-face interview with the author, June 2, 2021.

4. McCabe, interview.

5. Fry, interview.

6. Fry, interview.

7. "Witness: The Heysel Stadium Disaster."

8. PC G.S. Laird, *Football Liaison Report*, British Transport Police, June 3, 1985.

9. P. Clark, "I feel as though a relative has died," *Liverpool Echo*, June 1985.

10. Dan Kay, "Listen: Heysel remembered - by the Echo's news reporter in Brussels on the day," *Liverpool Echo*, May 29, 2015, https://www.liverpoolecho.co.uk/news/liverpool-news/listen-heysel-remembered---echos-9353718.

11. Tony Evans, "Heysel 30 Years: an eyewitness account of May 29, 1985 in Brussels," *The Anfield Wrap*, May 28, 2015, https://www.

theanfieldwrap.com/2015/05/heysel-30-years-an-eyewitness-account-of-may-29-1985-in-brussels/.

12. Evans, "An eyewitness account."
13. Evans, "End of the Innocence."
14. Evans, "End of the Innocence."
15. Mallinson, *The British Army.*
16. Evans, "End of the Innocence."
17. Atkinson and Roberts, "Podcast: Heysel 30 Years."

16. Carry On

1. Fry, interview.
2. Fry, interview.
3. Gruner and Lee-Potter, "I'm ashamed to come from Liverpool," May 30, 1985, *London Evening Standard.*
4. Laird, *Football Liaison Report.*
5. Sergeant P. White, *Football Liaison Report,* British Transport Police, May 31, 1985.
6. PC S. Jones, *Football Liaison Report,* British Transport Police, May 30, 1985.
7. PC M. Jones, *Football Liaison Report,* British Transport Police, May 31, 1985.
8. Laird, *Football Liaison Report.*
9. McGregor, *European Cup Final.*
10. McGregor, *European Cup Final.*
11. Ed Vulliamy, "Live by Aggro, Die by Aggro," *The New Statesmen,* June 7, 1985.
12. Caremani, *Heysel.*
13. The Anfield Wrap, "Oh God, what have we done."
14. The Anfield Wrap, "Oh God, what have we done."
15. The Anfield Wrap, "Oh God, what have we done."
16. Evans, "An Eyewitness Account."
17. T. Johnston, "Half-naked fans left girls crying," *Liverpool Echo,* June 11, 1985.
18. Johnston, "Half-naked fans."
19. Brouhon, *General Report.*
20. Brouhon, *General Report.*
21. Brouhon, *General Report.*
22. Brouhon, *Cabinet of the Burgomaster,* June 5, 1985.
23. Resende, *Personal Observation.*
24. Heysel and Hillsborough, Papers of Eric Heffer.
25. Paul Callan, "Shame," *Daily Mirror,* May 30, 1985.
26. Callan, "Shame."
27. Callan, "Shame."

28. *Daily Post*, "From the first provocation."

29. *Daily Post*, "From the first provocation."

30. Greg Miskiw, "The Grief," *The Sunday Mirror*, 2 June, 1985.

31. Evans, "End of the Innocence."

32. Evans, "End of the Innocence."

33. Record of proceedings of a session of the full senate, June 14, 1985.

34. Evans, "An Eyewitness Account."

35. Fry, interview.

36. Derek Brown, Charlie Burgess and Alex Scott, "Brussels counts soccer riot dead," *The Guardian*, May 30, 1985.

37. White, *Football Liaison Report*.

38. S. Jones, *Football Liaison Report*.

39. Evans, "An Eyewitness Account."

40. Gerry Ormonde, "Kopblog meets Tony Evans," *This is Anfield*, June 13, 2008, https://www.thisisanfield.com/2008/06/kopblog-meets-tony-evans/.

41. Ed Vulliamy, "Heysel stadium disaster: 'I saw the rows of bodies piled high,'" *The Guardian*, May 27, 2015, https://www.theguardian.com/football/2015/may/27/heysel-stadium-disaster-30th-anniversary

42. Callan, "Shame."

43. Callan, "Shame."

44. Callan, "Shame."

45. PC K. Sutton, *Football Liaison Report*, British Transport Police, June 1, 1985.

46. Inspector G.J. Fair, *Football Liaison Report*, British Transport Police, May 31, 1985.

47. White, *Football Liaison Report*.

17. Chinese Whispers

1. McCabe, interview.

2. Heysel, Papers of Eric Heffer.

3. Heysel, Papers of Eric Heffer.

4. Chief Inspector M. Griffin, *Football Liaison Report*, June 3, 1985.

5. Fry, interview.

6. Fry, interview.

7. Evans, "An Eyewitness Account."

8. "Abuse from drunken Reds fans," *Liverpool Echo*, June 11, 1985.

9. Evans, "Our Day of Shame."

10. Vulliamy, "Live by Aggro."

11. Vulliamy, "Live by Aggro."

12. Vulliamy, "Live by Aggro."

13. Vulliamy, "Heysel stadium disaster."

14. Vulliamy, "Heysel stadium disaster."

15. Caremani, *Heysel.*
16. Evans, "End of the Innocence."
17. Atkinson and Roberts, "Podcast: Heysel 30 Years."
18. Heysel, Papers of Eric Heffer.
19. The Anfield Wrap, "Oh God, what have we done."
20. The Anfield Wrap, "Oh God, what have we done."
21. Atkinson and Roberts, "Podcast: Heysel 30 Years."
22. Atkinson and Roberts, "Podcast: Heysel 30 Years."
23. *The Explosive 80s.*
24. Caremani, *Heysel.*
25. The Anfield Wrap, "Oh God, what have we done."
26. The Anfield Wrap, "Oh God, what have we done."
27. The Anfield Wrap, "Oh God, what have we done."
28. The Anfield Wrap, "Oh God, what have we done."
29. J. Dunstan, "Belgian police's cowardice - by PC," *Liverpool Echo,* June 11, 1985.
30. J. Dunstan, "Belgian police's cowardice - by PC."
31. Clark, "I feel as though a relative has died."
32. Steven Kelly, "The Belgian football tragedy: an eye-witness account," *Tribune,* June 7, 1985.
33. Kelly, "The Belgian football tragedy."
34. Popplewell, *Inquiry into Crowd Safety.*
35. Roosens, *Evidence of Mr Roosens.*
36. Popplewell, *Inquiry into Crowd Safety.*
37. Roosens, *Evidence of Mr Roosens.*
38. Popplewell, *Inquiry into Crowd Safety.*
39. John Foot, *Calcio: A History of Italian Football* (London: Harper Perennial, 2007).

18. Two-Match Ban

1. Correspondent to Dennis Howell, June 24, 1985.
2. Popplewell, *Inquiry into Crowd Safety.*
3. *Supplementary Report RE: Final Tie.*
4. URBSFA. Measures arising from the directive of the UEFA.
5. Meura, *8th Division City of Brussels Police Report,* May 31, 1985
6. Roosens, *Evidence of Mr Roosens.*
7. Griffin, *Football Liaison Report.*
8. Meura, *Police Report.*
9. Meura, *Police Report.*
10. Meura, *Police Report.*
11. Meura, *Police Report.*
12. Meura, *Police Report.*
13. Griffin, *Football Liaison Report.*

14. Sutton, *Football Liaison Report*.
15. Fair, *Football Liaison Report*.
16. Resende, *Personal Observation*.
17. Meura, *Police Report*.
18. Meura, *Police Report*.
19. Record of proceedings of a session of the full senate, June 14, 1985.
20. Ian Murray, "Soccer hooligans identified on video film," *The Times*, June 3, 1985.
21. "'Shot or knifed' riddle," *Daily Mail*, May 30, 1985.
22. "Chairman says NF to blame," *Liverpool Echo*, May 30, 1985.
23. "Second Gunman," *Mail on Sunday*, June 2, 1985.
24. *Mail on Sunday*, "Second Gunman."
25. Fry, interview.
26. The Parliamentary Committee, July 9, 1985.
27. Personal Opinion of SC/8
28. 8th Division of the Brussels Police, May 31, 1985.
29. The Parliamentary Committee.
30. *Letter from UEFA to LFC*, June 24, 1985.
31. *Letter from UEFA to LFC*.

19. "A Football Terracing Version of Dante's Inferno."

1. Bruce Grobbelaar, "'I wept for the dying'," *Sunday Mirror*, June 2, 1985.
2. "Witness: The Heysel Stadium Disaster."
3. Chisari, "'The Cursed Cup.'"
4. Chisari, "'The Cursed Cup.'"
5. "Witness: The Heysel Stadium Disaster."
6. "Witness: The Heysel Stadium Disaster."
7. "Witness: The Heysel Stadium Disaster."
8. Popplewell, *Inquiry into Crowd Safety*.
9. Popplewell, *Inquiry into Crowd Safety*.
10. David. Lacey, "Comment," *The Guardian*, May 30, 1985.
11. Shekhar Bhatia, "I saw our thugs start slaughter," *London Evening Standard*, May 30, 1985.
12. Foreign Office, Foreign Office Document, August 21, 1985, *UK: Italy Bilateral Relations Football Tragedy Brussels*.
13. "First Match," *Daily Mirror*, 1985.
14. *Heysel: Requiem For A Cup Final*, BBC Two, April 17, 2005, television broadcast.
15. Foot, *Calcio*.
16. *Daily Post*, "From the first provocation."
17. Roosens, *Evidence of Mr Roosens*.

18. *Report from LFC to UEFA.*
19. Match Programme, May 29, 1985.
20. Ian. Walmsley, "The Belgian in the Union Jack," *Liverpool Echo*, June 11, 1985.
21. Barbara Metcalfe and Andy Byrne, "Dazed fans tell of the bloodbath," *Liverpool Echo*, May 30, 1985.
22. Martin O'Shea, "Crush-then fights began," *Liverpool Echo*, June 11, 1985.
23. *Letter from LFC to UEFA.*
24. J.R. Hughes, "The Juventus thugs who wanted aggro," *Liverpool Echo*, June 1, 1985.
25. Hughes, "The Juventus thugs."
26. The Anfield Wrap, "Oh God, what have we done."
27. M. Johnson, "Italians started air raid," *Liverpool Echo*, June 11, 1985.
28. Patricia Myers, "My five hours of absolute hell," *Liverpool Echo*, June 11, 1985.
29. L. Colley, "A teenager's diary on day of agony," *Liverpool Echo*, June 11, 1985.
30. H. Harper, "Evertonian hooligan," *Liverpool Echo*, June 11, 1985.
31. J. Standing, *Liverpool Echo*, June 11, 1985.
32. The Anfield Wrap, "Oh God, what have we done."
33. D. Jackson, "They went berserk," *Liverpool Echo*, June 11, 1985.
34. *Daily Post*, "From the first provocation."
35. "The battle unit that charged and charged," editorial, *Liverpool Echo*, June 11, 1985.
36. Paul. Bennett, "Italians spitting through fence," *Liverpool Echo*, June 11, 1985.
37. Paul Kelso, "Liverpool still torn over night that shamed their name," *The Guardian*, April 2, 2005.
38. S. Keeling, "Fan ripped up three tickets," *Liverpool Echo*, June 11, 1985.
39. E. Winters, "Abuse from drunken Liverpool fans," *Liverpool Echo*, June 11, 1985.
40. McGregor, *European Cup Final.*
41. Griffin, *Football Liaison Report.*

20. Space

1. A. Anderson, "Flares fired into the Juventus section," *Liverpool Echo*, June 11, 1985.
2. J. Morris, "Weapon of fear – the flare," *Liverpool Echo*, June 11, 1985.
3. S. A. Avann and G.R. Avann, *Liverpool Echo*, June 11, 1985.
4. Johnston, "Half-naked fans."
5. Caremani, *The Truth.*

6. Chisari, "'The Cursed Cup'."
7. Martindale, "It all started with a banner."
8. "Witness: The Heysel Stadium Disaster."
9. McCabe, interview.
10. Caremani, *Heysel*.
11. Caremani, *Heysel*.
12. Morris, "Weapon of fear."
13. Fry, interview.
14. Fry, interview.
15. Fry, interview.
16. Fry, interview.
17. Fry, interview.
18. Fry, interview.
19. Caremani, *Heysel*.
20. Evans, "End of the Innocence."
21. Evans, "End of the Innocence."
22. Evans, "End of the Innocence."
23. Dunstan, "Belgian police's cowardice."
24. Dunstan, "Belgian police's cowardice."
25. Dunstan, "Belgian police's cowardice."
26. Burns, "Carnage."
27. Burns, "Carnage."
28. Chisari, "'The Cursed Cup'."

21. "Daddy, They're Crushing Me."

1. McCabe, interview.
2. *RBFA Report*.
3. Ian Hargreaves, "A Night of Horror," *Liverpool Echo*, May 30, 1985.
4. Brown, Burgess and Scott, "Brussels counts soccer riot dead."
5. S. Culligan, *Liverpool Echo*, June 11, 1985.
6. *The Explosive 80s*.
7. Meura, *Police Report*.
8. Colin Wells, "Terror ordeal for my children," *Liverpool Echo*, June 11, 1985.
9. Simon Hart, "Heysel disaster 30th anniversary: Italian journalist remembers a tragedy that was 'hidden' for so long," *The Independent*, May 29, 2015, https://www.independent.co.uk/sport/football/news/ heysel-disaster-30th-anniversary-italian-journalist-remembers-tragedy- was-hidden-so-long-10283163.html.
10. G. Ireland, "Italians in Reds' area," *Liverpool Echo*, June 11, 1985.
11. "Witness: The Heysel Stadium Disaster."
12. "Witness: The Heysel Stadium Disaster."
13. *The Explosive 80s*.

14. *The Explosive 80s.*
15. *The Explosive 80s.*
16. *The Explosive 80s.*
17. *The Explosive 80s.*
18. Vulliamy, "Heysel stadium disaster."
19. Vulliamy, "Heysel stadium disaster."
20. "Blood in the Stands," *Time*, June 10, 1985.
21. *Daily Post*, "From the first provocation."
22. *Daily Post*, "From the first provocation."
23. Heysel, Papers of Eric Heffer.
24. O'Shea, "Crush."
25. Vulliamy, "Live by Aggro."
26. Vulliamy, "Heysel stadium disaster."
27. Vulliamy, "Heysel stadium disaster."
28. Vulliamy, "Heysel stadium disaster."
29. Clark, "I feel as though a relative has died."
30. R. Guy, "Stamford Stomper," *Liverpool Echo*, June 11, 1985.
31. Guy, "Stamford Stomper."

22. The Wall

1. Tony Evans (@tonyevans92a), tweet, April 24, 2018, 5:39 p.m., https://mobile.twitter.com/tonyevans92a/status/988819785319301120.
2. Tony Evans, "Why Liverpool and Anfield will be tinged with contempt and hostility with AS Roma in town," *London Evening Standard*, April 24, 2018, https://www.standard.co.uk/sport/football/why-liverpool-and-anfield-will-be-tinged-with-contempt-and-hostility-with-as-roma-in-town-a3821746.html.
3. Grignet, *Evidence of Mr Grignet, Head of the Red Cross*, The Parliamentary Committee of Enquiry, July 9, 1986.
4. "The European Cup Final," *BBC News*, BBC1, May 29, 1985, television broadcast. Accessed as a YouTube video, posted by kinksterman, "European Cup Final Tragedy Heysel 1985," April 4, 2015, https://www.youtube.com/watch?v=5qpDvhPGUEo.
5. Brown, Burgess and Scott, "Brussels counts soccer riot dead."
6. Jeff Powell and Ian Walker, "Bloodbath," *Daily Mail*, May 30, 1985.
7. Gruner and Lee-Potter, "I'm ashamed to come from Liverpool."
8. A. McAllester, "The battle unit that charged and charged." *Liverpool Echo,*
9. Jackson, "They went berserk."
10. Chisari, "'The Cursed Cup'."
11. McCabe, interview.
12. McCabe, interview.

13. McCabe, interview.
14. McCabe, interview.
15. Johnston, "Half-naked fans."
16. Johnston, "Half-naked fans."
17. Alan Price, "Shame," *Daily Mirror*, May 30, 1985.
18. Price, "Shame."
19. Grobbelaar, "'I Wept for the Dying'."
20. Griffin, *Football Liaison Report*.
21. McGregor, *European Cup Final*.
22. Griffin, *Football Liaison Report*.
23. Greg Miskiw, "Rescued from a deadly mound," *Sunday Mirror*, June 2, 1985.
24. Hargreaves, "A Night of Horror."
25. Hargreaves, "A Night of Horror."
26. Andy Byrne, "Scouser who saved lives," *Liverpool Echo*, June 7, 1985.
27. Gruner and Lee-Potter, "I'm ashamed to be from Liverpool."
28. Miskiw, "Rescued from a deadly mound."
29. Miskiw, "Rescued from a deadly mound."
30. Miskiw, "Rescued from a deadly mound."
31. Bernaert, *Submission to the Minister of Interior*.
32. Grignet, *Evidence of Mr Grignet*.
33. Van Gompel, *Evidence given by Mr Van Gompel*.
34. McCabe, interview.
35. McCabe, interview.
36. Grignet, *Evidence of Mr Grignet*.

23. "Well, What an Unhappy Start?"

1. Sutton, *Football Liaison Report*.
2. Sutton, *Football Liaison Report*.
3. Powell and Walker, "Bloodbath."
4. Powell and Walker, "Bloodbath."
5. Brown, Burgess and Scott, "Brussels counts soccer riot dead."
6. Powell and Walker, "Bloodbath."
7. Brown, Burgess and Scott, "Brussels counts soccer riot dead."
8. Andy Byrne, "Girl's last moments," *Liverpool Echo*, May 30, 1985.
9. Byrne, "Girl's last moments."
10. Byrne, "Girl's last moments."
11. Byrne, "Girl's last moments."
12. Martindale, "It all started with a banner."
13. Martindale, "It all started with a banner."
14. Martindale, "It all started with a banner."
15. Fry, interview.
16. Fry, interview.

17. Bob Burns, "Heysel remembered - by the Echo's news reporter in Brussels on the day," *Liverpool Echo*, May 29, 2015, https://www.liverpoolecho.co.uk/news/liverpool-news/listen-heysel-remembered---echos-9353718.

18. Burns, "Heysel remembered."

19. Burns, "Carnage."

20. "TV chiefs rap UEFA," *Daily Mirror*, May 30, 1985.

21. *Daily Mirror*, "TV chiefs rap UEFA."

22. P. Sheridan and S. Usher, "Furious viewers attack the BBC," *Daily Mail*, May 30, 1985.

23. Sheridan and Usher, "Furious viewers attack the BBC."

24. *Daily Mirror*, "TV chiefs rap UEFA."

25. Sheridan and Usher, "Furious viewers attack the BBC."

26. "The European Cup Final," *BBC Sport*.

27. "The European Cup Final," *BBC Sport*.

28. "The European Cup Final," *BBC Sport*.

29. "The European Cup Final," *BBC Sport*.

30. "The European Cup Final," *BBC Sport*.

31. "The European Cup Final," *BBC Sport*.

32. "The European Cup Final," *BBC Sport*.

33. "The European Cup Final," *BBC Sport*.

34. "The European Cup Final," *BBC Sport*.

35. "The European Cup Final," *BBC Sport*.

36. Foot, *Calcio*.

37. Resende, *Personal Observation*.

38. Resende, *Personal Observation*.

39. Resende, *Personal Observation*.

40. Chisari, "'The Cursed Cup'."

41. Chisari, "'The Cursed Cup'."

42. Brouhon, *General Report*.

43. Brouhon, *General Report*.

44. Brouhon, *General Report*.

45. Brouhon, *General Report*.

46. Brouhon, *General Report*.

47. Brouhon, *General Report*.

48. Paul Kelso and Simon Hart, "'We should have refused to play final'," *The Guardian*, April 2, 2005, https://www.theguardian.com/football/2005/apr/02/championsleague2.

49. Powell and Walker, "Bloodbath."

50. Chisari, "'The Cursed Cup'."

24. "Some Had Already Taken a Shower."

1. Off the Ball, "Heysel is never ever mentioned."
2. "Bodies ordeal of soccer star's girlfriend," *Daily Mail*, May 31, 1985.
3. *Daily Mail*, "Bodies ordeal of soccer star's girlfriend."
4. Grobbelaar, "'I wept for the dying'."
5. Grobbelaar, "'I wept for the dying'."
6. Jackson, "Heysel: The Witnesses' Stories."
7. Jackson, "Heysel: The Witnesses' Stories."
8. Powell and Walker, "Bloodbath."
9. Powell and Walker, "Bloodbath."
10. Off the Ball, "Heysel is never ever mentioned."
11. Off the Ball, "Heysel is never ever mentioned."
12. Katie Dawson, "Heysel football disaster remembered 25 years on," *BBC News*, May 29, 2010, http://www.bbc.com/news/10176462.
13. Grobbelaar, "'I wept for the dying'."
14. *The Explosive 80s.*
15. Paul Fennessy, "'I hated myself... I got terribly down and lost my confidence, not just as a footballer but as a person'," *The 42*, May 26, 2018, https://www.the42.ie/jim-beglin-interview-4033956-May2018/.
16. John Hynes, "Chris Pile's story 30 years since Heysel," *A Golden Sky: A LFC Blog*, May 28, 2015.
17. Hynes, "30 years since Heysel."
18. Jo Dutton, "Heysel: Survivors tell their stories," *BBC News*, April 13, 2005,
      http://news.bbc.co.uk/1/hi/programmes/4415623.stm.
19. Chisari, "'The Cursed Cup'."
20. *The Explosive 80s.*
21. *The Explosive 80s.*
22. Jackson, "Heysel: The Witnesses' Stories."
23. "The European Cup Final," *BBC Sport.*
24. "The European Cup Final," *BBC Sport.*
25. "The European Cup Final," *BBC Sport.*
26. "The European Cup Final," *BBC Sport.*
27. "The European Cup Final," *BBC Sport.*
28. "The European Cup Final," *BBC Sport.*
29. "The European Cup Final," *BBC Sport.*
30. "The European Cup Final," *BBC Sport.*
31. "The European Cup Final," *BBC Sport.*
32. "The European Cup Final," *BBC Sport.*
33. "The European Cup Final," *BBC Sport.*
34. *The Explosive 80s.*
35. *The Explosive 80s.*
36. Chisari, "'The Cursed Cup'."
37. *The Explosive 80s.*

38. *The Explosive 80s.*

25. The Match

1. *The Explosive 80s.*
2. "The European Cup Final," *BBC Sport.*
3. "The European Cup Final," *BBC Sport.*
4. Grobbelaar, "'I wept for the dying'."
5. Powell and Walker, "Bloodbath."
6. "The European Cup Final," *BBC Sport.*
7. *The Explosive 80s.*
8. Fry, interview.
9. Off the Ball, "Heysel is never ever mentioned."
10. Off the Ball, "Heysel is never ever mentioned."
11. Nick Bunker, "Medics shocked at grim tool," *Liverpool Echo,* May 1985.
12. Bunker, "Medics shocked at grim toll."
13. Bunker, "Medics shocked at grim toll."
14. Bunker, "Medics shocked at grim toll."
15. *Heysel: Requiem For A Cup Final.*
16. *Heysel: Requiem For A Cup Final.*
17. Bunker, "Medics shocked at grim toll."
18. Bunker, "Medics shocked at grim toll."
19. Oliver Brown, "Heysel disaster of 1985 is football's forgotten tragedy and Liverpool and Juventus' minimal reaction prolongs hurt," *The Daily Telegraph,* May 28, 2015.
20. *The Explosive 80s.*
21. "The European Cup Final," *BBC Sport.*
22. "The European Cup Final," *BBC Sport.*
23. "The European Cup Final," *BBC Sport.*
24. *BBC Half Time News,* BBC1, May 29, 1985, television broadcast. Accessed as a YouTube video posted by killianM2, https://www.youtube.com/watch?v=XHetzhB8FNY.
25. Mike Gardner, "Soccer madness in Brussels," July 11, 2008, YouTube video, https://www.youtube.com/watch?v=fVCiRyoIC_E.
26. Hynes, "30 years since Heysel."
27. Dutton, "Heysel: Survivors tell their stories."
28. Jackson, "Heysel: The Witnesses' Stories."
29. *Heysel: Requiem For A Cup Final.*
30. *The Explosive 80s.*
31. Jackson, "Heysel: The Witnesses' Stories."
32. "The European Cup Final," *BBC Sport.*
33. *The Explosive 80s.*
34. *The Explosive 80s.*

35. "The European Cup Final," *BBC Sport*.
36. *Heysel: Requiem For A Cup Final*.
37. *Heysel: Requiem For A Cup Final*.
38. "The European Cup Final," *BBC Sport*.
39. Foot, *Calcio*.
40. Michel Platini, French TV Interview, May 29, 1985.
41. Platini, French TV Interview.
42. Dutton, "Heysel: Survivors tell their stories."
43. Hynes, "30 years since Heysel."
44. "The European Cup Final," *BBC Sport*.
45. Powell and Walker
46. Powell and Walker.
47. "The European Cup Final," *BBC Sport*.
48. Hynes, "30 years since Heysel."
49. *The Explosive 80s*.
50. *The Explosive 80s*.
51. Jackson, "Heysel: The Witnesses' Stories."
52. Jackson, "Heysel: The Witnesses' Stories."
53. Fry, interview.
54. McCabe, interview.
55. Grobbelaar, "'I wept for the dying'."
56. Grobbelaar, "'I wept for the dying'."
57. Ken Montgomery, "I May Quit Liverpool," *Sunday Mirror*, June 2, 1985.
58. J. Fraser, "Fighting mad soccer thug jailed for three years," *Daily Express*, 1985.
59. G. Parry, *The Guardian*, 1985.
60. Fraser, "Fighting mad soccer thug."
61. Parry, *The Guardian*.
62. Bert Millichip, unknown article, *The Guardian*, 1985.
63. *Evidence of Mr Van Doren Deputy Public Prosecutor*.
64. Deputy Prime Minister, Minster for the Interior and Civil Service, June 6, 1985.
65. *Evidence of Mr Glorie, Ministry of the Interior*.
66. *Evidence of Mr Van Doren*.

26. Italy

1. Ronald Singleton, "Marching gangs set fire to Union Jacks in Turin," *Daily Mail*, May 31, 1985.
2. "Hate call for Rome Embassy," *London Evening Standard*, May 30, 1985.
3. *London Evening Standard*, "Hate call for Rome Embassy."
4. Foot, *Calcio*.

5. David Selbourne, "Through Italian eyes," *New Society*, June, 1985.
6. Selbourne, "Through Italian eyes."
7. Singleton, "Marching gangs."
8. *London Evening Standard*, "Hate call for Rome Embassy."
9. Selbourne, "Through Italian eyes."
10. Foreign Office, *Liverpool/Juventus*, June 1, 1985, UK: Italy Bilateral Relations: Football Tragedy Brussels.
11. Selbourne, "Through Italian eyes."
12. Foreign Office, *Violence at the European Cup Final*, May 30, 1985, UK: Italy Bilateral Relations: Football Tragedy Brussels.
13. Foreign Office, *Violence at the European Cup Final.*
14. Source unknown.
15. Paul House, "Grief," *Daily Mirror*, May 31, 1985.
16. House, "Grief."
17. Patrick Bishop, Anne Spackman and Dalbert Hallenstein, "Giovacchino and his countrymen go home," *The Sunday Times*, June 2, 1985.
18. Bishop, Spackman and Hallenstein, "Giovacchino and his countrymen go home."
19. J. Woodcock, "Tears of a widow," *Daily Mail*, May 31, 1985.
20. House, "Grief."
21. Foreign Office, *Brussels Aftermath*, June 4, 1985, UK: Italy Bilateral Relations: Football Tragedy Brussels.
22. Foreign Office, *Brussels Aftermath.*
23. Foreign Office, *Liverpool/Juventus.*
24. Foreign Office, *Your Distress 31: Violence against British Tourist*, June 3, 1985, UK: Italy Bilateral Relations: Football Tragedy Brussels.
25. Andrew Golden and Geoff Garvey, "Wives' backlash terror," *Sunday Mirror*, June 2, 1985.
26. Foreign Office, *British Representation at the European Police Amateur Football Competition*, June 17, 1985, UK: Italy Bilateral Relations: Football Tragedy Brussels.
27. "Thatcher Bill Would Outlaw Alcohol at Soccer Stadiums," *Associated Press*, 1985.
28. T. Miles, "Anti-British backlash begins," *Daily Mail*, June 1, 1985.
29. Foreign Office, *Liverpool/Juventus.*
30. Foreign Office, *European Cup Final Disaster*, May 30, 1985, UK: Italy Bilateral Relations: Football Tragedy Brussels.
31. Miles, "Anti-British backlash begins."
32. Golden and Garvey, "Wives' backlash terror."
33. House, "Grief."
34. Foreign Office, *Your Distress 31.*
35. Singleton, "Marching gangs."
36. *London Evening Standard*, "Hate call for Rome Embassy."
37. Singleton, "Marching gangs."

38. *London Evening Standard*, "Hate call for Rome Embassy."
39. Singleton, "Marching gangs."
40. Singleton, "Marching gangs."
41. Foreign Office.
42. Foreign Office.
43. Foreign Office.
44. Foreign Office.
45. Foreign Office, *Violence at the European Cup Final*.
46. Foreign Office, *Liverpool/Juventus*.
47. Foreign Office, *Liverpool/Juventus: Italian Press Reactions*, June 4, 1985, UK: Italy Bilateral Relations: Football Tragedy Brussels.
48. House, "Grief."
49. Foreign Office, *Liverpool/Juventus*.
50. Miskiw, "The Grief."
51. George Armstrong, "Italian PM says Brussels riot has 'submerged UK in disgrace'," *The Guardian*, May 31, 1985.
52. Armstrong, "Italian PM."
53. Armstrong, "Italian PM."
54. Armstrong, "Italian PM."
55. Armstrong, "Italian PM."
56. Foot, *Calcio*.
57. Armstrong, "Italian PM."
58. Atkinson and Roberts, "Podcast: Heysel 30 Years."
59. House, "Grief."
60. Singleton, "Marching gangs."
61. Singleton, "Marching gangs."
62. Singleton, "Marching gangs."
63. Singleton, "Marching gangs."
64. House, "Grief."
65. House, "Grief."
66. C. Gammon, "A Soccer Riot: A Day of Horror and Shame."
67. Miskiw, "The Grief."
68. Chisari, "'The Cursed Cup'."
69. Chisari, "'The Cursed Cup'."
70. Foreign Office, *Interview Given by Prime Minister to Italian TV*, May 30, 1985, UK: Italy Bilateral Relations: Football Tragedy Brussels.
71. Foreign Office, Foreign Office Document, 1985, UK: Italy Bilateral Relations: Football Tragedy Brussels.
72. Miskiw, "The Grief."
73. Miskiw, "The Grief."
74. Miskiw, "The Grief."
75. Bishop, Spackman and Hallenstein, "Giovacchino and his countrymen go home."
76. Bishop, Spackman and Hallenstein, "Giovacchino and his countrymen go home."

77. Bishop, Spackman and Hallenstein, "Giovacchino and his countrymen go home."
78. Bishop, Spackman and Hallenstein, "Giovacchino and his countrymen go home."
79. Miskiw, "The Grief."
80. Miskiw, "The Grief."
81. Miskiw, "The Grief."
82. Bishop, Spackman and Hallenstein, "Giovacchino and his countrymen go home."
83. Miskiw, "The Grief."
84. Miskiw, "The Grief."
85. J. Earle, "Post-mortem order on football victims," *The Times*, 1985.
86. Earle, "Post-mortem order."
87. "Rome," *The Times*, June 4, 1985.
88. Foreign Office, *Liverpool/Juventus: Italian Press Reaction*.
89. Chisari, "'The Cursed Cup'."
90. Chisari, "'The Cursed Cup'."
91. Chisari, "'The Cursed Cup'."
92. Chisari, "'The Cursed Cup'."
93. Chisari, "'The Cursed Cup'."
94. C. Taylor, C. "Hate ends bride's dream honeymoon," *Liverpool Echo*, June 4, 1985.
95. Nick Bunker, "Italians welcome peace mission," *Liverpool Echo*, 1985.
96. Bunker, "Italians welcome peace mission."
97. "Fascists were behind riot in Brussels – Ken," *Daily Post*, 1985.
98. G. Andreotti, UK: Italy Bilateral Relations: Football Tragedy Brussels, June 18, 1985.
99. Ken. Jones, "United in Prayer," *Sunday Mirror*, June 2, 1985.
100. Jones, "United in Prayer."
101. Jones, "United in Prayer."
102. Jones, "United in Prayer."
103. Jones, "United in Prayer."
104. Jones, "United in Prayer."
105. Golden and Garvey, "Wives' backlash terror."
106. Golden and Garvey, "Wives' backlash terror."
107. Golden and Garvey, "Wives' backlash terror."
108. Golden and Garvey, "Wives' backlash terror."
109. Foot, *Calcio*.

27. Belgium

1. *The Explosive 80s*.
2. Foreign Office, May 30, 1985.
3. Callan, "Shame."

4. George Jones and Roger Ratcliffe, "One year FA ban not enough," *The Sunday Times*, June 2, 1985.

5. Jones and Ratcliffe, "One year FA ban not enough."

6. Jones and Ratcliffe, "One year FA ban not enough."

7. Brown, Burgess and Scott, "Brussels counts soccer riot dead."

8. "How many deaths is one soccer match worth?" *Liverpool Echo*, May 30, 1985.

9. Chisari, "'The Cursed Cup'."

10. Brown, Burgess and Scott, "Brussels counts soccer riot dead."

11. Brown, Burgess and Scott, "Brussels counts soccer riot dead."

12. Brown, Burgess and Scott, "Brussels counts soccer riot dead."

13. Record of proceedings of a session of the full senate, June 14, 1985.

14. Record of proceedings of a session of the full senate, June 14, 1985.

15. Record of proceedings of a session of the full senate, June 14, 1985.

16. Derek Brown, "Belgium bans every British team."

17. Brown, "Belgium bans every British team."

18. Glass, "Englishmen Abroad."

19. Glass, "Englishmen Abroad."

20. Foreign Office, May 30, 1985.

21. Foreign Office, *Document 22342-1, Prisons and Prisoners Repatriation and Deportation Football Hooliganism.* HO291/2060, 1985.

22. Murray, "Belgian aims to extradite soccer hooligans identified on video film."

23. Foreign Office, *Document 22342-1.*

24. gazza7558, "Medway Police banned from Europe 1985," February 28, 2015, YouTube video, accessed March 16, 2018, https://www.youtube.com/watch?v=tVLQscWeQB4.

25. gazza7558, "Medway Police banned from Europe 1985."

26. gazza7558, "Medway Police banned from Europe 1985."

27. gazza7558, "Medway Police banned from Europe 1985."

28. gazza7558, "Medway Police banned from Europe 1985."

29. gazza7558, "Medway Police banned from Europe 1985."

30. gazza7558, "Medway Police banned from Europe 1985."

31. Record of proceedings of a session of the full senate, 14 June 1985.

32. Record of proceedings of a session of the full senate, 14 June 1985.

33. Record of proceedings of a session of the full senate, 14 June 1985.

34. Record of proceedings of a session of the full senate, 14 June 1985.

35. Record of proceedings of a session of the full senate, 14 June 1985.

36. Record of proceedings of a session of the full senate, 14 June 1985.

37. The Times. June 4 1985.

38. Bob. Burns, "Howe jets in as Belgium fears terror campaign," *Liverpool Echo*, 1985.

39. "Inquiry on Soccer Riot Hears Reports of Errors," *The Associated Press*, 1985.

40. Brown, "Belgium bans every British team."

41. Ian Murray, "Belgium shares Heysel blame," 1985.
42. *Liverpool Echo*, "Belgians blast Liverpool FC."
43. Derek Brown, "Minister fights off resignation pressure after cup death report," *The Guardian*, 1985.
44. *Liverpool Echo*, "Belgians blast Liverpool FC."
45. *Liverpool Echo*, "Belgians blast Liverpool FC."
46. Murray, "Belgium shares Heysel blame."
47. *Liverpool Echo*, "Belgians blast Liverpool FC."
48. Murray, "Belgium shares Heysel blame."
49. Brown, "Minister fights off resignation pressure."
50. "Minister's resignation urged over Heysel riot," *Financial Times*, 1985.
51. Foreign Office, July 4, 1985.
52. Foreign Office, June 24, 1985.
53. *Financial Times*, "Minister's resignation urged."
54. *Financial Times*, "Minister's resignation urged."
55. *The Explosive 80s.*
56. Chris Rudd, "The aftermath of Heysel: The 1985 Belgian election," *West European Politics* 9, no. 2 (1986).
57. Rudd, "The aftermath of Heysel."
58. Rudd, "The aftermath of Heysel."
59. Rudd, "The aftermath of Heysel."

28. Liverpool

1. Derek Hatton, "My grief at TV Horror," *Liverpool Echo*, May 30, 1985.
2. "Sadness of Church Leaders," *Liverpool Echo*, May 30, 1985.
3. Metcalfe and Byrne, "Dazed fans tell of the bloodbath."
4. Metcalfe and Byrne, "Dazed fans tell of the bloodbath."
5. Metcalfe and Byrne, "Dazed fans tell of the bloodbath."
6. Gruner and Lee-Potter, "I'm ashamed to be from Liverpool."
7. Off the Ball, "Heysel is never ever mentioned."
8. Hynes, "30 years since Heysel."
9. Price, "Shame."
10. Metcalfe and Byrne, "Dazed fans tell of the bloodbath."
11. Hynes, "30 years since Heysel."
12. "Shanks will have turned in his grave," *Liverpool Echo*, May 30, 1985.
13. "The Brussels Disaster," *Liverpool Echo*, May 30, 1985.
14. *Liverpool Echo*, "How many deaths is one soccer match worth?"
15. *Liverpool Echo*, "How many deaths is one soccer match worth?"
16. *Liverpool Echo*, "How many deaths is one soccer match worth?"
17. *Liverpool Echo*, "How many deaths is one soccer match worth?"
18. "Comment," *Liverpool Echo*, May 30, 1985.
19. *Liverpool Echo*, "Comment."

20. *Liverpool Echo*, "Comment."
21. Hargreaves, "A Night of Horror."
22. Hargreaves, "A Night of Horror."
23. Hargreaves, "A Night of Horror."
24. "Our name must be cleared - Reds' fan," *Liverpool Echo*, May 30, 1985.
25. *Liverpool Echo*, "Our name must be cleared."
26. A.C. Ambrose, "Find the scum who did this," *Liverpool Echo*, June 11, 1985.
27. Ambrose, "Find the scum who did this."
28. Bennet and Woan, "The horror of Heysel stadium."
29. Bennet and Woan, "The horror of Heysel stadium."
30. Bennet and Woan, "The horror of Heysel stadium."
31. Nick Bunker, "The Mersey families who fear a backlash," *Liverpool Echo*, June 2, 1985.
32. Foreign Office, Foreign Office Document, May 31, 1985, UK: Italy Bilateral Relations: Football Tragedy Brussels.

29. Too Much on Their Plates

1. Foreign Office, *Visit by Liverpool Delegation to Turin*, June 4, 1985, UK: Italy Bilateral Relations: Football Tragedy Brussels.
2. Foreign Office, *Visit by Liverpool Delegation to Turin*.
3. P. Phelps, "Bid to heal wounds," *Liverpool Echo*, 1985.
4. Phelps, "Bid to heal wounds."
5. Nick Bunker, "Benvenuti," *Liverpool Echo*, June 1985.
6. Foreign Office, *Visit by Liverpool Delegation to Turin*.
7. Bunker, "Benvenuti."
8. Bunker, "Benvenuti."
9. "Tories relent over Turin mission," *Liverpool Echo*, June 7, 1985.
10. Foreign Office, *Visit by Liverpool Delegation to Turin*.
11. Foreign Office, *Visit by Liverpool Delegation to Turin*.
12. Bunker, "Benvenuti."
13. Bunker, "Benvenuti."
14. Alan Copps, "Soccer is not war, says Turin mayor," *Daily Telegraph*, June 18, 1985.
15. Copps, "Soccer is not war, says Turin mayor."
16. Bunker, "Benvenuti."
17. "Bon voyage message for peace mission," *Liverpool Echo*, June 14, 1985.
18. Andy Byrne, "Peace in their hearts," *Liverpool Echo*, June 14, 1985.
19. Byrne, "Peace in their hearts."
20. Derek Hatton, "Rebuilding job that we have got to do," *Liverpool Echo*, June 17, 1985.

21. Hatton, "Rebuilding job."
22. "All our love message for Turin," *Liverpool Echo,* June 17, 1985.
23. "Turin papers welcome jet of peace," *Liverpool Echo,* 1985.
24. *Liverpool Echo,* "Turin papers."
25. *Liverpool Echo,* "Turin papers."
26. D. Hope, "Hugs and kisses as peace mission arrives in Turin," *Daily Post,* 1985.
27. Hope, "Hugs and kisses."
28. Foreign Office, Foreign Office Document, June 19, 1985, UK: Italy Bilateral Relations: Football Tragedy Brussels.
29. Hope, "Hugs and kisses."
30. Hope, "Hugs and kisses."
31. *Liverpool Echo,* "Turin papers."
32. Byrne, "Scouser who saved eight lives."
33. Byrne, "Scouser who saved eight lives."
34. Byrne, "Scouser who saved eight lives."
35. Foreign Office, Foreign Office Document, June 1985, UK: Italy Bilateral Relations: Football Tragedy Brussels.
36. "Scousers 'warm and kind'," *Liverpool Echo,* June 17, 1985.
37. *Liverpool Echo,* "Scousers."
38. Nick Bunker, "City council leader breaks down as he says: 'We are sorry'," *Liverpool Echo,* June 18, 1985.
39. "Grief unites Turin and Liverpool," *The Times,* 1985.
40. Bunker, "City council leader."
41. Woodcock, "Tears of a widow."
42. Copps, "Liverpool brings its condolences."
43. Bunker, "City council leader."
44. Bunker, "City council leader."
45. Bunker, "City council leader."
46. "Let us still meet in rivalry and friendship," *Daily Post,* June 1985.
47. *Daily Post,* "Let us still meet."
48. *Daily Post,* "Let us still meet."
49. "Charity match may be on," *Daily Post,* 1985.
50. D. Hope, "The Sign of Peace," *Daily Post,* 1985.
51. Hope, "The Sign of Peace."
52. Foreign Office Document, June 19, 1985.
53. Foreign Office Document, June 19, 1985.
54. Hope, "Hugs and kisses."
55. Hugh Dalton, *Letter to M.A. Wicks at the British Consulate in Genoa,* June 20, 1985.
56. Hope, "The Sign of Peace."
57. Hope, "Hugs and kisses."
58. Foreign Office Document, June 19, 1985.
59. *Daily Post,* June 1985.
60. *Daily Post,* June 1985.

61. Foreign Office Document, June 19, 1985.

62. D. Hope, "Being here says more than words," *Daily Post*, 1985.

63. Hope, "Being here says more than words."

64. Hope, "Being here says more than words."

65. Hope, "Being here says more than words."

66. Hope, "Being here says more than words."

67. Hope, "Being here says more than words."

68. Hope, "Being here says more than words."

69. Copps, "Liverpool brings its condolences."

70. Copps, "Liverpool brings its condolences."

71. Copps, "Liverpool brings its condolences."

72. Copps, "Liverpool brings its condolences."

73. Copps, "Liverpool brings its condolences."

74. Copps, "Liverpool brings its condolences."

75. Copps, "Liverpool brings its condolences."

76. Copps, "Liverpool brings its condolences."

77. Foreign Office Document, June 19, 1985.

78. A. Dunn, "Liverpool sends Italian peace mission as unions prepare cash war at home," *The Guardian*, 1985.

30. "The Rubicon Had Been Crossed."

1. Foreign Office, *Message from the Prime Minister on Football Violence*, May 30, 1985, GRS 500, UK: Italy Bilateral Relations Football Tragedy Brussels.

2. Foreign Office, *Message from the Prime Minister.*

3. Foreign Office, *Message from the Prime Minister.*

4. Home Office, May 30, 1985.

5. Home Office, *Prisons and Prisoners Repatriation and Deportation Football Hooliganism*, HO291/2060.

6. Home Office, May 31, 1985.

7. Home Office.

8. Home Office.

9. Home Office, May 30, 1985.

10. Home Office.

11. Home Office.

12. Home Office.

13. Home Office.

14. Home Office.

15. Home Office.

16. Foreign Office, *Football: Message of Condolence*, May 1985, UK: Italy Bilateral Relations Football Tragedy Brussels.

17. Margaret Thatcher, *Press Conference after Heysel Stadium disaster*, May 30, 1985, Margaret Thatcher Foundation, https://www.

margaretthatcher.org/document/106060.

18. Foreign Office, *European Cup Final-Brussels-29 May 1985*, July 26, 1985, UK: Italy Bilateral Relations Football Tragedy Brussels.

19. Thatcher, *Press Conference after Heysel Stadium disaster.*

20. Thatcher, *Press Conference after Heysel Stadium disaster.*

21. Thatcher, *Press Conference after Heysel Stadium disaster.*

22. Thatcher, *Press Conference after Heysel Stadium disaster.*

23. D. McKie, "Thatcher set to demand FA ban on games in Europe," *The Guardian*, 1985.

24. McKie, "Thatcher set to demand FA ban."

25. McKie, "Thatcher set to demand FA ban."

26. McKie, "Thatcher set to demand FA ban."

27. Croker, *The First Voice.*

28. Croker, *The First Voice.*

29. McKie, "Thatcher set to demand FA ban."

30. Home Office, *Prisons and Prisoners.*

31. Home Office, *Prisons and Prisoners.*

32. McKie, "Thatcher set to demand FA ban."

33. *The Explosive 80s.*

34. *The Explosive 80s.*

35. *The Explosive 80s.*

36. *The Explosive 80s.*

37. *The Explosive 80s.*

38. *The Explosive 80s.*

39. *The Explosive 80s.*

31. Banned

1. "1985: English teams banned after Heysel," *BBC On This Day*, http://news.bbc.co.uk/onthisday/hi/dates/stories/may/31/newsid_2481000/2481723.stm.

2. Croker, *The First Voice.*

3. Jones and Ratcliffe, "One year FA ban not enough."

4. Jones and Ratcliffe, "One year FA ban not enough."

5. Jones and Ratcliffe, "One year FA ban not enough."

6. *BBC On This Day*, "English teams banned after Heysel."

7. *BBC On This Day*, "English teams banned after Heysel."

8. *BBC On This Day*, "English teams banned after Heysel."

9. *The Explosive 80s.*

10. Foreign Office, *Liverpool/Juventus.*

11. *BBC On This Day*, "English teams banned after Heysel."

12. Brian Scovell, "The price they to pay," *Daily Mail*, 1985.

13. Scovell, "The price they to pay."

14. Scovell, "The price they to pay."

15. Scovell, "The price they to pay."
16. Scovell, "The price they to pay."
17. Jones and Ratcliffe, "One year FA ban not enough."
18. Jones and Ratcliffe, "One year FA ban not enough."
19. Colin Hughes, "Italians 'partly to blame'," *The Times*, 1985.
20. Margaret Thatcher, *TV Interview for BBC* (*Heysel Stadium disaster*), 1985, Margaret Thatcher Foundation, https://www.margaretthatcher.org/document/105884.
21. "1985: Uefa bans English clubs from Europe," *BBC On This Day*, http://news.bbc.co.uk/onthisday/hi/dates/stories/june/2/newsid_2494000/2494963.stm.
22. *BBC On This Day*, "Uefa bans English clubs."
23. "Thatcher Bill Would Outlaw Ban Alcohol at Soccer Stadiums," *The Herald Tribune*, June 4, 1985.
24. FIGHTERS 1985, "BBC news – Heysel Stadium disaster," March 23, 2018, YouTube video, https://www.youtube.com/watch?v=sdUWsFrYBnc.
25. Staff from dispatches, "European Soccer Body Bans English Teams," *The Washington Post*, 1985.
26. Staff from dispatches, "European Soccer Body Bans English Teams."
27. *BBC On This Day*, "Uefa bans English clubs."
28. HC Deb, June 3, 1985, vol 80 cc21-33.
29. Ian Hargreaves, "World Ban," *Liverpool Echo*, 1985.
30. Hargreaves, "World Ban."
31. "Banned clubs chasing a lost cause," *Liverpool Echo*, 1985.
32. *Liverpool Echo*, "Banned clubs chasing a lost cause."
33. *Liverpool Echo*, "Banned clubs chasing a lost cause."
34. HC Deb, June 11, 1985, vol 80 cc.868-74.
35. HC Deb, June 11, 1985, vol 80 cc.868-74.
36. *Liverpool Echo*, "Banned clubs chasing a lost cause."
37. *Liverpool Echo*, "Banned clubs chasing a lost cause."
38. *Liverpool Echo*, "Banned clubs chasing a lost cause."
39. *Liverpool Echo*, "Banned clubs chasing a lost cause."
40. *Liverpool Echo*, "Banned clubs chasing a lost cause."
41. Home Office, *Prisons and Prisoners*.
42. Home Office, *Prisons and Prisoners*.
43. "FA kick out card plan hopes," *Liverpool Echo*, 1985.
44. *Liverpool Echo*, "FA kick out card plan hopes."
45. *Liverpool Echo*, "FA kick out card plan hopes."
46. "D-day on future of soccer," *Liverpool Echo*, 1985.
47. *Liverpool Echo*, "D-day on future of soccer."
48. *Liverpool Echo*, "D-day on future of soccer."
49. *Liverpool Echo*, "D-day on future of soccer."
50. *Liverpool Echo*, "D-day on future of soccer."
51. Home Office, Home Office Document, 1985.

52. Home Office Document, 1985.
53. Home Office Document, 1985.
54. Vulliamy, "Heysel stadium disaster."
55. Vulliamy, "Heysel stadium disaster."
56. Vulliamy, "Heysel stadium disaster."

32. Custard Creams

1. Ken Montgomery, "Anger," *Sunday Mirror*, June 2, 1985.
2. "Chairman says NF to Blame," *Liverpool Echo*, May 31, 1985.
3. Montgomery, "Anger."
4. The Anfield Wrap, "Heysel 30 Years: Why Did No-One See It Coming?" *The Anfield Wrap*, May 28, 2015, https://www.theanfieldwrap.com/2015/05/heysel-30-years-why-did-no-one-see-it-coming/.
5. The Anfield Wrap, "Why Did No-One See It Coming?"
6. Montgomery, "Anger."
7. Montgomery, "Anger."
8. Montgomery, "Anger."
9. Gareth Parry, "Fascists 'recruited on ferry'," *The Guardian*, May 31 1985.
10. Parry, "Fascists 'recruited on ferry'."
11. Jackson, "Heysel: the witnesses' stories."
12. Chris Rowland. *From Where I was Standing*. (GPRF Publishing. 2009).
13. Atkinson and Roberts, "Podcast: Heysel 30 Years."
14. Atkinson and Roberts, "Podcast: Heysel 30 Years."
15. Atkinson and Roberts, "Podcast: Heysel 30 Years."
16. FIGHTERS 1985, "Heysel Stadium Disaster (29 May 1985)," August 7, 2013, YouTube video, https://www.youtube.com/watch?v=xg8SzVizvtM.
17. Steen, "Interwoven tragedies."
18. Paddy Sheenan, "Heysel 30 years on - Peter Hooton: "If we had any idea people had died we would have walked out," *Liverpool Echo*, May 29, 2015, https://www.liverpoolecho.co.uk/news/heysel-30-years---peter-9254188.
19. Kevin Sampson, "My friendship with Mauro from Turin that survived the horror of Heysel," *The Guardian*, May 31, 2015, https://www.theguardian.com/commentisfree/2015/may/31/liverpool-juventus-heysel-tragedy.
20. Caremani, *Heysel*.
21. Image of Phil Neal, Michel Platini, and Ian Rush, 2005, Available from: https://th.bing.com/th/id/OIP.QX22IoT5SzRlCA7xsMj9bw-EsC3?pid=ImgDet&rs=1.

22. M. Daphinoff, *Letter from UEFA to LFC*, June 24, 1985.

23. Daphinoff, *Letter from UEFA to LFC*.

24. *Documents Annexed to Submissions to UEFA Appeal*, August 8, 1985.

25. *Documents Annexed to Submissions to UEFA Appeal*.

26. *Documents Annexed to Submissions to UEFA Appeal*.

27. *Documents Annexed to Submissions to UEFA Appeal*.

28. Atkinson and Roberts, "Podcast: Heysel 30 Years."

29. Atkinson and Roberts, "Podcast: Heysel 30 Years."

33. Our Cilla and the Proddy-Dogs

1. David Kennedy, *Merseyside's Old Firm? The Sectarian Roots of Everton and Liverpool Football Clubs* (Independently published, 2017).

2. Kennedy, *Merseyside's Old Firm?*

3. Kennedy, *Merseyside's Old Firm?*

4. Kennedy, *Merseyside's Old Firm?*

5. Kennedy, *Merseyside's Old Firm?*

6. Bob Waterhouse, "Is Everton Protestant or Catholic?" *Toffeeweb*, August 9, 2018, https://toffeeweb.com/season/18-19/comment/fanscomment/37054.html.

7. David Jeffery, "The Strange Death of Tory Liverpool: Conservative Electoral Decline in Liverpool, 1945-1996," *British Politics* 12 (2017).

8. Jeffery, "The Strange Death of Tory Liverpool."

9. P.J. Waller, *Democracy & Sectarianism: A political and social history of Liverpool 1868-1939* (Liverpool: Liverpool University Press, 1981).

10. Jeffery, "The Strange Death of Tory Liverpool."

11. Jeffery, "The Strange Death of Tory Liverpool."

12. Jeffery, "The Strange Death of Tory Liverpool."

13. Jeffery, "The Strange Death of Tory Liverpool."

14. Dunleavy, "Religious Sectarianism and Irish Nationalism."

15. Donald M. MacRaild, *Faith, Fraternity & Fighting: The Orange Order and Irish Migrants In Northern England, C.1850-1920* (Liverpool: Liverpool University Press, 2009).

16. Keith Roberts, "The rise and fall of Liverpool sectarianism. An investigation into the decline of sectarian antagonism on Merseyside," (PhD diss., University of Liverpool, 2015).

17. MacRaild, *Faith, Fraternity & Fighting*.

18. MacRaild, *Faith, Fraternity & Fighting*.

19. Tony Mason, "The Blues and Reds: A History of Liverpool and Everton Football Clubs," *The History Society of Lancashire and Cheshire* 13 (1985).

20. Roberts, "The rise and fall of Liverpool sectarianism."

21. "Mr T.P. O'Connor," Hansard, https://api.parliament.uk/historic-hansard/people/mr-tp-oconnor/index.html.

22. Waller, *Democracy & Sectarianism.*

23. MacRaild, *Faith, Fraternity & Fighting.*

24. MacRaild, *Faith, Fraternity & Fighting.*

25. MacRaild, *Faith, Fraternity & Fighting.*

26. MacRaild, *Faith, Fraternity & Fighting.*

27. MacRaild, *Faith, Fraternity & Fighting.*

28. John Belchem, "'The Church, The Throne and the People: Ships, Colonies and Commerce': Popular Toryism in early Victorian Liverpool," *Transactions of the Historic Society of Lancashire & Cheshire* 143 (1994).

29. Belchem, "'The Church, The Throne and the People'."

30. Jeffery, "The Strange Death of Tory Liverpool."

31. Roberts, "The rise and fall of Liverpool sectarianism."

32. Roberts, "The rise and fall of Liverpool sectarianism."

33. Dunleavy, "Religious Sectarianism and Irish Nationalism."

34. Dunleavy, "Religious Sectarianism and Irish Nationalism."

35. Kennedy, *Merseyside's Old Firm?*

36. Kennedy, *Merseyside's Old Firm?*

37. Jeffery, "The Strange Death of Tory Liverpool."

38. Kennedy, *Merseyside's Old Firm?*

39. Kennedy, David. "Introduction." *Soccer & Society*, 12:4, (Aug 2011): 471-473.

40. Jan Grace, "The Everton FC Collection," *Culture Liverpool*, https://www.cultureliverpool.co.uk/the-everton-fc-collection/.

41. Kennedy, David. "In the beginning God created Everton." *Soccer & Society*, 12:4, (2011): 481-490.

42. Mason, "The Blues and Reds."

43. Kennedy, David. "Houlding and the rise of factionalism." *Soccer & Society,* 12:4, (2011): 491-496.

44. Kennedy, David. "Houlding and the rise of factionalism."

45. Kennedy, David. "Houlding and the rise of factionalism."

46. Waller, *Democracy & Sectarianism.*

47. Jeffery, "The Strange Death of Tory Liverpool."

48. Waller, *Democracy & Sectarianism.*

49. Waller, *Democracy & Sectarianism.*

50. Waller, *Democracy & Sectarianism.*

51. Waller, *Democracy & Sectarianism.*

52. Kennedy, *Merseyside's Old Firm?*

53. Kennedy, *Merseyside's Old Firm?*

54. Kennedy, *Merseyside's Old Firm?*

55. Kennedy, *Merseyside's Old Firm?*

56. Roberts, "The rise and fall of Liverpool sectarianism."

57. Roberts, "The rise and fall of Liverpool sectarianism."

58. Kennedy, *Merseyside's Old Firm?*
59. Kennedy, *Merseyside's Old Firm?*
60. Kennedy, *Merseyside's Old Firm?*
61. Kennedy, *Merseyside's Old Firm?*
62. Kennedy, *Merseyside's Old Firm?*
63. Kennedy, *Merseyside's Old Firm?*
64. Kennedy, *Merseyside's Old Firm?*
65. Kennedy, David. "And then there were two: Everton and Liverpool football clubs, 1892–1902." *Soccer & Society*, 12:4, (2011): 523-537.
66. John Belchem, *Irish, Catholic and Scouse: The History of the Liverpool Irish, 1800-1939* (Liverpool: Liverpool University Press, 2007).
67. Roberts, "The rise and fall of Liverpool sectarianism."
68. Kennedy, David. "Red and blue and orange and green?" *Soccer & Society*, 12:4, (2011): 552-564.
69. Roberts, "The rise and fall of Liverpool sectarianism."
70. Kennedy, *Merseyside's Old Firm?*
71. Roberts, "The rise and fall of Liverpool sectarianism."
72. Roberts, "The rise and fall of Liverpool sectarianism."
73. Kennedy, *Merseyside's Old Firm?*
74. Roberts, "The rise and fall of Liverpool sectarianism."
75. Roberts, "The rise and fall of Liverpool sectarianism."

ACKNOWLEDGMENTS

Thank you to family and friends who I confided in. Thanks to Rowanvale, notably Ellie and Jaide. A massive thank you to Paul Fry and Eamonn McCabe who were so generous with their time and memories.

ABOUT THE AUTHOR

Paul McCallam is from Liverpool. He has a BSc in Psychology and a BA in History & Politics.

It would be good to hear your feedback.
mccapaul17@gmail.com

Printed in Great Britain
by Amazon

83256316R00294